Script Analysis for Actors, Directors, and Designers

Script Analysis for Actors, Directors, and Designers

Fourth Edition

James Thomas

ELSEVIER

AMSTERDAM • BOSTON • HEIDELBERG • LONDON • NEW YORK
• OXFORD PARIS • SAN DIEGO • SAN FRANCISCO • SINGAPORE •
SYDNEY • TOKYO

Focal
Press

Focal Press is an imprint of Elsevier
30 Corporate Drive, Suite 400, Burlington, MA 01803, USA
Linacre House, Jordan Hill, Oxford OX2 8DP, UK

Library of Congress Cataloging-in-Publication Data
Application submitted

British Library Cataloguing-in-Publication Data
A catalogue record for this book is available from the British Library.

ISBN: 978-0-240-81049-2

For information on all Focal Press publications
visit our website at www.elsevierdirect.com

11 12   5 4

Printed in the United States of America

Working together to grow
libraries in developing countries

www.elsevier.com | www.bookaid.org | www.sabre.org

ELSEVIER   BOOK AID
International   Sabre Foundation

For my respected colleagues at the Moscow Art Theatre School and for the great director Anatoly Efros. Their inspiring examples make a life in the theatre significant.

Contents

ix

Preface

New in this Edition

This edition contains new information about analysis of nonrealistic plays. Plays that depart from everyday reality in whole or in part, in content or in form, are being produced to a greater extent than ever. Because this type of writing does not coincide with observable reality, it is called nonrealistic. Throughout history much of dramatic literature has employed nonrealistic elements. Although some elements may be nonrealistic, the plays themselves do not of necessity assert anything against realism itself. Nonrealistic plays, on the other hand, assert something against realism. They assert that realism itself is artificial, outmoded, or even contrary to the laws of nature. The plays singled out in this new edition are labeled nonrealistic because they are assertively so. Several of them were included in earlier editions; however, they were treated there in terms of what they have in common with plays in general. This edition also addresses the special challenges nonrealistic plays present.

Nonrealistic plays have not displaced traditional or realistic works, and yet they are among the most representative plays of our time. Whether they will sooner or later become marginal and theatre will move in other directions remains to be seen. The reason for singling them out in this edition is to suggest that even novel and unusual developments in drama continue to employ the basic features of dramatic form (plot, dialogue, character, idea, tempo–rhythm–mood), although in nonstandard ways. If this is true, then formalist analysis and its derivative, action analysis, should be capable of providing ways to understand them. Furthermore, there should be no need for actors, directors, or designers to change their vocabulary, methods, questions asked, or means of coming to terms with the plays. The degree of difficulty is without doubt greater than with realistic or classic plays, but the danger of being "out of sync" with contemporary mentality is a worse problem. On balance, the difficulties encountered when trying to understand nonrealistic plays ought to be no greater than those encountered when trying to make sense of the contemporary world in general.

This edition also gives increased attention to script analysis for designers. In most discussions of script analysis, the director is mentioned quite frequently. Ever since Stanislavsky, and Vsevelod

Meyerhold, the role of the director has gained increasing importance. In fact, the notion of the director as the "primary creative thinker" has become so ingrained in us that it has become, in effect, the theatre's metanarrative, that is, a general explanation of all accumulated theatrical knowledge and experience. Under this metanarrative, designers concern themselves essentially with the technical requirements of the play and turn to the director for the interpretive elements of their work. But this metanarrative never was entirely true, even for those directors who supposedly created it. From Stanislavsky and Meyerhold to Peter Brook and Julie Taymor, script analysis has always been more than the work of directors, or of actors either. Theatre production has invariably worked best when all the members of the production team develop a personal relationship with the play itself as well as with their specific creative tasks in the production. The increased attention given to design issues in this edition is intended to reinforce to this point of view. As a further point, the term *mise-en-scene* in the book refers collectively to scenery, lighting, costumes, sound, and makeup. Elements in the play suggest the mise-en-scene, which in turn theatricalizes the play.

The new material goes together with routine editorial maintenance. I have continued to clarify inexact definitions, improve and update examples, and cull and update the Bibliography. The concepts of objectives, actions, and qualities have been reexamined to address the bothersome lack of clarity surrounding those terms. The revised Appendix includes additional questions for script analysis.

This Book and Its Point of View

This book is the outcome of teaching and directing experience acquired in theatre programs with a variety of educational objectives. In all of them, I found that at some point in the curriculum teachers require their students to analyze plays in a methodical fashion before the practical experience of acting, directing, and designing. Most theatre programs require at least one course devoted to this purpose. In the process of teaching these and related courses, I have examined theatre textbooks concerned with the craft of performance and literature textbooks concerned with the literary aspects of drama. I found very few intelligible, wide-ranging discussions of the dramatic potentials of a play explained in a way that is useful for actors, directors, and designers in their creative work. As a consequence, in too many cases, I found otherwise talented students unable to employ their talents to best advantage because they did not know how to study plays from a practical theatre point of view.

This book is designed to teach the serious theatre student the skills of script analysis using a formalist approach. By this, I mean first that it uses a standard system of classifications to study the written part of a play, excluding performance, scenery, and so forth. Formalist methodology also means that the book does not cover all the topics included in the usual dramatic literature textbooks. There is no extensive attention to dramatic forms or styles; no scrutiny of historical-critical theories or sociopolitical implications; and no attention to the life, mind, or personality of the author (although the book relates to all these matters). This approach is not new. We know how scientists adopt the practice of neglecting certain data outside their own spheres of interest. Likewise professional theatre artists tend to avoid outside details and turn instead to the play itself when they are looking for the key to their work. The scientist and artist know all the time that the neglected information exists, but they act as if it did not for the special purposes of their work. I admit that this kind of restricted approach can claim no scholarly pretensions. The aim is practical and intended first and foremost for the theatre.

Most of this book deals with play analysis, but since the acts of thinking and reading are very well connected with this process, I have provided an Introduction that I hope will make those activities a little clearer. It begins with a brief sketch of the heritage of formalist analysis and then offers general guidelines for reading and thinking about plays, including a new section on pattern awareness.

The largest portion of the book is involved with understanding the basic dramatic potentials of a play. I have attempted to keep the design simple. Chapter 1, Action Analysis, is a specially reduced adaptation of Chapters 2–6. Chapters 2–9 each treat one of the basic elements of drama initially described by Aristotle and later adopted and adapted by many other teachers, scholars, and theatre artists. Though all the elements depend on each other, of course, the method used is to select one element as the essence of the play for the time being and to disregard the others. This is what I believe is unique and what will prove the most useful about this book. By narrowing the point of view in this way, students can acquire the mental concentration needed to learn the individual parts of plays and their possibilities. The approach will in the end show that each element is inseparable from the whole meaning, an understanding that is the bedrock of artistic unity. When formalist analysis is done well, it can feel almost like the play is acting, directing, and designing itself.

A list of questions appears at the end of each chapter. They are important learning tools intended to stimulate creative thinking as actors, directors, and designers engage in the production process. By reviewing the topics one by one, readers will be certain to cover almost every important dramatic possibility found in a play. The Bibliography supplements and supports the point of view of the book and is also intended as a learning tool.

Play analysis is a practical skill that is best explained by concrete examples, but since this book is expected to be used with plays chosen by the teacher, I have tried to keep it self-contained. It is not necessary to read all the plays to make satisfactory use of it. Now as before I have tried to select titles that have achieved some popularity and influence. Four additional titles have been added to make the collection more representative of the current nonrealistic theatre scene: *The Birthday Party* (1964) by Harold Pinter, *Fefu and Her Friends* (1977) by Maria Irene Fornes, *Top Girls* (1982) by Caryl Churchill, and *Rosencrantz and Guildenstern are Dead* (1991) by Tom Stoppard. Additionally, *Machinal* by Sophie Treadwell replaces Eugene O'Neill's less familiar play, *The Hairy Ape*; and David Mamet's *American Buffalo* replaces David Rabe's *Streamers* for the same reason. To be sure, writers of the nonrealistic plays studied here have matured and followed up with later plays, but their mature writing is by and large more subtle and stylish, while their earliest works tend to be less difficult to understand. Nor is it certain at present which of any more recent plays will remain as valued as these over a longer period of time. Here is a list of the study plays:

Oedipus Rex (ca. 430 CE) by Sophocles
Hamlet (1600) by William Shakespeare
Tartuffe (1669) by Molière
The School for Scandal (1777) by Richard Brinsley Sheridan
The Wild Duck (1884) by Henrik Ibsen
Three Sisters (1901) by Anton Chekhov
Machinal (1928) by Sophie Treadwell
Mother Courage (1937) by Bertolt Brecht
Death of a Salesman (1949) by Arthur Miller
A Raisin in the Sun (1959) by Lorraine Hansberry
Happy Days (1961) by Samuel Beckett
The Birthday Party (1964) by Harold Pinter
Fefu and Her Friends (1977) by Maria Irene Fornes
American Buffalo (1977) by David Mamet
Top Girls (1982) by Caryl Churchill
A Lie of the Mind (1986) by Sam Shepard
The Piano Lesson (1990) by August Wilson

Rosencrantz and Guildenstern are Dead (1991) by Tom Stoppard
Angels in America (1992) by Tony Kushner

The scripts are available in single editions and anthologies, and plot summaries can be found at various sites on the Internet. I recommend selecting no more than three outside plays for specific study in class. For my part, I have had success using plays from our program's current production season, and applying the concepts in the book to those plays. For introductory level courses, realistic and classic plays have seemed to work best. Nonrealistic plays tend to require more experience in play reading and production. In any case, students say they benefit from the connection with ongoing production work.

Besides being a system of classification and an intellectual attitude, formalist analysis may also be used as means of entry into a play script. When analyzing plays, it is helpful to begin with a plan, and taken all together the classifications embody such a plan. This implies that students can go through them one by one, and in the beginning they are encouraged to do just that. Formalist analysis is an attempt to organize the study of a play, and the system of classifications is the necessary instructional basis of this organization. While this may seem schematic, if not uninspired, it should not be troubling, because a schematic or uninspired analysis is better than none at all. And after all, play analysis takes practice, just as any kind of analysis does. Intellectual muscles must be rigorously exercised if craftsmanship is to be developed so that talent can take wing.

This book can accommodate different teaching and learning strategies. Although it is purposefully organized and arranged, there is no absolute need to cover all the topics or to study them in the order they are presented. Some teachers may select fewer categories to form the organizing principles for their course; others may choose to assign the readings another way or to use the book as a foundation for other approaches to analysis. I mention just three points.

First, most of the book is within reach of serious beginning students, but the new material on nonrealistic plays and the material in Chapter 8 (Dialogue), Chapter 9 (Tempo, Rhythm, and Mood), and Chapter 10 (The Style of the Play) is perhaps better suited to more experienced readers. Nevertheless, beginners need to know what kind of knowledge is expected of them if they are to become serious about their future work in the theatre. For that reason, it is appropriate to introduce them to subjects that are important to professional actors, directors, and designers. Beginners may be tempted to disregard these chapters, but I hope not.

Second, it is a good idea for teachers to keep lessons moving and not become involved in prolonged study of individual plays. This may be accomplished if, instead of teaching the plays themselves, the teacher focuses on teaching the skills needed to analyze plays in general. It is not necessary to arrive at a conclusive analysis, only to study the analytical process itself. In fact, for teaching purposes it may be better if some conclusions remain unresolved. After all, at this stage there is no possibility of arriving at a conclusive, fully-justified analysis. Play analysis is no more than the first stage, the mental stage, of the production process. Rehearsal and the design studio still remain to test, correct, and supplement discoveries made during the initial analysis.

Third, a great deal can be gained by studying as many topics as possible in their original order. I have found that with enough practice most students sooner or later develop a mode of quick, automatic understanding. Sooner or later they are able to go to those topics that apply to their needs for the moment and minimize the rest.

Readers should gather from my remarks what they need to know about the scope of this book, but I wish to add a few more comments. There are many ways to understand plays, and this book is concerned with just one of them. Although much of the systematic writing about plays has been in this tradition, it is not hard to find objections to formalist analysis from those who favor other methods. Therefore, since we are concerned in this book with the closed context of the play itself, I emphasize that the attention given to this aspect does not imply that other kinds of analysis do not exist or are not important. I have just agreed temporarily to set them aside in favor of discovering the relationships expressed within the play itself. No single method can ever be completely true, of course, but I aim to convince readers that a large number of playable dramatic values can be discovered using this approach.

Writing a textbook on play analysis is a challenge. In part this is because there is no standardized vocabulary in the theatre as there is, for example, in music. There is not even total agreement about the most commonly used terms and definitions. As a rule, those who deal with plays on a everyday basis develop their own favorite aims, methods, and terms. It follows that there are a number of debatable terms and definitions involved. One of the purposes of this book is to address this lexical disorder by encouraging standardization of the vocabulary used in talking about theatre practice. In support of this goal, I have chosen to use traditional terminology, not because traditional terms are best, but because standardized terms are best. Traditional theatre vocabulary is satisfactory for teaching and practice at every level. The belief that innovative terms can somehow improve theatre teaching and practice is a notion that, in my opinion, few thoughtful teachers or practitioners would agree with.

Even so, and even though the topics and terms in this book have been carefully defined, it is not hard to find different, if not sometimes contradictory, meanings in the works of other writers and practitioners. Without a doubt we could devote a lot more thought to tracing the history of theatre terminology and establishing consensus definitions if we wished, but in a practical book it is not a good idea to test the patience of readers with too much theory. Besides, for working artists the conditions in the play itself are what is most important. I hope the terms and definitions as well as the comments about the plays are at least sound and practical. They are not meant to be authoritarian or to take the place of the teacher. Readers who learned about them elsewhere or in some other form may wish to use these definitions as a basis for comparison with their own instead of thinking of them as conclusive statements, of which there are very few in art anyway.

xvi

Acknowledgments

This book would not have been possible without the help of others, and the list of those whom I am obligated to is long. It begins with Francis Hodge, whose knowledge of play analysis and directing has set standards that in my opinion few have matched. He taught me (among many others) how to think seriously about plays and play production, and his approach to the analytical process (treated in *Play Directing: Analysis, Communication, and Style*) has helped to shape the general outline of this book. None of the errors found here should be attributed to him, but most of what is good and useful can be traced to his influence.

For the invaluable opportunity to attend their rehearsals, classes, and lectures and for their patience with my endless questioning, I would like to thank the artist–teachers of the Moscow Art Theatre School-Studio, notably Anatoly Smeliansky (Rector), Oleg Gerasimov (Emeritus), Ivan Moskvin-Tarkhanov (Emeritus), and especially Mikhail Lobanov, Sergei Zemtsov, Viktor Rizhakov, and Semyon Bulba. Diligent readers will discover that I have additional sources, probably more than I even know myself. Among them are the writings of George Pierce Baker, Roland Barthes, Eric Bentley, Michael Chekhov, Harold Clurman, Tom F. Driver, Mikhail N. Epstein, Francis Fergusson, John Gassner, Ihab Hassan, Kama Ginkas, Maria Knebel, Yuri Lotman, Vladimir Nemirovich-Danchenko, Frank McMullan, Konstantin Stanislavsky, F. Cowles Strickland, Georgi Tovstonogov, and Thornton Wilder.

Special mention should also be made of Anatoly Efros, whose works I have been privileged to translate. As a director and the paradigmatic modern heir of Stanislavsky, Efros' ideas and practices have not only influenced me, but should deservedly be a significant influence on theatre generations to come.

For supplemental information about nonrealism, I wish to acknowledge the writings of Roland Barthes, Eric Bentley, Lawrence Carra, Tom F. Driver, Maria Irene Fornes, William. H. Gass, Suzan-Lori Parks, and Vladimir Nabokov. For this edition, I would like to thank Weldon Durham for permission to adapt his Functional Analysis questions for designers, and John Devlin and Christine Frezza for their helpful comments on the manuscript.

I wish to acknowledge the following reprinted selections:

American Buffalo by David Mamet. Reproduced by permission of Grove/Atlantic, Inc.

Angels in America, Part One: Millennium Approaches by Tony Kushner. Reproduced by permission of Theater Communications Group, Inc.

Birthday Party by Harold Pinter. Reproduced by permission of Grove/Atlantic, Inc.

Death of a Salesman by Arthur Miller. Reproduced by permission of Viking Penguin, a division of Viking Penguin Books USA Inc.

Fefu and Her Friends by Maria Irene Fornes. Reproduced by permission of PAJ Publications.

Hamlet by William Shakespeare, *The School for Scandal* by Richard Brinsley Sheridan, and *The Wild Duck* by Henrik Ibsen reprinted in *Plays for the Theatre: An Anthology of World Drama*, Oscar G. Brockett, ed. (New York: Holt, Rinehart, and Winston, 1984).

Happy Days by Samuel Beckett. Reproduced by permission of Grove/Atlantic, Inc.

A Lie of the Mind by Sam Shepard. Reproduced by permission of Penguin Books Ltd.

Machinal by Sophie Treadwell. Reproduced by permission of the copyright holder.

Mother Courage and Her Children by Bertolt Brecht. Reproduced by permission of Pantheon Books, a division of Random House, Inc.

Oedipus Rex by Sophocles. Reproduced by permission of Harcourt Brace Jovanovich, Inc.

The Piano Lesson by August Wilson. Reproduced by permission of Penguin Books Ltd.

Rosencrantz and Guildenstern are Dead by Tom Stoppard. Reprinted by permission of Grove/Atlantic, Inc.

Tartuffe by Molière. Reproduced by permission of Penguin Books Ltd.

Introduction

The main task of an actor, director, or designer is to get excited about the play, and play analysis is a means of organizing the process of searching for this excitement. (Semyon Bulba, Faculty of Scenography, Moscow Art Theatre School)

What Is Formalist Play Analysis?

Although some readers may often have heard the term formal, they may not have a firm idea of what it means. This is understandable because it has taken on various meanings over time. Formal may be associated with the practice of doing something for appearance's sake as in a formal wedding. Or it may convey a feeling of primness and stiffness. Maybe readers harbor an unconscious feeling that formal means fixed, authoritarian, and inflexible. All these meanings have in common the notion of an arrangement that gives something its essential character or what Aristotle described as "the inward shaping of an object." The etymology of the word substantiates this. Formal is based on the idea of form or shape. The Latin word *forma* means something that shapes or has been shaped, but especially the shape given to an artistic object. The English word formula is related to it as are conformity, inform, reform, transform, and uniform.

Studying the origin of the word leads to the present meaning of *formalist analysis: the search for playable dramatic values that reveal a central unifying pattern which forms or shapes a play from the inside and coordinates all its parts.* Playable dramatic values are those features that energize actors, directors, and designers in their creative work. To accomplish its goal, formalist analysis uses a traditional system of classifications to break up a play into its parts to understand their purpose and relationship.

Some writers may call the formalist approach descriptive because it is concerned with describing a play in terms of its own internal artistic context. Or it may be called analytical because it analyzes the elements in a play as parts of an artistic totality. Others might describe this approach as Aristotelian because it is based on the parts of a play originally described by Aristotle. All of these are accurate. At the risk of seeming to split hairs, however, I should point out that formalist analysis is different from formal analysis, which means the study of a play in relation to the form or literary genre to which it belongs. Different, too, from formalistic analysis, which is based on the terms and concepts of the Russian Formalist critics (see below). In any event, the underlying assumption of formalist analysis is that the plays themselves ought to be studied instead of the abstract theories or external circumstances under which they were written. For theatre students especially, plays should not be merely a means to other kinds of studies, but rather the primary objects of attention.

Formalist analysis of drama is customarily associated with the principles and methods of Aristotle. His *Poetics* (335–322 CE) treats the six elements of drama (plot, character, dialogue, idea, "music," and production values), unity of action, probability, features of the tragic hero, plot requirements, and other subjects related to plays. Although the term poetics is derived from the same Greek source as the word poetry, in Aristotle's sense it more accurately means creatively making, constructing, and arranging an artistic work, in this case drama. The common sense conclusions he arrived at continue to influence Western literature and drama to the present day, and his expressions and descriptions have become part of our critical heritage.

From his survey of the writing, construction, and arrangement of the best plays of his time, Aristotle developed principles and methods for their analysis and evaluation. His work is the basis of the formalist approach. He summarized the basics of drama and analyzed their inner workings and possible combinations. He insisted on the importance of the independent, artistic nature of plays. He reduced concern with outside realistic or moral issues and emphasized instead strict attention to inner structural design, placing special emphasis on the importance of plot as a unifying feature. And his method was inductive — reasoning from detailed facts to general principles — rather than prescriptive. These four principles together make up the heart of the formalist tradition in criticism.

During the classical Roman period, and later during the Renaissance and the seventeenth century, scholars treated Aristotle's insights as rigid prescriptions. Inquiring into the historical reasons behind this happenstance is beyond the scope of this book, but we know now that the practical outcome left Aristotle with an undeserved reputation for pedantry, some of which lingers on to the present. As succeeding writers interpreted Aristotle with more insight and sensitivity, his reputation as a perceptive critic for the most part has been recovered.

Near the beginning of the twentieth century in Russia, scholar and critic Alexander Veselovsky extended the Aristotelian tradition by developing a system of defined aims and methods for the study of literature and drama. His system, like Aristotle's, was based on the importance of plot. Veselovsky was a member of the literary committee of Moscow's important Maly (Small) Theatre and promoted his principles among the theatre artists working there. His ideas influenced Vladimir Nemirovich-Danchenko, a member of the same committee and later cofounder of the Moscow Art Theatre with Konstantin Stanislavsky. Perhaps inspired by Veselovsky's emphasis on plot and artistic unity, Nemirovich and Stanislavsky promoted similar principles and methods among their own students. Significantly, their goal was practical, not scholarly: to help actors, directors, and designers understand and perform plays as logical and harmonious arrangements of actions.

Later on, near the period of the Russian Revolution (1917), formalist ideas began to be applied on an even larger scale by a group of critics known as the Russian Formalists. Headed by Viktor Shklovsky and Evgeny Zamyatin, the Formalists were characterized by their meticulous attention to the inherent artistic aspects of literature as opposed to its social or moral connections.

After 1928, Russian Formalism was suppressed in the Soviet Union for political reasons, but its major concepts and strategies can be found in the New Criticism, which first appeared during the 1930s and flourished during the 1940s and 1950s in the West. New Criticism was an American movement led by John Crowe Ransom, Allen Tate, and Robert Penn Warren, all of whom were writers and poets as well as critics. In his book, *The New Criticism* (1941), Ransom coined the term that identified this informal group, which also included R. P. Blackmur, Kenneth Burke, Cleanth Brooks, Robert B. Heilman, William K. Wimsatt, and Ivor Winters.

Like the Russian Formalists, the New Critics advocated meticulous study of the literary work itself. They disregarded the mind and personality of the author, literary sources, historical–critical theories, and political and social implications, which they considered to be outmoded, historical criticism. To emphasize their belief in the autonomy of the literary work itself, they referred to the writing as the "text" and termed their analytical approach "close reading." Their ideas were presented in four textbooks: Wimsatt and Warren's *Understanding Poetry* (1938), Brooks and Warren's *Understanding Fiction* (1943), Brooks and Heilman's *Understanding Drama* (1948), and Brooks and Warren's guide to methodology, *Modern Rhetoric* (1958). These textbooks helped to shift the focus of literary instruction away from external concerns and back to the work itself.

The Cambridge Critics led a comparable movement in English literary criticism. Influenced by poet T. S. Eliot, this group was led by William Empson and included F. R. Leavis, I. A. Richards, Caroline Spurgeon, and G. Wilson Knight. Knight's analyses of Shakespeare's plays, notably *The Wheel of Fire* (1930), were some of the major successes of the Cambridge Critics in the field of drama.

Many of the principles of the New Criticism were adopted by succeeding generations of American critics, including Francis Fergusson (*The Idea of a Theatre*, 1949), Elder Olson, Eric Bentley, Bernard Beckerman, Richard Hornby, and Jackson G. Barry, as well as theatre educators Alexander Dean, Hardie Albright, Lawrence Carra, William Halstead, F. Cowles Strickland, Curtis Canfield, Frank McMullan, Sam Smiley, and Francis Hodge, to name only a few. Among English-speaking theatre professionals, the members of the Group Theatre beginning in the 1930s adopted the analytical methods of the Moscow Art Theatre. Thus, formalist thinking also supports the creative principles of Stella Adler, Harold Clurman, Richard Boleslavsky, Robert Lewis, Mordecai Gorelik, Elia Kazan, Robert Lewis, Sanford Meisner, Lee Strasberg, and many of their students and followers, as well as Viola Spolin, Robert Cohen, Jean Benedetti, Charles Marowitz, Uta Hagen, and David Mamet. Among the most influential of Stanislavsky's followers in America was the actor and teacher Michael Chekhov (1891–1955), whose principles have become so well known in the world of film and television. After leaving Russia, Chekhov resided in Los Angeles, where he and his collaborator, George Shdanoff, taught several generations of actors a variant of Stanislavsky's principles based on the importance of the imagination and furthermore utilized a type of formalist analysis.

Beginning in the 1960s, drama and literature were influenced by movements in politics, psychoanalysis, sociology, anthropology, and religion in ways that seemed to defy traditional methods of criticism. Accordingly, a new generation of literary critics emerged who were dissatisfied with the self-imposed limits of the formalist approach. Within a decade more wide-ranging critical approaches appeared that were based on deconstruction, post-structuralism, hermeneutics, semiotics, cultural studies, and theories of reception and communication. Some of them have identified meanings previously unrecognized in plays, and sometimes their fresh interpretations have been promising. So far in the rehearsal hall, however, their results have not been consistently useful. Perhaps this is because they have emphasized taking apart (hence deconstruction) while theatrical production by definition must be concerned with putting together.

Moreover, some of the more recent literary theories are by intention always conditional. But as film director Andrey Tarkovsky said, it is risky for actors, directors, and designers never having to reach final conclusions. It is much too easy to settle for hints of intuition instead of thorough, consistent reasoning.

At any rate, even though literary criticism seems committed for the time being to sociopolitical interests outside the play, theatre practice must continue to rely on close study of the play itself. Some may argue that this approach is not better than any other method at its best. After all, there are certain plays and periods of history where considerations outside the script are important and should be studied. On the other hand, understanding the internal nature of the play is crucial to understanding its external context. More important in the theatre, plays must eventually exist in the practical realm of live performance and not just in the intellectual realm of scholarship. On stage, at least, the play itself is obliged to remain the final controlling factor. Formalist analysis corresponds with this point of view. It offers more than intellectual insights; it supplies practical suggestions that can energize actors, directors, and designers in their work.

To conclude, the principles of formalist analysis have endured in the theatre because they correspond with the nature of the thing to which they are applied. They are an outcome of how actors, directors, and designers think about plays, and they are based on the assumption that what these artists need to know about plays is what is important. Although we may not always be aware of it, the principles of formalist analysis help to make plays work out in performance. Without them, play scripts would seem unfinished and probably even unintelligible. Moreover, they are not just empty concepts to learn merely because generations of actors, directors, and designers have done so before. They are the keys that actors, directors, and designers use to check their work, to explore its possibilities, and find new directions in it. Formalist topics are not only the basis of the playwright's vision, but also a guide for actors, directors, and designers in the process of creation.

Action Analysis

This book also teaches a reduced type of formalist analysis called *action analysis*, which concentrates heavily on plot and pays comparatively less attention to the other elements of a play. This reduced type of analysis has its own interesting history and purpose. Stanislavsky developed action analysis during the later stages of work on his "system" of acting. He died before he could codify its principles, but his followers adopted and disseminated them. Among his followers was Maria Knebel (1898–1985), a personal student of both Stanislavsky and Michael Chekhov. A director, teacher, and author of influential books on acting, directing, and theatre pedagogy, Knebel started directing at the Moscow Art Theatre in 1935, and she was artistic director of the Central Children's Theatre 1950–1960, where the revival of the Russian theatre after Stalin began. From 1960–1985 she taught directing at the Lunacharsky State Institute for Theatre Training (GITIS, now RATI), which was founded by Vsevelod Meyerhold. There she made a conscious effort to preserve, maintain, and disseminate Stanislavsky's final principles in their undiluted form. The principles of action analysis described here are adopted from her writings. They were translated by this writer and are presented here in English for the first time.

According to Stanislavsky, the concepts of the super-objective and through-action are central to the creativity of the actor (and by extension, certainly, the director and designer). It is widely known that the Moscow Art Theatre originated the period of table work (analytical work done at the table prior to scenic rehearsals). During this period, the company, under the guidance of the director, subjected to careful analysis all the motives, implications, relationships, characters, through-action, super-objective, etc., of the play. Table work replaced the traditional practice whereby the author simply read the work to the company, after which everyone expressed their opinion of the play and then proceeded to work. Table work supplanted this confused state of affairs. Under the careful guidance of the director, table work made it possible to achieve artistic unity by studying the play deeply and defining its thematic and artistic issues. Table work later became common practice for all theatre organizations, from the largest professional companies to the smallest amateur performances.

Yet as early as 1905 Stanislavsky already had misgivings about the study method he had helped to develop. Since the director as artistic leader always needs to comprehend the future result of the work, the internal structure of the play must be made clear so that the director can imagine the path that will lead the actors and designers to the final result. For that reason, the director is prepared for work much more deeply and multi-dimensionally than the actor or designer in the first period of the company's work together. Stanislavsky saw that even the most patient and sensitive directors (including him) could not avoid becoming creative despots by their need to merge the actors and designers as soon as possible with the director's previously imagined impression of the play. Unintentionally, the practice of table work had begun to deprive the actors and designers of creative initiative. They were becoming passive recipients of the director's plan, which in any case seemed to offer all the right answers. Stanislavsky eventually became disenchanted with the unequal relationship that had unintentionally arisen between the director and the other members of the creative team. He wanted to find a way of working that would put everyone back into direct contact with the play. After further study and practice, he concluded that the easiest and most accessible way to grasp a play was through its plot. He worked out a way of working that combined intellectual analysis with physical action and which came to be known as "The Method of Active Analysis." (Sometimes this method is mistakenly called "The Method of Physical Actions." Though Stanislavsky occasionally used this term, we know now that it actually refers to the Sovietized version of Active Analysis, which played down the psychological parts of the process and played up the physical parts according to Marxist philosophy.)

In the usual way of rehearsing, the director guides the actors and designers toward their work by trying to stir their imaginations while talking about the contents of the play, the characters, the time period, environment, etc. Stanislavsky noticed that in the early stages of company work the actors and designers naturally perceive the director's ideas coolly. They are not prepared to digest someone else's ideas and feelings because they do not feel on firm ground yet and do not know what to accept or reject. For a true grasp of the essence of a play, intellectual as well as physical and emotional experiences are necessary. Stanislavsky criticized his earlier method, where everyone sits down with scripts and pencils and, under the prodding of the director, tries to penetrate the expressive life of the play. He believed that this approach separated the internal life of the play from the external and in doing so impoverished the results. He came to believe that intellectual preparation was necessary primarily to find the "skeleton" of the play, that is, to define the essential actions and their wellsprings. And as soon as everyone understands this much of the dramatic structure, early sensations of the theme, through-action, and mise-en-scene could begin to emerge almost of themselves. This type of rapid, plot-based analysis Stanislavsky called *mental reconnaissance*. As soon as this part of the work was finished, Stanislavsky suggested passing on to the next period of deeper analysis, which no longer exclusively occurred mentally but in the form of real physical action. This he called the period of *physical investigation*. At this point, everyone, including the designers, worked on the internal and external life of the play concurrently. In this way everyone experienced what Stanislavsky called "the psycho-physical unity" of the creative process. Active Analysis integrated mental reconnaissance with physical investigation by means of *etudes* (thematic improvisations) — performance etudes using the play's major events and the actors' words, and mise-en-scene etudes using the play's major events and the designers' sketches. In fact, the organization of Stanislavsky's home-studio made it possible for actors and designers to work together in this process.

A textbook on play analysis is not the place for a discussion of rehearsal or design-studio practice. It is enough to say here that *action analysis is the intellectual part of Stanislavsky's Active Analysis, the part he called mental reconnaissance*. Action analysis offers a big picture of the whole play quickly because it concentrates mainly on plot. Formalist analysis devotes a lot of attention to plot, too, but also a comparable amount to dialogue, character, idea, and tempo–rhythm–mood and style. Action analysis stresses the structural unity of the play, while formalist analysis provides a complete description of all the artistic mechanisms of the play. The first solves basic questions; the second approaches more complex issues. Except for certain learning purposes, there is no particular advantage to one method over the other. Both are necessary for a thorough understanding and in practice they are often used together. Curiously, the two approaches seem to reflect the different personalities of Stanislavsky and Nemirovich-Danchenko. As an actor and teacher, Stanislavsky was always more interested in the processes of learning and working than in performance as such. Possibly for that reason, he developed an approach that minimized table work and maximized physical work. Nemirovich was a playwright, critic, and director whose attention was always focused on the final product, the performance and its thematic significance. He was always committed to table work. The concept of the *seed* explained in Chapter 1 was initially his, although Stanislavsky adopted it, and it has been integrated into action analysis here. Since 1989, we have been learning more about the inner world of the early Moscow Art Theatre, about the working relationship between Stanislavsky and Nemirovich, and about the development of their creative principles. Sharon Carnicke's book, *Stanislavsky in Focus* (1998), is recommended for those who want to know more. Also valuable is *The Russian Theatre after Stalin* (1999) by Anatoly Smeliansky.

xxvi

This sums up what most actors, directors, and designers need to know about the heritage of formalist analysis and action analysis. The complete history, of course, is more complex than this. For example, the Freudian, Jungian, Marxian, Structuralist, Cultural Studies, and Postmodern critics whose ideas currently influence some of the more far-reaching methodologies are omitted from this survey. If the contributions of Freud, Jung, Marx, Sartre, Foucault, Lacan, and Derrida are understated, the position of the Russian Formalists and the New Critics regarding the independence of the text is a little overstated. As a matter of fact, apart from their theories, there are places in their writing that go beyond the literary work and into the areas of politics and morality. The survey is also responsible for another necessary exaggeration. By design, it leads the reader to feel a straight line of thinking that supports the formalist Aristotelian tradition. This is unlikely for a diverse group of thinkers dealing with such a complex subject. But having agreed about these oversimplifications, the survey is still adequate to establish the heritage of the formalist viewpoint. Those who wish to learn more may wish to refer to some of the books that have been written about the history of literary criticism. Among the more informative are *Russian Formalist Criticism: Four Essays* (1965) by Lee T. Lemon and Marion J. Reis, and *Literary Theory: An Introduction* (1996) by Terry Eagleton.

Dramatic Writing

Before beginning to study the principles of play analysis, it will be helpful to review some of the basic principles of reading in general. Initial learning about a play almost always begins with the written words of the script. But when we act, direct, or design a play, we not only read the play but also the play "reads us," so to speak. If we fall short in this respect, the results are there for everyone in the theatre to see. Therefore, what is done at the table before rehearsals and production conferences begin is crucial. If initial perceptions are wrong, every succeeding repetition reinforces the error. If initial perceptions are confused, every succeeding repetition increases the confusion. Persistent errors and extended confusion are certain to lead down the path of artistic failure. For these reasons alone, reviewing some of the basic principles involved with reading and thinking can help theatre artists approach their work with something worthwhile to say.

Special Expressiveness

Crucial differences exist between literature and drama that orthodox literary analysis is not equipped to address by itself. These differences go to the heart of drama as an independent art form. To begin with, literature uses words to illuminate actions and events, while drama uses actions and events to illuminate words. When plays are treated exclusively as literature, they are likely to be analyzed with the same principles as those applied to fiction, poetry, and other literary genres. This line of thinking undervalues the artistic legitimacy of theatre and drama, and indeed this book was written expressly as a challenge to it. Then too, dialogue in literature is supplemented with generous amounts of narration to explain plot, character, idea, and feelings not otherwise apparent. But when narration is employed in plays, it must not be merely literary, but first and foremost dramatic, which means it must convey action. Unlike the literary author, the dramatist cannot interrupt the action to offer supplementary information, add meanings, or clarify complex ideas without impeding the spirit of the play. When a narrator is present in a play, for example, or when background story is expressed, the words must continue to convey action in the specific context of the situation. (Stage directions are written in narrative form, of course, but they are not spoken by the actors and are not central to the action that is performed.)

Another feature that contributes to the special expressiveness of plays is their short length. Even in a very long play, the number of words is very small compared to those in a typical novel. Although plays employ far fewer words than novels, they must still contain at least as much dramatic potential as a complete novel to be theatrically compelling. Playwrights achieve this unique potency by infusing stage dialogue with a special expressiveness that is absent, or at least less significant, in fiction. It is true that stage dialogue often looks very much like its literary cousin. Sometimes it even sounds so ordinary that it seems as if it was written without any conscious effort at all on the part of the playwright. But this is a carefully crafted deception. The truth is that theatrical dialogue is a highly concentrated and powerful form of verbal expression. Speech is more condensed on stage and each word carries far more dramatic impact than in most other literature. Even a single utterance can pack a tremendous emotional wallop. "To Moscow..." "To be or not to be..." Because of the extra measure of expressiveness put into it by the playwright, there is probably more expressiveness per page in a play than in almost any other form of writing. Novelist Henry James, who was also a dramatist and a perceptive critic, maintained that playwriting required a more masterly sense of composition than any other kind of writing.

Concentrated dependence on dialogue as action and radical compactness together create the need and the opportunity for the special expressiveness in dramatic writing. It follows that actors, directors, and designers should learn to understand this special expressiveness to energize and illustrate every last ounce of it in production. Unfortunately, this does not always happen. Because the first experience of a play is a written script, the special expressiveness is both easy to overlook and difficult to recognize. There is an understandable confusion between the literary activity of reading and the theatrical activity of seeing, hearing, and feeling a play on the stage. Confusion is even more likely to occur with plays that have strong literary merit like those of Shakespeare, Samuel Beckett, Tom Stoppard, and other authors whose works are typically studied in dramatic literature courses. To avoid under-reading and misreading, theatre students should be aware of two important considerations about dramatic dialogue. First, the words in a script are far, far more expressive in a live performance than they are in the solitary, concentrated act of reading; and second, the words are only the tip of the iceberg, merely the visible part of what is happening deep inside a play. Energized acting, direction, and design are always required to unleash a play's potent expressiveness completely.

Pattern Awareness

Plays contain patterns that shape plot, character, dialogue, meaning, and atmosphere. The dictionary says that a pattern is a combination of qualities, acts, tendencies, etc., forming a consistent or characteristic arrangement. Play reading requires *pattern awareness*, which is the desire to seek and ability to find these essential patterns in a play. Pattern awareness means deepening the reading process by inquiring beyond surface appearances into underlying arrangements and operations. The patterns that play readers can recognize from this type of awareness shift continuously and run throughout the entire play. Pattern awareness also involves a change in the sense of time, a feeling of many things operating at once, resulting in a rich, lively interplay of characters, meaning, and events. Along with a broader sense of time is a related enlargement of thinking and analysis. The processes of reading, thinking, and analyzing at the level of pattern awareness require a special perspective. Traditionally we break down plays into parts — plot, character, dialogue, etc. — and learn to understand a play's complexity by focusing on only one small feature at a time. Pattern awareness demonstrates how all the parts fit together and how a play represents universal human experiences and feelings.

Historical awareness is a type of pattern awareness intimately associated with the modern era. Historical awareness here means not only a sense of history (a set of intellectual skills associated with the study of history) but also a process of converting the experience of time (past, present, and future) into the practical circumstances of everyday life. As Tom F. Driver rightly pointed out, historical awareness is itself a modern phenomenon and was a new way of thinking when it emerged early in the nineteenth century. To be a modern artist, in other words, means to live with an intense awareness of history, change, and the passage of time. Realism, the dramatic form that we associate most readily with modernism, arose from a feeling that life cannot depend forever on the thinking of the past or even the present. In form, certainly, realistic plays attempted to preserve the illusion of actual life "scientifically." In content, on the other hand, these plays made use of historical awareness, then new, to expose the repressiveness of institutions that was customarily kept hidden by "tradition."

In nonrealistic plays, pattern awareness often takes the form of *mythic awareness*. Myth is an important feature in Carl Jung's psychology and Northrop Frye's literary criticism, but its application in play analysis is broader and less specialized. Here myth simply means a traditional story that describes the psychology, customs, or ideals of a society. It has the related terms archetype (an original pattern on which all things of a similar kind are based) and ritual (a practice or pattern of behavior regularly performed in a set manner). Myths exist everywhere. They form part of a society's collective knowledge and therefore are characteristic features of a culture.

Sometimes too much emphasis is placed on such hidden meanings in plays, of course, but mythic awareness in the sense intended here is more than random myth hunting. In realistic and classic plays, events happen to one set of persons, at one moment in time, and in one place. Nonrealistic plays, in contrast, call special attention to the way each human being is both an individual and the representative of a group. Nonrealistic plays have developed specifically from the feeling that now more than ever we sense instinctively how each of us is part of a larger human experience in the world. Consider how often in public discourse we hear about concepts such as globalization, multiculturalism, and environmentalism, not to mention entities such as CNN, the United Nations, and the Internet. Thus, in nonrealistic plays mythic awareness is more than an accidental issue, as it is in realistic or historical plays. On the contrary, mythic awareness is an intentional attribute and a defining characteristic of nonrealism. Coincidentally, this is where nonrealistic plays connect with the very earliest forms of theatre. The dramatists of ancient Greece were expressing mythic awareness when they based their plays on stories about the gods and heroes of their religion. Medieval religious drama as well as much of the theatre of South America, Africa, Asia, and the Asian subcontinent can be traced to the same feeling.

In the West mythic awareness has been a comparatively modern phenomenon. It emerged close in time to World War I in response to the accidental coming together of Sigmund Freud's psychology, Albert Einstein's special theory of relativity, and the widespread disillusionment following the "war to end all wars." At the time a new view of the world began to appear that altered the basic features of the initial forms of modernism. The geniuses of this high modernism (James Joyce, Gertrude Stein, Pablo Picasso, Igor Stravinsky, Henri Matisse, and Samuel Beckett) expressed their vision of this emerging viewpoint partly by introducing a large-scale, collective sense of awareness into their works. Thornton Wilder was correct when he said that Joyce sought to situate his characters "among all those people who have lived and died, in all the periods of time, all the geography of the world, all the races, all the catastrophes of history" (Wilder, 176). Wilder was reaching for the same feeling when he wrote *The Skin of Our Teeth* and *Our Town*, two of America's most well-known nonrealistic plays.

Closer to our own time, Sam Shepard, author *A Lie of the Mind* and other nonrealistic plays, shares the same feeling:

In writing a play you can snare emotions that are not just personal emotions, not just catharsis, not just psychological emotions that you are getting off your chest, but emotions and feelings that are connected with everybody. Hopefully. It is not true all the time; sometimes it is nothing but self-indulgence. But if you work hard enough toward being true to what you intuitively feel is going on down in the play, you might be able to catch that kind of thing. So that you suddenly hook up with feelings that are on a very broad scale ... you start with something personal and see how it follows out and opens to something that's much bigger.... Then it starts to move in directions we all know, regardless of where we come from or who we are. It starts to hook up in a certain way. Those, to me, are mythic emotions. (*Dialogue*, April 1985, 58)

Shepard, Wilder, Bertolt Brecht, Samuel Beckett, Tom Stoppard, Harold Pinter, Tony Kushner, and Caryl Churchill, among many others, share similar feelings about the role of myth in contemporary playwriting, above all in nonrealistic plays. These writers are less interested in telling stories through accepted notions of plot and character than they are in revealing the broader meanings, the mythic content, beneath the surface of everyday life. Accordingly, the mythic patterns found in their plays are of more than passing importance. Such patterns serve to place these plays within a special view of the world. In practical terms, nonrealistic plays set up a constant alternation between everyday reality and large generalizations, relying on mythic awareness to "connect the dots" and help everything fit together. Awareness of patterns, history, and myth is one of the chief features of modern theatre. Even more, nonrealism in high-modern and late-modern theatre points toward the emergence of postmodern theatre, itself already on the move for some time.

Reading Plays

There are no hard and fast rules for reading plays, but certain mental skills are needed to understand the special kind of expressiveness they contain. The first important skill is that of analytical reading. Unfortunately, in its initial stages at least, analytical reading is hard work. Inexperienced amateurs tend to think that experienced professionals can sight-read a play the way some musicians sight-read a score, but this skill is as rare in the theatre as it is in music. A professional's analysis of a play is a long and painstaking process. In fact, a major characteristic of professionals is their recognition of the value of slow, methodical brain work.

Respect for Words

Another mental power consists of the ability to understand the many meanings of words and the dramatic force that may be expressed by them. Art students pay attention to shape and color; music students listen for pitch and timbre. Those who wish to make a living in the theatre need to develop an appreciation of the expressiveness and emotion inherent in words.

Facts, Implications, and Inferences

Mental power also means concern for literal facts and their connections. A fact is a verifiable assertion about a thing, and literal facts are those that are frankly stated in the dialogue as true. Literal facts in drama include identifications of people, places, actions, and objects, but they may also describe wishes as well as feelings and thoughts. Learning how to recognize hard facts is a basic test of artistic awareness. In the earliest readings of a play, the literal, verifiable facts need to be searched out to find what is objectively said. Furthermore, since plays are orderly arrangements by their nature, making logical connections among the facts is necessary for understanding the sequences and patterns found in them. We call these connections implications and inferences. Implications are hints or suggestions that are intended but not directly stated, and inferences are deductions from what is neither intended nor stated.

Remember the short scene in the garden from act 2 of Arthur Miller's play, *Death of a Salesman*. After a confrontation with his son Biff, Willy Loman decides to plant vegetables in his backyard garden late the same night. As in several earlier scenes, his absent brother, Ben, appears to him in a reverie, and they carry on a short dialogue. In this scene, the literal facts about planting a garden are important. We know that planting a garden requires certain external activities and special tools. Since these can be described precisely, this part of the action is easy to understand. Some of the literal facts involved with planting a garden are present: opening packages of seeds and reading the instructions, pacing off the rows for different kinds of plants, digging with a hoe, and planting the seeds in the ground. But most readers will see right away that planting a garden is not all that is happening here. There are things going on that are not connected with planting a garden. Planting is not done late at night with a flashlight, and a gardener does not carry on a conversation about life insurance with an imaginary figure the way Willy does. Willy is also possessed by a mysterious sense of urgency or anxiety in his task that prevents him from paying close attention to Ben. Obviously planting a garden is no longer what we normally think it is.

Implications and inferences now become important and they go beyond a literal reading of the scene. A closer examination of Willy's unusual actions relates them to his innermost feelings and thoughts, particularly his profound sense of personal failure as a father. He is no longer simply planting a garden; he is performing a ritual in preparation for his imminent death. The garden scene becomes an important clue to the meaning of the whole play, which is a conflict between Willy's misguided ideals as a salesman and his fatherly duty toward his son Biff. Therefore, although literal facts are a helpful starting point, implications and inferences need to be considered to arrive at a satisfactory understanding. Script analysis involves piecing the known and unknown together into a consistent and meaningful pattern just as detectives do in crime fiction.

Logical Thinking

Evidence of all kinds is important, but so is logical thinking. Unfortunately, unawareness of the creative capacities of logical thinking is widespread, especially among amateur artists. It can lead to the feeling that careful study of a play is stuffy and even creatively inhibiting. But experienced professionals appreciate that logical thinking can uncover dramatic possibilities that make plays come alive in a new way. There is another value to consider. Audiences are becoming smarter all the time because playwrights demand far more intelligence from them today than they did in the past. Ever since Vsevelod Meyerhold and Bertolt Brecht, a good number of modern plays have been fashioned to pull in the audience by inducing them to comprehend what is happening ideologically, not just to experience the play in a passive manner. Increasing emphasis has been placed on the semantic features of the play and a great deal of aesthetic pleasure comes from penetrating the secret thinking of the characters. Consequently, modern acting, directing, and design need to demand the most of audience understanding. If this is to occur, the artistic team needs to be at least one step ahead of the audience in its thinking. Unless the audience is given something exciting to think about, unless the artistic team understands and expresses the meaning of the play, the production cannot be considered truly modern in the creative sense.

Misleading Notions

Bringing some of the commonly misleading notions encountered in play reading out of the subconscious, where they often lurk, and into the open, can help readers to avoid accidental misreading. There are only a few pitfalls, and they are not difficult to understand. Most of them can be classified as nonsequiturs, either as conclusions that do not follow from the facts or as reasoning that does not make sense. Sometimes readers may need to revisit the principles of logical thinking before trying to deal more thoroughly with plays. The basics can be found in any good rhetoric textbook. With the help of a good teacher, this should be enough to fill in any gaps.

Affective Fallacy (Impressionism)

According to critic W. K. Wimsatt, this error results from confusion between the play and its results (what it is vs. what it does). It comes about when readers allow their favorite ideals or momentary enthusiasms or the momentary enthusiasms of the community to intrude on their judgment of the play. Maintaining enough emotional detachment is necessary to analyze a play correctly, but this is not always easy to do. After all, plays are meant to be emotional experiences, and many readers respond strongly to the emotional stimuli in them. Actors, directors, and designers, for example, respond in highly personal ways, as indeed they should. In the scene from *Death of a Salesman* cited above, it is possible that readers could be reminded of their own families. They might be drawn to conflate their own emotional memories with those of Willy Loman in the play. Or, alternatively, readers who sympathized with Willy's economic plight might be tempted to entangle their own point of view about economics with the economic world described in the play. Personal experiences like these can be interesting if readers are experienced artists or critics; but if not, they can lead to loose thinking or analytical lack of attention. At worst, a reader might become hopelessly, if unthinkingly, bogged down in self-analysis. Nonetheless, it is possible to maintain emotional distance and still respond emotionally to a play. The solution is to try to separate intimate personal responses from what is objectively there in the play. As director Elia Kazan said, "The first job is to discover what the script is saying, not what it reminds you of." Absolute objectivity is impossible, of course, but impartiality and the tracing out of both routine and unusual consequences needs to be maintained as much as possible.

Relativist Fallacy
Relativism is often known as the theory that all points of view are equally valid and depend on the individual. In the theatre, this would be like saying that all stage interpretations are equally well-founded. If this were true, there would be no way of writing a play rationally, reading it logically, or performing it effectively. If no example of acting, directing, or design is better than any other, then the work of any amateur or dilettante would be as good as that of any experienced professional. It is hard to understand how this belief could be held without denying the excellence of Tom Stoppard, Meryl Streep, Peter Brook, Ming Cho Lee, and many others indeed.

This misconception is called the relativist fallacy. It arose as a correct, though excessive, reaction against the Victorian notion that Western society was superior to any other. It led for awhile to the counter-belief that no society could be judged from the viewpoint of any other. At the present time most of us recognize that every society has its good and bad points and that any society can go bad and lead to abuses that are simply wrong. The same principle is true in the sphere of art. The point of view of this book is that it should be possible to show what a play is and how it might be understood as a basis for acting, directing, or design. If this is true, then the quality of plays and their production does not depend merely on your opinion or mine, but on diligent study and extensive practice under the guidance of honest and experienced teachers and mentors.

Fallacy of Faulty Generalization

Some readers are inclined to this reading error when they jump to a conclusion without having enough evidence. When a reader uses "all" or "never" in statements about the play with only a casual concern for the information in the play itself, further close reading will normally correct the mistake. But even more deadly in play reading is inattention to contrary examples. If, after reading *Hamlet*, for instance, a reader resorts to the worn-out generalities about "the melancholy prince" or "the man who could not make up his mind," he should test the conclusions with contradictory evidence. A little scrutiny will show that Hamlet is cheerful while welcoming the Players, and he is decisive while dealing with the Ghost. A few contrary illustrations like these should be enough to disprove the original sweeping assertions.

Fallacy of Illicit Process (Reductiveness)

This kind of error reduces complex issues to one thing, which is a frequent mistake even among experienced play readers. Reducing Hamlet to the Freudian "Oedipus Complex" is an extreme instance. So is thinking that *Mother Courage* is nothing but an anti-war play, that *A Raisin in the Sun* is a plea for racial integration, *A Lie of the Mind* is a plea against spousal abuse, that *Angels in America* is a defense of homosexuality, or *Three Sisters* is about the decline of the Russian intelligentsia. The spoken or implied phrase "nothing but" is the giveaway. The motive behind attempts to reduce a play to less complex equivalents is generally disparagement.

Genetic Fallacy

Related to reductiveness is the genetic fallacy or the fallacy of origins, which is an attempt to reduce a play to its sources in the historical world of the artist in order to explain it. There is for any play a large body of secondary writing about its circumstances, the author's life and times, and so forth. Much of this writing is pedantic in the extreme and full of banalities. For example, the question is not what does *Death of a Salesman* tell us about Arthur Miller's personal life or about American society after World War II, but rather what does it tell us about itself? There may be some connections between a play and some external features in the life and world of the author, but they are not as important as people believe them to be. Seldom does a point-to-point correlation exist, and although formalist analysis teaches the fundamental unity of plays, it also teaches that plays are complex independent objects deserving intellectual respect. Readers should exercise caution before attempting to trace the meaning of a play to a tendency observed in the life or times of the author.

Fallacy of the Half-Truth (Debunking)

This error in logic occurs when readers use the same explanation for everything, with negative implications. In this way, the author, play, or character is discredited or debunked. Henrik Ibsen's plays often suffer from this fallacy among readers. To say that Ibsen wrote grim Victorian social dramas carries the unspoken meaning to others that his plays are (1) gloomy and humorless, (2) the result of psychological neuroses in the author's temperament, and (3) Victorian journalism masquerading as drama. Readers holding this opinion see Ibsen's plays as boring, depressing, and outdated. Another example is the statement that: "nothing really happens in Samuel Beckett's plays — there's no plot." What is the hidden meaning behind this half-truth? The remedy for automatic cynicism is to study the script more than once and with an open mind. This is not just a question of finding any reasonable explanation and verifying it in the script but also of testing what connects to what against many points in the script.

Frigidity (Insensitivity)

The next error turns in the opposite direction. Frigidity is author John Gardner's term for not showing enough concern about the characters or situations. Frigidity here means not treating the feelings in the play with the humane respect they deserve. Frigidity also includes the inability to recognize the seriousness of things in general. The standard of comparison is the respect any civilized person should show under the circumstances. Frigidity occurs when pulling back from genuine feeling through irony or sarcasm, or when only looking at the surface trivialities in a conflict, playing the jester. Unfortunately, it is one of the chief characteristics of the current scene. It can lead actors, directors, and designers to less concern for the characters, conflict, and meaning of a play. The error is also frigidity when actors, directors, or designers knowingly go into a production less than fully prepared. Frigidity is one of the worst errors possible in play reading and is often the root cause of other errors.

Theatre is based on the sympathy we should have for other people's problems, for their pain. It has been said many times that drama opens minds and stimulates the empathetic imagination by allowing us to understand the world through eyes other than our own. This is even truer for actors, directors, and designers whose responsibility it is to theatricalize the preconditions for empathy in the spectators. The ability to penetrate a spatial barrier and enter an object for a moment of complete identification — this is essential for an artist and it is precisely the paralysis of this faculty that leads to the problem of frigidity.

Imitative Fallacy

According to poet and critic Ivor Winters, to say that a work of literature is justified in employing, let's say, lack of communication to express a lack of communication, is merely an indirect justification for bad reading or bad writing. In fact, all feeling, if surrendered to, is a mode of "miscommunication," just as it may be a mode of loving, hating, flying, fearing, etc. Playwriting is not only a means of capturing feelings but also arranging them in dramatic form, and play reading is an attempt to understand this process in order to communicate it. To the extent that any play or reading of a play produces a real lack of communication, real boredom, or real chaos, it fails in its intention to work satisfactorily on stage.

Intentional Fallacy

This is another of Wimsatt's formulations that is central to the principles of formalist analysis. It means trying to determine what the author's so-called intention was and whether it was fulfilled, instead of attending to the work itself. Examples of this are easy to find because of the modern vogues for complicated literary criticism and the resulting frequency with which artists insist on writing about their own works. Take the situation of Bertolt Brecht. No one can measure the amount of misunderstanding that has resulted from misapplication of his theoretical writings to productions of his plays (alienation effect, epic theatre, and so forth). Wimsatt in *The Verbal Icon* argues that a work of art is detached from the author the moment it is finished. After that, the author no longer has the power to "intend" anything about it or to control it. Wimsatt's opinion, however, should be taken as a warning more than as a strict rule. As with the other reading errors, the antidote to use against the intentional fallacy is repeated close reading of the play itself before attempting to make a definitive statement about the author's intention.

Biographical Fallacy

This is the belief that a play can be understood by claiming it is really about events in the dramatist's life. This type of approach distances itself from the play and goes instead into the playwright's biography to find people, places, and things that seem to be similar to features in the play. And then it claims that the play is actually a picture of those people, places, and things. In its extreme form this is a fallacy because it does not consider that playwrights use their imaginations when they write, and that they can imagine improbable or even impossible things. It is common to say, for instance, that Sam Shepard wrote about the West because he has lived there for much of his life. But if living in the West were all that was required to write plays, many more people would be writing them. What about the plays Shepard wrote that do not take place in the West? But someone might add that Shepard was also a musician, but then so are many other people, and where are their plays? Biography can be potentially useful for actors, directors, and designers in their work, but it can never be a satisfactory argument alone for the interpretation of a production. The real problem is that biographical study might become a substitute for the hard work of studying the play itself. It could completely overlook the imaginative work of the playwright.

Literal-Mindedness

Related to frigidity is the error of evaluating everything in the play on the basis of its literal resemblance to real life. When it is used as a negative judgment, a statement like "the Angel in *Angels in America* and Sutter's ghost in *The Piano Lesson* are not plausible because modern science tells us there are no such things as angels or ghosts" is a typical if crude example. This kind of thinking is a possible sign of a limited imagination as much as anything else. It may stem from misunderstanding the idea of reality in acting, sometimes called emotional honesty. But the quality of observed reality in a play has little connection with the play's potential for expressing psychological truth. A play, after all, can be unrealistic in all its external features and still permit honest acting. A simple door can be different from one play to another, depending on the artistic plan of the production. In one play, it can be realistic while in another the actor can enter by appearing out of the darkness in a spotlight. Emotional honesty and theatrical reality are separate and distinct issues and do not contradict one another. Whatever the source of the confusion, however, the lesson is that everyday reality is irrelevant to understanding a play as an artistic experience. Each play creates its own special "reality."

Secondhand Thinking

This error is a corollary of the intentional fallacy. Although it is not a logical fallacy as such, it can still be troublesome for novice play readers. It stems from relying too much on other people's opinions, especially when dealing with difficult material. The methods of the college classroom and the contemporary interest in radical criticism have not discouraged the habit. Unfortunately, addiction to the judgments, even of experienced critics, and even when they are accurate, can inhibit self-confidence and independent thinking. Artists, especially young artists, should beware of cutting themselves off from new experiences, feelings, or words by relying too much on established opinion rather than on direct contact. To permit the free exercise of imagination, script analysis should initially be a solo experience. Experts can safely be consulted afterward.

Over-Reliance on Stage Directions

Secondhand thinking also extends to stage directions, which are notes incorporated in a script or added to it to convey information about its performance not already evident in the dialogue itself. Ordinarily they are concerned either with the actor's movements on stage or with scenery and stage effects. Plays written in the past tended to keep stage directions to a minimum, but over the years their use grew more widespread until, by the end of the nineteenth century, they were often long and very elaborate. The prefaces to George Bernard Shaw's plays, for instance, often run on for dozens of pages and contain explicit — if sometimes amusingly misleading — information for actors, directors, and designers. There is some evidence among modern playwrights, however, of a reversal of this trend.

But stage directions may not always belong to the author. According to the practice of most play publishers today, stage directions are as likely to be written by the original stage manager and taken from the ideas of the original director and the scenery, costumes, and lighting of the original designers; or else written by the literary editor of the text (as in the case of Shakespeare, for example). Even when we are certain the author has written the stage directions, it is prudent to recall the advice of the influential designer and thinker, Edward Gordon Craig, about the reliability of stage directions. In his essay "On the Art of the Theatre," Craig contended that stage directions are an "infringement" on the artistic rights of actors, directors, and designers. From this he concluded that playwrights should cease using them altogether! Craig's prejudices are notorious, of course, and his position on this subject was extreme. He did have a point, however. Stage directions are intended to supplement the dialogue, not replace it. They should not be confused with the play itself. Many professional actors, directors, and designers as well as producers and agents will seldom read stage directions, any stage directions. They want to work with the play itself and allow it to tell them everything they need to know, which is the point of view of this book.

In Conclusion

In the theatre, we do not always get the chance to choose the plays we act, direct, or design. And even when we do, the plays themselves do not always sustain our initial interest as much as we would like them to. Professional analysis — the approach introduced here and taught in the following chapters — is a method for placing actors, directors, and designers in a sustained creative state. It is not only a means of help; it is also a practical skill. It is like a basic grammar. It should permanently take root in us so that we do not have to think about it at the moment of creativity. Professional analysis is not a command or a required style, however. It is not necessary to force it, but to allow the door to open for itself...   xli

CHAPTER 1

Action Analysis

Why action analysis? In the Introduction we said that formalist analysis proceeds by gathering lots of detailed information from the play and then drawing general conclusions about the whole work. It uses a systematic collection of close-ups to assemble at last the big picture. Because it attempts to cover all the dramatic potentials of a play, formalist analysis is time-consuming and thorough. This attention to detail almost guarantees its practical success. Unfortunately, attention to detail is also lengthy and loaded with ins and outs. In the middle of a project readers can become so involved in the details that at times they lose sight of the whole play. They cannot see the forest for the trees. At some point they may need to step back and consider what result their project is leading to. The method of action analysis offered in this chapter provides that opportunity. Action analysis is a reduced type of formalist analysis based primarily on the events in the plot. It is not intended as a shortcut to creativity, however. It may be quicker and simpler than formalist analysis, but by the same token it is also less complete. Action analysis and formalist analysis are meant to complement each other. They are arranged so that they operate together to obtain the level of knowledge necessary for professional work.

Action analysis will also introduce readers to some of the features of formalist analysis treated at more length starting with the next chapter. For example, to evaluate the events accurately, it will be necessary to consider the given circumstances (Chapter 2), background story (Chapter 3), action (Chapter 4), and structure (Chapter 5), which are the lifeblood of a play. By determining the main events from which the behavior of a character develops, readers will begin to understand the motives behind the actions and start to learn about character (Chapter 6). In addition, learning the sequence of the events and its logic, readers will come to an understanding of the main idea that governs the play (Chapter 7). The close association between action analysis and formalist analysis also means that each method can be learned and used in any order the reader's needs require.

Events

The easiest and most accessible way to come to terms with a play is through the events in the plot. That is why action analysis starts with the process of identifying and explaining the play's events and then builds on this foundation. An *event* is something that generally would not or should not happen. As a result, it changes everything, causes new ideas and feelings in a character, forces a character to see life in a new way, and changes the direction of a character's life. The bigger the event, the bigger the change is. To distinguish an event from an ordinary fact is quite simple. Stanislavsky suggested looking back on any stage of our own life and trying to remember what the main event was in this interval of time and understand how it was reflected in our relations with others. Of course, it is easy to appreciate what this or that event is in one's own life. But just try to appreciate the value of a similar fact not for oneself but for another person, and how mistaken we can be in our estimation of the fact from the other person's

2

point of view. Even for that of a close friend or relative, it is not very easy. Empathy — the capacity to recognize or understand another's state of mind or emotion — is necessary to appreciate what is important in someone else's life. And for empathy to be real, it is necessary for us to study all the circumstances that predetermined the given fact, all the motives that led the person to perform this or that action. It would be necessary to interview this person and obtain some very personal information for this purpose.

So it is with actors, directors, and designers, who by definition must work with unfamiliar characters. How do we learn what constitutes a major event or a passing episode under these circumstances? For this purpose it is necessary to remove the specified fact from the play, and after that try to understand how it would affect the life of the characters. Again, empathy. What would happen, for example, if Ophelia did not allow her father and Claudius to eavesdrop on her conversation with Hamlet? She would have another destiny. Sad and unfair, perhaps, but not tragic. There would not have been the shock of rejection from Hamlet that extinguished Ophelia's last hope. She would not have suffered the terrible truth of her isolation that led her to suicide. Ophelia's sad destiny in the play is linked to her role in the eavesdropping scene. Understanding what constitutes a dramatic event requires readers to think eventfully (consistent with the action), instead of just verbally (consistent with the dialog).

Action analysis also requires a special understanding to be able to distinguish the essential events from the less essential. A simple illustration will help to explain. An express train traveling, for example, from Boston to Washington, D.C. stops only at major cities along the way: New York, Philadelphia. But there is also a local train, which stops at the medium-size cities: Hartford, New Haven, Baltimore, etc. To study the regions lying between the major cities — between Boston and New York or between Philadelphia and Washington, D.C. — the traveler needs to stop at the smaller cities, where one contains shopping districts, another suburbs, a third hills and valleys, a fourth lakes and rivers, a fifth factories, etc. It is also possible for the traveler to get off the train and take an intercity bus, stopping at each small town, village, or rural community along the way. There the traveler can obtain an even better understanding of the regions lying between Boston and Washington, D.C. Then again, it is also possible for a non-stop train to travel straight from Boston to Washington, D.C. without any stops along the way. A feeling of great momentum and speed will be the result. But this "train" is for the rich — the geniuses, as Stanislavsky put it. We might say that the express train is action analysis (Chapter 1),

3

while the local train is formalist analysis (Chapters 2–7) and the inter-city bus is advanced formalist analysis (Chapters 8–10). Most of us do not need to concern ourselves with the nonstop train.

Sequence of External Events

The sequence of events begins with a list of the most important external events in their original order. *External events* are the basic social interactions that are taking place, for example, arrivals or departures, meetings, announcements, discussions, quarrels, etc. External events exist on the primary, material level of the play; however, they must be significant in the context of the play and not just routine. There is no need to be too exacting when describing the external events at this point, as long as the descriptions are generally accurate. The goal of action analysis is not to be exhaustively thorough, but to obtain a rapid picture of the whole play as fast as possible. Shakespeare's plays make the learning process somewhat easier to manage because they are crowded with events and are also divided into formal scenes. As a result, it is possible to consider most scenes as a single external event, at least for learning purposes. *Hamlet* will be the example used here.

What happens in 1,1 (shorthand for act 1, scene 1)? Several small external events occur in the scene: the changing of the guard, the arrival of Horatio, the appearance of the Ghost, a discussion about the previous appearance of the Ghost, the second appearance of the Ghost, a discussion about Denmark's preparations for war, and a decision to tell Hamlet about the Ghost. These are simple socio-physical activities — arrivals, departures, discussions, and decisions — of the kind found in everyday life under a variety of circumstances. But they are significant because they are happening for the first time, relate to Hamlet personally, and may have a bearing on Denmark's volatile political environment. At this point they are described in the fewest words possible, short and to the point. Brevity and an absence of literary language are essential goals in action analysis. Short, clear-cut descriptions are closest to simple human behavior, which is a merit of action analysis.

The next question to ask is which one of the six or seven smaller events in 1,1 form the essence of the whole scene. What single event sets the scene apart and defines its vital purpose in the play? Let's review the circumstances. All the characters in the play are important at some point, of course, but for the moment most readers would agree that the guards Francisco, Barnardo, and Marcellus, are less essential here than Horatio and the Ghost. Horatio is Hamlet's classmate and closest friend from the University of Wittenberg, and the Ghost provides the grounds for the scene. Earlier, Marcellus told Horatio about the prior appearance of the Ghost, but the skeptical Horatio did not believe him. That is why Marcellus has asked him to come and see for himself. A wise rehearsal room proverb says, "Anything of importance on stage happens either for the first time or the last time." First times and last times entail beginnings and ends, which are dramatic by their nature. This particular scene shows Horatio's first encounter with the Ghost. In fact, it is his first experience with anything supernatural. Moreover, as Hamlet's closest friend and confidant, Horatio would be the first to tell him about the event. Evidently, the main point of the scene is Horatio's encounter with the Ghost. Therefore, we could describe the chief external event of 1,1 as "Horatio encounters the Ghost."

Using an "express" way of thinking, the external events in *Hamlet* could be listed like this:

1,1. Horatio encounters the Ghost
1,2. Claudius takes over the throne
1,3. Laertes departs for France
1,4. Hamlet encounters the Ghost
1,5. Hamlet learns that Claudius murdered his father
2,1. Polonius gives instructions to Reynaldo
2,2. Hamlet plans to trap Claudius
3,1. Claudius eavesdrops on Hamlet and Ophelia
3,2. The "mousetrap scene"
3,3. Claudius attempts to pray
3,4. Hamlet reproaches Gertrude
4,1. Claudius takes action against Hamlet
4,2. Hamlet is captured by Rosencrantz and Guildenstern
4,3. Claudius sends Hamlet to England
4,4. Hamlet crosses paths with Fortinbras
4,5. Laertes returns to Elsinore
4,6. Horatio learns that Hamlet has returned
4,7. Claudius and Laertes conspire to murder Hamlet
5,1. Hamlet learns about Ophelia's death
5,2. Hamlet agrees to a sporting duel with Laertes
5,3. Hamlet slays Claudius

This is quite a short and snappy summary of a very complex play. Some may argue that it is too short; others may disagree with some of the descriptions. No matter. Action analysis is not intended to be complete or perfect, just rapid and functional. As well, the descriptions offered here are not intended to be definitive but simply demonstrations of the thinking process involved. Besides, sometimes a short and snappy point of view is useful for seeing through the avalanche of words in a play, above all a play by Shakespeare. Whatever the case may be, more analysis and rehearsal lie ahead to fine-tune any over-hasty or misguided conclusions. True, many less essential events have been omitted, but at least this summary gives a satisfactory outline of the external events, which at this point is all that is needed to proceed with the next stage of action analysis.

Reviewing the Facts

This stage of action analysis is explained by its title. *Reviewing the facts* means coming to terms with the basic specifics of the play. As a process, it occurs at random intervals throughout action analysis, and one good time to address it occurs after defining the external events. Notice that we already performed a quick review of the facts for 1,1 when attempting to define the basic external events for that scene. A similar thinking process led to identification of the other external events listed above for the play.

This stage of action analysis asks readers to understand the characters as specific people who are living in a specific set of circumstances. To do so, it is necessary to purge any memories of what other actors, directors, or designers may have done with the play in the past or what anyone may have written about it. Other people's ideas can come later, after readers have reached their own understanding. Reviewing the facts in this way, readers will start to understand for themselves the conditions that generate the events, plus the words and characters that illustrate them. Reviewing the facts means answering the questions: who, what, where, when, why, and how, including everything that happened before the play begins and offstage between acts and scenes. In the formalist analysis taught in the following chapters, those conditions are called given circumstances, background story, external and internal action, and character. Action analysis does not require careful identification of these conditions in the same thorough way as format analysis does. All that is needed at present is to ask, who, what, where, when, why, and how in any convenient order. Study the questions as a skeptical district attorney would do when cross-examining a deceitful offender, inquiring and probing and not taking anything for granted.

Seed

Action analysis also looks for a special pattern that is latent but unidentified in the external events up to now. At first, it may seem that literary scholars have already covered this ground. A search for *Hamlet* in the Modern Language Association database, for example, lists over three thousand articles on subjects (patterns) ranging from Afterlife and Allegory to Violence and Wordplay. *Hamlet* contains many, many patterns, but there is a difference between a pattern as a literary motif and the special kind of pattern sought here in action analysis. The dictionary states that a motif is "a recurring prominent thematic element." Searching for interesting motifs is standard practice in literary scholarship, where the goal is basically intellectual insights. The question for actors, directors, and designers is not what motifs take account of, not what motifs include, but what they exclude. The point is that motifs cover just part of a work. In the theatre, the whole play has to be produced, not just the parts that match up with a certain motif. By relying too much on literary motifs, actors, directors, and designers sometimes assume that the rest of the work is merely padding for the sake of entertainment. Or worse, lapses on the part of the dramatist. Or worse still, they might apply additional literary motifs to fill the "vacant" parts, a practice that would undermine the artistic unity of the play.

7

The question clears up as soon as we think about the nature of pattern in drama. While a motif may illuminate two, three, or four events or more, the special pattern sought in play analysis, in action analysis, ought to illuminate the entire play. The creative processes of actors, directors, and designers involve a steady, consecutive embodiment of this pattern into a unified representation. Action analysis accelerates the process by using an analytic concept called the *seed*, which provides a concise vision of the whole play. Formalist analysis reveals such a pattern using the concepts of super-objective and main idea, which will be covered in subsequent chapters.

Stanislavsky's partner and co-founder of the Moscow Art Theatre, Vladimir Nemirovich-Danchenko, devised the concept of the seed. Nemirovich was a playwright, critic, and superior director in his own right and in 1943 he established the Moscow Art Theatre School. He never trusted that it was possible to begin creative work on a play without everyone — actors and designers as well as director — having a clear vision of the seed, of the whole, before them. Maria Knebel, a personal pupil of both Stanislavsky and Nemirovich, wrote about the seed:

The concept of the seed occupies a leading position in Nemirovich-Danchenko's system of creative insights. Correctly established by the director, the seed first of all promotes a "vision of the whole," it helps to construct the performance based on a harmonic unity of all its parts. The seed should resonate through each episode, Nemirovich-Danchenko said, and he required that all the participants of a production, whether playing a small or large role, should be strongly connected to everyone else by a common striving to produce on stage this essence of the author's plan, for the sake of which the play was brought to life, for the sake of which the theatre selected and produced it.

(Knebel, 181–182)

The seed, then, is the "essence of the author's plan," the basic subject of the play, the central issue "for the sake of which the play was brought to life." A seed in nature is a source of development or growth, and the seed of a play is the source of its development and growth as a creative work. In Shakespeare, there is an enormous amount of details, digressions, and consequences piled on top of each other, many of which have only a distant connection to the seed. This is because the original seed has matured, so to speak, into a giant, impressive redwood tree. We might also say that the smaller the mature tree is, the simpler the original play. The smallest trees are no more than everyday clichés or newspaper anecdotes. In the finest and subtlest plays, however, it is possible to lose sight of the original seed, but it is always there nonetheless. Today we might think of the seed as the play's DNA, because it contains the "genetic instructions" used in the development and operation of every part of the play.

The seed can generally be traced to one of society's moral commandments to respect a Greater Good, to honor one's family, as well as sanctions against idolatry, murder, infidelity, stealing, dishonesty, greed, etc. Of course, commandments like "You shall not kill" are very elementary. And if that is all the seed is, then it could be a simple newspaper story stating "Mr. Jones killed Mr. Smith. He was captured, put on trial, and sent to prison." Not very interesting, probably, except for Messrs. Jones and Smith. But what about a big, complicated story such as *Hamlet*? Here a huge number of variations, digressions, resulting ideas, and observations are heaped together, showing little obvious connection either with each other or with its innermost moral commandment, whatever it might be.

Nemirovich-Danchenko used an example from his stage adaptation of Leo Tolstoy's novel *Anna Karenina* (1876) to explain the concept of the seed. Tolstoy's story is about a tragic, adulterous love affair, and Nemirovich said that the seed for his production was "passion." Clearly, this seed can be traced to the commandment "You shall not commit adultery." Passion explains the nature of Anna's violation of this commandment besides revealing society's attitude toward it. However, we barely perceive this so visibly in the pages of the novel because we become so involved in the particulars of life presented there. So much is happening from page to page as we observe how the characters under- or overrate the influence of this moral commandment in their lives or when they try to offer extenuating circumstances to explain it away. Much of the action has little obvious connection to the seed of passion, but all the same the seed is what holds it all together.

Which moral commandment is found at the core of *Hamlet*? The most obvious choice would be "You shall not kill," stemming from Claudius' murder of King Hamlet. However, an attentive reading of 1,2 shows that something more is troubling Hamlet, something he feels even before he learns that his father was murdered. Hamlet suggests what this something is when his mother reproaches him for mourning his father's death too long and in such a public manner:

```
QUEEN. Good Hamlet, cast thy nighted colour off,
     And let thine eye look like a friend on
        Denmark.                                           9
     Do not for ever with thy vailed lids
     Seek for thy noble father in the dust.
     Thou know'st 'tis common. All that lives
        must die,
     Passing through nature to eternity.
HAMLET. Ay, madam, it is common.
QUEEN. If it be,
     Why seems it so particular with thee?
HAMLET. Seems, madam, Nay, it is. I know not
     'seems.'
     'Tis not alone my inky cloak, good mother,
     Nor customary suits of solemn black,
     Nor windy suspiration of forc'd breath,
     No, nor the fruitful river in the eye,
     Nor the dejected havior of the visage,
     Together with all forms, moods, shapes of
        grief,
     That can denote me truly. These indeed seem,
     For they are actions that a man might play;
     But I have that within which passeth show-
     These but the trappings and the suits of
        woe.
```

Hamlet is offended that anyone would think he was capable of falsely "seeming" anything, much less his feelings for his father. The accusation is particularly hurtful because it comes from his mother, whom Hamlet loves but already suspects of deceit. At the end of the scene he expresses his troubles in a famous soliloquy ("O, that this too, too solid flesh would melt..."). He cannot grasp why his mother would so soon forget her first husband — whom she "seemed" to love — and then straight away marry his brother, Hamlet's uncle. How could she change her affections so quickly? Either she was lying then or she is lying now. What is troubling Hamlet is the lack of sincerity in Gertrude, Claudius, and everyone who assented to this entire repugnant state of affairs. The starting place for the seed can be traced to the commandment "You shall not lie." Murder, coveting another man's goods (the throne), and coveting another man's wife are certainly present in the play, but in Shakespeare's treatment of the story they all originate from "You shall not lie."

From the violation of this moral commandment comes the seed of idealism. Let's explain. The dictionary defines idealism as the practice of forming behavioral standards from abstract ideas and, for better or worse, living under their influence. An idealist is (1) a person who represents things as they might or should be rather than as they really are, (2) someone whose conduct is influenced by ideals that often conflict with practical considerations, and/or (3) someone who has fallen in love with an idea and thus allows his/her life to be thrown away, eaten away. Hamlet is all of these. He is a supreme idealist, perhaps the most prominent example of an idealist in all of dramatic literature. Moreover, his idealism is far-reaching because he places his ideals, in this case his passionate devotion to the truth, above all other considerations regardless of the consequences.

And so, if idealism is an accurate explanation of the seed, by definition it should influence every event and every role in the play. This is where reviewing the facts comes into play again. Earlier, we reviewed the facts to identify the external events. At this point, we will review the facts in an attempt to identify and verify the seed of idealism.

Hamlet has returned from the University of Wittenberg to attend his father's funeral and his uncle's coronation. Hamlet is a prince, he is young, and he has led a privileged and protected life. He loves to read, listen to music, and attend the theatre. Moreover, he is under the influence of the bookish idealism he learned at college, including the study of philosophy, for which he has a special fascination. He is inexperienced in love. He is inexperienced in other aspects of the real

10

world as well, in particular the rough and tumble world of big-time politics and statecraft. On the other hand, Hamlet is no fool. He may lack real-world experience, but he makes up for it with superior intelligence, sensitivity, and perception. In fact, he is almost a poet or philosopher in his sensitivity to the subtleties of human behavior. He is also loyal and kind. In 3,2, Ophelia, who is in love with him of course, considers him noble, a courtier (gentleman), soldier (an excellent fencer), scholar, and handsome, witty, poetic, athletic, and fashionable. He attracts attention wherever he goes. Even the common people of Denmark love and admire him. Prince Hamlet!

Yet for all his obvious personal advantages, it seems as though he comes from another planet. In fact, Hamlet has come from another planet, from the future, from the renaissance, where idealists live that believe in human dignity and the potential of mankind. Here on earth in the present he is attempting to come to terms with his father's old-fashioned feudal ideals, the ideals of the present. But his biological and intellectual systems cannot tolerate the atmosphere of lies, murder, corruption, capricious love, disloyalty, hypocrisy, apathy, philistinism, sin, etc., that characterize much of human life on earth, or at least it may be so in Denmark. He lives in a bubble and has to breathe a special kind of pure air to survive — the air of idealism. He is a perfectionist with high standards. If he loves, it must be pure love. His friendships must be loyal and without constraint. If he feels an emotion, it must be genuine, never forced or feigned. If he speaks, it must always be the absolute truth. Even his mastery of fencing must be letter perfect. And what a ruthless conscience he has to keep watch over his high ideals. What is worse is that he expects others to hold the same ideals and he can be cruel to them if they do not live up to his standards. If the truth were told, Hamlet might even be a little proud of his ideals. Maybe he feels himself to be an exceptional individual to have such lofty standards. ("...I have that within which passeth show.") Doesn't he accept the dueling challenge as an opportunity to show off just a little in front of Claudius? Unfortunately, Hamlet's ideal world does not exist, either in Denmark or anywhere else on this earth. It is a figment of his untested and over-heated idealism. He becomes aware of this in the end, of course. Nevertheless, even though his idealism may have been extreme and unworkable, he comes to understand that he stood up for something important — the pursuit of truth. Paraphrasing a modern politician, Hamlet might have said: "Extremism in the defense of truth is no vice!"

This review of the facts shows how the seed grows and develops into a large, impressive tree, blossoms with ideas, and becomes a

11

play. There will never be uniformity of opinion about *Hamlet* and there may be other ways to describe its seed. Most readers would grant, however, that idealism in one form or another appears to resonate throughout the entire play. No matter what, this formulation may serve to explain the concept of the seed, how it can be identified, and how it can serve to unify play, performance, and mise-en-scene (scenery, lighting, costumes, sound, makeup).

Sequence of Internal Events

The seed works to connect every moment of the play to a single subject. If this is true, then idealism should connect to all the external events described before. In other words, idealism should appear in a pre-existing form inside each external event of *Hamlet*. Indeed, an *internal event* is defined as the expression of the seed growing within an external event. Here is another place to review the facts, this time to learn if the seed is actually present throughout the entire play, and if so, how it expresses itself. In 1,1, Horatio encounters the Ghost. The focus of the seed here is on Horatio, who, as Marcellus tells us, does not believe in ghosts. Horatio, like Hamlet, is a student at the University of Wittenberg, where he learned about the principle of "rational truth" only just emerging at the time and became fascinated by it. And since there is no place for ghosts in rational thought, Horatio does not believe in them. The guards, Barnardo and Marcellus, are less educated, perhaps, but they possess more everyday know-how. They have actually seen this Ghost and in any case they are not well-informed skeptics. They are less idealistic than Horatio, less guided by abstract book knowledge, and more in touch with the way things are presented to them in real life, whether rational or irrational. In this scene, Horatio's idealism comes face to face for the first time with something it cannot explain. He calls it a "thing" and an "illusion" because he cannot bring himself even to say the word ghost. Horatio becomes unnerved because the existence of the Ghost is contrary to his sense of rational truth. Accordingly, we may title the internal event in 1,1, "The Ghost defies Horatio's idealism." This is a way of saying that the irrational presence of the Ghost contradicts Horatio's rational ideals. What he learned at the University of Wittenberg does not hold true in the real world of Denmark. The intellectual focus of the play is already underway by means of the seed of idealism.

In 1,2, Hamlet learns about the Ghost from Horatio. A short time before, Hamlet's idealism received a shock in the form of his mother's hasty marriage to his uncle, Claudius. He thought his mother was idealistically devoted to his father, whom Hamlet loved deeply, idealistically. How could she forget her husband, her apparent ideal, so soon? Now Hamlet learns from his best friend that a ghost has appeared and that it resembles his father. Since Hamlet goes to the same philosophy classes at the University of Wittenberg as Horatio, he does not believe in ghosts either. Horatio even feels a little ridiculous telling him about it, but after all, it looked like Hamlet's father, the former king, and it seemed to be searching for someone. Perhaps it was searching for Hamlet? Also, could it be that the Ghost has something to say about Denmark's current political crisis? In any case, Hamlet must be told. Actually, five shocks to Hamlet's idealism occur in this scene: the throne usurped by Claudius, mourning for his dead father cut short, an unfaithful mother, his return to Wittenberg forbidden by Claudius, and now what seems to be the ghost of his father. The seed continues to be working powerfully.

We have been reviewing the facts to connect the external events with the seed of idealism. The goal here is to continuously verify the presence of the seed. The result is the following sequence of external and internal events, in which the seed is italicized for emphasis.

1,1. External: The Ghost appears
    Internal: The Ghost defies Horatio's *idealism*
1,2. External: Claudius takes over the throne
    Internal: Claudius censures Hamlet's *idealism*
1,3. External: Laertes departs for France
    Internal: Polonius exposes his hypocritical *ideals*
1,4. External: Hamlet meets the Ghost
    Internal: The Ghost incites Hamlet's *idealism*
1,5. External: Hamlet learns that Claudius murdered his father
    Internal: The Ghost challenges Hamlet's *idealism*
2,1. External: Reynaldo departs for France
    Internal: Ophelia fears Hamlet has rejected her *idealistic* love
2,2. External: Hamlet welcomes the Players
    Internal: Hamlet plans to put his *idealism* into action
3,1. External: Claudius eavesdrops on Hamlet
    Internal: Hamlet warns Ophelia against betraying her *ideals*
3,2. External: The "mousetrap scene"
    Internal: Hamlet celebrates the apparent success of his *idealism*
3,3. External: Claudius attempts to pray
    Internal: Hamlet attempts to put his *ideals* into action

3,4. External: Gertrude appeals to Hamlet
Internal: Hamlet scolds Gertrude for betraying her *ideals*

4,1. External: Claudius takes action
Internal: Claudius fortifies his *cynicism* (a cynic believes that the primary motive of human behavior is self-interest, which is an obvious defiance of *idealism*)

4,2. External: Rosencrantz and Guildenstern capture Hamlet
Internal: Hamlet ridicules the *cynicism* of R and G

4,3. External: Claudius sends Hamlet to England
Internal: *Idealistic* Hamlet openly defies *cynical* Claudius

4,4. External: Hamlet crosses paths with Fortinbras
Internal: Hamlet compares his *idealism* with that of Fortinbras

4,5. External: Laertes returns to Elsinore and observes Ophelia's madness
Internal: Laertes' rash *idealism* and Ophelia's defeated *idealism*

4,6. External: Horatio learns that Hamlet has returned
Internal: Horatio fears that Hamlet has given up his *ideals*

4,7. External: Claudius and Laertes conspire to murder Hamlet
Internal: Claudius *cynically* manipulates Laertes' *idealism*

5,1. External: Hamlet learns about Ophelia's death
Internal: Hamlet recognizes that his *idealism* has led to Ophelia's death

5,2. External: Hamlet agrees to a sporting duel with Laertes
Internal: Hamlet comes to terms with his *idealism*

5,3. External: Hamlet slays Claudius
Internal: Hamlet defends himself and his newly compassionate *ideals*

All the internal events show an underlying connection with the seed of idealism, satisfying the purpose for which the seed was proposed in the first place. Idealism is the basic subject that holds everything together. Forcing the seed to the surface in this way makes it possible to act, direct, and design a play not according to an assortment of motifs, but according to the singular unity of all its parts. Notice, too, that the seed has been obtained from the facts of the play itself and has not been imposed from any outside sources.

Three Major Climaxes

A vision of the whole play has begun to come into view. The next task is to find the *three major climaxes*, a process that helps to give the play a sense of forward movement. Regardless of its complexity, simplicity, or style, the plot of every play goes through three stages in which it emerges, develops, and concludes. The first stage dramatizes the overall goal of the main character, the second stage shows the hardships encountered by the main character in pursuit of this goal, and the third stage enacts how the main character comes to terms with the play's particular reality. A climax is an event of highest dramatic tension, a major turning point in the action. The beginning, middle, and end comprise the three major climaxes, which by definition are the single most important events in each of the play's three stages of development. Michael Chekhov believed that identifying the three major climaxes is vital because it exposes the basic outline of the play, which is also one of the purposes of action analysis. The progress from each climax to the next gives the play a sense of forward motion. The principle of forward motion holds true even for plays that seem to show little evidence of a plot or movement as such.

As long as Hamlet remains ignorant of how his father died, he has no concrete reason to take decisive action. Claudius has taken the throne away from him, of course, but Hamlet cannot do anything about that problem for the reason that Claudius is already in power. In addition, Hamlet has made it clear to us that he is less upset about the political issues at stake than he is about the personal ones. It is not the throne that is on his mind at first, but the atmosphere of cynicism that seems to have taken over the court. This does not stop Claudius from worrying that Hamlet is after the throne, however, because Claudius believes that Hamlet must be motivated by cynical self-interest, like himself.

For the first major climax, readers would be drawn to the scene where Hamlet's idealistic energies begin to materialize. This would be 1,5, where the Ghost reveals the circumstances of his murder and challenges Hamlet to take revenge. Here is when the seed of idealism breaks through and begins to grow. Here we begin to see the evil that had been lurking around King Hamlet in the intrigues of Claudius, Gertrude, and Polonius. Here Hamlet has come face to face for the first time with absolute hypocrisy. He makes note of this extraordinary discovery in his journal:

```
HAMLET.   O  most  pernicious  woman!  [i.e.,
          Gertrude]
       O villain, villain, smiling, damnèd villain!
          [i.e., Claudius]
       My  tables — meet it is I set it down
          [i.e., in his journal]
```

> That one may smile, and smile, and be a
> villain.
> At least I am sure it may be so in Denmark.

Learning about his father's murder provides Hamlet with grounds to take decisive action. His ideal world, so comfortable at the University of Wittenberg up to now, begins to break down. Act 1, scene 5 corresponds to our understanding of a climax because the tension of the external events reaches maximum emotional temperature. It incorporates the entire external plot up to that moment and points forward to the middle phase of the play's development. A climax should also be a vivid expression of the internal life of the play. If the first major climax is 1,5, how does the seed, the expression of the play's inner life, operate there? Hamlet's idealism suffers its first major setback. It is one thing for Claudius and Gertrude to be indifferent to King Hamlet's death; it is another thing for them to have murdered him. Another point worth noting in 1,5 is the idealism of the Ghost, King Hamlet. The assassinated King expects his son, the Prince and heir apparent, to fulfill his royal responsibilities, his royal ideals. This creates a new conflict of ideals, which Hamlet does not foresee the consequences of when he swears to discharge his father's command:

> HAMLET. Remember thee?
> Yes, from the table of my memory
> I'll wipe away all trivial fond records,
> All saws of books, all forms, all pres-
> sures past
> That youth and observation copied there,
> And thy commandment all alone shall live
> Within the book and volume of my brain,
> Unmixed with baser matter. Yes, by heaven!

Hamlet vows to give up his bookishness and devote himself to revenging his father's murder. But revenge is an ideal, too, although it belongs to an earlier epoch. Starting in 1,5, a clash emerges between King Hamlet's old-fashioned feudal ideals and Prince Hamlet's renaissance humanistic ideals. Idealism itself is being placed on trial.

The beginning and end of the play are polar opposites; not always, but more often than not. What is revealed in the beginning changes into its opposite at the end; what lies in between is the movement from the beginning through to the end. Opposites by definition are different, which means they should be easier to recognize than the in-between points. That is why we will look for the climax at the end, the third major climax, before trying to find the middle climax.

There is not much doubt that the most important scene in *Hamlet* is 5,3, when all the forces of the play clash and the future of Denmark is determined. There is little doubt either that 5,3 is the climax of the external events, or the third major climax. Four deaths, the collapse of the monarchy, a family dynasty shattered, and a change of national leadership would be considered a climactic event under any circumstances.

An earlier event, that in 5,2, is also worth examining for what it helps us to understand about the seed and how it works. When Hamlet describes his sea adventures to Horatio, the episode does not seem to be dramatic in the usual sense because it is narrative for the most part and does not exhibit much external action. However, Hamlet has returned to Denmark a changed person. He tries to explain to Horatio the change that has taken place in him:

> **HAMLET.** Sir, in my heart there was a kind of fighting
> That would not let me sleep. Methought I lay
> Worse than mutinies in the bilboes. Rashly,
> And praised be rashness for it — let us know,
> Our indiscretion sometimes serves us well
> When our deep plots do pall, and that should learn us
> There's a divinity that shapes our ends,
> Rough-hew them how we will —

17

To paraphrase: "I felt all locked up inside, Horatio. I could not sleep at night. It was worse than being shackled in chains like a prisoner. I know that I impulsively sent Rosencrantz and Guildenstern to their deaths, and a little while ago I impulsively fought with Laertes at Ophelia's grave. But sometimes impulsiveness can be a good thing. Sometimes accidental blunders work out better in the end than all the elaborate plotting and planning we could perhaps do. This should teach us a lesson: there is something indescribable that shapes our destinies, no matter how much our own idealistic plans may interfere."

A few moments later Osric delivers Claudius's invitation for a sporting duel with Laertes, which we know is designed to lead to Hamlet's death. Hamlet understands that Osric is Claudius's lackey and that he will report everything said here to Claudius. But Hamlet only pokes fun at Osric's manners; he does not openly scorn him as he did Rosencrantz and Guildenstern earlier in the play when they found themselves in a similar position. Osric is just a fool, not a representative of all the evil in the world (as Hamlet once thought of Rosencrantz and Guildenstern). The change in Hamlet's former intolerance of any sort of hypocrisy surprises Horatio. A few moments later, Hamlet accepts Claudius's challenge, but confesses a shiver of foreboding. Horatio worries that Hamlet could still be in shock from recent events; he should be looked after in case he does something, well, impulsive:

> HORATIO. If your mind dislike anything, obey it. I will forestall their repair hither and say you are not fit.
> HAMLET. Not a whit, we defy augury. There is a special providence in the fall of a sparrow. If it be now, 'tis not to come; if it be not to come, it will be now; if it not be now, yet it will come. The readiness is all. Since no man of aught he leaves knows, what is't betimes? Let be.

18

"If you have a bad feeling about this challenge," Horatio seems to say, "then please do not go through with it. I will tell the King that you do not feel well." "Never mind," replies Hamlet, "I do not believe in my so-called intuition anymore. Reality has taught me to no longer trust my overheated idealism. I must learn to adjust myself to reality and not try to force reality to adjust itself to me. Whatever will happen will happen. Living, being ready for life, is what matters. Anyway, since no one can know what happens after he dies, why should we agonize over it? We must try to live as honestly as we can. Let everything else happen as it will." Hamlet's inner life has changed. He used to be impossibly idealistic, both about his own behavior and that of others. He is still idealistic and honorable, but now his idealism has been tempered by personal experience and self-reflection. He instinctively rejects his father's old-fashioned ideals. He is less selfish and more compassionate. Note, too, that Hamlet does not speak in verse at this point, but in plain prose, which indicates that he is speaking from his heart, without using courtly phrases.

Could this event actually be the third major climax? Despite the obvious thematic importance of this scene in the play, our choice for the third major climax continues to be 5,3, as we discussed before. The words about Hamlet's change of heart in 5,2 are as yet only words. Hamlet's change of attitude still has to be tested in a real-life situation. Hamlet does not go to the duel with revenge in mind. If Claudius had not caused Gertrude's death in the next scene, perhaps Hamlet might have reconciled himself to things as they are and returned to Wittenberg. But when Gertrude dies and Laertes tells Hamlet about the poisoned rapier (Hamlet will die in a few moments, like his mother), then Hamlet acts without hesitation. He feels he must take a public stand against this wickedness. Act 5, scene 2 is thematic and narrative, while 5,3 thematic and theatrical. In a play, the true beginning and end ought to illuminate each other not just thematically, but for the most part theatrically (in action).

The middle is the part of the play where Hamlet's plans expand and develop. Hamlet's fanatical pursuit of the truth characterizes this part of the play. It is fitting that the distinguishing event involves a company of actors. Hamlet's scenes with the Players form a thematic group related to idealism, his and theirs mutually, but the issues are too multifaceted to be treated at length here. It is enough to say that Hamlet admires the actors for their professional idealism, their ability to become engaged by the ideals of characters they have never even met, and by the moral impact of their work on an audience's conscience (on their ideals). "Players are the only honest hypocrites," says Hamlet. In other words, the Players are in some sense from the same planet that he is from. Thus, the second major climax is the "dumb show," "play-within-a-play," or "mousetrap scene" in 3,2, where Claudius reveals his guilt while watching the players enact "The Murder of Gozago." Externally, 3,2 is a crowd scene that involves the entire court, fanfares, color, torches, pageantry, etc. Internally, it marks the collapse of Claudius' cynical plotting (he tries to pray for forgiveness after this scene) and the apparent victory of Hamlet's idealistic search for the truth.

19

However, it is not until Hamlet kills Polonius, and later Rosencrantz and Guildenstern, and (indirectly) Ophelia that he begins to comprehend how his fanatical, impossible idealism has deformed him. He always thought of himself, and prided himself, as a good person, humane and thoughtful, yet now he has committed acts he considered evil in the past. In the graveyard scene, he begins to recognize how a scrupulous person like himself could be driven by honorable ideals to behave like those cynics who corrupted the royal court of Elsinore. In 5,2, he apologizes to Laertes (for being responsible for the death of Polonius and Ophelia), then in 5,3 he sacrifices himself in the name of compassionate idealism (out of kindness, really) and of course for his own spiritual salvation. His death refutes Claudius's cynical world view and for that reason it just might bring about fundamental changes in people's lives, and, with any luck, change the course of Denmark's history. That is why he insists that Horatio should not die too, but live on to tell Hamlet's story to future generations:

```
HAMLET. As th' art a man
        Give me the cup [i.e., of poison]. Let go.
            By heaven, I'll ha't!
        O God, Horatio, what a wounded name,
        Things  standing  thus  unknown,  shall  I
            leave behind me!
        If thou didst ever hold me in thy heart,
        Absent thee from felicity awhile,
        And in this harsh world draw thy breath in
            pain,
        To tell my story.
```

It is no accident that Hamlet's next utterance is about the arrival of warlike Fortinbras, who promises to honor Hamlet's death with a soldier's funeral. Should this moment be treated approvingly or ironically?

Theme

Earlier we said that a motif is "a recurring prominent thematic element." However, the dictionary also states that a theme is a "unifying or dominant idea, a motif." A motif and a theme sound like the same thing, and for literary purposes they may be identical. But for actors, directors, and designers there is an important difference: a motif covers just part of a work, while the theme covers the whole work. Like the seed, the theme passes through the entire play, a condition that leads to its definition here: the *theme* is the play's response to the seed, what the play shows about the seed. It is directly expressed in the actions of the main character and indirectly in the actions of the supporting characters. We will return to *Hamlet* to explain this further.

The three major climaxes provide the best path to understanding the theme of the play. Each climax is the dramatic focus of its corresponding part of the play and includes the entire external and internal action up to that point. Let's review the facts. Three climaxes mark Hamlet's line of development in the play: (1) Hamlet commits himself to revenging his father's murder; (2) Hamlet ruthlessly pursues the truth and in doing so he is responsible for the deaths of some innocent people and the disruption of the entire state of Denmark; (3) as a result, a new self-awareness emerges in Hamlet. Evil is destroyed, but at what cost, and will it ever return? The play is a test, or an exhibit, of Hamlet's idealism.

But many plays share the same seed, the same basic subject of idealism. What distinguishes them is their response to the seed, their outlook toward the basic subject. What does the play *Hamlet* show about the character Hamlet's idealism? Hamlet begins in a state of emotional agitation; he has an overheated sense of right and wrong. His awkward and destructive progress from this idealism of his toward a more sensible and humane awareness of life as it really is — this development constitutes the action of the play. The development of a conscience. If the theme is the play's point of view about idealism, then the theme of *Hamlet* can be expressed, if just for our narrow purpose here, as *impossible idealism*. In Shakespeare's plays everything generally works out all right in the end, but he was not a moralist or a preacher. His plays do not promote a point of view, such as "submitting to the status quo" or "resigning oneself to one's fate." They reflect the prevailing spirit of his time: that the established order (Providence) is in the end wise and benevolent. For Shakespeare, living in the world means coming to terms with reality, not merely as it is in our own minds or in books, but as it is in its earthbound human entirety.

Be that as it may, ever since Polish critic Jan Kott's book, *Shakespeare our Contemporary*, many readers have treated Shakespeare as a moralist with an ironic sensibility, in other words as a modernist. According to this point of view, Shakespeare's plays expose idealism as a cruel hoax foisted on us by a universe that is fickle, irrational, and mean-spirited. This interpretive point of view is intelligent, and perhaps outdated already. But it needs to be brought up here to remind readers that the purpose of play analysis is not to obtain the definitive interpretation of a play, but at all times an accurate and consistent one. Our instructional example in this chapter treats idealism in Shakespeare as a positive impulse: idealism can be distorted, but in time it will be tempered by contact with real life. This tends to be the consensus view concerning Shakespeare's plays. In any case, we have shown how the three major climaxes in *Hamlet* illustrate different stages in the development of the theme of impossible idealism.

Super-Objective

One of the advantages of defining the three major climaxes is learning what gives the play a sense of forward motion. Without this feeling, a play remains flat and uninteresting in performance. But while the theme is a satisfactory summary statement of the play's ideology, it remains just that — a fixed summary, a conclusive statement of the play's action. In performance, however, the theme needs to reveal itself progressively, through the events the characters perform over the course of time. The *super-objective* is a concept that embraces the theme, but also provides a sense of forward motion to our understanding of the play. The super-objective is the main character's all-inclusive goal; it is the theme expressed in terms of what the main character is striving to accomplish. Sometimes it is said that the super-objective originates from the play itself instead of from the main character, but this is a distinction without a difference. The overall meaning of a play is always embodied in its main character in any case. Supporting characters also have their super-objectives (all-inclusive goals), but they are less essential in action analysis because they are thematically subordinate to that of the main character.

Hamlet's super-objective is "to put things right," or put another way, "to find out why things have gone wrong." He wishes to determine why the world does not operate according to his ideals and then he wants to change the world so that it does so. He states his super-objective in the script: "O cursed spite / That ever I was born to set it right!" (1,5,215–216).

A review of the facts shows that Hamlet attempts to set things right throughout the entire play, even after he returns to Denmark the second time. He puts things right by agreeing to carry out the Ghost's demands; by rebuking the lies and hypocrisy of Polonius, Rosencrantz and Guildenstern, Ophelia, Gertrude; and above all by exposing Claudius in the "mousetrap scene." Hamlet's impossible idealism drives him to imagine that with enough effort he will set everything right in Denmark just by revealing it as wrong. Instead, to his dismay, he uncovers more deceit, lust, corruption, apathy, sycophancy, intrigue, and stupidity everywhere he turns. The only characters that provide him with any genuine help, with any real truth, are the Ghost, Horatio, the Players, the Gravedigger, and Yorick, the deceased court jester who was his childhood friend. Hamlet has an impossible amount of wickedness to set right; however, this does not deter him from his super-objective.

Through-action

At this point we are seeking to understand Hamlet as a complete story once again, as the account of a specific character performing a specific action within specific circumstances. The *through-action*, sometimes called the through-line of action or unbroken line, fulfills this purpose. The through-action has often been discussed in the writing of Stanislavsky and his followers. The description Sharon Carnicke provides in her informative book, *Stanislavsky in Focus*, is a representative example. She defines the through-action as "A unifying, overall action that relates all moment-to-moment actions throughout the play to each other" (181). While this definition is accurate, it does not lead to the heart of the matter. It still remains somewhat abstract because it does not distinguish the through-action from the theme, seed, and super-objective, which also serve to link all the actions to each other in their own way. It might be more helpful to think of the through-action as a one-sentence description of the main conflict, expressing what the main character does in the play to accomplish his/her super-objective. Though the through-action implies a super-objective, it does not openly express it, only the means used to accomplish it. Incidentally, the through-action is also an important concept in film and television where it is called the premise or sometimes the logline.

23

Idealism, Hamlet's impractical nature, the corruption in Denmark, and the concepts of truth and self-awareness found in *Hamlet* are useful formulations up to a point. Their abstract separation from concrete instances is helpful for obtaining a vision of the whole. But helpful as they are, they are still abstractions. To be effective for actors, directors, and designers, these concepts need to be translated from the abstract to the concrete, from the realm of ideas back to the realm of real human behavior evident in the play itself. The through-action makes it possible for these concepts to become concrete, which is one step closer to the physical expression necessary for performance.

We need to review the facts again and look with fresh eyes at the actions that showed us the way to the external events, seed, internal events, three major climaxes, theme, and super-objective in the first place. The difference is that now we have a sense of the whole play in which to frame the story. Remember that reviewing the facts means asking who, what, where, when, how, and why. Who is Hamlet? Young, idealistic, devoted to art, philosophy, theology, and poetry. What is he doing? Searching for dishonesty and trying to eliminate it. Where is he doing it? In the corrupt royal court of Denmark. When is he doing it? At a turbulent time when Denmark is threatened by war from abroad and when his cynical uncle has taken over the throne. How does he do it? At times, sensitive and unfeeling, elegant and clumsy, impulsive and brooding, anguished and elated, graceful and without grace or finesse, tender and violent. Why is he doing it? His conscience forces him to do it, and his father, whom he is devoted to, has ordered him to do it. It is a moral and royal duty.

Hamlet learned about art, literature, theology, and philosophy at the University of Wittenberg, where he lived for the most part untouched by real life. Outside the university setting, he meets up with a reality that is as unfamiliar and unexpected as it is appalling to him. Hamlet was not equipped for this confrontation with real life after being isolated from it at the university, which itself may have had an unrealistic view of the outside world. After going through torment at court, Hamlet loses faith in the advanced ideals he learned about in the classroom. They could not conform to practical reality. Then he returns to the point where he started, washed up on the shores of Denmark, "naked and alone," with only his personal experience left to support him. He has learned for himself that ideals are important aspirations, but that the real world is a sinful and human place after all. This knowledge is the foundation for his new strength and the importance of his story to the world. Hamlet has learned how to face insanity and corruption without becoming insane and corrupt himself. In fact, he has even become more humane in the process.

Reviewing the facts leads to a description of the through-action as a concise account of what basically happens in the play: a sensitive, idealistic prince provokes dangerous discord in the palace of his uncle, a criminal usurper. This one-sentence description of the through-action contains all the parts of action analysis in dormant form. It suggests Hamlet's super-objective, but does not openly express it, only the means Hamlet uses to accomplish it — provocation. It hints that Hamlet could do a lot of damage with his idealistic provocations, not just to himself but also to others and to his country. From within the limits of this statement we can also work out the seed, theme, super-objective, and even find clues about the three major climaxes. Moreover, this account of the through-action also preserves the tragic tone of the play. Not everyone may agree with this description of the through-action, but at least its purpose and the working process behind it should be apparent.

Counter Through-action

Adjacent to the through-action and running in the opposite direction to it, passes a *counter through-action* that is opposed to it. Every

24

action in a play, as in life, meets with a counter-action, which either challenges or strengthens it. The counter through-action is the source of the conflict in the play. Without it there is no play in the ordinary sense, because there is no conflict.

Hamlet's principal opponent is Claudius. Determining the counter through-action involves the same thinking process as the through-action, except that it is concerned with the story of the principal opponent of the main character (antagonist) instead of the main character (protagonist). Who is Claudius? Brother of the deceased king and uncle to the heir-apparent prince. He is also the new husband of his brother's widow. What is he? A clever and cynical murderer and usurper. Where is he doing it? In a palace in feudal Denmark that is threatened by war. When is he doing it? After the mysterious death of the former king, who was a legendary warrior. How does he do it? By murdering the king with the tacit backing of court insiders. Why does he do it? For power and the former king's wife. This analysis leads to the following description of the counter through-action: a feudal usurper undermines the provocations of an idealistic prince, who is his nephew and rightful heir. In this statement, notice the attention to the feudal morality of the world of the play, which provides a challenge to Hamlet's renaissance idealism and strengthens it by contrast. Again, this definition is not meant to be authoritative, simply an object lesson on the process used to determine the counter through-action.

Action Analysis and Nonrealistic Plays

Realistic and classic plays, in the vein of *Death of a Salesman* or *Hamlet*, are written in a standard manner, with the intention that all the parts fit plausibly together and everything is readily understandable. At this point it would be a good idea to go through the process of action analysis again, but this time using a nonrealistic play, which presents different analytical challenges. *Happy Days* by Samuel Beckett will be the play studied for this purpose. *Happy Days* is one of a group of plays, written largely in the 1950s and 1960s, collectively labeled "Theatre of the Absurd," of which Beckett was the leading figure. Many people find "Absurdist" and nonrealistic plays in general impossibly hard to understand. Why do these authors have to write in such a difficult way? Why so many literary and theatrical tricks? Why are all those complicated things going on all the time? Why do they use so many formal patterns in their writing? Consequently, to understand Absurdist and other assertively nonrealistic plays, there is an obvious need for well-informed actors, directors, designers, and, of course, audiences — well-informed both in the sense of understanding the dramatic and theatrical issues involved and in the sense of understanding the wellspring from which the nonrealistic impulse arises. This makes *Happy Days* an excellent play to begin the study of nonrealistic plays in general. Granted that these plays may be more difficult to understand than realistic or classic plays, all the same action analysis — and later, formalist analysis — can successfully be used to release their theatrical potentials just as with any other type of play. The challenge consists of closer reading and even closer reasoning throughout the course of analysis. The following breakdown of *Happy Days* will skip through the rationale behind the basic concepts and thinking processes involved since they have already been explained above.

Sequence of External Events

An event was defined earlier as a conflict, something significant that changes someone because in general it would not or should not happen. Nonrealistic plays like *Happy Days* seem to challenge this definition because so little happens in them that is significant in the accepted sense. In fact, one widespread feature of nonrealistic plays is the comparative insignificance of their events. Many of these plays have found a way to conceal the outline of the plot or the plot is so subtle that the entire play may consist of trivial events like so many of those found in *Happy Days* — awaking, rummaging through an ordinary shopping bag, recollecting trivial episodes from the past, casually chattering, etc. Nevertheless, these plays would fall apart without at least a minimal plot, which, like all plots, is composed of events, conflicts.

Ever since the plays of Anton Chekhov, our understanding of what constitutes a dramatic event has had to go through a re-evaluation. Chekhov showed that under certain circumstances even the tiniest events can have significant consequences. Today this way of thinking has become part of the air we breathe. Think of how the delicate balance of nature's ecology can be upset by something as small as a one percent change in the earth's ozone layer or a one degree change in global temperature. A hundred years ago few of us would have concerned ourselves with something as small as a one percent or one degree change, even if it could be measured with the scientific instruments of that time. Today we not only have the instruments (ask why), we also know how much our well-being depends on these tiny conditions. In *Happy Days* the tiny conditions need to be examined very closely indeed. Because they are so different from what we believe to be dramatic, they can get away from our attention. Think of how the form of the humble soup can escaped serious artistic attention before Andy Warhol.

Initial readings of *Happy Days* suggest again that actors, directors, and designers need to exercise a special kind of understanding, not just to identify the events, but also to distinguish the essential from the less essential. Referring to the travel example at the beginning of the chapter, *Happy Days* seems to contain no big cities to arrest the traveler's attention but only a succession of small, bus-stop towns and villages, each one with much the same look and feel as the other. If this were true, however, the play in performance would be as boringly repetitious as our imaginary trip. The solution to this problem is to avoid reading what critics say about a play and turn instead to the play itself, to examine the countryside, as you might say, with the sharp eye of an experienced traveler.

Winnie and Willie are first of all husband and wife, and it is from this understanding that analysis of the play should commence. Otherwise stated, *Happy Days* is about a marriage, and the curious digressions, meditations, and assorted diversions throughout the play should not distract from this basic fact. A typical day in the life of Winnie and Willie's marriage is much the same as that of any other middle-aged couple: waking up; dressing and grooming; small talk about current events, shared memories, and life's little troubles; settling in with routine daily activities; and to end with, getting ready for bed. A close look at *Happy Days* reveals just this sequence of external events repeated twice — first with Winnie and Willie and then for the most part Winnie alone.

27

Act One (day one: Winnie is embedded up to her waist in a mound of earth. Willie is out of sight behind her.)

1. Winnie awakes
2. Willie awakes
3. Winnie takes care of her appearance
4. Winnie and Willie's light conversation
5. Winnie and the revolver
6. Winnie and the parasol
7. Winnie and Willie prepare for the "night"

Act Two (day two: Winnie is embedded up to her neck. Willie has apparently disappeared.)

8. Winnie awakes without Willie, but pretends he is still there

9. Winnie mentally goes through the first parts of her daily routine
10. Winnie mentally goes through the remaining parts of her daily routine
11. Willie emerges from his "room" and goes to Winnie

As you would expect, many interesting and entertaining situations have been purposely omitted from this list. With a nonrealistic play like *Happy Days*, it is more important than ever to pass over the less essential events for the time being and pay attention to the most important blocks of action to grasp the basic story: two days in the life of Winnie and Willie.

Reviewing the Facts

At this point it is time to pause and get our bearings by reviewing the facts. Winnie and Willie are a middle-aged married couple going through what appears to be a typical day or two in their life together. They look to be performing routine everyday activities interrupted by humdrum exchanges of shared experiences, although they are doing so in a strange environment unlike any ordinary realistic household. Why they are in this unusual situation or how they got this way is not made clear, nor is the passage of time, which is apparently static. Although the situation seems boring and impossible, Winnie in fact conducts herself with unflagging optimism, while Willie behaves with relative indifference. This sums up as much as we know at this point.

Seed

To identify the seed, it is helpful to recall that it starts with one of ethical precepts found in the common moral imperatives of society. Prominent among them is the imperative to tell the truth, which is the issue at stake in *Happy Days*. Winnie is in effect "lying" about her reality. There is no reason for her to be happy, and yet she is. Her life is impossible. It is evident that Winnie's image of both Willie and their life together is in conflict with reality. Moreover, since her picture of the situation interferes with her capacity for self-awareness, it could be comparable to lying. Nevertheless, she is so used to this lie that she has come to believe it is real, necessary, and important. Now, a dream is a succession of involuntary images that pass through the mind at night while we are asleep. But a dream can also be voluntary; something indulged in while we are awake, such as a daydream or reverie about something longed for, a deep aspiration. This second meaning is what concerns us here. Winnie is living in a dream (some would say nightmare). She has created a dream life for herself in a world that is otherwise unfit to live in. The seed, the basic subject, of *Happy Days* is dreams of this nature.

Let's review some of the facts to check the accuracy of this seed. One of the most puzzling features of *Happy Days* is Winnie's unthinking belief that Willie is a model husband when for sure he is otherwise. Critics point out that Winnie is a creature of habit and that she uses habit as a defense against the depressing reality of her marriage and her situation in general. Yet Winnie's habits may also show that she is motivated by a certain dream image of Willie and their life together. She prays daily, gives careful attention to her appearance, wears becoming clothing and jewelry, uses a lady's parasol to protect her from the sun, is conscientious about her hairdo, wears a fashionable hat, treats Willie politely (usually), enjoys poetry and music up to a point, is a skilled and gracious light conversationalist, etc. All for Willie and their life together, or at least for their dream life together. She disapproves of Willie's bad habits, of course — wearing no clothes, enjoying pornographic postcards, vulgarly cleaning his nose, etc. Regarding his behavior and her environment in general, however, she is eager to excuse things and tries never to complain about things she cannot change — all features of her dream image of Willie and their relationship.

There may be different ways and means to explain the basic subject of *Happy Days*, but most readers would agree that Winnie's dream life resonates throughout the entire play. In any case, this interpretation can serve to explain the process of discovering the seed, a process that serves realistic and nonrealistic plays alike. It is only that identifying the seed for a nonrealistic play like *Happy Days* requires a special effort at close reading and close reasoning. Above all, a special effort has to be made to see these plays with empathy, namely, from the point of view of the main character instead of from that of an ironic or unsympathetic observer.

Sequence of Internal Events

If the seed of the play is dreams, there should be evidence of it in all the external events. In the first external event, Winnie awakens and begins her day. She says her morning prayers, grooms herself, checks on Willie's welfare, and expresses her gratitude to the Divinity that nothing significant has changed in her life. "So much to be thankful for," she says. We may title the first internal event: Winnie begins another happy day in her dream world. It makes no difference that we believe she should behave otherwise; it is her view that matters here.

29

In the second event, Winnie awakens Willie while she continues her grooming. As he raises his head behind the mound of earth and begins his day, we notice that he is bald and naked (not youthful, stylish, or handsome), that she has struck him in the head when she tossed away her medicine bottle, and that he settles in to read the obituaries from the newspaper. These circumstances can be seen as a parody of a middle-aged married couple long accustomed to each other's habits and eccentricities. Any sense of parody, however, escapes Winnie's notice. Willie reads that an old acquaintance of theirs, Reverend Carolus Hunter, has died, which prompts Winnie's recollection of a dalliance she had in her youth, perhaps with Hunter. This memory in fact enhances her dream life (she was courted in her youth by an important person!) and Willie's status in her eyes (he was the man she chose over Hunter to be her husband!). The second internal event is that Winnie's dream husband awakes and makes her happy with his amusing conversation.

Continuing to verify the presence of the seed of dreams in this manner, the result might be a sequence of internal events like the following. Note that the seed is exposed on purpose and included in the statement of each internal event (and italicized for emphasis here).

1. External: Winnie awakes
   Internal: Winnie begins another happy day in her *dream* world
2. External: Willie awakes
   Internal: Winnie's *dream* husband awakes and joins her for another happy day
3. External: Winnie looks at the naughty postcard
   Internal: Winnie's *dream* falters, but she holds onto it
4. External: Willie retires to his hole
   Internal: Winnie's *dream* falters, but she holds onto it
5. External: Winnie and the revolver
   Internal: Winnie's *dream* falters, but she holds onto it
6. External: Winnie and the parasol
   Internal: Winnie's *dream* falters, but she holds onto it
7. External: Winnie's memory of Shower and Cooker
   Internal: Winnie's *dream* falters, but she holds onto it
8. External: Winnie and Willie prepare for bed
   Internal: Winnie's *dream* falters, but she holds onto it
9. External: Winnie awakes without Willie, but pretends he is still there
   Internal: Winnie's *dream* falters, but she holds onto it

10. External: Winnie mentally goes through the first parts of her daily routine
    Internal: Winnie's *dream* falters, but she holds onto it
11. External: Winnie mentally goes through the remaining parts of her daily routine
    Internal: Winnie's *dream* falters, but she holds onto it
12. External: Willie crawls to Winnie
    Internal: Winnie's *dream* falters, but she holds onto it

Winnie always has to reinforce her dream of happiness because it is so pathetic and pointless. The internal events are repetitive, of course, and Chapter 7 will explain the rationale behind this feature of nonrealistic plays. At this point, though, it is enough to verify that the seed of dreams is continuously present in each external event. Moreover, this conclusion is supported by facts from the play itself, and not drawn from literary commentary about the play.

Theme

The theme is the play's viewpoint about the seed. This is another way of saying that the theme is the mind-set of the main character about the seed, since a play is in effect the biography of its main character. In *Happy Days*, the main character is Winnie, of course, and her mind-set about the seed of dreams is most sharply defined in her relationship with Willie. Willie's first appearance reassures Winnie that her dream is safe and sound, at least for the moment. His second appearance reassures her of this once again as they prepare to retire at the close of the day. And his final appearance (after a mysterious absence) pacifies her fear that her dream may have collapsed. These events show that Winnie seeks her happiness — her dream world — through Willie. His presence is essential for her happiness. His crude behavior, his indifference, and the isolation of their relationship have no affect on her rose-colored image of him. These seeming contradictions only serve to confirm and strengthen her dream-picture of him, of her life, and indeed of her entire world.

Winnie is insensitive to obvious facts because her dream is illogical and misguided — absurd. Accordingly, the theme is *absurd dreams*. *Happy Days* does not necessarily illustrate the meaninglessness of existence or the incapability of human communication. It illustrates how her absurd dreams have made the existence of Winnie and Willie meaningless and uncommunicative. Her absurd dreams have deadened her consciousness and blocked fulfillment of her potential as a human being. She is trapped in a dream world.

Some might say that Winnie is "whistling in the dark," being cheerful and optimistic in a situation that does not warrant cheerfulness or optimism. Others might say that she is "fiddling while Rome burns," behaving heedlessly and irresponsibly in the midst of a crisis, in the midst of a meaningless existence. The latter was a popular view of *Happy Days* and the themes of Absurdist plays fifty years ago when these plays first appeared on the scene. But the world changes and art changes along with it, and so today it is possible to see that *Happy Days* and Absurdist plays in general are as much about absurd personal dreams as they are about the so-called meaninglessness of existence. Of the two interpretations, both are "right," in the sense that they are not imposed from outside but emerge from close reading of the play itself. Moreover, both readings are truthful, in the sense that they reflect genuine feelings many of us have at moments in our lives. This seeming paradox — two different themes that are both "right" — is a useful object lesson about the issue of artistic interpretation.

Three Major Climaxes

Traditional dramatic form has a beginning, middle, and end, but *Happy Days* seems to start in the middle of things and end without a feeling of closure. It is all middle, apparently, without a conventional beginning or end. Yet in spite of everything, the beginning, middle, and end are there. They may be small and "insignificant," but without them the play would fall apart. *Happy Days* asks us to re-evaluate our understanding of what constitutes a beginning, middle, and end.

Starting in reverse order, the third major climax — the formal end — is without doubt Willie's appearance in the final event of the play. Is it safe to assume that Willie might also play a part in the first and second major climax? Compared to Winnie's trivial activities, Willie's entrances and exits are fairly dramatic events. They provide Winnie with her sole assurance of happiness. In all probability, the first, second, and third major climaxes involve Willie as well:

- First major climax: Willie's first entrance (at the back of the earthen mound) begins Winnie's happy day
- Second major climax: Willie's second entrance (still at the back of the mound) concludes Winnie's happy day
- Third major climax: Willie's third entrance (in front of the mound) revives Winnie's happy day after she fears he has left her

Willie's first appearance marks the formal beginning of the play's action. His second appearance (after briefly retiring to his hole to avoid sunburn) marks the formal middle of the play, the point where the action begins to move toward the third major climax. The placement of the second major climax at the end of act 1 is a conventional piece of dramatic writing. It is a time-honored way of concluding the first act while pointing in the direction of what is to come. For most of the second act Winnie does not see or hear from Willie and fears he may be gone. When Willie reappears, it restores Winnie's faith in her dream, marking the end of the play. *Happy Days* is a nonrealistic play, but its formal beginning, middle, and end (an arrival marks the beginning, an arrival marks the middle, and another arrival marks the end) are indispensable for playwriting in general. That the ending still lacks a conventional sense of closure is an issue that action analysis is not equipped to deal with. The ending as a feature by itself is treated in more detail in Chapter 5, Progressions and Structure.

Super-Objective

The super-objective, the main character's overall goal, helps to establish a sense of forward motion in the play. The difficulty in nonrealistic plays like *Happy* Days is to find a super-objective to guide this sense of forward motion in the direction of an actable path. One obvious choice of super-objective for Winnie would be to live happily and without complaint. As Stanislavsky and many others have pointed out, however, such empty, generalized feelings as "to live happily" lack artistic truth on stage. To work effectively in performance, a play must illustrate a specific attitude toward a specific condition or person, an attitude from which truthful feelings can emerge. Truthful feelings cannot be performed directly, but are the summary by-products of preceding conditions. Such shapeless feelings as happiness arise from concrete circumstances in Winnie's life, and actors, directors, and designers feel the need to work out concrete, human ways to theatricalize them.

The solution to this problem is to be unyielding about asking specific questions: What exactly is Winnie unable to understand? What is she happy about? What is her husband indifferent about? A reader's intuition can be helpful as far as it goes, but specific conditions that relate to the world of the play must still be found. Close reading shows that Willie's presence seems to confirm something for Winnie, to reassure her of something, to support her belief in something. What could Willie's mere presence represent for Winnie? The answer is — her dream. Winnie's super-objective is to uphold her dream world at all costs. If her dream world gives way, if Willie should disappear, her entire world would collapse, which it does temporarily in act 2 where

33

she struggles to keep it going. Winnie's habits are little rituals she uses to keep her dream alive. Unfortunately, her circumstances — an empty marriage and an empty existence — are incompatible with her super-objective. The contradiction between her absurd dream of happiness and the unhappiness of her life is precisely the meaning and enter-tainment value of the play.

Through-action

The through-action is a concise, one-sentence description of the main conflict. This may sound easy, but as we can see from our earlier search of the through-action in *Hamlet*, it can be a tricky process to extract the substance of a play and shape it into a satisfactory one-sentence through-action. This is even truer for nonrealistic plays, where so little seems to be happening or where what is happening seems to be so con-fusing and mysterious. Indeed, that is why focalizing the story into the form of a through-action is twice as important in nonrealistic plays.

A simple review of the facts discloses the following. Who is Winnie? A married, middle-aged woman. What is she doing? Keeping herself attractive and respectable through routine daily hab-its. Where? In a desolate, uninhabited locale (a picture of her outer and inner life). When? Timeless, without beginning or end (again, her outer and inner life). Why? To maintain her dream of happiness. How? Bravely and with spirit, though sometimes downcast. Think of a woman living in an empty marriage with an indifferent husband and in an indifferent world, and then think of the artificial reality she must create for herself to survive. Accordingly, the through-action might be stated in this way: a middle-aged wife trapped in a hope-less marriage tirelessly reactivates herself and her apathetic husband. Is this through-action too simple-minded for such a play as *Happy Days*? Is Winnie trapped in a hopeless marriage or a cosmic crisis? Is Winnie's through-action cheerful and optimistic or heedless and irre-sponsible? Is *Happy Days* a thoughtful parody of a domestic comedy or an illustration of the callous indifference of Providence? One clue may be Winnie's surprise at the end when she sees what Willie looks like after his unexplained absence. Coincidentally, at the time of this writing *Happy Days* is playing in New York, where actress Fiona Shaw is performing the role of Winnie as a "deluded celebrity."

Counter Through-action

The relationship between Winnie and Willie creates a clash of pur-poses, a conflict. It may be a low-key conflict, but it is a conflict nonetheless. It arises from Winnie's absurd dream and Willie's inability or unwillingness to live according to it. Willie is unlike Winnie's dream image of him, and he is (deliberately?) unresponsive to her efforts to sustain their relationship beyond the minimum of reluctant coexistence. The conflict between them is never hostile, of course. Winnie is too compliant and Willie is too indifferent for outspoken disagreements to occur. But even so, there is opposition between them, and it might be described in the form of this counter through-action: an apathetic husband refuses to accept his wife's attempts to reactivate their relationship. If this counter through-action is accurate, then what might Willie's intention be when he reappears at the end? What kind of clothing is he wearing, and why is he "dressed to kill"? In nonrealistic plays it is essential to take the mise-en-scene (costume, in this event) into account more than ever.

Summary

Action analysis of *Hamlet* and *Happy Days* began with a list of concrete events, then switched back and forth between abstract ideas (seed and theme) and concrete events (three major climaxes, super-objective), and concluded with the world of concrete behavior (through-action and counter through-action). The outcome is a no-nonsense vision of the whole, a speedy way of getting to the professional inner workings of a play. By concentrating on the events of the plot as it does, action analysis enables us to see the progress of the dramatic action, the thematic core, the conflict, and the basic storyline of the play. Action analysis establishes a firm foundation with which to begin rehearsals and director–designer conferences. If action analysis is done at the beginning of the study process, it helps actors, directors, and designers to maintain a point of reference during the more detailed method of script analysis taught in the following chapters. If it is done in company with formalist analysis, it can help to show how everything in a play is interconnected. The reduced, concentrated nature of action analysis leads to an appreciation of how plays are written, how they work in terms of practical theatre, and how much special ability it takes to write even a modestly successful play. Yet by no means is action analysis complete in itself.

35

Prior experience with action analysis is not required for the method of formalist analysis taught in the following chapters. Both approaches are formalist in the sense that they acknowledge the importance of form (the arrangement of parts) in a play, and they depend on information from the play itself instead of outside sources. The next chapters will show how formalist analysis starts from the very beginning, without preparation, building fact upon fact, until the overall unity of the play emerges almost by itself. Even so, added insights can be gained in formalist analysis by building on knowledge gained from prior action analysis. Thus, for readers who wish to combine the findings of action analysis and formalist analysis, Chapters 2 though 7 provide appropriate added questions.

Questions

1. *Sequence of External Events.* What are the most important external events, those that change characters the most? How are they arranged in order? Descriptions should be short and snappy, without resorting to abstract or literary words. What do the external events suggest about the mise-en-scene? How could the mise-en-scene contribute to the effectiveness of the external events?

2. *Review of the Facts.* Who are the most important characters in each event? What are they doing in practical terms? Where are they doing it, in what physical environment? When are they doing it? Why are they doing it? How are they doing it, in what manner emotionally? Again, thinking should be short and snappy, not bookish.

3. *Seed.* To begin with, look for the basic moral commandment violated in the play. Is it murder, adultery, slander or lying, honor between parents and children, or the attitude toward the Divinity? What subject, based on this commandment, provides the creative impulse behind the play? A few words, or even one word, will be enough to describe the seed. (The seed is an extremely important concept, but it can be difficult to accept and deal with in a determined way. Stick-to-itiveness will pay off in the end.) What does the seed suggest about the mise-en-scene? How could the mise-en-scene contribute to the effectiveness of the seed?

4. *Sequence of Internal Events.* Look for the latent connection between the seed and each external event. Short and snappy, always using the seed itself in the formulation. What elements of the mise-en-scene are suggested by the internal events? How could the mise-en-scene contribute to the effectiveness of the internal events?

5. *Three Major Climaxes.* What are the three major climaxes (the three events of highest dramatic tension or emotional temperature; the three major turning points in the action; the beginning,

middle, and end)? What do the three major climaxes suggest about the mise-en-scene? How could the mise-en-scene contribute to the effectiveness of the three major climaxes?

6. *Theme.* What is the main character's response to the seed, toward the basic subject of the play? In other words, what does the play demonstrate about the seed? How do the three major climaxes show the progressive development of the theme, its beginning, middle, and end? What does the theme suggest about the mise-en-scene? How could the mise-en-scene contribute to the effectiveness of the theme?

7. *Super-Objective.* The super-objective is best stated as a future action, a goal the main character is striving to achieve. How is the super-objective expressed through the unfolding action of the main character? What is the course of action, progress, or path of the super-objective as it develops in the actions of the main character? What does the super-objective suggest about the mise-en-scene? How could the mise-en-scene contribute to the effectiveness of the super-objective?

8. *Through-action.* State the main conflict of the play in one concise sentence — the story of a particular character performing a particular action under particular circumstances. How are the seed, theme, and super-objective latent within the through-action? What does the through-action suggest about the mise-en-scene? How could the mise-en-scene contribute to the effectiveness of the through-action?

9. *Counter Through-action.* What counteraction interferes with the through-action of the main character, both challenging and strengthening it? What storyline runs adjacent to the through-action, but in the opposite direction? What is the source of the main conflict in the play? What does the counter through-action suggest about the mise-en-scene? How could the mise-en-scene contribute to the effectiveness of the counter through-action?

CHAPTER 2

Given Circumstances

This chapter begins the study of formalist analysis, which is the foundation for action analysis studied in the previous chapter. Unlike action analysis, which is rapid and sketchy, formalist analysis is slow and detailed. Like the first years of medical study that involve the close study of anatomy and how the body works, formalist analysis studies the form (anatomy) of plays and how plays work. Formalist analysis asks readers not to cling to any ideas of their own about the play or characters, but to allow the play to come to them and identify itself piece by piece. Readers have ideas, of course, but they are asked to set them aside and let the play speak to them. Readers should also try to forget about previous theories — for the time being there is just the reader and the play.

The Introduction referred to Aristotle's Poetics, in which it was said that plays consist of six elements that set them apart from other artistic forms: plot, character, idea, dialogue, tempo-rhythm-mood (Aristotle's "music"), and mise-en-scene (scenery, costumes, lighting, properties, sound, makeup). Aristotle arrived at this scheme in his study of how the parts of a play operate. He did not mean that all plays have these elements in the same amount or in the same way. One play may have more or fewer events in its plot than another, more complicated or simplified characters, and more or less attention devoted to mise-en-scene. Aristotle meant that all these elements are present in one form or another in all those works we call plays. Because this is a book about script analysis, however, we are primarily concerned here with the written part of a play. We will not deal directly with the practice of acting, directing, or design in themselves, but with the playwright's text, which is always the starting point for theatricalization by actors, directors, and designers.

The beginning of all plays is the unique combination of present and past that Stanislavsky called the *given circumstances*. Others use different terms — social context, foundations of the plot, playwright's setting, texture, local detail, or literary landscape. They all mean the same thing. Given circumstances are the specific conditions in which the action of the play occurs.

Novice play readers sometimes consider given circumstances as the trivial, uninteresting things they can pass over. The impulse may be unthinking, but it acknowledges something important. At first glance, the given circumstances may not seem as exciting or useful as are the other parts of a play, for example, the characters or setting. They are simple things — so obvious that the impulse is to take them for granted, like the air we breathe. Yet assumptions that are most familiar are often hardest to recognize as important; again, like the air we breathe. Actually, the given circumstances are as vital to a play as plot, character, and all the other features. They put the characters and audience into the "here and now" of the action. Without the given circumstances, characters would exist in an abstract never-never land without any connection to real life. Given circumstances work as silent, invisible yet potent forces. They influence the characters, increase tensions, create complications, create the environment, suggest the mise-en-scene, and move the plot forward. Moreover, given circumstances always contain important clues to other parts of the play. They may seem trivial, but they are precisely the details that make it possible to know what makes the plot go and the characters tick. Bringing each given circumstance into focus will help to explain how it operates. This can happen only after careful analysis forces it to stand up and be identified.

This chapter is concerned with the given circumstances that take place in the present, on stage, before the audience. They spring from the time and place of the play along with the conventions, attitudes, and manners behind and around it. Under this heading, we will be concerned with eight subtopics: time, place, society, economics, learning and the arts, politics and law, spirituality, and, to end with, the world of the play. In the next chapter, we will turn to the given circumstances that exist in the past, the unseen background story, which includes everything that happened before the play begins.

Time

Time in the given circumstances has three aspects: (1) the time of the play's writing, (2) the time in which the action of the play is set, and (3) the time that passes during the course of the action.

Time of Composition

40

The *time of composition* is not strategic in the earliest stages of script analysis because it is not part of the written play. It will become more valuable when it is studied in connection with the biography of the author, the conditions of the author's era, and the place of the play within the body of the author's works. Although knowledge of the author's life, world, and work is necessary for a complete understanding of any play, too much attention to these issues at this early point can even be distracting. Sometimes confusion can arise between what is learned about a play from outside sources and what is objectively in it. It is perhaps better to set aside external matters for a later time when the process of script analysis is further along.

Time of the Action

In many plays it is important to know the *time of the action*, that is, the exact time, season, and year in which the action is set. This knowledge is not just for the sake of realism or bookish accuracy but also to be aware of the entire dramatic situation. The exactitude of the information available about time depends on the play. For instance, in *Death of a Salesman* there are references in Willy Loman's flashbacks to the boxer Gene Tunney and the football player Red Grange. These names establish the year of those scenes at about 1927 when Tunney was heavyweight champion and Grange played football for the Chicago Bears. Two years later the stock market crashed, ushering in the Great Depression — important time information in this play about the American dream of financial success. References to the time period in *Machinal* — a telephone switchboard, adding machines, typewriters, Telephone Girl, slang ("hot dog!," "sweetie,""sweet papa"), and the Mexican Revolution — establish the time of the action as the decade of the 1910s, an era of immense national confidence prior to World War I. It was also the decade of revolution in Russia. The last days of the archconservative lawyer, Roy Cohn, depicted in *Angels in America*, set this play's action in 1986. At that time Cohn was dying of AIDS-related illness, and the United States Attorney General had published the first official report about AIDS. For the first time the enormous magnitude of the AIDS epidemic began to be reflected in public discourse. This year was also the beginning of Ronald Regan's second term as president, which many considered a signal of the end of the American liberal ideal. The year 1986 can therefore be seen as the end one era and the beginning of another.

Gene Tunney, the Great Depression, economic boom and political unrest, Roy Cohn, and public awareness of the AIDS epidemic are important in these plays not merely because they help to establish the historical context, but because they set in motion, stand out against, or reinforce the conflicts among the characters and inform the creative work of designers. For these reasons, the time of the action is a crucial issue. The time of the action should be determined by searching the dialogue for direct statements or references to historical people, places, or things. Stage directions and playwrights' notes offer added information about the time of the action, but they are not as dependable or influential as time stated in the dialogue itself. Since stage directions and extra notes are only one vision of the play, actors, directors, and designers looking forward to a genuinely contemporary production will normally withhold study of them until settling on their own interpretation first.

Dramatic Time

Dramatic time is the total of the time that passes during the on-stage action plus the time during intervals between acts and scenes. Some plays permit very precise determination. In *The Wild Duck*, it is possible, without the help of stage directions, to identify the passage of dramatic time almost to the hour, including the time of day and day of the week for each act. But dramatic time can also be compressed or expanded to accommodate theatrical needs. Several days pass in *The Piano Lesson*, months in *Hamlet*, and years in *Three Sisters* and *Mother Courage*. Time moves forward and backward in *Death of a Salesman*, and stands still in *Happy Days*. In *A Lie of the Mind*, time moves in random leaps.

There is an interesting assortment of information about dramatic time in the opening lines of *Hamlet*:

> BERNARDO. Who's there?
>
> FRANCISCO. Nay, answer me. Stand and unfold yourself.
>
> BERNARDO. Long live the King!
>
> FRANCISCO. Bernardo?
>
> BERNARDO. He.
>
> FRANCISCO. You come most carefully upon your hour.
>
> BERNARDO. 'Tis now struck twelve; get thee to bed, Francisco.
>
> FRANCISCO. For this relief much thanks. 'Tis bitter cold, And I am sick at heart.
>
> BERNARDO. Have you had quiet guard?
>
> FRANCISCO. Not a mouse stirring.
>
> BERNARDO. Well; good night.

Although Francisco is on guard duty, Bernardo speaks the first line. Why? Because he is nervous to begin with and then becomes frightened when Francisco makes a noise in the dark as he paces back and forth during his watch. Then Francisco challenges him, "Nay, answer *me*." Francisco, after all, is the one who is on guard duty. "Stand and unfold yourself," he says, from which we understand that it is night and Bernardo is coming toward him wrapped in a cloak. The cloak is needed because it is winter, a fact that is confirmed a moment later when Francisco says "Tis bitter cold." Another comment by Bernardo indicates the time of day — "Tis now struck twelve" — and specifies the time as midnight. The passage ends with Bernardo's expression of "good night" to further emphasize the lateness of the hour (and his eagerness to get away). They are all afraid of something. Imaginative actors, directors, and designers should be able to grasp the mysterious atmosphere Shakespeare has established as the cold winter night enfolds the jumpy, frightened characters.

Ibsen uses some of the same methods for expressing dramatic time in this selection from act 2 of *The Wild Duck*:

> (*A knocking is heard at the entrance door.*)
>
> GINA. (*rising*) Hush, Ekdal — I think there's someone at the door.
>
> HJALMAR. (*laying his flute on the bookcases*) There! Again!
>
> (*Gina goes and opens the door.*)
>
> GREGERS. (*in the passage*) Excuse me —
>
> GINA. (*starting back slightly*) Oh!
>
> GREGERS. Doesn't Mr. Ekdal, the photographer, live here?
>
> GINA. Yes, he does.
>
> HJALMAR. (*going toward the door*) Gregers! You here after all? Well, come in then.
>
> GREGERS. (*coming in*) I told you I would come and look you up.
>
> HJALMAR. But this evening — Have you left the party?
>
> GREGERS. I have left the party and my father's. Good evening, Mrs. Ekdal. I don't know whether you recognize me?
>
> GINA. Oh, yes, it's not difficult to know young Mr. Werle again.
>
> GREGERS. No, I am like my mother, and no doubt you remember her.
>
> HJALMAR. Left your father's house, did you say?
>
> GREGERS. Yes, I have gone to a hotel.
>
> HJALMAR. Indeed. Well, since you're here, take off your coat and sit down.
>
> GREGERS. Thanks. (*He takes off his overcoat.*)

43

Gregers' statement, "I told you I would come and look you up," refers to something he said to Hjalmar at the dinner party, an event we already know occurred earlier the same evening. Its use at this point is not just a way of maintaining continuity of time by connecting this scene with a prior incident in the play, but also indicates that Gregers has rushed over to Hjalmar's house straight after arguing with his father. Hjalmar's reply "But this evening — Have you left the party?"

and Gregers' responses "I have left the party" and "Good evening, Mrs. Ekdal" reinforce the continuity of time, confirm the time of the current scene, and underscore Hjalmar's surprise at the fact of Gregers's unexpected, late-night arrival. We see also that Gregers is wearing an overcoat because it is winter. The season is important enough for Ibsen to remind us about it again in the accompanying stage directions, which we know he wrote himself. The point is that the environment is cold, that Gregers is a mysterious late-night visitor, and, besides that, he is more or less a stranger.

In the opening scene of *A Raisin in the Sun*, dramatic time is stated in the dialogue, observed in the characters' actions, and confirmed in the stage directions. Ruth mentions it three times. Travis gets out of bed and exits to the bathroom, and then Ruth warns Walter Lee about being late for work. Ruth's interest in the time shows that it is her duty to keep the family operating successfully.

> RUTH. Come on now, boy, it's seven thirty.
> (*He sits up at last, in a stupor of sleepiness.*)
> I say hurry up. Travis! You ain't the only person in the world got to use a bathroom. (*The child, a sturdy, handsome boy of ten or twelve, drags himself out of bed and almost blindly takes his towels and "today's clothes" from the drawers and a closet and goes out to the bathroom, which is in an outside hall and which is shared by another family or families on the same floor. RUTH crosses to the bedroom door at right and opens it and calls in to her husband.*)
> Walter Lee!... It's after seven thirty! Lemme see you do some waking up in there now. (*She waits.*) You better get up from there, man! It's seven thirty I tell you. (*She waits again.*) All right, you just go ahead and lay there and next thing you know Travis be finished and Mr. Johnson'll be in there and you'll be fussing and cussing around here like a mad man! And be late too! (*She waits, at the end of her patience.*) Walter Lee — it's time to get up!

44

Careful detective work searching for the passage of time in the dialogue will pay handsome dividends later on when dealing with more complicated issues.

Place

The next subdivision of given circumstances is *place* — the physical environment. Some directors and designers feel that the mise-en-scene should illustrate the physical environment realistically, while others believe it should illustrate the play's inner spirit. Formalist analysis does not argue for or against either of these viewpoints. A realistic picture of the physical environment may work for some plays and an abstract scenic metaphor for others, while for others it may be a combination or something entirely different. What is important is that the physical environment in any configuration influences the action, characters, and environment. Therefore it is an extremely important part of the entire experience of the play.

General Locale

The first topic under the heading of place is *general locale*, that is, the country, region, or district in which the action is set. Instructions about the general locale are often available in the front notes and stage directions, but readers should always validate them in the dialogue as much as possible, if not discounting them sometimes for the sake of genuine originality. This passage from *Hamlet* contains references to the city of Wittenberg, where Hamlet has been studying, as well as to Denmark, his native country and the geographical setting for the action:

> CLAUDIUS. For your intent
> In going back to school in Wittenberg,
> It is most retrograde to our desire;
> And we beseech you bend you to remain
> Here, in the cheer and comfort of our eye,
> Our chiefest courtier, cousin and our son.
> QUEEN. Let not thy mother lose her prayers, Hamlet.
> HAMLET. I shall in all my best obey you, madam.
> CLAUDIUS. Why, 'tis a loving and a fair reply.
> Be as ourself in Denmark.

In addition to these locales, the play also contains references to Poland, Norway, England, and France. The motive for including all these locales is more than topographical accuracy. Readers should ask themselves: Why Wittenberg? Why Norway? Why England? What was Shakespeare getting at by naming so many countries?

The emotional associations evoked by the general locale can also contribute to the emotional life of the entire play. Playwrights take advantage of this to add extra meaning to their works. Few can read *Machinal*, for example, without sensing the emotional associations of life in a large, busy metropolis such as New York City. *Death of a Salesman* contains several examples of emotions associated with the general locale, as in this passage when Willy Loman laments the decline of the neighborhood around his home in Brooklyn.

> WILLY. The street is lined with cars. There's not a breath of fresh air in the neighborhood. The grass don't grow anymore, you can't raise a carrot in the back yard. Remember those two beautiful elm trees out there? They should've had a law against apartment houses. Remember when I and Biff hung the swing between them?

In this excerpt from *A Raisin in the Sun*, Mama Younger announces that she has made a down payment on a new home. Her family has been living in a crowded tenement on Chicago's south side. They are delighted about the prospect of a place of their own. There are negative associations connected with the soon-to-be neighborhood, however, which everyone knows to be a white suburb.

> RUTH. Oh, Walter...a home...a home. (*She comes back to Mama.*) Well — where is it? How big is it? How much it going to cost?
> MAMA. Well —
> RUTH. When we moving?
> MAMA. (*smiling at her*) First of the month.
> RUTH. (*throwing her head back with jubilance*) Praise God!
> MAMA. (*tentatively, still looking at her son's back turned against her and RUTH*) It's — it's a nice house too...

(She cannot help speaking directly to him.
An imploring quality in her voice, her
manner, makes her almost like a girl now.)
Three bedrooms — nice big one for you and
Ruth...Me...and Beneatha still have to share
our room, but Travis have one of his own —
and *(with difficulty)* I figure if the — new
baby — is a boy, we could get one of them
double-decker outfits...And there's a yard
with a little patch of dirt where I could
maybe get to grow me a few flowers...And a
nice big basement...

RUTH. Walter, honey, be glad —

MAMA. *(still to his back, fingering things on the*
table) 'Course I don't want to make it sound
fancier than it is...It's just a plain
little old house — but it's made good and
solid — and it will be ours. Walter Lee -
it makes a difference in a man when he can
walk on floors that belong to him...

RUTH. Where is it?

MAMA. *(frightened at this telling)*Well — well —
it's out there in Clybourne Park —
(RUTH's radiance fades abruptly, and
Walter finally turns slowly to face his
mother with incredulity and hostility.)

MAMA. *(matter-of-factly)* Four-o-six Clybourne
Street, Clybourne Park.

RUTH. *Clybourne Park?* Mama, there ain't no
colored people living in Clybourne Park.

MAMA. Well, I guess there's going to be some now.

Playwrights choose general locales to evoke emotional associations as well as for realism and authenticity. In *A Lie of the Mind,* the general locales are remote towns in Oklahoma and Montana, depicted in the play as inhospitable regions attractive to society's loners. *American Buffalo* takes place in Chicago. What emotional and technical associations do these general locales evoke?

Specific Locale

The *specific locale* is the particular place in which the stage action occurs. A reader's first impulse is to rely on stage directions for information about the specific locale. And published scripts often do include notes and diagrams of the scenery, such as the lengthy description of Doaker Charles's kitchen and parlor in *The Piano Lesson* or the even lengthier description of the transparent multi-level Loman house in *Death of a Salesman*. Scenery notes and diagrams can be interesting and useful, even if out of date, but they are normally the editor or stage manager's description of the first professional production and usually not the author's own. This may not be a problem for those who are reading a play for study purposes, but it is a serious issue for designers or directors who are preparing for a truly contemporary interpretation. Modern theatre calls for distinctive mise-en-scene for each and every production, meaning that editorial notes about an earlier production generally should not be used as a guide.

Dialogue is always a more productive source of information about the specific locale. Statements like, "So this is your quarters, Hjalmar — this is your home" in *The Wild Duck* and "Lord, ain't nothing so dreary as the view from this window on a dreary day, is there?" in *A Raisin in the Sun* are the best kind of references about the specific locale in those plays. They identify, but they also emotionalize. Some plays may also include details about the architectural layout. Mrs. Sorby instructs the servants in act 1 of *The Wild Duck*, "Tell them to serve the coffee in the music room, Pettersen." Anfisa opens act 3 of *Three Sisters* by saying:

> ANFISA. They're sitting down there under the
> stairs now. "Please come upstairs," I
> tell them. "We can't have this, can we?"
> They're crying. "We don't know where
> father is," they say. "He might have been
> burnt to death." What an idea! Then there
> are those other people out in the yard as
> well, they're in their nightclothes, too.

Little by little the Prozorov family is displaced from one specific locale in their house to another, until at last they are completely pushed out by Natasha. This sense of displacement is experienced by the characters on both sides of the conflict and is central to the meaning of the play.

Specific locale can also be identified through inference. In this passage from *The School for Scandal*, Charles Surface is about to auction his family portraits to pay his debts. He points to the paintings in the portrait gallery of his eighteenth-century house where the sale takes place.

> (*Enter* CHARLES SURFACE, SIR OLIVER SURFACE, MOSES, *and* CARELESS.)
>
> CHARLES SURFACE. Walk in, gentlemen, pray walk in — here they are, the family of the Surfaces up to the [Norman] Conquest.
>
> SIR OLIVER (*disguised as* MASTER PREMIUM). And, in my opinion, a goodly collection.
>
> CHARLES SURFACE. Ay, ay, these are done in the true spirit of portrait painting; no volontère grace or expression. Not like the works of your modern Raphaels, who give you the strongest resemblance, yet contrive to make your portrait independent of you; so that you may sink the original and not hurt the picture. No, no; the merit of these is the inveterate likeness — all stiff and awkward as the originals, and like nothing in human nature besides.
>
> SIR OLIVER. Ah! We shall never see such figures of men again.
>
> CHARLES SURFACE. I hope not. Well, you see, Master Premium, what a domestic character I am; here I sit of an evening surrounded by my family.

49

When Charles says, "Walk in, gentlemen, pray walk in," we imagine him entering a picture gallery and inviting the others to follow. When he says, "Here they are, the family of the Surfaces up to the Conquest," he is pointing to the paintings. His sarcastic description of the paintings ("The merit of these is the inveterate likeness — all stiff and awkward as the originals, and like nothing in human nature besides.") is a clue to what the style of the paintings should evoke.

Society

In science, a closed system is an assembly of objects in the state of isolation from the outside environment. Plays show social groups living together under a closed system, too; closed because the playwright has isolated the society of the play from the world of objective reality. In this section we will seek information about *society*, the closed social system of the play, which influences the characters' behavior and environment.

Arthur Miller believed that the playwright's choice of social groups determines the form of the play. Communication among family members, he said, is different from that with strangers, and private behavior is different from public. Interest in the family leads to writing realistic plays dealing with personal and private subjects, while interest in social groups outside the family leads to nonrealistic forms that treat public subjects. Miller's observations are intriguing, but they should not be applied too rigidly. The implications that result from the choice of social groups are numerous and complex, and there are some obvious contrary examples. In any case, his observations help us to understand how the choice of social groups, the meaning, and the environment of the play are interconnected.

50 Families

The most common social group, and the most important one in the majority of modern plays, is the *family*. This is logical because we are all sons, daughters, sisters, and brothers before we are anything else. And since the family is the most basic social unit, playwrights cannot stray too far from it without losing touch with their audiences. The dramatic importance of families lies in the emotional quality that attends specific social relationships, such as love between husband and wife, pressures between parent and child, and competition among siblings.

Seven family members are identified in the garden scene from *Death of a Salesman* that we looked at in the Introduction. They are Willy's father, Willy as a father, Willy's wife, Willy's sons Biff and Happy, Willy's brother Ben, and Ben as the uncle of Biff and Happy. Almost every member of the Loman family and their family relationship to each other is identified in the scene. This leads to certain expectations about family relationships that may be confirmed or perhaps refuted in the play.

Claudius's opening lines in *Hamlet* explain his (apparent) relationship to his deceased brother, King Hamlet, and above all his new relationship to his brother's wife, Gertrude, a relationship many readers would interpret as dishonorable, if not incestuous. Once more, expectations associated with family relationships provide the grounds for future conflicts.

> CLAUDIUS. Though yet of Hamlet our dear brother's
>   death
>   The memory be green, and that it us befitted
>   To bear our hearts in grief, and our whole
>   kingdom
>   To be contracted in one brow of woe,
>   Yet so far has discretion fought with nature
>   That we with wisest sorrow think on him
>   Together with remembrance of ourselves.
>   Therefore, our sometime sister, now our
>   queen,
>   The imperial jointress to this warlike
>   state,
>   Have we, as with a defeated joy,
>   With an auspicious and a drooping eye,
>   With mirth in funeral and dirge in marriage,
>   In equal scale, weighing delight with dole,
>   Taken to wife.   51

The thematic issue behind the complex family relationships in *The Piano Lesson* may seem complex to grasp at first, but upon closer examination the families form an unbroken bond going all the way back to slavery times. This bond exerts a powerful influence on the characters and opens a window into the basic subject, or "lesson," of the play. Characters that ignore these family roots risk losing their identities as free and independent human beings.

Families form the heart of such dissimilar plays as *Oedipus Rex, Tartuffe, Three Sisters, A Lie of the Mind, Mother Courage,* and *Angels in America.* A study of these examples indicates how universal the attraction of family groups can be, in modern drama most of all. Family love, its absence, or its distortion can be found at the heart of many, many plays.

Love and Friendship

Friendships are sympathetic social bonds outside the family. We find vivid examples of friendship in David Mamet's play *American Buffalo,* where the social group is defined by the perceived friendships among a group of petty criminals. An important friendship exists between Hamlet and Horatio in *Hamlet;* Gregers Werle and

Hjalmar Ekdal in *The Wild Duck*; Walter, Willy, and Bobo in *A Raisin in the Sun*; Willy and Charley in *Death of a Salesman*; and Roy Cohn and Louis Ironson in *Angels in America*. As with family relationships, friendships point to emotional and behavioral expectations that may be confirmed, or just as often refuted or tested in the play.

Love identifies another kind of social group outside the family. Love entails not just the dominant heterosexual form but all forms, including homosexual love, the love of a parent for a child, love between siblings, and above all obsessive or destructive love. There are many examples in the study plays: Oedipus and Jocasta, Hamlet and Ophelia, Tartuffe and Elmire, Mrs. Sorby and Mr. Werle (*The Wild Duck*), Mother Courage and the Chaplain, Winnie and Willie (*Happy Days*), Louis Ironson and Prior Walter (*Angels in America*), Berniece and Avery (*The Piano Lesson*), and Jake and Beth (*A Lie of the Mind*), to name a few. Apart from the family unit, friendship and love are among the most dramatic social groups found in plays. Readers should have little difficulty finding more examples and determining how they affirm or refute customary expectations. Make a note that in modern plays love can at the same time confirm and refute such expectations, a paradox that for some readers may obscure the real issues at stake. Jake's love for Beth in *A Lie of the Mind* is a case in point. Jake is an example of a lover-abuser, and Beth's behavior abets that of her abuser. Some readers may deny that real love can exist in such an abusive relationship as theirs. The point is that in spite of everything, real, mature love somehow manages to emerge from their abusive relationship.

Occupation

Occupation forms another social group outside the family. This group is defined by what characters do to earn a living and their interactions with others having the same or different occupations. Office workers and businessmen form the central occupational group in *Death of a Salesman* and *Machinal*, for instance, as do professional soldiers in *Mother Courage* and *Three Sisters*. Occupational groups also occur in classic plays, where we might not expect to encounter such social issues. Professional actors, soldiers, and gravediggers are represented in *Hamlet*; process servers in *Tartuffe*; and moneylenders in *The School for Scandal*. Information about occupational groups provides clues to the characters' motives and suggests emotional values that could be underscored in the play. Why does *Angels in America* feature attorneys, doctors, religious and other lettered figures and those who serve or support them?

Social Rank

Social rank distinguishes a character's position or standing in society, differences which in general stem from wealth, power, formal education, or other material issues. It is based on a fortunate group whose members are accustomed to giving orders and having them carried out by those from lower social ranks. Characters of lower social rank show deference to those of higher rank by using formal titles and various kinds of submissive behavior, such as bows, curtsies, salutes, and special forms of address. We observe this at work in *Hamlet*, for example, where Claudius and Gertrude address Hamlet by his given name. All the others, including Ophelia and Horatio, say "Prince Hamlet" or "my lord."

Although distinctions of social rank can be found in many other classic plays like *Oedipus Rex*, *Tartuffe*, and *Three Sisters*, they are seldom the subject of explicit attention there (*The School for Scandal* is a notable exception). Distinctions of social rank were a normal part of everyday life in the past and are still customary in many regions of the world. When such distinctions are taken for granted because of the play's general locale or time period, no special need exists to provide explanations in the dialogue. In such cases, information about social rank needs to be deduced from the characters' behavior. There may not be much information about the inner workings of the class system in *Hamlet*, *Tartuffe*, or *Three Sisters*, but class distinctions are nevertheless of paramount importance. In other words, projecting modern, classless social behavior into historical plays can lead to misreading. Sometimes it will be necessary to supplement script analysis with outside information or devise contemporary substitutions to communicate the thematic significance of distinctions of social rank.

Social rank may not work the same way in the present as it did in the past, but it still exists and can be just as forceful and repressive. While aristocratic birth was the main source of high status in the past, today it often appears as an outcome of education, financial or political power, ethnicity, or sexual orientation, and in these forms it may be easier for modern readers to comprehend. For example, social rank based on money turns up in *The Wild Duck*, *Mother Courage*, *Death of a Salesman*, *The Piano Lesson*, and *Three Sisters*; social rank based on education is found in *Three Sisters*; ethnic discrimination influences the social rank of the characters in *A Raisin in the Sun* and *The Piano Lesson*; and social rank associated with sexual orientation is a feature of *Angels in America*. Understanding obvious and hidden social rank is essential in these and other modern plays.

53

Social Standards

Social standards are the codes of conduct and shared beliefs regarded as necessary by the characters and to which they are expected to conform. Examples of modern social standards include belief in individual rights, prohibitions against dishonesty and antisocial behavior, and belief in working for a living and being a useful member of society, but there are many others, just as powerful though less obvious, from other times and places. Social standards do not need to be proven or even stated in most plays because characters accept them as true without question. Characters believe in them and conversely their behavior and beliefs are conditioned by them. Social standards are often so important that violation produces shock, horror, moral revulsion, indignation, and ostracism, and even justifies the use of more extreme penalties to enforce conformity. A certain dominant group enforces these standards at the same time as secondary groups reinforce (or challenge) the dominant group and its standards.

In former times, social standards were determined by established religion, class, politics, inherited family position, and national culture. In classic plays, the characters' behavior tends to be controlled by religious, aristocratic, or nationalistic standards — royal power, for example, in *Oedipus Rex*, *Hamlet*, and *Tartuffe*. In contemporary society, the overt influence of such forms of social control has lessened. At the present time it is the social standards of science and business, the idea of equality, and the social standards of the media and the dominant middle class that collectively determine the standards of belief and behavior for most people. The powerful influence of social standards may be distasteful to those who consider themselves independent-minded, but understanding and dealing with these influences in plays is necessary nonetheless. Today the unwritten codes dictated by social standards are often the only principles that characters take seriously enough to cause conflicts.

One way social standards make themselves known is through the use of euphemisms in the dialogue. A euphemism is an inoffensive term that is substituted for an offensive one. Thus euphemisms are evidence of social standards at work through avoidance of unacceptable words, those that point to highly charged social issues. Examples may be found in *The Wild Duck*. In the first scene the servant Jensen, referring to Mr. Ekdal, says to Pettersen, "I've heard tell as he's been a lively customer in his day." They both understand that "lively customer" is a euphemism for someone who is a womanizer. In the climactic scene at the end of act 1, Gregers accuses his father

54

of having been "interested in" their former household servant Gina Hansen. In this context, "interested in" is a euphemism for sexual relations. Both Gregers and Mr. Werle use euphemisms when referring to the deceased Mrs. Werle. Gregers refers to her "breakdown" and her "unfortunate weakness." Mr. Werle says that she was "morbid" and "overstrained." He also says, "her eyes were — clouded now and then." These are euphemisms for alcoholism and possibly drug addiction, which were almost as common in the late nineteenth century as they are today, unfortunately, even though social standards of that time prohibited speaking openly about them.

Social standards are disclosed through other kinds of verbal clues, too. When Jensen says earlier, "I've heard tell..." it is a hint that there is serious gossip about Werle's family, and gossip stems from violation — or apparent violation — of narrow-minded social standards. This is confirmed later when Mr. Werle explains to Gregers why he did not provide more help to Old Ekdal. He says, "I've had a slur cast on my reputation ... I have done all I could without positively laying myself open to all sorts of suspicion and gossip." Then, referring to the fact that Mrs. Sorby is living with him, he says, "A woman so situated may easily find herself in a false position in the eyes of the world. For that matter, it does a man no good either." Mr. Werle is controlled by a fear of scandal. It could ruin his position in business and society. More evidence of this veiled type of social control occurs when Hjalmar confesses that he "kept the window blinds down" when his father was in prison. Euphemisms and other kinds of hints in *The Wild Duck* show the existence of powerful social standards concerning marriage, sex, alcohol, drugs, mental health, politics, business affairs, and even relations between labor and management. The reward for conforming to these standards is economic success and social acceptance; the penalty for violation is malicious gossip, public scandal, social ostracism, and even prison.

Social standards frequently construct a harsh and unforgiving world. The old saying that sticks and stones can break our bones but words can never hurt us is not true in plays. Words, above all epithets and slurs, are used to condemn violations of prevailing social standards, and they have the power to inflict serious damage. They can cause shame, embarrassment, and guilt and they tend to work very effectively in plays. Notice this harsh exchange of epithets between Roy Cohn, a Jewish lawyer, and Belize, a black homosexual hospital worker, from *Angels in America*. The topic is Belize's demand for access to Roy's unauthorized supply of the then scarce and expensive AIDS drug AZT.

55

BELIZE. You expect pity?

ROY. (*a beat, then*) I expect you to hand over those keys and move your nigger ass out of my room.

BELIZE. What did you say?

ROY. Move your nigger cunt spade faggot lackey ass out of my room.

BELIZE. (*Overlapping starting on "spade"*) Shit-for-brains filthy-mouthed selfish motherfucking cowardly cocksucking cloven-hoofed pig.

ROY. (*Overlapping*) Mongrel. Dingo. Slave. Ape.

BELIZE. Kike.

ROY. Now you're talking!

BELIZE. Greedy kike.

ROY. Now you can have a bottle. But only one.

These offensive epithets emphasize the outsider status of Cohn as a Jew and Belize as a black and a homosexual. They are intended to offend and insult. In this episode the words hurt so much that they almost transcend offensiveness by calling attention to the fact that both characters share a hidden bond, the regrettable bond of exclusion from mainstream society. On a similar note, why is Baron Tuzenbach considered an outsider in *Three Sisters*?

Economics

Economics is concerned with the large-scale monetary system the characters live under and the smaller scale financial transactions in which they may be engaged. It may seem that the study of economics is far from our stated principle of fixing on the play itself, but economics is more important in script analysis than it first appears. Among the study plays, *Tartuffe*, *The School for Scandal*, *The Wild Duck*, *The Hairy Ape*, *Mother Courage*, *Death of a Salesman*, *A Raisin in the Sun*, *Three Sisters*, *The Piano Lesson*, *American Buffalo*, and *Angels in America* all share a deep concern with money. Sometimes economic issues appear where we least expect them, for example in the plays of Anton Chekhov. In *The Cherry Orchard*, it is important to identify information about real estate development, mortgages, banking, borrowing and lending, agricultural marketing, and the daily financial affairs of a large country estate, not to mention the economic impact of the law passed in 1861 freeing the serfs. Andrey's unauthorized mortgage of the Prozorov estate is a significant financial issue in *Three Sisters*. Gaining or losing money (for the most part losing it) has been and continues to be one of the favorite plot resources for dramatists.

According to economists, there are four principal financial systems. Mercantilism is colonialism with national control of manufacturing and exports. In a laissez-faire economic system, business is permitted to follow the unwritten "natural laws" of economics. Private property, profit, and credit form the basis of capitalism. Socialism calls for public ownership of manufacturing, public services, and natural resources. These four economic systems seldom exist in isolation, but usually operate in various combinations.

Capitalism is a system that many of us are familiar with and one we often encounter in the plays we read. Since capitalism is based on individual freedom and free enterprise, it can be rewarding for successful entrepreneurs, but it can be very hard on those with limited financial talent, influence, or resources. In *Death of a Salesman*, Willy Loman struggles to live within a capitalist system dominated by powerful, unfeeling business interests. His economic concerns consist of meeting the regular payments for his refrigerator, automobile, life insurance, and home. Willy's personal economics are so important to him that they are elevated to almost symbolic status in the play. In the kitchen of Joe Meilziner's famous scenic design, for example, the Hastings refrigerator (always breaking down) is the lone appliance.

Mercantilism is the economic system in *The School for Scandal*. The important economic issues are the loans made to Charles Surface based on his credit from the family's colonial imports, the auction of his family home and its furnishings, and the sizable financial resources controlled by Sir Oliver Surface. International trading, which plays a major role in mercantilism, influences the timing of Charles's loans and the well-timed arrival of Sir Oliver. In *Machinal*, the First Man's revolutionary adventures in Mexico indicate deeply held socialist principles, principles which also filter through the dehumanizing capitalist environment of the play by implication. Economics can be an important issue in script analysis, but a word of caution. Because economics is an issue close to each of us, special care should be taken against projecting personal economic convictions or experiences into a play. As with the other analytical concepts, readers should search for conditions that are actually present in the play.

57

Politics and Law

The term *politics and law* refers to governmental institutions and activities, including the rules of conduct or legislation established by political and legal authorities. Political and legal conditions rely for their enforcement on the mutual consent of the governed (the characters). Consequently, their importance in plays is identified through the respect or disregard that the governed characters show for political and legal matters. In *Oedipus Rex*, the public oath Oedipus undertakes to track down the murderer of Laius is an example of an important political condition. For him and the population of Thebes, this oath has the force of law. Moreover, the absolute political authority of Oedipus is understood and accepted by everyone without question. There is no need for him to explain or justify himself.

Politics is at work in the pact made between King Hamlet and King Fortinbras that Horatio discloses in 1,1 of *Hamlet*. Horatio informs his companions that this pact has serious political consequences for Denmark and Norway. First, Denmark has gained political control of Norway; second, young Fortinbras of Norway has raised a military challenge against Claudius to regain his country's independence; and third, Claudius has responded by placing Denmark on military alert. Danish weapons makers are working around the clock to prepare for an impending war. The feeling of war is in the air, and everyone is frightened and tense.

Politics plays a significant role in *Angels in America*, too. Roy Cohn is a successful lawyer and political power broker. His desire to influence political decisions at the highest level forms the basis of his relationship with Joe Pitt. Louis Ironson, Prior's faithless companion, is a political liberal who is very much interested in current politics. Joe Pitt and his family are political conservatives who admire and respect the conservative political values that were on the rise in America in 1986. *Angels in America* consists in large part of dramatic illustrations of the complex dynamics formed by the mixture of these opposing political ideologies.

Learning and the Arts

According to philosophers, *learning and the arts* are among humanity's highest forms of social activity. Every society has its knowledge-workers and artists, or at least it has people who spend a large part of their time dealing with intellectual life and the arts. The life of the mind — sometimes referred to as "the greater good" — is protected in most societies because in significant ways it helps to shape the course of life in general. Although there may be no specialized professional roles for learning or art, learning and the arts play a substantial role in creating culture in its broader sense, too. Intellectuals and artists often try to influence political action and advocate social change, for example.

Learning itself is not reserved for scholars and artists. It may appear in nonprofessional ways, besides. At one limit of the learning spectrum are characters with formal schooling and refined artistic taste. Hamlet, for example, is most at home in Wittenberg, which is an isolated intellectual and artistic environment. He is the product of a humanistic education that taught him to appreciate poetry, philosophy, and theatre. He prefers the life of the mind to the life of action exemplified by Claudius, Fortinbras, and Laertes. He is out of place in practical and warlike Denmark. At the other end of this spectrum are uneducated characters or those who may even condemn the life of the mind. The characters in *American Buffalo* are not formally educated, but they do display a deep respect for criminal, "street" wisdom. In fact, it is Don's blind respect for the street wisdom he sees in Teach that leads to his disenchantment at the end. In *A Raisin in the Sun*, Walter Lee Younger has been denied ordinary learning opportunities. As a result, he is scornful of the educational dreams of his sister, Beneatha, as well as those of her college friend, George Murchison. In *Death of a Salesman*, Willy Loman preaches against formal schooling. He encourages the cultivation of a winning personality because he believes this is what has made him a successful salesman. School is for losers, he says.

On the other hand, formal education does not always go hand-in-hand with wisdom either. Gregers Werle is the most educated character in *The Wild Duck*, yet he is helpless in carrying out even the simplest of chores such as lighting a stove. He also lacks the kind of humane wisdom possessed by Gina, the uneducated former housemaid and wife of Hjalmar who is one of the targets of his idealistic scheming. Humane wisdom, without the advantages of a formal education, also characterizes Mama Younger in *A Raisin in the Sun* as well as Boy Willie in *The Piano Lesson*. Anfisa, the former serf and now household servant in *Three Sisters*, is perhaps the wisest and most well-adjusted character in the play. It is the educated characters in that play that cannot understand what is happening to them. Likewise with *Hamlet*.

59

Spirituality

In its narrowest sense, *spirituality* entails the formal religious features in a play. More broadly, spirituality includes any beliefs in divine, spiritual, or supernatural powers that are obeyed, worshiped, or respected. It can be identified through the presence of religious organizations, ceremonies, and traditions, and in spiritual values espoused by the characters.

Spirituality as such does not figure in *American Buffalo, A Lie of the Mind,* or *Death of a Salesman.* Spirituality plays a small but strategic role in *The Wild Duck* through the character of Reverend Molvik, in *Mother Courage* through the Chaplain, and in *Happy Days* through Winnie's repeated prayers. Spirituality is very important in *A Raisin in the Sun, The Piano Lesson,* and *Angels in America. Oedipus Rex* contains many religious references, including prayers by the Chorus. *Hamlet* also includes important spiritual conditions, particularly references to religious ceremonies, traditions, and beliefs. Because Ophelia committed suicide, her funeral was unsanctioned by the established Church. *Tartuffe* is about the duplicity of certain religious groups that were influential in Moliere's time.

Sometimes characters may be guided by spiritual considerations that remain hidden or unspoken. It is worth noting as well that the absence of spirituality (or of any given circumstance for that matter) can be as significant as its presence. Like "the dog that didn't bark" from a well-known Sherlock Holmes mystery, absence can become an important issue in certain situations. There is no mention of spirituality in *Three Sisters, American Buffalo,* or *Death of a Salesman,* for example. What changes might the introduction of spiritual values induce in these plays? Readers should be on the alert for any evidence or absence of spirituality in characters' actions as well as in their words.

60

The World of the Play

The cumulative effect of all the given circumstances creates *the world of the play.* The characters reveal this world through their behavior more than their words. They show whether the reality they inhabit is a world that is a heaven, a purgatory, or a hell; whether it is good or bad, welcoming or unwelcoming, amusing or frightening, benign or dangerous, lovable or hateful.

At the beginning of this chapter, there was a statement that without living through and theatricalizing the given circumstances, the play and its characters would exist in an abstract world without any connection to real life. How many times has an audience experienced the feeling of looking into such a psychological, social, or environmental void while watching a play? This occurs when productions devote insufficient attention to understanding and illustrating the given circumstances that govern the world of the play. To create that world it is necessary to identify the given circumstances and understand which ones exert the most influence over the characters and their environment.

In *Oedipus Rex*, spiritual forces control the characters. Their world is a fearful place dominated by unpredictable and unforgiving gods who do not hesitate to send plagues and famines to punish those who disregard them. The world of *Hamlet* also is inhospitable. As punishment for his sins, King Hamlet has been condemned to wander among the living, and to suffer the fires of purgatory among the dead, until his murder is avenged and the criminal is brought to justice. For his part, young Hamlet is compelled by his world to undertake a violent and bloody revenge that he is morally unable to perform. Since strong political forces are at work in the play too, the reader will have to determine whether the world of *Hamlet* is predominantly a spiritual or political one. The world of *Tartuffe*, on the other hand, is obviously controlled by religion and politics working in concert. Orgon suffers at the hands of Tartuffe throughout most of the play, but at the end the King uses his political power to set everything right again. The characters in *The Piano Lesson* live in a harsh economic, social, and political world, but also one whose harshness can be made less severe by a sympathetic spirituality.

The dramatic worlds of many modern plays are dominated by social considerations that can be as cruel and unforgiving as could be the gods of old. The world of the play is dissimilar in each of the two parts of *Angels in America*. A rough and unfeeling form of justice governs the world of part one, while a humane form of forgiveness governs part two. In *The Wild Duck*, a petty financial crime leads to the social ruin of the Ekdal family. In *Death of a Salesman*, Willy Loman is the victim of a world dominated by unfeeling, profit-hungry commercial interests. The coarse and impulsive ideology of petty crooks controls the special world of *American Buffalo*. Outmoded, distorted, and forgotten ideals control the world of *Happy Days* and *A Lie of the Mind*.

Studying the world of the play also offers an opportunity to acquire an initial sense of the characters and environment. As observed before, the world of the play is formed by the given circumstances

61

that control the characters and their environment. Accordingly, the characters' relationship to their world reveals their individual distinctiveness, just as it suggests the distinctiveness of the mise-en-scene. Different characters in a play will exhibit different responses to their world. In fact, their responses toward the given circumstances, toward their world, actually delineate their identity. Every character in *Tartuffe*, for example, has a distinguishing response to the religious values that define their world, and their individual responses in turn determine their behavior. To Orgon religion means extravagant public devoutness. He admires Tartuffe for this characteristic, which he interprets as saintliness. He hopes that Tartuffe will teach him how to achieve peace of mind and how to stop worrying about what he views as his family's irreligious behavior. According to Orgon, Tartuffe must take the family under control and teach them how to behave faithfully. The other characters express their own points of view toward religion. For Madame Pernelle, it means social status and respectability; Elmire views religion as a private affair of conscience; Dorine considers it a refuge for gossips; for Cleante religion is "pious flummery" (flattery); Marianne sees religion as a tiresome family duty; and for Tartuffe religion is a con game and a means to easy wealth. It is only the King who seems to believe that religion equates with virtuous conduct! Thus each character expresses a different response to the spiritual–political ideals that control the special world of this play.

Given Circumstances in Nonrealistic Plays

Given circumstances in nonrealistic plays identify the who, what, where, when, why, and how of the play's world much as they do in realistic and classic plays. The difference is in their purpose. Standard plays (those written with the intention that all the parts fit plausibly together and everything is readily understood) are about particular people, places, and events; that is why their given circumstances are driven by plot and character (the human focus of the play). Nonrealistic plays are about generalized people, places, and events; hence their given circumstances are driven by theme (the intellectual focus of the play). The essentials of plot and character are not neglected, of course, but they are treated in a different way and function in a different way than they do in standard plays. Later chapters will explain more about this issue. The point here is that since realistic plausibility is not the main concern in nonrealistic plays, playwrights are free to create any imaginable sort of given circumstances they wish, as long as they manage vividly to harmonize the given circumstances with the theme. The examples below represent the wide range of theme-driven given circumstances found in the nonrealistic study plays.

Timelessness

Time in nonrealistic plays is free from the constraints of clock or calendar, emphasizing timelessness instead of a particular time. Nor is time always arranged in sequential order as it is in most standard plays. In *Angels in America*, dream-like and hallucinatory episodes (illustrating the inner life of certain characters) exist outside of normal time and interrupt the sequential flow of the action on a regular basis. *Happy Days* and *Rosencrantz and Guildenstern are Dead* take place completely outside of normal time; their world is timeless. *Top Girls* begins with a timeless episode in which present-day characters interact with historical and legendary characters, and continues with later scenes in which time in Marlene's outer life jumps back and forth from past to present, further suggesting timelessness. Acts 1, 2, and 3 in *Fefu and Her Friends* are sequential; however, timelessness is suggested when each of the four scenes of act 2 are performed four times at once in four different locales, suggesting their timelessness. In addition, Julia experiences timeless, dream-like visions (her inner life) and is even able to transport herself through time and space. *Mother Courage* employs a so-called epic approach to the passage of time, meaning that each scene is autonomous and does not necessarily connect to the next sequentially, but is instead a timeless facet of the main subject, in the manner of a mosaic or montage (a pattern of meaning).

63

Unlocalized Place

In nonrealistic plays place is treated in a generalized manner to draw attention away from the particular toward the universal. Details of place are often suggested but not always clarified, and the places are frequently unlocalized, meaning that no specific place is intended. An unlocalized patch of scorched earth identifies the locale of *Happy Days*. *Rosencrantz and Guildenstern are Dead* occurs in no identifiable place at all. Even the so-called ship in act 2 is unlocalized, and Stoppard parodies the conventions of a specific realistic locale to emphasize the fact. The setting for *Fefu and Her Friends* appears to be a specific place (Fefu's home), but upon closer inspection its "tasteful mixture of styles" is a generalization without particulars, a locale too simple and clean, and with an atmosphere of something gone wrong (like an Edward Hopper painting). *Mother Courage* takes place in empty, unlocalized or generic locales (a result of war's desolation), which could be anywhere or anytime. *Machinal* and *Angels in America* take place in generic urban locales: an office, a hall, a corridor, a hotel, an apartment, a park, a bedroom, a restaurant. Their settings could be (and sometimes have been) made realistically specific, but this approach would undoubtedly compromise the wider meaning of these plays.

Myth

Nonrealistic plays regularly make use of mythic awareness in the given circumstances (see information about myth in the Introduction). Recall that myth means a traditional story that describes the psychology, customs, or ideals of a society. In this manner, myth works to introduce a large-scale, collective sense of awareness into a play.

Note the examples of mythic associations found in some of the nonrealistic study plays. The definitions are from *The New Dictionary of Cultural Literacy*.

Machinal makes use of myths about society and politics.

The Organization Man: someone who subordinates his personal goals and wishes to the demands of the organization for which he works.

Liberation Movement: freedom movements that arise in certain nations to expel dictatorial powers, often by means of guerrilla warfare.

Mother Courage makes use of myths about society and economics.

Survival of the Fittest: the idea that social progress results from conflicts in which the fittest or best adapted individuals or entire societies would prevail.

Capitalism: an economic and political system characterized by a free market for goods and services and private control of production and consumption.

Invisible Hand: belief that individuals seeking their economic self-interest actually benefit society more than they would if they tried to benefit society directly.

A Lie of the Mind makes use of myths about society.

Prodigal Son: a wandering son returns home for forgiveness after an errant life.

The Frontier: new and untested opportunities.

Mark of Cain (from the *Bible*): — an individual's or humankind's sinful nature.

Pioneer Mentality: the attainment of a livelihood for oneself and for one's family, hard labor, and solid material achievement as the true marks of patriotic spirit.

Top Girls makes use of myths about economics and society.

The Free Market: the production and exchange of goods and services without interference from the government.

Feminism: women should have the same economic, social, and political rights as men.

Survival of the Fittest: as above.

Fefu and Her Friends makes use of myths about society as well as learning and the arts.

Middle Class: desire for social respectability and material wealth and emphasis on the family and education.

Intelligentsia: intellectuals who form a vanguard or elite.

WASP: *white Anglo-Saxon Protestant* — a member of what many consider to be the most privileged and influential group in American society.

65

Angels in America makes use of myths about spirituality and politics.

Democracy: a system of government in which power is vested in the people.

Annunciation: announcement made by the angel Gabriel to Mary, the mother of Jesus, that she was going to bear a son; Gabriel also revealed the sacred laws of the Koran to Muhammad.

Liberalism: a viewpoint or ideology associated with free political institutions and religious toleration, as well as support for a strong role of government in regulating capitalism and constructing a social support system.

Conservatism: a general preference for the existing order of society, and an opposition to efforts to bring about sharp change.

The Birthday Party makes use of myths about politics and law.

Power Elite: a small, loosely knit group of people who tend to dominate policymaking, includes bureaucratic, corporate, intellectual, military, and government elites who control the principal institutions and whose opinions and actions influence the decisions of the policymakers.

Power Corrupts: an observation that a person's sense of morality lessens as his/her power increases.

Happy Days makes use of myths about society, spirituality, and learning and the arts.

"The Waste Land" (from a poem by T.S. Eliot): — the fragmented and sterile nature of the modern world.

Shangri-La: an ideal refuge from the troubles of the world.

"The Inferno" (from *The Divine Comedy*): — a hot and terrible place or condition.

It should be emphasized that we are not promoting arbitrary "myth hunting" here. Myth in nonrealistic plays serves the very specific purpose of illustrating aspects of theme, which Chapter 7 will study in more detail.

Theme World

We said earlier that each play creates its own closed system, its own world. It follows from this that nonrealistic plays create their own worlds too, although the given circumstances governing their worlds are determined more by thematic issues than by plot or character. In other words, the given circumstances in nonrealistic plays create literally a *theme world*. "Theme park" is a term used to describe an amusement park that is designed to carry a theme throughout the park, and theme world describes a world that is designed to carry a theme throughout the play. For example, the given circumstances of *Machinal* are controlled by economics and social standards, working together to create a theme world of mechanized conformity. The theme world of *Mother Courage* is controlled by the dehumanizing economics of war capitalism. *Happy Days* is controlled by distorted social standards, creating a theme world of absurd dreams. *The Birthday Party* is a political theme world controlled by a nameless, menacing power. In *Fefu and Her Friends* middle-class intellect and culture coproduce a theme world of true feelings dangerously suppressed. *Top Girls* illustrates a socioeconomic theme world of self-centered ambition. The myth-centered given circumstances in *A Lie of the Mind* produce a theme world of distorted, irrational ideals. Learning and social standards govern the given circumstances of *Rosencrantz and Guildenstern are Dead*, producing a theme world of irrational uncertainty. And the theme world of *Angels in America* is controlled by politics, law, and social standards, forming the picture of a broken-down civilization. These examples are for teaching purposes, of course, and not intended to be authoritative. The lesson is that given circumstances in nonrealistic plays should be closely analyzed for what they reveal about the theme. Any clash with standard realistic expectations needs to be theatricalized to illustrate theme.

Summary

This chapter contained a review of the given circumstances that readers should try to identify in the study of plays. We also attempted to discover the dramatic potentials within each given circumstance. It is not too much of an exaggeration to say that after the given circumstances are accurately and thoroughly identified, the rest of the play will begin to fall into place more or less by itself. Of course, not all the given circumstances will be equally useful on every occasion. But as in most situations, over time readers will develop their own instincts for what is most useful and when. Because these instincts are among the unteachable skills of play analysis, this text cannot equip students with them. It can do no more than point the way.

Questions   67

1. *Time.* In what year and season does the action occur? Can the passage of time during the play be determined? The time between the scenes and acts? The hour of day for each scene? Each act? What features of time suggest the mise-en-scene? How could the mise-en-scene contribute to the effectiveness of these features?
2. *Place.* In what country, region, or city does the action occur? Are any geographical features described? In what specific locale does the action occur? What is the specific location for each scene, including the ground plan and other architectural features if possible? What features of place suggest the mise-en-scene? How could the mise-en-scene contribute to the effectiveness of these features?
3. *Society.* What are the family relationships? What are the friendships and love relationships? What occupational groups are depicted? What social ranks are represented? What are the social standards, the behavior expectations? Are they spoken about or implied? Are they enforced openly or indirectly? What social group controls the social standards? What are the rewards for conformity? What are the penalties for violating social standards? What features of society suggest the mise-en-scene? How

could the mise-en-scene contribute to the effectiveness of these features?

4. *Economics.* What is the general economic system in the play? Any specific examples of business activities or transactions? Does money exercise any control over the characters? Who controls the economic circumstances? How do they exert control? What are the rewards for economic success? The penalties for violating the economic standards? What features of economics suggest the mise-en–scene? How could the mise-en-scene contribute to the effectiveness of these features?

5. *Politics and Law.* What is the system of government that serves as the background for the play? Any specific examples of political or legal activities, actions, or ceremonies? Do politics or law exercise any control over the characters? Who controls the political and legal circumstances in the play? How do they exert control? What are the rewards for political and legal obedience? The penalties for violating the political and legal standards? What features of politics and law suggest the mise-en-scene? How could the mise-en-scene contribute to the effectiveness of these features?

6. *Learning and the Arts.* What is the general level of culture and artistic taste in the characters? Any examples of intellectual or creative activities? Any characters more or less educated or creative than others? Does intellect or culture exercise any control over the characters? Who controls the intellectual and artistic circumstances in the play? How do they exert their control? What are the rewards for intellectual and creative activity? What are the penalties for violating intellectual and artistic standards? What features of learning and the arts suggest the mise-en-scene? How could the mise-en-scene contribute to the effectiveness of these features?

7. *Spirituality.* What is the accepted code of religious or spiritual belief? Any examples of religious or spiritual activities or ceremonies? Does spirituality exercise any control over the characters? Who controls the spiritual circumstances in the play? How do they exert control? What are the rewards for spiritual conformity? What are the penalties for violating the spiritual standards? What features of spirituality suggest the mise-en-scene? How could the mise-en-scene contribute to the effectiveness of these features?

8. *The World of the Play.* Describe the special world of the play, the closed system, the distinctive universe created by the collective given circumstances. How does the world of the play influence

the conduct and attitude of characters in the play? What are the different points of view expressed by the characters toward their world? How does the world of the play suggest the mise-en-scene? How could the mise-en-scene contribute to the effective illustration of the world of the play?

9. *After Action Analysis.* Search for the play's seed/theme at work in the given circumstances. How does the seed/theme relate to the given circumstances? Why did the playwright choose these specific given circumstances from the whole range of other possibilities to illustrate the seed/theme? In what way would the use of different given circumstances change the seed/theme, and vice versa? In what way does connecting the seed/theme with the given circumstances and mise-en-scene contribute to the effectiveness of the play?

69

CHAPTER 3

Background Story

Now that we have studied the present, we can turn our attention to the past. The lives of the characters begin long before they appear on stage, and their pasts are indispensable for understanding their present lives. Every dramatic story has a past, but the conventional time and space features of the theatre require special writing skill to illustrate all of it through dialogue in action. Playwrights employ a unique kind of narration to reveal the past while the stage action continues to advance. The common term for this dramatic convention is *exposition*, but sometimes it is also referred to as previous action or antecedent action. The word exposition comes from the Latin root *exposito*, meaning to put forward or to expose, and it has proven useful because exposition is a way of exposing the unseen parts of a play.

Unfortunately, the abstract term exposition often calls up an unthinking response. According to scholars, exposition tells the spectators what they need to know about the past to understand what they are going to see. As such, it is considered a literary disadvantage because it seems to interfere with the forward progress of the play. It involves a certain amount of dullness, but skillful dramatists are able to handle it without unduly holding up the action. But this way of thinking about the past carries unpleasant overtones. It leads to the impression that the past is a clumsy literary requirement that obstructs the flow of the plot. The clumsiness increases when scholars talk about protactic characters, such as the Chorus in classical Greek tragedies or certain servants in modern plays, introduced, it is said, purposely to disclose exposition.

Actors, directors, and designers cannot not let the matter rest here because what exposition means to us is vital for a full-scale understanding of a play. We should attempt to understand the past in a way that makes it dramatically compelling, not a clumsy literary obstacle to overcome. To do this requires several important adjustments to a reader's way of thinking about a play. First, the notion that what has already happened is somehow dull and undramatic must be set aside. After all, for the characters themselves, it is just the opposite. To them the past is not dull and unexciting, but rather their own lives — everything good and bad that has happened to them. Second, the past should be understood as an integral part of the play, not a clumsy encumbrance. It helps in understanding the characters that are themselves talking about the past, it creates moods, generates conflicts, and strongly influences the environment and mise-en-scene. And to repeat what was said in the Introduction, drama is not a graceless, second-class form of literature. It is an independent art with its own purpose and principles, including its own special way of dealing with the past. Third, to be reminded of the dramatic potentials and potencies of the past, replace the static term exposition with the more energetic term *background story*. For actors, directors, and designers background story in no way interferes with the flow of the action. On the contrary, it propels the action forward in explosive surges and with an increasing sense of urgency. While we are on the subject, the term backstory has been used often to refer to what we are calling here background story. Backstory is actually a film and television term referring to a behind-the-scenes look at the making of motion pictures and televisions shows. For example, actors, directors, producers, and other film and television figures provide informative inner-circle backstories about the events that affected each production and their lives. This distinction deserves to be preserved.

Background story involves everything that happened before the beginning of the play, before the curtain goes up. Time and again it is crucial to know what went on prior to the stage action. In *Oedipus Rex* the fate of Jocasta's infant son is an example. Did Jocasta bind the infant's feet and turn him over to a household servant with orders to abandon him? Where did the Corinthian Messenger obtain the infant he gave to King Polybus and Queen Merope? He claims to have obtained the infant from one of Laius' herdsmen. But why did the herdsman give the baby to him in the first place? Did the infant belong to the herdsman? If not, who gave it to him and why? Is the shepherd the same herdsman who gave the infant to the Corinthian Messenger? If the answer is yes, why is he unwilling to acknowledge it? All these questions and many more about the background story are decisive in the plot of *Oedipus Rex*.

The past becomes even more complicated when it is employed as Ibsen did, for example, in *The Wild Duck*. In the excerpt from act 1 that follows, Gregers Werle has returned home after a long absence. He has a sharp disagreement with his father about the fate of the Ekdal family, whose patriarch, the elderly Lieutenant Ekdal, used to be a business partner and close friend. But we should guard against hasty value judgments about the past. The real truth should not always depend on the recollections of Gregers, his father, or on those of any other single character. By the way, it is a good idea to get into the habit of underlining or highlighting the background story as we do here to distinguish it from the onstage action.

GREGERS. How has that family been allowed to go so miserably to the wall?

WERLE. You mean the Ekdals, I suppose?

GREGERS. Yes, I mean the Ekdals. Lieutenant Ekdal who was once so closely associated with you?

WERLE. Much too closely; I have felt that to my cost for many a year. It is thanks to him that I — yes I — have had a kind of slur cast upon my reputation.

GREGERS. (*softly*) Are you sure that he alone was to blame?

WERLE. Who else do you suppose?

GREGERS. You and he acted together in that affair of the forests —

WERLE. But was it not Ekdal that drew the map of the tracts we had bought — that fraudulent map! It was he who felled all the timber illegally on government ground. In fact, the whole management was in his hands. I was quite in the dark as to what Lieutenant Ekdal was doing.

GREGERS. Lieutenant Ekdal himself seems to have been very much in the dark about what he was doing.

WERLE. That may be. But the fact is that he was found guilty and I was acquitted.

GREGERS. Yes, I know that nothing was proved against you.

72

Since the views of the past presented by these two characters are incompatible or at least incomplete, readers are obliged to form their own accounts. This requires understanding what happened and why in a very detailed way. It also means knowing whose version of the past is more accurate and how much of it is reliable. In the excerpt here, the characters disagree about the reasons for the decline of the Ekdal family. Gregers blames his father for it, while Mr. Werle seems to lay the blame on Lieutenant Ekdal, Werle's former business partner. Later in the play, Lieutenant Ekdal offers still another version to his son, Hjalmar, and to his daughter-in-law, Gina. Whose version is authentic? Who benefits from each version? In such cases, readers should examine each version of the background story skeptically, as trial lawyers examine a witness in court.

Technique

Let's first study the basic techniques that playwrights use to disclose background story and later consider some ways of identifying it. By approaching the topic in this way, it should be easier to understand the workings of background story in plays as a whole.

Background story tends to appear in three ways: in extended passages near the beginning of a play, in fragments distributed throughout the action, or buried beneath the onstage action. There is no advantage in craftsmanship or plausibility in any single method. The choice depends on the author's goals and the practical requirements of the play. Playwriting fashions also play a part. All these methods have been used in a wide assortment of plays, can be used simultaneously, and are capable of revealing the past without interrupting the flow of the action or disturbing the play's plausibility.

73

Historical Technique

In classic plays (those written before the emergence of realism), the background story tends to appear in extended passages near the beginning. Note how this operates in *Hamlet*. In the last chapter we studied 1,1 for its political content. Horatio's speech to Marcellus consists of 29 lines explaining the reasons behind Denmark's preparations for war. In the next scene, Claudius has a speech of 34 lines expressing his gratitude to the court for their support during the recent transfer of power. He also explains his strategy for dealing with the political threat posed by Fortinbras. More background story is disclosed at the end of the scene. In a famous soliloquy of 50 lines, Hamlet reveals his feelings about his father's recent death and his mother's hasty remarriage. In 1,3 Laertes says farewell to Ophelia in a speech of 34 lines, meanwhile warning her not to be misled by Hamlet's fondness for her. Besides being a warning to Ophelia, this is also background story. In 1,4 the Ghost appears again, and then in a discourse of 50 lines in 1,5 he discloses the circumstances of his murder. At this point of the play, the characters have revealed most of the background story in five speeches totaling about 200 lines. In a similar manner, the opening scenes in *Oedipus Rex*, *Tartuffe*, and *The School for Scandal* reveal almost the entire background story in those classic plays, too.

The technique of placing the background story at the beginning has advantages and disadvantages. On one hand, it focuses attention because it collects all the essential facts of the background story together near the beginning in the play. This permits the dramatist to devote the remainder of the play to the development of onstage (present) action, which is a considerable writing and performance benefit. On the other hand, extended narration can be a burden on actors and audiences because it is essential to express all the important background information in jam-packed speeches, while at the same time maintaining emotional honesty and logical consistency. Audiences must digest most of the background story at one time and note who the important characters are and what they did. And they must bear it in mind throughout all the action that follows.

Modern Technique

In the early part of the nineteenth century another way of disclosing background story began to appear. It was a time when the scientific spirit was beginning to influence the world at large, even as in the theatre it influenced a new playwriting style, the well-made play. The chief architect of this style was the French author Eugene Scribe, who managed to introduce some of the thinking and practices of science into the craft of playwriting. In place of the rather free and imaginative treatment of background story found in classic plays, Scribe began to employ the then novel scientific principles of cause and effect, as he said, to make the "accidental seem necessary." Time, place, and action were to operate according to "realistic" (scientific) rules. Scribe's well-made plays contained scandalous secrets in the background story and then disclosed them as the action progressed. His plays also included meticulously coordinated patterns of action and deception, a climactic scene in which the unknown parts of the background story are revealed to opposing characters, and a

74

plausible resolution in which a new balance is established among the opposing forces. Scribe's formulaic methods assured box office success. He wrote over 400 of these well-made plays and his work was a major influence on the development of modern drama worldwide. Much of playwriting today is still of the well-made variety, particularly in film and television.

In well-made plays some of the background story continued to appear at the beginning as it had in classic plays, but now most of it was divided into smaller portions, shared among a larger number of characters, and disclosed in bits and pieces throughout later scenes. This was done to achieve realistic plausibility, that is, to achieve the illusion of authenticity. Scholars call this way of treating background story the retrospective method because the onstage action moves forward in time while the past moves backward in time. The key to its effective use was to avoid revealing the most important facts of the background story until as late as possible in the action, at the point when its disclosure was most dramatically effective. Although the absence of traditional long speeches of background story seems to provide well-made plays with a more credible sense of everyday reality, its initial use by playwrights was somewhat awkward by later standards. A typical well-made play, for example, employed an opening scene in which two minor characters, typically servants, performed household duties while gossiping about their employer's past. This type of opening was so widespread in nineteenth-century plays that it came to be called the below-stairs scene because it almost always involved servants, whose living quarters in those times were located downstairs.

An interesting point about the retrospective method is that it was the rediscovery of a historical model that had remained by and large unused for almost 2,400 years. Few dramatists ever handled it better than Sophocles did in *Oedipus Rex*, whose plot is a murder mystery told retrospectively. A "detective" (Oedipus) searches for a murderer by inquiring into the past, and step-by-step discovers that the criminal turns out to be himself. In spite of its very early date of composition, *Oedipus Rex* remains an excellent example of retrospective technique.

Henrik Ibsen learned to understand the well-made play and its retrospective style while he was managing director at a theatre in Norway. He produced many of Scribe's plays there and drew from this experience in writing his earliest realistic plays. Scribe was a skillful craftsman, but Ibsen was also an artist and he brought an artistic sensibility to his writing. For example, in the opening of Ibsen's play *The Wild Duck*, the old family servant, Petersen, and a hired servant, Jensen, gossip about the prominent members of society present at the dinner party in another room. This is a representative below-stairs scene, but Ibsen added a special refinement. Unlike Scribe and other writers of well-made plays, Ibsen seldom treated his secondary characters as simple functionaries to disclose background story. Pettersen and Jensen are distinctive personalities in their own right and each has his own special motives for gossiping about the dubious "pillars of society" present at the dinner party in the adjoining room. Thus, Ibsen's background story is artistic as well as dramatic, in the sense that it reveals as much about the present (the self-serving hypocrisy of Petersen, Jensen, and the townspeople) as it does about the past.

Like any true artist, Ibsen was always testing and refining his methods. In his later plays, he withheld much of the important background story from earlier scenes, distributing it instead in fragments throughout the play. As time went on, Ibsen and other early modern dramatists (namely, Anton Chekhov, August Strindberg, and George Bernard Shaw) became extremely proficient at this method. They learned how to distribute the background story in ever subtler bits and pieces throughout their plays, and they knew where and how to place the information so that its disclosure would be almost inconspicuous yet as dramatic as possible. In their best works, no single piece of background story is revealed until it is of maximum service to the action — in other words, until it has maximum influence on the characters. The past unfolds one small fact at a time with inspired shrewdness for dramatic tempos and rhythms.

Minimalist Technique

In an increasing number of contemporary plays the background story seems inadequate to motivate the onstage behavior of the characters. In these plays, the background story is so altered, reduced, or concealed that it is almost impossible to perceive without very close reading, and a feeling of uncertainty and elusiveness often goes along with it. As in, did it really happen, or do the characters only imagine that it happened, or is someone being untruthful? *American Buffalo* is a prime example. Who was the mysterious coin collector who purchased the five-cent American buffalo coin from Don? Who is Fletch, the pivotal character everyone knows and respects but whom we never see? What happened between Teach and Gracie and Ruthie to make him so angry with them? How did Don come to respect Teach so devotedly, a respect that leads to disaster for him and Bob? How did Don come to own the junk shop? The answers to these questions and more are central to the play, and they can be found in the play, but it takes a great deal of careful reading to find them because they are suggested but seldom spoken about. Also required is a firm belief in the importance of the background story to the characters.

Use of such minimalist background story is a radical extension of the modern retrospective method. The main difference lies in reducing the quantity of background story to a bare minimum and then disclosing what remains through intricate, complicated hints in preference to, but without getting rid of, candid narration. Minimalist background story requires patient and imaginative analysis (including pattern awareness) to unearth every last ounce of information. It also requires close attention to tempo, rhythm, and mood in performance to illuminate every veiled hint and casual allusion these plays depend on for their effects. What cannot be spoken needs to be illustrated through the subtle interplay of vocal pauses, facial expressions, physical gestures and postures, and mise-en-scene.

Identification

Background story takes on several forms: events, character descriptions, and feelings. Which is most important depends on the nature of the play, the characters, and the situations in the play.

Events

A *background story event* is something significant that happened in the past, something vital to the play and involving a conflict of some kind. Past events of this type are important because they provide the source material for onstage conflicts. Here are some background passages that contain significant events.

Two crucial background story events are disclosed in Mama Younger's statement to her son, Walter, in *A Raisin in the Sun*, "Son — do you know your wife is expecting another baby?" The significant events for Walter are (1) Ruth is pregnant and (2) he did not even know about it.

Another example is Hjalmar Ekdal's confession in *The Wild Duck* that his father, Old Ekdal, "considered" suicide when he was sentenced to prison. Hjalmar tells his friend, Gregers Werle, "When the sentence of imprisonment was passed — he had the pistol in his hand." In the narrow-minded provincial society of this play, Old Ekdal's misdeed ruined him and fated his family to social isolation.

In *Oedipus Rex*, when Oedipus asks who found him as an infant, the Corinthian Messenger discloses a significant event, "It was another shepherd that gave you to me." At this moment Oedipus finds out that he is not the son of Polybus and Merope as he thought, which leads him to the discovery that he murdered his father and married his mother.

In *Mother Courage*, the Recruiter discloses a significant background story event when he says to the Sergeant, "The General wants me to recruit four platoons by the twelfth." The significant fact that the General will have him shot if he does not enlist 90 new men by the end of the week explains why the Recruiter does not show much sympathy for reluctant recruits later in the play.

Sally says to her mother, Lorraine, in *A Lie of the Mind*, "Right then I knew what Jake had in mind." "What?" asks Lorraine. "Jake had decided to kill him." What is significant here is the cold, hard reality of Jake's violent temperament, regardless of that fact that his mother thinks in a different way about him.

Background stories are composed of dramatic events like these. Yet no character's account of past events should always be taken at face value. It is not that characters sometimes lie; they tell their own versions of the truth as they see it. Even a lie told as a truth, however, can be revealing if it is studied with care. In Hjalmar Ekdal's scene discussed above, his inadvertent use of the word "considered" instead of "attempted" when he speaks about his father's experience is revealing. For one thing, a considered suicide, with its suggestions of self-dramatization, is different from an attempted suicide. And even though the considered event itself was real enough, it is not as important as the selfish use Hjalmar makes of it at this moment in the play. It does not show Hjalmar's sympathy for his father as much as it shows the personal embarrassment he felt about his father's disgrace. This example illustrates how background story can reveal significant information that may be otherwise overlooked in a play.

Character Descriptions

Discussing the events of the past often leads to *character descriptions* of those who performed them. This element of the background story is as important to designers as it is to actors and directors.

In *Tartuffe*, Orgon offers this description of his daughter's suitor: "I had promised you to Valere, but apart from the fact that he's said to be a bit of a gambler, I suspect him of being a free thinker." Orgon heard from someone that Valere was a gambler, and Orgon already suspected Valere's liberal opinions from previous encounters with him.

In *Hamlet*, Horatio reveals to Hamlet his memory of deceased King Hamlet's character: "I saw him once; he was a goodly king." It is significant that Hamlet's father was known to be a wise and principled person, in contrast to his brother, Claudius. Or at least these two characters think so.

Joseph Surface receives this admiring character description from Sir Peter Teazle in *The School for Scandal*: "Joseph is indeed what a youth should be — everyone in the world speaks well of him." Teazle's description turns out to be false.

Speaking to Gregers Werle in *The Wild Duck*, Dr. Relling says of Lieutenant Ekdal: "The old lieutenant has been an ass all his days." Relling's description turns out to be true.

Willy Loman recalls his brother Ben in *Death of a Salesman*: "There was the only man I ever met who knew all the answers." Later on we learn that Ben is in fact a huckster and Willie has merely been deceived by his impressive boasting.

Mama Younger in *A Raisin in the Sun* remembers her deceased husband: "God knows there was plenty wrong with Walter Younger — hard-headed, mean, kind of wild with women — plenty wrong with him. But he sure loved his children." Walter Younger's decency is contrasted with the dishonesty of his son, Walter Jr., who plans to expropriate his father's life insurance money.

79

Doaker speaks about his niece, Berniece, to Boy Willie in *The Piano Lesson*: "She still got [her husband] Crawley on her mind. He been dead three years but she still holding on to him. She need to go out here and let one of those fellows grab a whole handful of whatever she got. She act like it done got precious." Berniece is in danger of becoming a professional widow.

Feelings

Characters reveal their *past feelings* in a variety of ways.

In *The Wild Duck*, when Hjalmar Ekdal's father went to prison for fraud, it was also an embarrassing time for Hjalmar: "I kept the blinds drawn down over both my windows. When I peeped out I saw the sun shining as if nothing had happened. I could not understand it. I saw people going along the street, laughing and talking about indifferent things. I could not understand it. It seemed to me that the whole of existence must be at a standstill — as if under an eclipse." To which Gregers Werle adds, "I felt that too, when my mother died." Hjalmar and Gregers share a moment of sentimental self-dramatization.

In *Death of a Salesman*, Willy Loman tells Linda how he often feels lonely when traveling on the road: "I get so lonely — in particular when business is bad and there's nobody to talk to. I get the feeling that I'll never sell anything again." His loneliness on the road leads him to seek the comfort of other women.

When the Young Woman in *Machinal* asks, "But Ma — didn't you love Pa? her Mother replies, "I suppose I did — I don't know — I've forgotten — what difference does it make — now?" The absence of real human feeling between her mother and father surprises and saddens the Young Woman.

The emotional frustrations of Walter Younger Jr.'s past express themselves through sense impressions in *A Raisin in the Sun*: "Sometimes it's like I can see the future stretched out in front of me — just plain as day. The future, Mama. Hanging over there at the edge of my days. Just waiting for me — a big, looming blank space — full of nothing." Walter has the emotional feelings of a poet.

Lorraine's repressed feelings about her husband's disappearance are the subject of these remarks to her daughter, Beth, in *A Lie of the Mind*:

LORRAINE. Wonder? Did I ever wonder? You know a man your whole life. You grow up with him. You're almost raised together. You go to school on the same bus together. You go through tornadoes together in the same basement. You go through a war together. You have babies together. And then one day he just up and disappears into thin air. Did I ever wonder? Yeah. You bet your sweet life I wondered. But you know where all that wondering got me? Nowhere. Absolutely nowhere. Because here I am. Alone. Just the same as though he'd never even existed.

Lorraine's tangled and conflicting feelings are typical of the background story in Sam Shepard's plays.

These examples show that past feelings expressed through the background story are also valuable for beginning to understand the characters engaged in present action on stage.

Background Story at Work

To learn how past events, character descriptions, and feelings work together in longer passages of dialogue, we will consider examples of classic, modern, and minimalist technique. Past events, feelings, and character descriptions are underlined.

Historical Technique

Hamlet belongs to that group of plays in which the background story appears in long passages early in the play. The murder of King Hamlet is the single most significant background story event. In 1,5 the Ghost discloses the circumstances surrounding this event in several lengthy speeches. Background story in this scene is a seamless merging of past events, feelings, and character descriptions. The Ghost begins by disclosing the physical pain he has suffered in purgatory since his death.

> GHOST. <u>I am thy father's spirit,</u>
> <u>Doom'd for a certain term to walk the</u>
> <u>night,</u>
> <u>And for the day confin'd to fast in fires,</u>
> <u>Till the foul crimes done in my days of</u>
> <u>nature</u>
> <u>Are burnt and purg'd away.</u>

In the next 11 lines he explains that he is prohibited from telling Hamlet what purgatory is really like, nevertheless he describes how Hamlet would feel if he knew what his father has been suffering.

> GHOST. <u>But that I am forbid</u>
> <u>To tell the secrets my prison-house,</u>
> <u>I could a tale unfold whose lightest word</u>
> <u>Would harrow up thy soul, freeze thy young</u>
> <u>blood,</u>
> <u>Make thy two eyes, like stars, start from</u>
> <u>their spheres,</u>
> <u>Thy knotted and combined locks to part,</u>
> <u>And each particular hair to stand on end,</u>
> <u>Like quills upon the fretful porpentine.</u>
> But this eternal blazon must not be
> To ears of flesh and blood.

Now the Ghost discloses that he was murdered, which is the pivotal event of the background story. He adds the feeling that blood ties and incest made the crime even worse.

> GHOST. List, List, O, List!
> If thou didst ever thy dear father love—
> HAMLET. O God!

```
GHOST.  Revenge his foul and most unnatural
        murder.
HAMLET. Murder!
GHOST.  Murder most foul, as in the best it is;
        But this most foul, strange, and unnatural.
```

A few lines later, the Ghost picks up the thread of the background
story events once again.

```
GHOST. Now, Hamlet, hear;
       'Tis given out that, sleeping in my
       orchard
       A serpent stung me; so the whole ear of
       Denmark
       Is by a forged process of my death
       Rankly abused; but know, thou noble youth,
       The serpent that did sting thy father's
       life
       Now wears his crown.
HAMLET. O my prophetic soul!
        My uncle!
```

The Ghost adds a character description of Claudius, condemning the incestuous relationship with Gertrude and the murder of his
own brother.

```
GHOST. Ay, that incestuous, that adulterate
       beast,
       With wicked witchcraft of his wits, with
       traitorous gifts —
       O wicked wit and gifts that have the power
       So to seduce — won to his shameful lust
       The will of my most seeming virtuous
       queen.
```

Now follows 11 lines contrasting King Hamlet's idealistic love of
Gertrude with Claudius's cynical lust.

```
GHOST. O Hamlet, what a falling off was there,
       From me, whose love was of that dignity
       That it went hand in hand even with the vow
       I made to her in marriage; and to decline
       Upon a wretch whose natural gifts were poor
       To those of mine!
```

The next 16 lines are a vivid account of the murder itself.

```
GHOST. But soft! Methinks I scent the morning
       air.
       Brief let me be. Sleeping within my orchard,
       My custom always of the afternoon,
       Upon my secure hour thy uncle stole,
       With juice of cursed hebona in a vial,
       And in the porches of mine ears did pour
       The leprous distillment; whose effect
       Holds such an enmity with blood of man
       That  swift  as  quicksilver  it  courses
       through
       The natural gates and alleys of the body;
       And with a sudden vigour it doth posset
       And curd, like eager droppings into milk,
       The thin and wholesome blood. So did it
       mine;
       And a most instant tetter bark'd about,
       Most lazar-like, with vile and loathsome
       crust,
       All my smooth body.
```

Seven lines of religious feelings develop from these.

```
GHOST. Thus was I, sleeping, by a brother's
       hand
       Of life, of crown, of queen, at once
       dispatch'd;
       Cut off even in the blossom of my sin,
       Unhousl'd [no Holy Communion], disap-
       pointed, unanel'd [no final rites];
       No reck'ning made [no confession], but
       sent to my account
       With all my imperfections on my head.
       O, Horrible! Horrible! most horrible!
```

The Ghost concludes the scene by challenging Hamlet to revenge his murder. The background story in this scene has been disclosed by a single character in a few long speeches composed of an artful blend of events, feelings, and character descriptions.

Modern Technique

In *A Raisin in the Sun,* several different characters disclose the past retrospectively and in small fragments. This scene between Walter

Jr. and his wife, Ruth, also occurs near the beginning of the play. It centers on Walter's scheme for buying a liquor store with his buddies Bobo and Willie. Their project will require $10,000 from his father's life insurance. In this argument between Walter and Ruth, background story events, character descriptions, and feelings mix together. The passage requires attentive reading to unravel this complicated mixture and grasp its significance in the action to come. Underlining identifies the background story references.

WALTER. You want to know <u>what I was thinking 'bout in the bathroom this morning?</u>

RUTH. No.

WALTER. <u>How come you always got to be so pleasant?</u>

RUTH. <u>What is there to be pleasant 'bout?</u>

WALTER. You want to know what I was thinking 'bout in the bathroom or not?

RUTH. <u>I know what you was thinking 'bout.</u>

WALTER. (*ignoring her*) <u>'Bout what me an' Willy Harris was talking about last night.</u>

RUTH. (*immediately — a refrain*) <u>Willy Harris is a good-for-nothing loud mouth.</u>

WALTER. <u>Anybody who talks to me has got to be a good-for-nothing loud mouth, ain't he? And what you know about who is just a good-for-nothing loud mouth? Charlie Atkins was just a "good-for-nothing loud-mouth" too, wasn't he? When he wanted me to go into the dry-cleaning business with him. And now — he's grossing a hundred thousand dollars a year. A hundred thousand dollars a year! You still call him a loud mouth?</u>

RUTH. (*bitterly*) Oh, Walter Lee.
(*She folds her head on her arms over the table.*)

WALTER. (*rising and coming over to her and standing over her*) <u>You tired, ain't you? Tired of everything. Me, the boy, the way we live — this beat up hole — everything. Ain't you? So tired — moaning and groaning all the time, but you wouldn't do nothing to help, would you? You couldn't be on my side that long for nothing could you?</u>

RUTH. Walter, please leave me alone.

WALTER. A man needs for a woman to back him up...

RUTH. Walter—

WALTER. Mama would listen to you. You know she listen to you more than she do me and Bennie. She think more of you, too. All you have to do is just sit down with her when you drinking your coffee one morning and talking 'bout things like you do — (*He sits down beside her and demonstrates graphically what he thinks her methods and tone should be.*) —you just sip your coffee, see, and say easy like that you been thinking 'bout that deal Walter Lee is so interested in, 'bout the store, and all, and sip some more coffee, like what you saying ain't really that important to you — and the next thing you know, she be listening good and asking you questions and when I come home — I can tell her the details. This ain't no fly-by-night proposition, baby. I mean we got it figured out, me and Willy and Bobo.

RUTH. (*with a frown*) Bobo?

WALTER. Yeah. You see, this little liquor store we got in mind cost seventy-five thousand and we figured the initial investment on the place be 'bout thirty thousand, see. That be ten thousand each. Course, there's a couple of hundred you got to pay so's you don't spend the rest of your life just waitin' for them clowns to let your license get approved—

RUTH. You mean graft?

WALTER. (*frowning impatiently*) Don't call it that. See there, that just goes to show you what women understand about the world. Baby, don't nothing happen in this world 'less you pay somebody off!

RUTH. Walter, leave me alone! (*She raises her head and stares at him vigorously — then*

85

says, more quietly.) Eat your eggs, they gonna be cold.

WALTER. (*straightening up from her and looking off*) That's it. There you are. Man say to his woman: I got me a dream. His woman say: eat your eggs. (*sadly, but gaining in power*) Man say: I got to take hold of this here world, baby! And a woman will say: Eat your eggs and go to work. (*passionately now*) Man say: I got to change my life. <u>I'm choking to death, baby!</u> And his woman say— (*in utter anguish as he brings his fists down on his thighs*) —Your eggs is getting cold!

RUTH. (*softly*) <u>Walter, that ain't none of our money.</u>

WALTER. (*not listening at all or even looking at her*) This morning, I was lookin' in the mirror and thinking about it...I'm thirty-five years old; I been married eleven years and I got a boy who sleeps in the living room— (*very, very quietly*) and all I got to give him is stories about how rich people live...

RUTH. Eat your eggs, Walter.

WALTER. Damn my eggs...damn all the eggs that ever was!

RUTH. Then go to work.

WALTER. (*looking at her*) See — I'm trying to talk to you 'bout myself — (*shaking his head with the repetition*) —and all you can say is eat them eggs and go to work.

RUTH. (*wearily*) <u>Honey, you never say anything new. I listen to you every day, every night, and every morning, and you never say nothing new.</u> (*shrugging*) <u>So you would rather be Mr. Arnold than be his chauffeur. So — I would rather be living in Buckingham Palace.</u>

WALTER. <u>That's just what is wrong with the colored women in this world...Don't understand about building their men up and</u>

> making 'em feel like they somebody. Like
> they can do something.

RUTH. (*dryly, but to hurt*) There are colored
men who do things.

WALTER. No thanks to the colored woman.

RUTH. Well, being a colored woman, I guess I
can't help myself none.

A fine piece of realistic writing and an excellent example of modernist background story, this passage, and indeed Hansberry's entire play, will reward careful study.

Minimalist Technique

A smaller amount of background story is found in *A Lie of the Mind* compared to the examples above. Only two previous events could be considered significant in the sense understood here: Jake's abuse of his wife, Beth; and the death of Jake's father. In 1,1 and 1,3 Jake discloses the entire story about Beth through several long speeches in the standard historical manner. After those two scenes, her life and character are clear to us. But the story of Jake's father is disclosed in minimalist fashion. Only a minimal amount of concrete information is disclosed about him. We do not even learn his name. Moreover, the disclosures are revealed guardedly — through hints, curtailed anecdotes, indirect references, discarded objects, "character transformations," etc. The father's life and character are an enigma, and yet his spirit exerts a strange power over his family.

In 1,7 Jake seems to have forgotten all about his father until he finds himself back at the family home in his childhood bedroom. He is traumatized by guilt from abusing his wife, and his mother, Lorraine, tries to nurse him out of his depression. All of a sudden Jake stops and stares at the dusty models of World War II airplanes hanging from the ceiling above his bed. References to his father begin to emerge, but they are vague and incomplete. Again, background story is underlined.

JAKE. I can't stay here.

LORRAINE. Why not? You never shoulda' left in
the first place. This was the first room you
ever had to yourself.

JAKE. Where were we before?

LORRAINE. You mean, before here?

JAKE. Yeah. Where were we before?

LORRAINE. You-name-it-U.S.A. Those were the days we chased your Daddy from one airbase to the next. Always tryin' to catch up with the next "Secret Mission." Some secret. He was always cookin' up some weird code on the phone. Tryin' to make a big drama outa' things. Thought it was romantic I guess. Worst of all was I fell for it. (JAKE wanders around the space, trying to recognize it.)

JAKE. What code?

LORRAINE. Oh, I can't remember them now. There was lots of 'em. It was so many years ago. He'd make 'em all up.

JAKE. Why'd he use a code?

LORRAINE. He said it was because they didn't want him to reveal his location.

JAKE. Did you believe him?

LORRAINE. Yeah. Why shouldn't I of?

JAKE. Maybe he was lyin'.

LORRAINE. Why would he do that?

JAKE. So you wouldn't know what he was up to. That's why.

LORRAINE. That was back when we were in love.

JAKE. Oh.

LORRAINE. That was back before things went to pieces.

JAKE. (Still moving around the space.) But we finally tracked him down, huh?

LORRAINE. Yeah. 'Course we tracked him down. Turned out to not be worth the trip, but we found him all right.

JAKE. Where?

LORRAINE. Different places. You were pretty little then.

JAKE. Little.

LORRAINE. Just a spit of a thing. I used to pack you to sleep in a dresser drawer. You were that tiny.

JAKE. You didn't close the drawer. Did ya'?

LORRAINE. No. 'Course not.

What attracts attention in this passage is Lorraine's reluctance to delve into any particulars about her husband, Jake's father. Jake presses her for more information, but she redirects his questions away from his father and back to her own relationship with Jake. Their hesitant behavior is evidence of the father's lingering influence on his wife and son. The form of Jake's curiosity about him is also intriguing. What is the specific nature of his emotional response here? Has he forgotten his childhood? And if so, why? Did he love his father and does he miss him now? Why does Jake tell his sister later on that he has made a determined effort not to be like their father? The minimalist treatment of the father in the background story raises more questions about the present than it answers about the past, which is the purpose of this technique.

Background Story in Nonrealistic Plays

Nonrealistic plays tend to have short and simple character histories and are more likely to reveal information about the world of the play, its closed system, than about plot or character. The actual process of disclosure may be in long speeches, bits and pieces, uncertain and elusive hints, or any combination of these. Whatever the case may be, background story in nonrealistic plays tends to be limited and perform a different function than it does in realistic plays. We will explain more about this below, but first some examples.

The background story in *Machinal* contains only a handful of references to Helen's earlier life at home with her family. It was a time when she believed her mother and father were in love. The Young Man, with whom she has a brief affair, discloses a little about his involvement in the Mexican Revolution, which started in 1910 and was the first of the major armed struggles for freedom in the twentieth century. Though not eventful in the usual way, the background story nevertheless establishes that Helen lives in a loveless world, and that a lover of hers is among those who are fighting for freedom in that world. That Helen is a stranger in this strange land we learn first and foremost from her onstage actions.

In *Mother Courage* (and other plays of his) Brecht makes a point of neutralizing the influence of background story by disclosing it with explanatory placards at the beginning of each scene. His intention is to do away with background story as a motivating factor and concentrate instead on what is happening to the characters in the present. He wants to focus the audience's attentions on the characters' concrete present choices rather than the insubstantial influence of the past.

Winnie chatters about a few background story events in *Happy Days*. The dances, friendships, love affairs, visits from strangers, deaths, etc., she talks about in her one-sided conversations with Willie are not so much significant background story events as signs that life for them has been an endless series of broken dreams extending back into time without end.

The key events in the background story of *The Birthday Party* consist of Stanley's ruined career as a pianist, his retreat to a seaside boarding house run by Meg and Petey, and a vague prior relationship he had with Goldberg and McCann, which for some reason causes them to track him down and take him away to someplace unpleasant. Once again, the background story is not as important as the cruel power that Goldberg and McCann exercise in the present over Stanley as well as Petey, Meg, and Lulu.

In *Fefu and Her Friends* a group of women gather to plan a children's education project. According to the playwright, the play was set in 1935 because that era was "pre-Freud." In other words, it was a time when the past did not play a crucial role in one's self-image and people tended to accept each other at face value without always interpreting each other or themselves in light of the past. The normal questions of realism (who these characters are, how they became what they are, etc.) are less important than how the characters come to terms with what is happening to them on stage in the present.

The opening scene in *Top Girls* could be considered a scene of background story, in that it illustrates the choices made by a selection of free-thinking female characters from art and history. All are women who overcame major obstacles to achieve distinction. Excepting that in each case when they had an opportunity to choose genuine emancipation, they opted for power instead. This pattern establishes the perspective for us to observe Marlene as she follows the same path throughout the present action of the play.

Rosencrantz and Guildenstern are Dead is one of those plays with almost a complete absence of background story. We know as little about the two title characters here as we do about Shakespeare's original models. The play's meaning revolves around the uncertainty of the present, not the certainty of the past. In fact, it is Guildenstern's notions about the past that restrain him from seeing the present as it is.

Angels in America is in many ways a summary example of nonrealism on the question of background story. Its subject is "beautiful systems dying, old fixed orders spiraling apart" (1,3). Established principles of democracy, politics, law, religion, family, friendship — all are depicted in a state of collapse. At first glance, the background story appears to be conventional in terms of its quantity and manner of disclosure. In contrast to conventional practice, however, the focus is not on what happened in the past, but on the fact that the old world — the world of progress, justice, and benevolent Providence — is coming to an end. The question to ask is how the characters come to terms with their reality at this point in time. Will Joe Pitt and Louis Ironson choose to be passive bystanders (victims) of history or active builders of the future?

The tendency shown here is toward more onstage action and less background story, toward more action and less narration. Changes in form like this do not happen by themselves or in a social vacuum. They are a product of the deep feelings of individual artists confronting the general trends of a particular period of time. Then again, a textbook on script analysis is not the place to spend too much time thinking about the influence of history on dramatic form. We can only observe how the issue is treated by playwrights in their work. It is enough to say that in their search for a way to express a present-day view of the world, certain playwrights began to test realism's emphasis on background story. Initially, as we stated earlier, they began to minimize and conceal the background story as much as possible. When this path became exhausted, they began to turn away from realism to nonrealism, and by doing so they also changed the accepted (realistic) wisdom that emphasized background story so much in first place.

Summary

We have been reviewing the topic of background story, noting how it is treated, and studying the adjustments playwrights have made to accommodate particular technical needs and cultural shifts. We have seen that, since the background story is crowded with significant information, it is essential to know as much about it as possible, sometimes in exhausting detail. Another important part of learning about background story is the understanding that for theatre artists it involves much more than the dry theoretical term exposition. Most readers who have followed the discussion so far should see that background story in plays is as dramatic as onstage action. Often it is more so.

Questions

1. *Technique.* Is the background story disclosed in long speeches? In short statements? In subtle hints and veiled allusions? How

reliable are the characters who disclose the background story? Is the background story disclosed near the beginning of the play? Throughout the entire play? Any disclosed near the end of the play? How much background story is there compared to onstage action? Where does the action of the play begin in relation to the background story? In relation to the end of the action?

2. *Identification.* What specific events are disclosed in the background story? How long ago did they occur? What is the original chronology of events? In what order are the events disclosed in the play? Besides events, are there any character descriptions in the background story? Any feelings or sensory impressions? In what ways are they interrelated with the events in the background story? Write a complete report of each character's background story. Provide a complete report of the background story as told by all the characters.

3. *Mise-en-scene.* What does the background story suggest about the mise-en-scene? How could the mise-en-scene contribute to the effectiveness of the background story?

4. *After Action Analysis.* Search for the play's seed/theme in the background story. How does the seed/theme influence the events, character descriptions, and feelings in the background story? In what way does associating the seed/theme with the background story contribute to the effectiveness of the play?

CHAPTER 4

External and Internal Action

The word *plot* comes from two sources: the Old French word *complot*, meaning a secret scheme, and from the English word *plat*, meaning a plan or map. It has an added sense of its parts being packed together. Plot has parallel meanings related to secret intrigues or conspiracies and to suspense. Aristotle believed that plot was the first principle and the soul of drama. He described it as the imitation of the dramatic action (action performed with a significant goal in mind) and the arrangement of the incidents. He also said that the most effective plots have a beginning, middle, and end and represent single complete dramatic action.

Critics continue to debate Aristotle's statements about plot, but that is not of concern at this moment. Most audiences — including actors, directors, and designers — expect some kind of plot, even if it is not apparent why they do. In essence, plot means the story line, the sense that things are moving, that the play is getting somewhere, and that events are moving forward. In this basic sense, plot serves to sustain interest in how everything does or does not come together in the end. It evokes the questions "What happened?" "What is happening?" and "What is going to happen?"

It is not necessary at this time to define plot more than this, but someone who tried would be obliged to deal with at least four fundamental features: (1) external action, (2) internal action, (3) progressions, and (4) structure. A plot could be weak or lacking in one of these features, but there would be a sense that something was missing or strange. A play with such a feeling seldom accomplishes what is expected, at least from a conventional point of view. External and internal action will be the organizing principles of this chapter. Chapter 5 will deal with the progress and structure of the plot.

External Action

The first responsibility of plot is to provide the *external action* needed to carry out the story in concrete terms. This is plot on its most basic level, the level of what the characters are physically doing on stage. Stanislavsky and his followers refer to this property of the plot as the "first plan." They are interested in the way external action can be used to stimulate the actor's imagination. They maintain that for an actor the life of a play should start with basic physical actions and then proceed to deal with internal, or psychological, actions — unconscious creativity by means of conscious physical action. The external action is also a major source of information about the environment and mise-en-scene.

Once again when reading for personal study, it is perfectly acceptable to supplement the dialogue with the stage directions for information about external action. In most cases, stage directions are more or less an accurate record of the original production. If analysis is intended for a new performance, however, great care should be exercised when using the stage directions as an authority for anything, including the mise-en-scene. Formalist analysis relies on the dialogue as much as possible. And even when there is no obvious external action in the dialogue, as a rule it can be discovered by deduction without consulting other people's suggestions. Most of the interpretive external action created by professional directors, or the mise-en-scene created by professional designers, does not come from the stage directions anyway, but rather from information found in the dialogue itself.

Entrances and Exits

Entrances and exits in drama are equivalent to attack and release in music: they start and stop the stage action. The questions they answer are who is or was or will be on stage and by what means. In film and television, there is little need for writing entrances or exits in the dialogue because the camera follows the characters wherever they go. In a play, however, all the characters must come to the stage to perform their actions before a stationary audience. Thus, stage action always starts with an entrance and concludes with an exit (or a curtain or blackout, which is essentially the same thing). The "French Scene" is a feature closely linked with entrances and exits and will be treated in the next chapter.

Entrances and exits differ from one another in their characters and situations, but they all share the same general features. Reading the dialogue in the literal sense is helpful to illustrate this precept, but dialogue is not always interpreted in a literal sense, of course, for performance. The following simple example from *Oedipus Rex* shows Sophocles presenting an important entrance. Notice the use of repetition for dramatic reinforcement.

CHORUS. He is coming. Creon is coming.

Shakespeare infuses emotion into the following two examples from *Hamlet*. The entrance is Horatio's warning to Hamlet of the appearance of the Ghost; the exit is the Ghost's disappearance.

HORATIO. Look, my lord, it comes!

*

GHOST. Adieu, adieu, adieu! Remember me.

Moliere includes both emotion and mise-en-scene in this exit from *Tartuffe*.

ORGON. I'm so incensed...I shall have to go
outside to recover myself.

Ibsen's talent for innuendo may be seen at work in the following entrance from *The Wild Duck*. Here Gina Ekdal reproaches her father-in-law for his tardiness, but she is also hinting that he has been drinking again. In the second example, Ibsen has concluded a family dispute with an exit that also involves information about character motivation. The third passage shows Ibsen using an exit to provoke a feeling of suspense, for what's going to happen next.

GINA. How late you are today, Grandfather!

*

GREGERS. When I look back upon your past I
seem to see a battlefield with shattered
lives on every hand.

WERLE. I begin to think that the chasm that
divides us is too wide.

GREGERS. (*bowing with self-command*) So I have
observed, and therefore I take my hat
and go.

WERLE. You are going? Out of the house?

GREGERS. Yes. For at last I see my mission in life.
WERLE. What mission?
GREGERS. You would only laugh if I told you.

*

GREGERS. Put on your hat and coat, Hjalmar; I
   want you to come for a long walk with me.

In this exit from *A Raisin in the Sun*, Mama Younger expresses her approval of Beneatha's new boyfriend, who has just departed.

MAMA. Lord, that's a pretty thing just went
   out of here!

Chekhov seldom wrote entrances or exits directly in the dialogue of his plays. Characters entering and exiting unannounced is one of the features that contributes to an apparent sense of aimlessness in his dramas. Examples of traditional entrances and exits, however, are not lacking. This passage from *Three Sisters* begins with an unannounced entrance by Andrey Prozorov (ahn-DRAY PRO-zuh-rof) and Dr. Chebutykin (cheh-boo-TEE-kin) and ends with a statement about their exit. A few moments before this, both characters hurried off stage to avoid an embarrassing situation; now they plan to escape to the club for an evening of cards. In this short *on-the-way scene* (a scene wherein the characters pass from one locale to another), the characters reveal meaningful information about themselves.

(ANDREY *and* CHEBUTIKIN *come in quietly.*)
CHEBUTYKIN. I never got around to marry-
   ing because my life has just passed like
   lightning, and besides I was madly in
   love with your mother and she was married
   already.
ANDREY. One shouldn't get married, indeed one
   shouldn't. It's a bore.
CHEBUTYKIN. Yes, yes, that's a point of view,
   but there is such a thing as loneliness.
   You can argue about it as much as you
   like, but loneliness is a terrible thing.
   Though actually of course it doesn't
   matter.
ANDREY. Let's hurry up and get out of here.
CHEBUTYKIN. What's the rush? There's plenty of
   time.

```
ANDREY. I'm afraid my wife might stop me.
CHEBUTYKIN. Oh, I see.
ANDREY. I won't play cards tonight; I'll just
    sit and watch. I feel a bit unwell. I get
    so out of breath, is there anything I can
    do for it, Doctor?
CHEBUTYKIN. Why ask me? I don't know, dear
    boy. I don't remember.
ANDREY. Let's go out through the kitchen.
```

The distinctive terseness of David Mamet's dialogue is seen at work in this entrance from *American Buffalo*.

```
TEACH. (appears at the doorway and enters the
    store) Good morning.
BOB. Morning, Teach.
```

A short time later Bob is sent out for coffee, an English muffin, and plain yogurt. Notice Don's immediate defense of Bob after he leaves, which is a sign of his special concern for Bob. As for Teach, a few moments before this he warned Bob not to say anything to Ruthie about last night's card game, in which he lost money to her. Yet now he denies it had any importance for him. It is a sign of further impulsive behavior from him still to come.

```
DON. And plain if they got it.
BOB. I will. (Exits.)
DON. He wouldn't say anything.
TEACH. What the fuck do I care...
```

Entrances and exits deserve careful study. Who is coming and going and who is here are some of the most basic parts of the plot. Arrivals and departures significantly affect the course of action and obviously the mise-en-scene. Moreover, as seen in the passage from *Three Sisters* and *American Buffalo*, the surrounding dialogue can also reveal valuable information about character.

Blocking

Blocking is the movement and positioning of the characters on stage. The spatial relationships among the characters are necessary to clarify the story and reveal emotional mind-sets. The ability to visualize blocking and mise-en-scene while reading is one of the basic skills of play analysis. Characters in plays attract and repel each other like polarized magnets: they are close to each other in climactic or affectionate moments but remain apart in moments of lower tension. Much of this type of blocking is motivated from within the play itself, and with attentive reading it can be recognized as such in the dialogue.

Here are some examples of indigenous blocking, that is, external action required for the execution of the plot. Such instances as these are necessary to show the logic of the basic events, motivate them, and suggest the mise-en-scene. In the first line, Oedipus provides a picture of the stage positions of the Chorus, some of their costume accessories, and a scenic piece. The words "strewn" and "before" (in this translation, at least) indicate that the characters are located around the *thymele* (central altar), which was a standard architectural feature of classical Greek theatres.

> OEDIPUS. My children...
> Why have you strewn yourselves before
> these altars
> In supplication, with your boughs and
> garlands?

Hamlet's following line in the "mousetrap scene" (3,2) is both a stage direction and an erotic pun. Ophelia is seated on the floor before the Players' makeshift stage. Hamlet asks permission to rest his head on her knees while watching the play.

> HAMLET. Lady, shall I lie in your lap?

In this line from *Tartuffe*, Elmire instructs Orgon to hide under the table. Besides identifying an element of the mise-en-scene, her insistence at this point shows that Orgon is reluctant to join in her scheme to entrap Tartuffe.

> ELMIRE. Help me to bring the table up. Now get
> under it... You shall see in due course.
> Get under there and, mind now, take care
> that he doesn't see or hear you.

A moment before the line from *Death of a Salesman* below, Biff has discovered his father in a hotel room with another woman. Willy pushes her into the bathroom because he does not want his son to see her.

> WILLY. All right, stay in the bathroom here,
> and don't come out. I think there's a law
> in Massachusetts, so don't come out.

In *A Raisin in the Sun*, the Nigerian student, Joseph Asagai, visits Beneatha's apartment. Her family is packing for their move to Clybourne Park. It is not a particularly significant entrance in itself, but his line contains information about the mise-en-scene as well as a little of the charm that makes his character so attractive to Beneatha.

```
ASAGAI.  I came over...I had some free time.
         I thought I might help with the packing.
         Ah, I like the look of packing crates!
         A household in preparation for a journey.
```

Use of Properties

A third type of external action is the *use of properties* (objects held in the hand). Properties tend to be among the few things that are actually real in a performance, and as such they provide an important link with the real world as well as opportunities for design and illustrative stage business. Like blocking, the use of properties has both a logical and a dramatic aspect. Logic is served when characters use properties to carry out the story or identify the given circumstances; dramatic potential is released when properties are used for the expression of feelings, relationships, theme, and environment.

99

After Hamlet has spoken with the Ghost, he asks his friends not to reveal what they have seen. His line shows that he is using a sword on which his friends are expected to place their hands ceremoniously.

```
HAMLET.  Swear by my sword
         Never to speak of this that you have heard,
```

This line from *The School for Scandal* requires close attention to the context of the improvised auction about to take place. There are three references to properties: a chair used as the auctioneer's pulpit, a parchment showing the family tree, and the same parchment used as an auctioneer's gavel.

```
CHARLES.  But come, get to your pulpit, Mr.
          Auctioneer; here's a gouty old chair of my
          grandfather's will answer the purpose....
          What parchment have we here? Oh, our gene-
          alogy in full. Here, Careless, you shall
          have no common bit of mahogany, here's the
          family tree for you, you rogue! This shall
          be your hammer....
```

Hjalmar's warning to Hedvig about the pistol in *The Wild Duck* is an external action that prepares future plot information. This practice is called loading, funding, or foreshadowing — terms that refer to the accumulation dramatic potential prior to a significant action.

> HJALMAR. Don't touch that pistol, Hedvig! One
> of the barrels is loaded, remember that.

Avery's blessing near the end of *The Piano Lesson* shows the properties taking on additional meaning as part of a holy ritual.

> AVERY. Seem like that piano's causing all the
> trouble. I can bless that. Berniece, put
> me some water in that bottle... Hold this
> candle. Whatever you do, make sure it
> don't go out.

In *Three Sisters,* Olga removes clothing from a wardrobe and heaps it into Anfisa's arms. Olga is distracted by the fire in town and neglects to see that poor old Anfisa is exhausted. A few moments later Anfisa breaks down in the belief that she will lose her position with the household because she has grown too old to work.

> OLGA. Here, this gray one — take it.... And
> this one here.... The blouse too.... And
> take this skirt, Anfisa.... What is it, my
> God, Kirsanovsky Street is burned to the
> ground.... Take this.... Take this....
> The poor Vershinins were frightened....
> Their house nearly burned up. They must
> spend the night here.... We can't let them
> go home.... At poor Fedotik's everything
> got burned, there's nothing left....
> ANFISA. You'll have to call Ferapont, Miss. I
> can't carry...

An unusual property in *American Buffalo* is the pig leg-spreader, a device for holding the animal's legs apart for ease of handling. It is only named in the stage directions, not the actual dialogue, but the presence in Don's junkshop of a device used to disembowel pigs plays an illuminating role in the relationship between him and Teach.

> TEACH. (*holds up the dead-pig leg-spreader*):
> You know what this is?
> (*Pause.*)

```
BOB. Yeah.
TEACH. What is it?
BOB. I know.
    (Pause.)
TEACH. Huh?
BOB. What?
TEACH. Things are what they are.
```

Even Teach does not know what the object is or what it is used for, which is the point — he is a fraud.

Special Activities

Special activities are those outside the usual range of external actions found in a play; that is, beyond standing, sitting, eating, drinking, smoking, walking, talking, arriving, and departing, etc. As a rule, they also require extra rehearsal time. Examples include combat, musical performance, dance, acrobatics, and other activities that require special knowledge or skill on the part of the performers. When playwrights make an effort to describe special activities in their plays, it is because they have endowed those activities with playable dramatic values.

Hamlet's unintentional murder of Polonius is a turning point in the play and must be performed as such, not as a matter-of-fact accident. Polonius, of course, has been hiding where he can eavesdrop (behind a curtain, in most performances). Hamlet kills him with a weapon, whose characteristics will depend on the period in which the performance is set.

```
POLONIUS. (behind) What ho! help, help, help!
HAMLET. (draws) How now! a rat?
    Dead for a ducat, dead!
    (kills POLONIUS with a pass through the
    arras)
    POLONIUS. (behind) O, I am slain!
```

Mrs. Sorby's piano playing is the subject of this passage from *The Wild Duck*. When she goes into an adjoining room, she begins to play a tune. Her cheerful music continues in the background throughout the following scene, where it serves as an emotional counterpoint to the quarrel between Gregers and his father.

```
GUEST. Shall we play a duet, Mrs. Sorby?
MRS. SORBY. Yes, suppose we do.
GUESTS. Bravo, bravo!
```

A Nigerian folk dance is the subject of these lines in *A Raisin in the Sun*. As well as dance skills, the characters need both space to dance and probably selected costume accessories to foreground the special nature of the action.

> RUTH. What kind of dance is that?
> BENEATHA. A folk dance.
> RUTH. What kind of folks do that, honey?
> BENEATHA. It's from Nigeria. It's a dance of welcome.

Cleaning up the debris from last night's poker game could be considered one of the special activities in *American Buffalo*. At first glance, the special activity here may not seem particularly important, but a closer look shows that it relates to the deeper meaning of the play. Note that Teach lost at cards last night and that he trashes the junkshop at the end of the play as well. This passage is a representative example of the kind of cleaning up after the fact that Don has always had to deal with in his relations with Teach.

> DON. Don't tell me you're sorry. I'm not mad at you.
> BOB. You're not?
> DON. (*Pause.*) Let's clean up here.

Understanding these and other special activities will help readers to appreciate their dramatic potential as well as their importance in the mise-en-scene.

Internal Action

Plot is often understood as a completely external happening. According to this viewpoint, plays with strong plots contain plenty of entrances and exits, fights and hazards and rescues, secrets and lies, crimes and misdemeanors, and similar types of clever and interesting external actions. But this is a misunderstanding. Plot is more than a collection of inventive external activities; for besides its external features, it also occurs inside the characters, changing their internal as well as external circumstances. This internal dimension of the plot is referred to here as *internal action* (psychological action) to distinguish it from external action (physical action). Stanislavsky's followers sometimes refer to the internal action as the "second plan" of the play.

It is important to point out here that this sense of duality — the split between external life and internal life — is an invented exercise intended to aid in understanding the separate features of a play. On stage, in performance, in rehearsal, at the table doing play analysis, as in real life, body and mind are one entity, an understanding that is the basis of psychologically truthful performance.

Internal action concerns the psychological lives of the characters — their mental, spiritual, and emotional impulses. When internal action is expressed *openly in the dialogue*, it appears in three forms: assertions, plans, and commands. There is nothing unusual or mysterious about these forms. They simply describe the attitude of the character toward what is being said. They are similar to the grammatical principle of mood, whether making an assertion (indicative mood), posing a future plan (subjunctive mood), or giving a command (imperative mood). In the following section, the way internal action is expressed in the words of the characters will be examined. Internal action also has nonverbal characteristics that will be discussed in the next chapter.

Assertions

Assertions are the simplest forms of internal action in the dialogue. In one way or another, they appear on almost every page of a script. The basic principle needs little explaining. Normally, an assertion is the plain statement of a fact, a declaration that something is true or false. "This car is red." Plays contain a few ordinary assertions like these too. In a play, however, assertions not only *say* something, they also *do* something. "I now pronounce you man and wife." Assertions produce changes in characters, in the course of the action. They may take the form of ordinary statements, but they actually need to do something to be worth our attention as assertions.

Several examples follow in which the dialogue is understood literally, but obviously there are times when dialogue should not be read this way. As we said in the last chapter, sometimes characters deceive themselves or lie. Even these occasions are instructive, however, because dialogue must be read literally before it can be read in other ways. We must know the truth before we can know if a statement is false or not.

In 1,2 of *The School for Scandal*, Rowley announces to Sir Peter Teazle the surprise arrival of wealthy Sir Oliver Surface in London. How and from where does Rowley enter?

> ROWLEY. Sir Oliver is arrived, and at this
> moment is in town.

103

Rowley's announcement involves four clear assertions: a person (Sir Oliver), an event (is arrived), a time (at this moment), and a place (in town). These assertions are significant. Sir Oliver, the rich uncle of the brothers Charles and Joseph Surface, plans a ruse to prove to his friend, Sir Peter Teazle, that Joseph is a hypocrite and Charles is honest.

The following moment from *The Wild Duck* asserts an important event: that Hedvig Ekdal has shot herself, a fact that reveals her father to be a fool and his friend, Gregers Werle, a heartless zealot. Note how repetition increases the impact of this assertion.

> RELLING. What's the matter here?
> GINA. They say Hedvig shot herself.
> HJALMAR. Come and help us!
> RELLING. Shot herself!

Assertions involving moral or criminal offenses grow to become accusations. In this selection from *Oedipus Rex*, Oedipus asserts (accuses) Teiresias of conspiring with Creon to murder old King Laius. Teiresias is angered by this triple assertion of treason, conspiracy, and murder, and responds by asserting (accusing) Oedipus himself of being the murderer. These two accusations are assertions about a significant event that forms the heart of the play.

> OEDIPUS. I'll tell you what I think:
>   You planned it, you had it done,
>   You all but killed him with your own hands:
>   If you had eyes, I'd say the crime was yours,
>   And yours alone.
> TEIRESIAS. So? I charge you, then,
>   Abide by the proclamation you have made:
>   From this day forth
>   Never speak again to these men or to me;
>   You yourself are the pollution of this country.

Assertions also appear when Damis asserts (accuses) Tartuffe of attempting to seduce Elmire, who is Tartuffe's wife and Damis' step-mother. Damis' assertions involve a person (Tartuffe) and an event (seduction). Note also in this passage that the number of words devoted to advancing the plot is quite small. Most of the words describe Damis' feelings about Tartuffe, Orgon, and Elmire — Damis is an emotional young man.

> DAMIS. We have interesting news for you, father. Something has just occurred which will astonish you. You are well repaid for your kindness! The gentleman sets a very high value on the consideration you have shown for him! He has just been demonstrating his passionate concern for you and he stops at nothing less than dishonoring your bed. I have just overheard him making a disgraceful declaration of his guilty passion for your wife. She, in kind-heartedness and over-anxiety to be discreet was all for keeping it secret but I can't condone such shameless behavior. I consider it would be a gross injustice to you to keep it from you.

In *The Piano Lesson* Berniece asserts (accuses) that Boy Willie played a part in the death of her husband, Crawley, three years ago. Crawley's unfortunate death has had a significant influence on Berniece's misguided outlook on life.

105

> BERNIECE. You killed Crawley just as sure as if you pulled the trigger.
>
> *
>
> Crawley ain't knew you stole that wood.
>
> *
>
> All I know is Crawley would be alive if you hadn't come up and got him.
>
> *
>
> Crawley's dead and in the ground and you still walking around here eating. That's all I know. He went off to load some wood with you and ain't never come back.
>
> *
>
> He ain't here, is he? He ain't here!
>
> *

He ain't here, is he? Is he?

*

He ain't here.

*

You come up there and got him!

Three characters and five assertions appear in this passage from *Mother Courage*. First, Swiss Cheese asserts he did not steal the payroll. Second, the Sergeant asserts Mother Courage was an accomplice in the theft. Third, Swiss Cheese asserts she had nothing to do with it. Fourth, Swiss Cheese asserts he is innocent. Fifth, Mother Courage asserts she does not even know Swiss Cheese. The moment moves quickly, but it is significant because it shows Mother Courage denying her own son, even if for understandable reasons. Swiss Cheese will be shot if he is guilty, in which case Mother Courage will be shot too if she acknowledges him as her son.

> (*Voices are heard from the rear. The two men bring in* SWISS CHEESE.)
>
> SWISS CHEESE. Let me go. I haven't got anything. Stop twisting my shoulder, I'm innocent.
>
> THE SERGEANT. He belongs here. You know each other.
>
> MOTHER COURAGE. What makes you think that?
>
> SWISS CHEESE. I don't know them. I don't even know who they are. I had a meal here, it cost me ten hellers. Maybe you saw me sitting here, it was too salty.
>
> THE SERGEANT. Who are you anyway?
>
> MOTHER COURAGE. We're respectable people. And it's true. He had a meal here. He said it was too salty.
>
> THE SERGEANT. Are you trying to tell me you don't know each other?
>
> MOTHER COURAGE. Why should I know him? I don't know everybody. I don't ask people what their name is or if they're heartless; if they pay, they're not heathens.

Assertions can also hide behind apparent trivialities. When Teach inquires about the Don's secret scheme with Bob to steal some rare coins, Don attempts to cover up something important by asserting it is not important.

```
TEACH.  So what is this thing with the kid
     [i.e., Bob].
     (Pause.)
     I mean is it anything, uh...
DON. It's nothing... you know...
TEACH. Yeah.
     (Pause.)
     It's what... ?
DON. You know, it's just some guy we spotted.
TEACH. Yeah. Some guy.
DON. Yeah.
TEACH. Some guy.
DON. Yeah.
     (Pause.)
```

In any form, assertions are crucial components of the plot. They induce changes in the characters and function as internal anchors that mark the progress of the plot. Professional practice ensures that seemingly elementary information such as this is always pointed up in performance and mise-en-scene.

107

Plans

A *plan* is any detailed method for doing something, developed in advance. Some plans are very simple, as in "First we'll meet at Mike's house, then we'll go to the movies." Or they may be elaborate, with complex sets of dependent actions leading to a final goal, like the plans for landing an astronaut on the moon. Plans are the most practical and economical means for advancing the plot, and are found in plays everywhere. Sometimes it is hard to tell the difference between plans (things that really happen or are expected to really happen) and dreams (fantastic notions, hopes, or reveries that probably will never turn out). As the following examples show, playwrights have made use of plans in a wide assortment of situations.

An illustration of a simple and direct plan occurs in *Mother Courage* when Anna Fierling determines to hide the platoon's cash box. She wants to protect her son from being accused of the theft.

```
MOTHER COURAGE. I'd better get the cash box
     out of here, I've found a hiding place.
```

> All right, get me a drink. (KATRIN *goes*
> *behind the wagon*.) I'll hide it in the
> rabbit hole down by the river until I can
> take it away. Maybe late tonight. I'll go
> get it and take it to the regiment.

Hamlet's well-known statement also describes a plan — in this case, one that has profound consequences. An event in the background story sets up the plan.

> HAMLET. I have heard
>   That guilty creatures, sitting at a play,
>   Have by the very cunning of the scene
>   Been struck so to the soul that presently
>   They have proclaim'd their malefactions;
>   I'll have these players
>   Play something like the murder of my father
>   Before mine uncle. I'll observe his looks;
>   I'll tent him to the quick. If'a do blench,
>   I know my course.
>   The play's the thing
>   Wherein I'll catch the conscience of the
>   King.

Later in the play Claudius arranges a counter-plan with Laertes to use an unbated foil (no protective button on the point) tipped with poison to murder Hamlet. Shakespeare is praised for his skill in maintaining the rhythm of his blank verse even while he is relating basic, first-plan plot information as described here.

> CLAUDIUS. But good Laertes,
>   Will you do this? Keep close within your
>   chamber.
>   Hamlet return'd shall know you are come
>   home.
>   We'll put on those shall praise your
>   excellence,
>   And set a double varnish on the fame
>   The Frenchman gave you; bring you, in fine,
>   together,
>   And wager on your heads. He, being remiss,
>   Most generous, and free from all contriving,
>   Will not peruse the foils; so that with ease
>   Or with a little shuffling, you may choose

> A sword unbated, and, in a pass of practice,
> Requite him for your father.

In *Tartuffe*, the servant, Dorine, prepares an elaborate counter-plan to frustrate Orgon's initial plan to marry off his daughter, Mariane, to Tartuffe. Mariane's boyfriend, Valere, will help to carry out Dorine's plan.

> DORINE. We'll try everything we can. Your father can't be serious and it's all sheer rubbish, but you had better pretend to fall in with his nonsense and give the appearance of consenting so that if it comes to the point you'll more easily be able to delay the marriage. If we can only gain time we may easily set everything right. You can complain of sudden illness that will necessitate delay; another time you can have recourse to bad omens — such as having met a corpse or broken a mirror or dreamt of muddy water. Finally, the great thing is that they can't make you his wife unless you answer "I will." But I think, as a precaution, you had better not be found talking together. (*to* VALERE) Off you go and get all your friends to use their influence with her father to stand by his promise. We must ask his brother to try once again, and see if we can get the stepmother on our side.

In *The Wild Duck* Gregers' advice to Hedvig proves to be a fatally misguided plan because it results in her death.

> GREGERS. (*coming a little nearer*) But suppose you were to sacrifice *The Wild Duck* of your own free will for his sake?
>
> HEDVIG. (*rising*) *The Wild Duck*!
>
> GREGERS. Suppose you were to make a free-will offering, for his sake, of the dearest treasure you have in the world?
>
> HEDVIG. Do you think that would do any good?
>
> GREGERS. Try it, Hedvig.
>
> HEDVIG. (*softly, with flashing eyes*) Yes, I will try it.

> GREGERS. Have you really the courage for it,
> so you think?
> HEDVIG. I'll ask grandfather to shoot *The Wild*
> *Duck* for me.
> GREGERS. Yes, do. But not a word to your mother
> about it.
> HEDVIG. Why, not?
> GREGERS. She doesn't understand us.
> HEDVIG. *The Wild Duck!* I'll try it tomorrow
> morning.

Three Sisters is about plans that never materialize, that is, dreams. But one plan that does materialize, unfortunately, is Solyony's duel with Tuzenbach, which is explained to Andrey and Masha in this passage spoken by Dr. Chebutykin.

> CHEBUTYKIN. Solyony began to pick on the Baron
> and he lost his temper and insulted him,
> and it finally got to the point where
> Solyony had to challenge him to a duel.
> (*Looks at his watch.*) It's time now, I
> believe. At half-past twelve, in the for-
> est over there, the one we can see from
> here, beyond the river...Oh, well, who
> really cares. Solyony imagines he's the
> poet Lermontov and he even writes verses.
> Now a joke is a joke, but this is the
> third duel for him.

Plans for the coin theft in *American Buffalo* always seem to have a sense of uncertainty or reluctance about them, even though they go into elaborate detail. Mamet's penchant for terse colloquial speech is also in evidence.

> TEACH. Then I guess I'll go home, take a nap,
> and rest up. Come here tonight and we'll
> take off this fucking fruit's coins.
> DON. Right.
> TEACH. I feel like I'm trying to stay up to
> death...
> DON. You ain't been to sleep since the [card]
> game?
> TEACH. *Shit* no, then that dyke cocksucker...

DON. So go take a nap. You trying to kill
    yourself?
TEACH. You're right, and you do what you think
    is right, Don.
DON. I got to, Teach.
TEACH. You got to trust your instincts, right
    or wrong.
DON. I got to.
TEACH. I know it. I know you do.
    (*Pause.*)
    Any body wants to get in touch with me,
    I'm over at the hotel.
DON. Okay.
TEACH. I'm not at the *hotel*, I stepped out for
    coffee. I'll be back one minute.
DON. Okay.
TEACH. And I'll see you around eleven.
DON. O'clock.
TEACH. *Here.*
DON. Right.
TEACH. And don't worry about anything.
DON. I won't.
TEACH. I don't want to hear you're worrying
    about a God-damned thing.
DON. You won't, Teach.
TEACH. You're sure you want Fletch coming with
    us?
DON. Yes.
TEACH. All right, then, so long as you're
    sure.
DON. I'm sure, Teach.
TEACH. Then I'm going to see you tonight.
DON. Goddamn right you are.
TEACH. I'm seeing you later.
DON. I know.
TEACH. Good-bye.
DON. Good-bye.
TEACH. I want to make one thing plain before I
    go, Don. I am not mad at you.
DON. I know.
TEACH. All right, then.
DON. You have a good nap.

```
TEACH. I will.
    (TEACH exits.)
DON. Fuckin' business…
    (Lights dim to black.)
```

Plans are productive internal actions to study because they appear in the dialogue explicitly as plans and they provide the engine for the plot. Their treatment seldom varies. First the characters discuss the tactical details, then they put them into effect — or sometimes not, as in some of the study plays already discussed.

Commands

A *command* is a statement containing a specific authoritative requirement, a statement with a built-in feeling of necessity. "Silence!" The following examples demonstrate different kinds of commands.

When Claudius commands Hamlet to leave for England, he is expressing his authority as king.

```
CLAUDIUS. Hamlet, this deed, for thine espe-
    cial safety —
    Which we do tender, as we dearly grieve
    For that which thou hast done — must send
    thee hence
    With fiery quickness. Therefore prepare
    thyself;
    The bark is ready, and the wind at help,
    Th' associates tend, and everything is bent
    For England.
HAMLET. For England!
```

Orgon takes advantage of his paternal authority when he commands his daughter, Mariane, to marry Tartuffe.

```
ORGON. What have you to say about our guest
    Tartuffe?
MARIANE. What have I to say?
ORGON. Yes, you! Mind how you answer.
MARIANE. Oh dear! I'll say anything you like
    about him.
ORGON. That's very sensible. Then let me hear
    you say, my dear, that he is a wonderful
    man, that you love him, and you'd be glad
    to have me choose him for your husband. Eh?
```

Mama Younger expresses another kind of parental authority in this command from *A Raisin in the Sun*. In the previous moment, her daughter, Beneatha, has rejected the need for God in her life. Observe the special activity, too.

> (MAMA *absorbs* BENEATHA's *speech, studies her daughter and rises slowly and crosses to Beneatha and slaps her powerfully across the face. After, there is only silence and the daughter drops her eyes from her mother's face, and Mama is very tall before her.*)
>
> MAMA. Now — you say after me, in my mother's house there is still God. (*There is a long pause and* BENEATHA *stares at the floor wordlessly.* MAMA *repeats the phrase with precision and cool emotion.*) In my mother's house there is still God.
>
> BENEATHA. In my mother's house there is still God. (*a long pause*)
>
> MAMA. (*walking away from* BENEATHA, *too disturbed for triumphant posturing. Stopping and turning back to her daughter.*) There are some ideas we ain't going to have in this house. Not as long as I am the head of this family.
>
> BENEATHA. Yes, ma' am.

113

Here is a string of commands issued by Teach and Don to each other in *American Buffalo*. They are talking about the robbery Don has been planning with Bob. Notice the back-and-forth direction of the commands. First Teach is the "cat" and Don is the "mouse," and then the roles are reversed. Mamet uses parentheses to indicate slight changes of outlook on the part of the speaker.

> TEACH. Can we get started? Do you want to tell me something about coins?
> (*Pause.*)
>
> DON. What about 'em?
>
> TEACH. A crash course. What to look for. What to take. What to *not* take. (*... this they can trace*) (*that isn't worth nothing...*).
> (*Pause.*)
> What looks like what but it's more *valuable...* so on...

```
DON. First off, I want the [rare Buffalo-head]
    nickel back.
TEACH. Donny...
DON. No, I know it's only a fuckin' nickel...
    I mean big deal, huh? But what I'm saying
    is I only want it back.
TEACH. You're going to get it back. I'm going
    in there for his coins, what am I going to
    take 'em all except your nickel? Wake up.
```

Commands push the play forward with events the characters must strive to carry out. Attentive reading will also disclose the existence of *driving characters*, strong-willed characters who introduce the plans and commands necessary to advance the plot.

External and Internal Action in Nonrealistic Plays

External Action

Nonrealistic plays employ external action (entrances and exits, blocking, and use of properties) similar to their realistic and classic counterparts. It is in the treatment of special activities (activities beyond the normal and everyday) that nonrealistic plays come into their own. Because the guiding principle is theme instead of plot or character, and because realistic plausibility is not an issue, there is no limit to the type and variety of special activities found in nonrealistic plays. Anything that illustrates the theme is apt to turn up. Here are some examples of special activities from the study plays.

In episode one of *Machinal*, the Telephone Girl, Adding Clerk, Filing Clerk, and Stenographer behave like mechanical robots when they ridicule Helen for arriving late to work. This special activity highlights the dehumanizing influence of the world of the play.

```
TELEPHONE GIRL. You're late
FILING CLERK. You're late.
ADDING CLERK. You're late.
STENOGRAPHER. And yesterday!
FILING CLERK. The day before.
ADDING CLERK. And the day before.
STENOGRAPHER. You'll lose your job.
HELEN. No!
STENOGRAPHER. No?
    (Workers exchange glances.)
```

HELEN. I can't!

STENOGRAPHER. You can't?

(*Same business.*)

FILING CLERK. Rent — bills — installments — miscellaneous.

ADDING CLERK. A dollar ten — ninety-five — $3.40 — 35¢ — $12.60.

In *Happy* Days, Winnie's position fixed in a mound of earth is a special activity indeed. Her blocking is not explained in the dialogue, but Willie's blocking is explained here.

(WILLIE *collapses behind the slope, his head disappears,* WINNIE *turns towards the event.* [...] *She cranes back and down.*)

WINNIE. Go back to your hole now, Willie, you've exposed yourself enough. (*Pause.*) Do as I say, Willie, don't lie sprawling there in this hellish sun, go back into your hole. (*Pause.*) Go on now, Willie. (WILLIE *invisible [to the audience] starts crawling towards hole.*) That's the man. (*She follows his progress with her eyes.*) Not head first, stupid, how are you going to turn? (*Pause.*) That's it... right round... now back in. (*Pause.*) Oh I know it is not easy, dear, crawling backwards, but it is rewarding in the end. (*Pause.*) You have left your Vaseline behind. (*She watches as he crawls back for the Vaseline.*) The lid! (*She watches as he crawls back towards the hole. Irritated.*) Not head first, I tell you! (*Pause.*) More to the right. (*Pause.*) The right, I said. (*Pause. Irritated.*) Keep your tail down, can't you! (*Pause.*) Now. (*Pause.*) There. (*All these directions loud. Now in her normal voice, still turned towards him.*) Can you hear me? (*Pause.*) I beseech you, Willie, just say yes or no, can you hear me, just yes or nothing. (*Pause.*)

WILLIE. Yes.

Few special activities appear openly in the dialogue of *Happy Days*, but quite a number are found in the stage directions, where it is frequently necessary to seek them out in nonrealistic plays. Elements of the mise-en-scene that directly influence special activities in this play include an expanse of scorched earth rising to a mound, a woman embedded in center of the mound, a piercing bell announcing the passage of time, unchanging white light, a fake landscape for a backdrop, and a parasol that bursts into flames. Close reading is necessary to understand the thematic issues that lie behind these special activities.

The special activities in *Fefu and Her Friends* begin with a pretended shooting:

> FEFU. (*Walks to the French doors. Beckoning* CHRISTINA.) Pst! (FEFU *gets the gun as* CHRISTINA *goes to the French doors.*) You haven't met Phillip. Have you?
>
> CHRISTINA. No.
>
> FEFU. That's him.
>
> CHRISTINA. Which one?
>
> FEFU. (*Aims and shoots.*) That one!
>
> (CHRISTINA *and* CINDY *scream.* FEFU *smiles proudly. She blows on the mouth of the barrel. She puts down the gun and looks out again.*)
>
> CINDY. Christ, Fefu.
>
> FEFU. There he goes. He's up. It's a game we play. I shoot and he falls. Whenever he hears the blast he falls. No matter where he is he falls. One time he fell in a puddle of mud and his clothes were a mess. (*She looks out.*) It's not too bad. He just dusting off some stuff. (*She waves to* PHILLIP *and starts to go upstairs.*) He's all right. Look.

Later on, the characters — all educated, articulate, adult women — engage in a juvenile water fight. Julia, confined to a wheelchair from a mysterious hunting accident, appears in a featureless room with leaves on the floor and suffers from hallucinations that insult her gender. Later on she walks without her wheelchair and materializes before a frightened Fefu. At the end of the play, Fefu shoots at a rabbit offstage, killing both it and — puzzlingly — Julia as well. These

116

and other special activities in *Fefu and Her Friends* have perplexed many critics, but close reading reveals that they are written to express the thematic issue at the heart of the play, a thematic issue which needs to be identified and theatricalized.

Top Girls is well-known for its nonrealistic opening scene, a special activity in which Marlene hosts a dinner party celebrating her promotion to manager of an employment agency for women. The time is the present, but her guests are Pope Joan (a women disguised as a man and who was said to be Pope, AD 854–856), Isabella Bird (a Victorian explorer), Dull Gret (a figure from Breughel's 1562 painting "Mad Meg"), Lady Nijo (mistress of a Japanese emperor and later a nun), and Patient Griselda (a character from Chaucer's *Canterbury Tales*). Marlene and the other characters introduce themselves and chat about their lives, as if such a nonrealistic situation were the norm.

In *A Lie of the Mind*, Jake undergoes special activities in the form of nonrealistic "transformations." He alternates between two different personalities — one childlike and kind, the other mean-spirited and brutish. His transformations are not explained in the dialogue. They just happen, without attempting to hide them behind a façade of realistic plausibility. At one point (between scenes) Jake travels on foot from Oklahoma to Montana, wearing only his underwear and his father's Air Force flight jacket, and wrapped in an American flag. At the end of the play he forsakes his wife and turns her over to his brother, Frankie. Simultaneously, her mother and father fold that American flag.

The premise of *Rosencrantz and Guildenstern Are Dead* is a nonrealistic special activity in itself: two characters from *Hamlet* display a life quite apart from their specified roles in Shakespeare's play. Moreover, Guildenstern gives the impression of being intellectually equipped to deal with the philosophical implications of their situation. The play itself begins with a prolonged run of heads in a game of coin toss.

Angels in America is also known for its nonrealistic special activities. Mr. Lies, a travel agent, appears to Harper Pitt in a valium-induced reverie and offers to take her some place safe, which turns out to be Antarctica:

HARPER. Oh! You startled me!

MR. LIES. Cash, check or credit card?

HARPER. I remember you. You're from Salt Lake City. You sold us the plane tickets when we flew here. What are you doing in Brooklyn?

MR. LIES. You said you wanted to travel...

HARPER. And here you are. How thoughtful.

MR. LIES. Mr. Lies. Of the International Order of Travel Agents. We mobilize the globe, we set people adrift, we stir the populace and send nomads eddying across the planet. We are adepts of motion, acolytes of the flux. Cash check or credit card. Name your destination.

HARPER. Antarctica, maybe. I want to see the hole in the ozone. I heard on the radio...

In other reveries Prior Walter's ancestors appear before him in his bedroom; Harper Pitt talks to Prior Walter in a "mutual dream scene," although they have never met each other before; Prior Walter hears voices speaking in biblical Hebrew, a language unknown to him; and of course the famous Angel appears before him at the end of the play.

Special activities in nonrealistic plays appear energetically and without warning. There is no obvious reason why this should be so. At one moment the action is realistically plausible, at another the characters are involuntarily pushed into readjustments, at a third mysterious unplanned impulses arise, a fourth is seen through the fun-house mirror of parody, etc. And all this happens before any reasonable explanations are offered. Explanations may follow, or may be attempted, or they may not. There is no obvious reason, but shifting the viewpoints conveys a different awareness, a new view from this or that side. It is a way of seeing another, fresher reality alongside the ordinary one.

Sometimes the surprising nature of the special activities in nonrealistic plays can distract from the substance of their purpose, but they are intended for more than entertainment value. They are guided by theme instead of realistic or traditional concerns with plot plausibility or character consistency. In their boldness, they are open declarations against the built-in expectations of realism and other conventional playwriting assumptions.

Internal Action

Internal action in nonrealistic plays often seems trifling, enigmatic, repetitive, or contrary to the rules of common sense. As with special activities, the nature and variety of examples depends on the mind of the playwright coming to grips with the theme. To get the right idea about internal actions in nonrealistic plays, it is crucial to remember the guiding principle is theme rather than plot or character.

Helen and other characters make several assertions about the apparently trivial issue of hands in *Machinal*.

> TELEPHONE GIRL. Why did you flinch, Kid?
> HELEN. Flinch?
> TELEPHONE GIRL. Did he pinch [you]?
> HELEN. No.
> TELEPHONE GIRL. Then what?
> HELEN. Nothing! — Just his hand.
> TELEPHONE GIRL. Oh — just his hand — (*Shakes her head thoughtfully.*) Uh-Huh.
> HELEN. He says he fell in love with my hands.
> HELEN. It's my hands got me a husband.
> HELEN. [at the hospital, in a fit of delirium after giving birth to a baby girl she doesn't want] God? No matter — it doesn't matter — everybody loves God — God is love — even if He's bad they got to love Him — even if He's got fat hands[i.e., like her husband's] — fat hands — no no — he wouldn't be God — His hands make you well — He lays on his hands *
> (*The* FIRST MAN *is holding* HELEN'S *hand across the table.*)
> HELEN. When you put your hand over mine! When you just touch me!
> FIRST MAN. You got mighty pretty hands, honey. This little pig went to market. This little pig stayed home. This little pig went —
> HELEN. (*laughs*) Diddle diddle dee. (*Laughs again.*)
> FIRST MAN. You got awful pretty hands.
> HELEN. I used to have. But I haven't taken much care of them lately. I will now.

119

Helen is captive in an unfeeling, mechanical world, and her hands and hair are internal idealizations of her repressed humanity. In the end, she murders her husband after failing in a desperate attempt to make him into a real human being. Later on, in one final effort to salvage her humanity, she attends to her hands and hair: "Did you see that," says a Reporter as Helen is strapped into the electric chair. "She fixed her hair under the cap — pulled her hair out under the cap."

Enigmatic assertions indicating internal action are found everywhere in *Fefu and Her Friends*.

FEFU. My husband married me to have a constant reminder of how loathsome women are.
(JULIA *takes the remaining slug out of the gun. She lets it fall on the floor.*)

JULIA. She's [Fefu] hurting herself. (JULIA *looks blank and is motionless. She notices* JULIA'S *condition.*)

CINDY. (*to* CHRISTINA). She's absent.

CHRISTINA. What do we do?

CINDY. Nothing, she'll be all right in a moment.

EMMA. Do you think about genitals all the time?

FEFU. No, I don't think about genitals.

EMMA. I do, and it drives me crazy.

FEFU. I am in constant pain. I don't want to give in to it. If I do I am afraid I will never recover. [...] as if normally there is a lubricant...not in the body... a spiritual lubricant... it's hard to describe... and without it, life is a nightmare, and everything is distorted. — A black cat started coming into my kitchen. He's awfully mangled and big. He is missing an eye and his skin is diseased. At first I was repelled by him, but then, I thought, this is a monster that has been sent to me and I must feed him. And I fed him. One day he came and shat all over my kitchen. Foul Diarrhea. He still comes and I still feed him. — I am afraid of him. (EMMA *kisses* FEFU.) How about a little lemonade?

EMMA. Yes.

FEFU. How about a game of croquet?

EMMA. Fine.

(PAULA *stands in the doorway to the living room with a bottle of spoiled milk from the kitchen.*)

120

PAULA. (*In a low-keyed manner.*) Anyone take
  rotten milk? (*Pause.*) I'm kidding. This one
  is no good but there's more in there...
  (*Remaining in good spirits.*) Forget it.
  It's not a good joke.
JULIA. It's good.
PAULA. In there [i.e., the kitchen] it seemed
  funny but here it isn't. It's a kitchen
  joke. (*As she exits shrugging her shoul-
  ders.*) Bye.

In part 3, the character of Emma reads from "The Science of Education" by the famous educator Emma Sheridan Fry. She reads, "Environment knocks at the gateway of the senses. A rain of summons beats upon us day and night." Unknown to the characters, Emma Fry's assertions and other cryptic statements and events in the play are just that: warnings from the "environment" (theme) about the unacknowledged turmoil of the characters' inner lives.

In *A Lie of the Mind* just about everyone makes foolish plans that misfire. It is worthwhile to study several of them to see how strange — plausible but strange — they actually are. The primary event in the background story is Jake's shocking abuse of his wife, Beth — not unrealistic itself, but all the same an unsettling beginning for a play about love. Jake's brother, Frankie, begins the succession of foolish plans by arranging to visit Beth's family home and report her condition back to Jake. Jake is dazed as well from the beating, and his mother, Lorraine, has come to take care of her favorite child.

121

FRANKIE. If you could take him [Jake] for a
  couple of days, Mom, I could get back and
  find out what happened with Beth. You think
  you could do that? I just need a couple
  of days. I gotta' find out for sure what's
  going' on.
LORRAINE. I'm gonna' take him on a permanent
  basis. I'm not even gonna' let him outa'
  his room for a solid year. Maybe that'll
  teach him.

Why does Frankie insist on traveling all the way from Oklahoma to Montana instead of telephoning? After all, a telephone was used in the first scene. Why does Lorraine insist on such extreme measures instead of taking Jake home to let him recover? These plans are foolish because they are guided by foolish assumptions (thematic issues).

In the hospital Beth is recovering under the dutiful eye of her brother, Mike. Their parents, Baylor and Meg, arrive to find out what happened and take Beth home, which is five hundred miles away. Baylor is a rancher with an insensible plan of his own.

> MIKE. I wish you'd have called me or something before you came down [to the hospital].
> BAYLOR. Why should I call you?
> MIKE. She's having a kind of rough time right now, Dad. She needs a lot of rest.
> BAYLOR. Listen, I got two mules settin' out there in the parkin' lot I gotta' deliver by midnight. I'm supposed to be at the sale by six tomorrow mornin' and those mules have to be in the stalls by midnight tonight.
> MIKE. You brought mules down here?
> BAYLOR. Yeah. Why not? Might as well do a little business long as I'm gonna' be down in this country anyway. That all right by you?

Back in Oklahoma Lorraine has hidden Jake's pants to ensure he does not run away from home. Despite her foolish plan, Jake plans to escape anyway by concealing his sister, Sally, under the covers in his bed and then traveling to Montana to see Beth for himself.

> JAKE. (Tucking blanket around SALLY then pulling pillow over her head.) Now when she [their mother] comes in, in the morning — She'll come in with the breakfast. She'll come in and she'll say somethin' like: "Rise and shine — it's Coffee Time!" You just stay under the pillow. You kinda' moan or somethin' — make a few little movements, but don't say anything to her.
> SALLY. You're gonna' try to get to Montana in your underpants with an American flag [a keepsake from his father's Air Force funeral] wrapped around your neck?
> JAKE. I'll travel by night.
> SALLY. Oh boy, Jake. I hope ya' make it.

JAKE. I'll make it all right. There's nothin'
    gonna' stop me. Not Frankie or Mom or that
    Family of Beth's or— (*He stops and stares
    into space.*)

Meanwhile in Montana again, Frankie is mistaken for a deer and
shot in the leg by Baylor, who brings him into the house to recover.
Beth herself is recovering her mental faculties after the severe beating
from Jake. When she sees Frankie, she plans to transform him into
a kinder, gentler embodiment of Jake. Soon after this she plans to
marry Frankie.

BETH. Pretend to be. Like you. Between us we
    can make a life. You could be the woman.
    You be. [...] (*Moving toward FRANKIE.*) You
    could pretend to be in love with me. With
    my shirt. [She's wearing her father's hunt-
    ing shirt.] You love my shirt. This shirt
    is a man to you. You are my beautiful woman.
    You lie down. (BETH *moves in to FRANKIE and
    tries to push him down on the sofa by the
    shoulders. FRANKIE resists.*)

123

Lorraine and Sally dispose of old family memorabilia as they prepare for a visit to Ireland, Lorraine's ancestral home. Sally is skeptical about Lorraine's foolish travel plan and delays by questioning
what will become of the discarded items. Another foolish, or at least
eccentric, plan is the result.

SALLY. How're we gonna' haul this junk outa'
    here, Mom.
LORRAINE. We're not gonna' haul it. We're
    gonna' burn it.
SALLY. I know, but we've gotta' get it outa'
    the house somehow.
LORRAINE. What for?
SALLY. Well, what're we gonna' do, burn the
    house down?
LORRAINE. Why not? (*Pause. SALLY stares at
    LORRAINE.*)
SALLY. We're gonna' burn the whole house down?
LORRAINE. That's right. The whole slam bang.
    Oughta' make a pretty nice light, don't
    ya' think? Little show for the neighbors.

(SALLY *starts to laugh.*) What's so damn funny?
> (*SALLY stops laughing.*)

SALLY. How're we gonna' do it?

LORRAINE. Well, ya' light one a' them Blue
> Diamond stick matches and toss it in there
> and run.

SALLY. You mean we're just gonna' run away and
> let it burn?

(LORRAINE *picks up a box of wooden matches and
> approaches the pile of junk.*)

LORRAINE. Nah — maybe we won't run. Maybe we'll
> just stand out there on the front lawn, the
> two of us, and watch it burn for a while.
> Sing a song maybe. Do a little jig. Then
> we'll jus turn and walk away. Just walk.

SALLY. Well, we're not gonna' have any place
> to come back to, Mom.

LORRAINE. Who's comin' back?

These plans are excessive and ill-advised in terms of commonsensical action and consistent psychology, but they are nonetheless plausible in terms of their thematic associations.

In *The Birthday Party*, certain internal actions in the dialogue suggest mysterious crimes and misdemeanors, emotional anxieties, and pointed insults, which imply something beyond the realistic appearance of the play. The mysteries begin with Stanley's emphatic questioning (commanding) of Meg when she informs him that two visitors will soon be arriving at the seaside boarding house. The reason for the choosing extended passages will be made clear below.

MEG. I've got to get things in for the two
> gentlemen.

(*A Pause. STANLEY slowly raises his head. He
> speaks without turning.*)

STANLEY. What two gentlemen?

MEG. I'm expecting visitors.

(*He turns.*)

STANLEY. What?

MEG. You didn't know that, did you?

STANLEY. What are you talking about?

MEG. Two gentlemen asked Petey [her husband]
> if they could come and stay for a couple
> of nights. I'm expecting them.

STANLEY. I don't believe it.

MEG. It's true.

STANLEY. (*moving to her*) You're saying it on purpose.

MEG. Petey told me this morning.

STANLEY. (*grinding out his cigarette*) When was this? When did he see them?

MEG. Last night.

STANLEY. Who are they?

MEG. I don't know.

STANLEY. Didn't he tell you their names?

MEG. No.

STANLEY. (*pacing the room*) Here? They wanted to come here?

MEG. Yes, they did.

STANLEY. Why?

MEG. This house is on the [approved] list.

STANELY. But who are they? I mean, why....?

MEG. You'll see when they come.

STANLEY. (*decisively*) They won't come.

MEG. Why not?

STANLEY. (*quickly*) I tell you they won't come. Why didn't they come last night, if they were coming?

MEG. Perhaps they couldn't find the pace in the dark. It's not easy to find in the dark.

STANLEY. They won't come. Someone's teasing you. Forget all about it. It's a false alarm. A false alarm.

Why is Stanley so curious about the unidentified visitors? His mood changes when he learns about them, and he becomes anxious and overbearing. Later, when Goldberg and McCann meet up with Stanley, an everyday exchange of pleasantries morphs into a series of menacing commands by McCann.

(McCANN *is sitting at the table tearing a sheet of newspaper into five equal strips. It is evening. After a few moments* STANLEY *enters. He stops upon seeing* McCANN, *and watches him. He then walks towards the kitchen, and speaks.*)

STANLEY. Evening.

McCANN. Evening.

> (*Chuckles are heard from outside the back door, which is open.*)

STANLEY. Very warm tonight. (*He turns towards the back door, and back.*) Someone out there?

(*McCANN tears another length of paper. STANLEY goes into the kitchen and pours a glass of water. He drinks it looking through the hatch. He puts the glass down, comes out of the kitchen and walks quickly towards the door, left. McCANN rises and intercepts him.*)

McCANN. I don't think we've met.

STANLEY. No, we haven't.

McCANN. My name's McCann.

STANLEY. Staying here long?

McCANN. Not long. What's your name?

STANLEY. Webber.

McCANN. I'm glad to meet you, sir. (*He offers his hand. STANLEY takes it, and McCANN holds the grip.*) Many happy returns of the day. (*STANLEY withdraws his hand. They face each other.*) Were you going out?

STANLEY. Yes.

McCANN. On your birthday?

STANLEY. Yes. Why not?

McCANN. But they're holding a party for you here tonight.

STANLEY. Oh, really? That's unfortunate.

McCANN. Ah no. It's very nice.

> (*Voices from outside the door.*)

STANLEY. I'm sorry. I'm not in the mood for a party tonight.

McCANN. Oh, is that so? I'm sorry.

SATNLEY. Yes, I'm going out to celebrate quietly, on my own.

McCANN. That's a shame.

Stanley's unexpected curiosity in the first passage and McCann's quiet persistence in the second show how simple questions can become threatening commands in certain nonrealistic circumstances.

Several features give these passages their characteristic "Pinteresque" (vaguely ominous) atmosphere. The first feature is repetition. Under standard conditions, two visitors arriving at a boarding house would not cause any special concern. But here twenty-eight lines are devoted to affirming the simple question of their arrival. Stanley's excessive talk is the clue. An ordinary situation involving the conversation of two guests talking about a birthday party for one of them is likewise extended beyond customary length. The second feature is trivial topics of conversation. The characters talk about simple everyday things and repeat clichés ("That's a shame," "It's very nice," "I don't believe it," etc.) with philosophical earnestness. The third feature is simple physical activities performed with unwarranted seriousness. McCann is methodically "tearing apart" the newspaper, presumably to soothe his nerves, but the implied threat of violence does not escape Stanley's notice. As soon as Stanley spots McCann, he goes into the kitchen for "a glass of water" (to regain his composure). A few moments later, McCann grips Stanley's hand beyond the expected time limit (a threat) for a normal handshake. *The Birthday Party* is about abuse of power, and the commands here are examples of that power in action. Furthermore, the fact that the commands are delivered behind a façade of innocent conversation makes the abuse of power even more worrisome to contemplate. These passages of internal action are object lessons about the way in which routine commands and plans can be transformed for thematic ends.

Summary

External and internal actions are crucial for understanding plot in all its dimensions. External action includes entrances and exits, blocking, use of properties, and special activities that contribute to the basic story as well as the mise-en-scene. Internal action consists of assertions, plans, and commands that comprise the psychological story, which of course influences the mise-en-scene as well. Every assertion, plan, and command contributes to the forward motion of the plot. Accordingly, actors and directors need to "point" these moments (reinforce them theatrically) to make sure the characters express the necessary plot information. Designers who are sensitized to the function of entrances and exits in the plot may find it easier to determine their most expressive form and placement within the scenic space. In other words, once the external and internal actions are understood, there is an obligation to illustrate them as powerfully as possible on stage, through performance or mise-en-scene or both working in harmony or counterpoint. Fortunately, we are aided in this by the emotional dynamics and arrangement of the plot, which will be discussed in the next chapter.

Questions

1. *External Action.* Identify the entrances and exits in the dialogue. How does each one contribute to the development of the plot? Are there any movements or positions of the characters stated in the dialogue? What function do they play in forwarding the plot? Are there any practical uses of properties in the dialogue? Are there any special activities in the dialogue, like dancing, fighting, cooking, or anything else besides regular blocking or use of properties? Do they advance the plot or do they have some other purpose? What does the external action suggest about the mise-en-scene? How could the mise-en-scene contribute to the effectiveness of the external action?

2. *Internal Action.* Locate and highlight all the important assertions about people, places, things, and events that take place in the present action. Are there any detailed plans for doing something? How do they advance the plot? Any commands issued by a power figure? Any official orders given by someone exercising personal, political, or military authority? Are there any directions or instructions in the form of supervision or teaching? Describe how each of these internal actions moves the story ahead. What does the internal action suggest about the mise-en-scene? How could the mise-en-scene contribute to the effectiveness of the internal action?

3. *After Action Analysis.* Search for the play's seed/theme in the external and internal actions. How does the seed/theme influence the external and internal actions? Why did the playwright choose these specific external and internal actions from the whole range of possibilities? How would the play be different with other external and internal actions? In what way does associating the seed with the external and internal actions help the play grow and develop?

CHAPTER 5

Progressions and Structure

There is a continuous growth that is designed to ensure maximum dramatic effect in a play. Actors, directors, and designers concerned with professionalism need to understand and theatricalize this growth and the particular way it shows itself in their creative work. For if all the events give the impression of being equally important, or if their relationship to each other or to the play as a whole is misinterpreted, the result will be artistic disorder and an uninteresting performance. A production that is flat (lacking in emotional dynamics) is a sign that too little attention has been given to the vital issue of continuous, calculated growth.

129

Progressions

Plays are written to create the impression that things are moving, that they are getting somewhere. By this we do not always mean a chronological movement but sometimes a psychological one. Even in a play without much obvious external action, one like *Three Sisters*, perhaps, or *American Buffalo*, the plot is always advancing. The feeling of forward motion comes from the dramatist's method of always making the next event more interesting and significant than the last. We are uncomfortable when our interest in the play declines or if there is a feeling of repetition. We are not even satisfied to maintain the same level of interest. Forward motion is a fundamental necessity of plot.

But a plot does not progress at the same rate throughout the entire play. That would be almost as uninteresting as no forward motion at all. What happens is this: a topic is introduced and developed to an emotional peak, and then a new topic is introduced that begins to grow toward another peak. Emotional intensity may suspend a little after the peak, but interest will not fade because a new topic will emerge almost immediately and begin moving toward another peak. This is how a play moves forward in *progressions*, which rise, crest, and fall away like waves at the seashore.

Progressions are arranged in groups according to their size, called beats, units, scenes, and acts. Literature employs progressions too, called sentences, paragraphs, and chapters. In drama as in literature, progressions help to create interest, maintain suspense, develop the story logically, and bring everything to a satisfactory conclusion. The study of progressions begins by understanding how a play subdivides itself into a chain of storytelling pieces. After this has been learned, it becomes possible to determine the logic connecting them. From this process, the plot and its forward motion will start to become apparent.

Since progressions are also related to character, some readers may be concerned that we do not discuss character objectives and actions at this point in the book. The principal reason is learning ease. In this chapter, we are interested in the basic storytelling function of progressions, and the main task is to identify them by studying the external features of the story. Some of the descriptions we will use are not actions or objectives in the sense employed by Stanislavsky and his followers. Plot may be discussed without always using Stanislavsky's vocabulary for analyzing characters. A reasonable explanation of the external actions of the characters is satisfactory at this point and saves time. Chapter 6 will consider how progressions also have internal features that influence the characters. There is no pressing need to stick with this strategy. Readers who wish to study character objectives and actions before learning about beats and units can jump ahead to Chapter 6 for that information, and then return to this chapter later on.

Beats

The smallest dramatic progression is called a *beat*. In a play, beats work like paragraphs in prose, but without the indentations that are their visible identification marks. However, the purpose of beats is identical to that of a paragraph, namely, to introduce, develop, and conclude a single topic that adds to the progress and growth of the work. Any collection of associated lines can compose a beat as long as they express a single, complete topic (or action, objective, or conflict as we will see in Chapter 6). A typical beat consists of about six lines of dialogue, but many are longer or shorter, and some contain only physical or psychological action with little or no dialogue. The requirements are very flexible. The length, internal arrangement, and purpose will vary according to the playwright's intentions and the work at hand.

Beats are indispensable features of playwriting and as a result can be identified objectively in the script. Ideally, different readers analyzing the same play should arrive at the same pattern of beats. Unfortunately, we are so accustomed to seeing dialogue flow uninterrupted on the page that we may not realize how much the practice of grouping by beats is intended to help our understanding. But the effect of dialogue without beats would be like a passage of prose without paragraphing. It would be almost impossible to make sense of a continuous river of dialogue undivided into beats. Disregarding beats means always having to deal with countless unrelated lines of dialogue. Script analysis identifies beats and forces them into the open where they can be articulated by actors, directors, and designers.

Consider this piece of advice about beats. Even though beats are present in the script, it is easy to become confused when trying to identify them. Beats are there for a reason, but good playwrights are crafty and inventive with their writing. Even though they should ensure that their subject is always clear, in practice many of them disguise what is happening to a certain extent. After all, plays are meant to be art, not science. A special illusive or indefinite quality is often part of the playgoing experience. Readers should make allowances for beats that aim at artistic effects where the playwright's objective is to keep the audience guessing, for the sake of a delayed surprise, for example. Even when authors do not try to conceal their technique, learning about beats can still be frustrating initially. It is natural to experience confusion in the beginning because learning to recognize beats takes practice. Readers should try not to become trapped in endless mental gymnastics, but make an educated guess, then move ahead and test the results at rehearsal. The first part of the rehearsal period is generally used to identify and explain the progressions in the play anyhow.

To understand beats, we will look at the opening moments of David Mamet's play, *American Buffalo*. The setting is morning at Don's resale shop in Chicago. The play begins in the middle of a scene between Bob and Don. Beats are not openly identified in a play, and so we have illustrated them here with a dotted line marked

131

through the script. Marking beats is a useful practice to get into the habit of finding them. As a further point, studying the words of one character at a time can make the topics of conversation and their associated beats easier to recognize.

Beat 1

> DON. So?
>   (*Pause.*)
>   So what, Bob?
>   (*Pause.*)
> BOB. I'm sorry, Donny.
>   (*Pause.*)
> DON. All right.
> BOB. I'm sorry, Donny.
> DON. Yeah.

Beat 2

> BOB. Maybe he's still in there.
> DON. If you think that, Bob, how come you're in here?
> BOB. I came in.
>   (*Pause.*)
> DON. You don't come in, Bob. You don't come in until you do a thing.
> BOB. He didn't come out.
> DON. What do I care, Bob, if he came out or not? You're s'posed to watch the guy, you watch him. Am I wrong?
> BOB. I just went to the back.
> DON. Why?
>   (*Pause.*)
>   Why did you do that?
> BOB. 'Cause he wasn't coming out the front.

This passage consists of two beats. We said before that an important storytelling function of beats is the disclosure of a new topic. In the first beat, the topic is Bob's apology. The beat rises to a small peak when Don says "All right," and it ends when he says "Yeah." It contains five lines.

The second beat begins with Bob's line, "Maybe he's still in there." Bob justifies his behavior and Don shows him where he went wrong. He specifies this in his line "You're s'posed to watch the guy." The beat lasts for nine lines.

To summarize the topics of these two beats:

Beat 1: Don reprimands Bob
Beat 2: Don lectures Bob

There may be other ways to describe these two beats, but at least the reasons for choosing these descriptions should be clear. Notice this important feature, too, almost a law of dramatic writing: in each beat, the characters are restricted to one small topic, and after that topic is finished, there is no longer any need to talk about it. The characters may discuss additional issues related to the original topic, but they will never repeat the topic in the same way or with the same intention. Without this economy, the dialogue we have just studied would have a negligent, unfinished feeling about it.

Units

Beats follow each other without a break but are not lined up end-to-end without connections. They work together with one another in the development of larger progressions called *units*. In other words, while a beat is a group of related lines, a unit is a group of related beats. Compare beats with musical measures (groups of related notes), and units with musical phrases (groups of related measures). What distinguishes beats from units is their relative size and influence in a play. A unit is larger and more influential because it contains several beats.

Some writers maintain the distinction between units and beats, while others use the two terms interchangeably. Can these two points of view be reconciled? To clarify the question, it will be helpful to look at the historical picture. Following the practice of the Russian Formalist critics, Stanislavsky and Nemirovich employed the procedure of subdividing a play into its component pieces. Stanislavsky explained the process in *An Actor's Work* (aka *An Actor Prepares* and *Building a Character*), where, in the Russian edition, he spoke of these subdivisions as *kouski*, meaning bits or pieces. He did not make any further size distinctions except to speak of large pieces (*bolshiye kouski*), medium pieces (*sredniye kouski*), and small pieces (*malyenkiye kouski*). In the first English translation of *An Actor Prepares*, Elizabeth Hapgood designated the larger pieces as units and the smaller ones as bits. According to Hapgood, the term beat first appeared when Russian teachers of Stanislavsky's system in America used the same English terms, but mispronouncing the word bit as "beet" because there is no "ih" sound in Russian speech. American actors heard the word "beat," and of course associated it with its musical counterpart, to which it bears some similarity.

Stanislavsky was interested in the larger progressions (units), and Hapgood's English terms were chosen to represent his viewpoint. He maintained that analysis of beats (smaller bits and pieces) might be necessary now and then to disclose the subtleties within a unit, but he did not believe in dealing with more subdivisions than necessary. There are two lessons here: (1) beats are subdivisions of units, and (2) it is easier to come to terms with a smaller quantity of large progressions than a larger quantity of small progressions. These are historical distinctions, of course, and they should always be adapted to suit one's own needs.

To explain units, we will study the remaining beats that make up the first unit of *American Buffalo*.

Beat 3

> DON. Well, Bob, I'm sorry, but this isn't good enough. If you want to do business...if we got a business deal, it isn't good enough. I want you to remember this.
>
> BOB. I do.
>
> DON. Yeah, now...but later, what?
> (*Pause.*)
> Just one thing, Bob. Action counts.
> (*Pause.*)
> Action walks and bullshit talks.

Beat 4

> BOB. I'm sorry.
> DON. Don't tell me that you're sorry. I'm not mad at you.
> BOB. You're not?
> DON. (*Pause.*) Let's clean up here.

Beat 3 contains three lines. It consists of Don's lesson for Bob and concludes with a "street" maxim, "Action walks and bullshit talks."

SCRIPT ANALYSIS FOR ACTORS, DIRECTORS, AND DESIGNERS

The fourth beat ends the episode with four lines in which Bob acknowledges his mistake. The line after the pause begins the next beat.

The focus of the unit seems to be Bob's mistake and Don's lesson for him. In outline form, the composition of the unit can be described as follows:

Unit 1: Don warns Bob about his mistake
Beat 1: Don reprimands Bob
Beat 2: Don lectures Bob
Beat 3: Don cautions Bob
Beat 4: Don reinforces the lesson for Bob

Readers can draw a further lesson from the fact that the unit studied here ends with a decisive physical action (Don and Bob start to clean up the debris around the poker table), although this may not occur in all cases. In addition, there may be disagreement about the exact wording used in this summary. Some of the beats, for example, may not be considered actions or objectives in the strict sense of Stanislavsky, but merely loose descriptions of the events. But at least this summary should make the basic principle at stake understandable. Each beat has a distinct identity and it also interacts with other beats in the logical development of its enclosing unit, which itself is distinct from other units. And everything connects together under a single topic, in this case Bob's mistake.

Moving on in the script, four units of action elapse before Teach arrives at the junk shop:

Unit 1: Don reproaches Bob for failing to do his job
Unit 2: Don praises Fletcher as an example for Bob to follow
Unit 3: Don corrects Bob's false impression of Fletcher
Unit 4: Don advises Bob against his unhealthy eating habits

The content is identified by the topics of conversation revealing Don in his self-appointed role as Bob's mentor. Like most ordinary garden-variety units in modern realistic plays, each of these consists of about one page of printed dialogue in the sort of acting script published by Samuel French or Dramatists Play Service. The playing time for each is about two minutes. Such a premeditated way of describing units may seem too clinical at first, but there is no need to be concerned about it at this point. There are always exceptions. The length of a unit is based on the practical requirements of storytelling before an audience. Once more, because units have no clear identification marks or fixed length and seldom have a clear indication of any physical action, they are not always obvious in the text. Identifying them can laborious, if not challenging, but the effort is rewarded in the logic and clarity of the performance.

Formal Scenes and French Scenes

A *scene* is a collection of units marked by a change of time or place and its units are related in such a way that they form a tiny play in themselves. This is one reason why scenes are popular choices for acting and directing classes as well as design projects: they are miniature, self-contained plays. A scene is similar to a unit since its action is continuous and its locale is constant, but a scene is composed of several units and is therefore longer and more substantial than a unit. Moreover, the ending of a scene is stronger and more decisive than a unit because the consequences of the action it contains are greater. In fact, the emotional strength of the ending is one of the features that give a scene its characteristic identity. Many plays, whether classic or modern, are divided into scenes in a formal manner (scene 1, scene 2, etc.), as found, for example, in *A Lie of the Mind, Mother Courage, The School for Scandal,* and many others. Greek tragedies do not contain formal scenes; scenes are nonetheless identified in them by alternating choral odes with episodes.

Reading seventeenth-century French plays by Pierre Corneille, Jean Racine, and Moliere, there would seem to be dozens of formal scenes in each act. Of course, this is not entirely true. It was the convention of that time to consider a new scene through any new arrangement of characters on stage. Hence a *French Scene* is created anytime a character enters or exits. Plays no longer designate French Scenes as such, but the term is still used in the same sense. Modern plays "hold the situation" longer to make the most of emotional shadings, and therefore tend to have fewer events than their classic counterparts. This practice results in fewer formal scenes and longer individual scenes, but it does not do away with the need for entrances and exits. And so the term French Scene continues to be used as a convenient reference for any new arrangement of characters on stage. Important, too, for suggestions about the mise-en-scene.

American Buffalo is a good case in point to learn how French Scenes work to advance the plot. Since the entire play takes place in a single locale (Don's junk shop) and since the time in each act is continuous, each act is really one long scene. And yet each act is still divided into identifiable French Scenes by means of its entrances and exits. Formal scenes and French Scenes, like beats and units,

136

coordinate with each other to advance the plot. To understand this, we might look at act 1, which contains seven French Scenes.

The external subject of the act as a whole is the pending theft of the rare coins. In the first French Scene Don grouses at Bob for slipping up on their planning for the theft. Then Teach arrives to complain about an associate's lack of professionalism while Bob goes for coffee. Next, Teach and Don grumble about their meager takings recently. After that, Bob returns and briefs Don about the man with the rare coins and then goes back to the restaurant for some missing items. In the fifth French Scene Teach interrogates Don about the robbery plan, which Teach was unaware of. In the next French Scene Don releases Bob from the robbery plan under pressure from Teach. The seventh French Scene consists of Teach and Don planning the robbery for that evening. Briefly sketched out, the French Scenes in act 1 look like this:

Act 1 French Scenes:

1. Bob and Don (Don warns Bob against making any mistakes on the job)
2. Bob, Don, and Teach (Teach complains about Ruthie, and Bob goes for coffee)
3. Don and Teach (Bob and Teach complain about their meager takings)
4. Don, Teach, and Bob (Bob brings news to Don about their pending robbery)
5. Don and Teach (Teach probes Don about the job and warns against using Bob)
6. Don, Teach, and Bob (Don releases Bob from his part in the planned robbery)
7. Don and Teach (Don and Teach plan the robbery)

Readers should be able to grasp the logic and economy of this act as it develops through these seven French Scenes. Each French Scene has its own special topic, and though they are all related, no single topic is overworked on the way to the imminent robbery of the coins.

Acts

The largest progression in a play is called an *act*, whose action can either be continuous or be divided into formal scenes or French Scenes. An act is characterized further by the dramatic quality of its ending. The first and middle acts of a play will convey a clear expectation of something important to come in the final act. And the final act will use all the dramatic potentials of the theatre to create a strong feeling of closure.

The Roman author Horace (65–68 CE) was the first to identify acts as divisions of a play. His thinking was based on an understanding of the divisions found in classical Greek tragedies (typically five episodes). Owing to his influence, the five-act arrangement became the accepted standard for centuries. Shakespeare did not arrange his plays into acts (that was done later by literary scholars); however, a number of his plays seem to divide themselves into five parts. The practice of writing plays in four or three acts developed during the nineteenth century, and at the present time full-length plays with two or even one act have become widespread. Today, long one-act plays are produced regularly. There are many reasons put forward for this historical trend: this is the end of a stylistic era; we have seen it all, have no time, have more important things to do, and require more detailed understanding, new techniques, or a deeper penetration of character psychology. Whatever the reason and despite the evident historical trend, the impulse to subdivide a play into large, semi-independent masses of action has not gone away. Most playwrights continue to collect scenic progressions into acts or their equivalents.

The next logical step with *American Buffalo* is to assemble the related French Scenes into acts. Since the analytical routine has already been described, let's pass over the in-between explanations and simply collect the French Scenes into their enclosing acts. At this advanced point in analyzing progressions, individual details should be suppressed and situations described in broad terms to see the big picture. Once again, there is no need to be too concerned with verbal nuances, only with describing the progress of the plot.

Act 1: (Morning) Don allows Teach to supervise the robbery

1. Don and Bob (Don warns Bob against making any mistakes on the job)
2. Don, Bob, and Teach (Teach complains about Ruthie and Bob goes for coffee)
3. Don and Teach (Bob and Teach complain about their meager takings)
4. Don, Teach, and Bob (Bob briefs Don with news about their pending robbery)
5. Don and Teach (Teach probes Don about the job and warns against using Bob)

6. Don, Teach, and Bob (Don releases Bob from his part in the planned robbery)
7. Don and Teach (Don and Teach plan the robbery)

Act 2: (11:15 that evening) Don realizes Teach is a fraud

1. Don and Bob (Bob arrives and asks Don to buy a rare coin)
2. Don, Bob, and Teach (Teach arrives and insists that Bob must leave)
3. Don and Teach (Teach instructs Don how they will carry out the robbery)
4. Don, Teach, and Bob (Bob brings news about Fletcher and Teach strikes him fatally)
5. Don and Bob (Bob apologizes and Don looks after him)

After studying the entire play, it becomes clear that the focal point of its meaning is Don. The play may be understood as the story of a person deceived by his own misplaced ideals. Don respected Teach because he believed him to be a criminal expert as well as a mentor and friend, but, to his dismay, Don came to realize that Teach was no more than a brutal, ignorant thug. Unfortunately, the injury and probable death of his troubled protégé, Bob, was the price Don had to pay for this lesson. We observe how each French Scene illustrates one single step in Don's descent from self-confident mentor to grief-stricken friend and chump. It is necessary to point out here how logical and economical are all the progressions, which is a result of very skillful writing. Readers should be able to understand the thinking behind these French Scene descriptions even though they may not agree with them in every case. Acts are coherent groups of related formal scenes or French Scenes. To appreciate their role in storytelling, it is necessary to understand how each scene contributes to its enclosing act, just as each unit contributes to its enclosing scene, and each beat to its enclosing unit.

139

Digressions

A *digression* is something that departs from the main subject. In plays, digressions are actions that deviate (or seem to) from the logical advance of the plot. They have no apparent influence on the main storyline. Digressions can be found in many plays. Nonrealistic plays make extensive use of them (see below), but for the moment we are concerned with their presence in classic and realistic plays. The choral odes in *Oedipus Rex* are a good example. In classic Greek drama, the odes (lyric poems) sung and danced by the chorus are not part of the story itself, but digressions intended to reinforce thematic issues in the play. We accept the odes without question because they are intelligible pauses in the action with their own special logic. *Hamlet* contains digressions, too, by and large in the form of soliloquies, but sometimes in other forms as well. Hamlet's "advice to the players" (3,2) and the graveyard scene (5,1) are digressions in the sense discussed here. We accept them also as plausible breaks in the action because they clearly deal with the thematic issues at stake. Other examples are the engagement party in act one of *The Wild Duck*, Cleante's defense of religious tolerance in *Tartuffe*, and the gossip scene in 1,1 of *The School for Scandal*. The poetic history lessons and Wining Boy's conversation with the ghosts of the yellow dog at the railway station are digressions in *The Piano Lesson*. All these moments are considered digressions because they deviate from the progress of the plot, but they are plausible in spite of this, and we tend to accept them on that basis.

Formalist analysis is based on the premise that plays are unified works of art. That what unifies them is their main idea, which controls and directs everything toward itself. And that by this means everything in a play serves this idea. What makes the digressions in classic and realistic plays plausible is the ability of the playwright to "smooth them out" by carefully associating them with the main idea. Actors and designers follow through with an equivalent impulse in performance and mise-en-scene. In other words, digressions are fine-tuned to highlight their connection with the main idea. Correspondence with the main idea is so important in realistic and classic plays that Stanislavsky devoted part of a chapter to the issue in *An Actor's Work*. He warns there against the "dangerous phenomenon" of interrupting the main idea with "minor tasks" (digressions) that could "distort" the main idea of the play. "When you force [digressions] or some other extraneous goal into a play," he says, "it's like a canker on a beautiful body and often deforms it beyond recognition." The play becomes "crippled." Stanislavsky proposes that such digressions should be "grafted" onto the main idea so that they "cease to exist independently" and re-emerge in a way that makes the main idea stronger (pp. 316–318).

The message here is that to produce a play, in particular a realistic or classic play, actors, directors, and designers should not rest until they have found the main idea for everything, including any supposed digressions from the plot. Not just a "concept" to attach to a production, but a main idea to which every zigzag in the action, every implication, and every digression is attached. And having found this main idea, all the bits and pieces and digressions need to relate to it so unmistakably that it really is a main idea instead of a mere notion from which digressions and other features hang loosely with no support from within the play itself. Even then, of course, finding the main idea and subordinating to it everything including the digressions is no assurance of a successful production. But it does eliminate lots of possible mistakes. Chapter 7 will discuss the main idea and its associated features in more detail.

Structure

The arrangement of the parts of the plot and their relationship to each other and to the whole play is called its *structure*. Just as literary critics sometimes speak of the gestalt, or unified pattern, of the whole work, we can speak of the beats, units, scenes, and acts comprising the harmonious structure of a play. Regardless of their size or arrangement, each of these structural parts continues to perform its assigned function in the play as a whole. The main difference in the structure from one play to the next is in the arrangement and relative emphasis devoted to each of its parts.

Some drama textbooks suggest that the structure of the plot consists of rising action, climax, and falling action. These terms come from the German dramatist and novelist Gustav Freytag (1816–1895), who represented the parts of a play as a pyramid, the so-called Freytag Pyramid (Freytag, 114). His inspiration was probably Horace, but in any case, according to Freytag's way of thinking, plays consist of five distinct parts separated by three crises in the following way:

1. Introduction (exposition)
   a. First crisis (inciting action)
2. Rising action
3. Climax (turning point)
   a. Second crisis
4. Falling action (return)
   a. Third crisis
5. Catastrophe (denouement or resolution)

Each part may consist of several scenes or a single scene, but the climax, according to Freytag's arrangement, is a single big scene somewhere in the middle of the play. Freytag points out that Shakespeare often used this type of pyramidal structure. In *Hamlet*, for example, he arranged what Freytag argues is the climax in the middle of a five-part structure. The first half of the play (up to this climax) shows Hamlet searching for conclusive proof of Claudius' guilt. Then, after the mousetrap scene, Hamlet sets in motion the second half of the play, which leads to the deaths of Ophelia, Polonius, Rosencrantz and Guildenstern, Gertrude, Laertes, Claudius, and that of Hamlet himself.

Freytag described many accurate and useful playwriting fundamentals, but he was not always clear about his terms and definitions, such as the distinction between climax and crisis, or catastrophe and denouement or resolution. Consequently, succeeding generations have adjusted his terms in various ways to suit their needs. Despite the standing of Freytag's ideas, however, there is no law of playwriting that requires such a balanced methodical arrangement. A more practical approach would be to consider the typical dramatic structure not as a symmetrical pyramid but rather as a line ascending upward at an angle, interrupted by one or more less important events in each act, and terminating with the most important event, followed by a feeling of closure. *Oedipus Rex, Tartuffe, Death of a Salesman, A Raisin in the Sun*, and *The Piano Lesson* are examples of plays with such uneven rising structures. Their major climaxes appear at or near the end of the final act. Certain nonrealistic plays, like *Machinal, Happy Days*, and perhaps *Top Girls*, employ a structure that is free of traditional climaxes, but more about this later. The structure of most standard plays reveals several high-tension climaxes whose placement varies from one work to another.

Point of Attack

Now that we have considered the general nature of structure, we will explore its individual parts. Their features and arrangement help to determine the relative amount of restriction or freedom in the development of the story.

The first part of the structure to consider is the *point of attack*, the moment when the play begins in relation to the timeline of the background story at one end and the end of the play at the other. When the onstage action begins late in the background story and close to the final climax, the play is said to have a *late point of attack*. *The Wild Duck* has such an arrangement. The onstage action shows the last few days of a story that began more than nineteen years before. A play with a late point of attack like *The Wild Duck* compresses a great deal of background story and onstage action into a brief dramatic time frame. Because of this compression, plot freedom — the range and variety of actions available to the playwright — is restricted because of the requirement to narrate so much background story. *The Wild Duck* is a modern realistic play, but the use of a late point of attack is not restricted to the modern era or to the style of realism. *Oedipus Rex, Tartuffe,* and *The School for Scandal* also demonstrate late points of attack. What is the relative importance of background story in each?

Conversely, a play shows an *early point of attack* when there is little background story and a long stretch of dramatic time between the opening curtain and the final climax. The background story for *Hamlet* begins a few weeks before the start of the play, while the onstage action covers a period of several months. Once again, the treatment of the point of attack is independent of the play's historical period or style. *Machinal, Mother Courage,* and *Angels in America* also have early points of attack. Because of the longer onstage dramatic time involved, the plot is freer (the range of doable actions is greater) and the play projects a sensation of being more voluminous. There is less moment-to-moment tension and a looser arrangement of parts than is found in plays with a late point of attack. The treatment of the point of attack is characteristic of the temperaments of individual playwrights as well as writing fashions in vogue when they wrote.

143

Primary Event

The *primary event* is the most important incident in the background story, one that so energizes the characters that it produces in them the conditions necessary for the play to take place. And since the primary event is part of the background story, it is therefore narrated and not performed. Here are some examples of primary events from the study plays:

Oedipus Rex (a deadly plague descended on Thebes)
Hamlet (Claudius murdered King Hamlet)
The Wild Duck (Gregers' father became engaged to Mrs. Sorby)
Three Sisters (General Prozorov, the father of the three sisters, died)
Machinal (Mr. Jones decided to propose to the Young Woman)
Death of a Salesman (Biff was fired from his job for stealing)
The Birthday Party (Stanley was prevented from playing a concert)
American Buffalo (a stranger paid Don ninety dollars for a five-cent coin)
A Lie of the Mind (Jake murdered his drunken father)
Rosencrantz and Guildenstern are Dead (the title characters were summoned by a messenger from the King)

Notice the prominence of life-changing events. Primary events are always powerful dramatic situations in themselves, but they are not always as obvious as one might think. For example, think about the engagement of Gregers' father in *The Wild Duck* or Stanley's canceled piano concert in *The Birthday Party*. Primary events are crucial for generating the initial state of tension with which every play should begin. They can also provide opportunities for rehearsal improvisations to implant the conditions of the play forcefully in the imaginations of the performers.

Inciting Action

The *inciting action* is the single event in the play that sparks the main action, the main conflict. It occurs at that point in the play when something happens to the leading character that sets that main conflict in motion. The inciting action then becomes the chief driving force, the "big bang," for all the succeeding action of the play. In *Hamlet*, the inciting action occurs in the fifth scene when the Ghost tells Hamlet about the murder and challenges him to take revenge. The inciting action in *Oedipus Rex* occurs in the Prologue when Creon informs Oedipus of the Oracle's warning. In *The School for Scandal* it happens in 1,2 when Sir Oliver Surface returns to London. The inciting action of *The Piano Lesson* occurs at the moment when Boy Willie first appears. In *American Buffalo*, it is when Teach arrives. The inciting action may take on different forms, but it always appears somewhere near the beginning of the play for the simple reason that it initiates the main conflict. It may be an incident, an idea, a wish, a feeling, or a plan in someone's mind. In any case, the main conflict can begin only after the inciting action takes place. It forms the transition between the introductory material and the body of the play, and its placement in the overall structure helps to shape the emotional dynamics of the play.

Conflicts

On the stage as in real life, all planned human behavior encounters oppostion as it tries to reach a goal. Characters meet up with those who have opposing wishes, or they run into opposing events, or they may even question their own goals. The dictionary defines *conflict* as incompatibility or interference, as of one idea, desire, event, or activity with another. And in drama, conflicts are the counter-movements in the plot created by these opposing motives and events. The conflicts are what produce the increasing levels of tension in the play.

The plot thickens and becomes more complex, and the internal tensions begin to surface. Different parts of the play begin to connect, and it feels as if the play is moving ahead.

Conflicts arise from the presence of two elements: (1) obstacles and (2) complications. An *obstacle* is something that obstructs or hinders the progress of a character's goal. Obstacles motivate characters and advance the story, but it makes little difference what they are as such. They can be nonspecific or left open to interpretation, such as the city of Moscow (*Three Sisters*), a character's hands (*Machinal*), an executive promotion (*Top Girls*), or a hunting accident (*Fefu and Her Friends*). Very frequently obstacles are physical objects, such as insurance money (*A Raison in the Sun*), an old coin (*American Buffalo*), a wild duck (*The Wild Duck*), or a piano (*The Piano Lesson*). The most important physical obstacle in a film is humorously called a McGuffin, as, for instance, the famous Maltese falcon in the film of the same name. In short, anything that serves the purpose will do. The point is that whatever the obstacle may be, and even though it does not have any inherent effect on the story, its vital importance is accepted without question by the characters. Obstacles in turn create *complications*, which are unexpected changes in existing plans, methods, or attitudes — things that make a situation more difficult to deal with. Without obstacles and complications there might be a potential for conflict, but there would be no chance for that conflict actually to occur.

145

To explain we will review the conflicts found in 1,1 of *A Raisin in the Sun*. The action takes place in the living room of the Youngers' small apartment on Chicago's South Side, a low-income, African-American neighborhood. It is Friday morning and, as everyone knows, on Friday paychecks are distributed. On stage are Walter Younger, Jr., his wife and son, and his mother and sister. Below each numbered conflict are listed its related obstacle and complication.

1. Conflict: Ruth objects to Walter's scheme to buy a liquor store with his father's life insurance money
    a. Obstacle: insurance money
    b. Complication: Walter has to persuade his wife to let him have the insurance money
2. Conflict: Ruth disapproves of Walter's friends
    a. Obstacle: Walter's friends
    b. Complication: Walter has to persuade his wife that his friends are responsible people

3. Conflict: Ruth refuses to give Travis an extra fifty cents for school
   a. Obstacle: fifty cents (money)
   b. Complication: Walter has to deal with being financially embarrassed before his son
4. Conflict: Ruth objects to Walter's endless talk about becoming a big success
   a. Obstacle: employment
   b. Complication: Walter has to deal with Ruth's lack of faith in him
5. Conflict: Walter objects to Beneatha's (costly) ambition to become a doctor
   a. Obstacle: dreams (aspirations)
   b. Complication: Walter has to persuade Beneatha that her ambition is foolish
6. Conflict: Mama fears that her plans for the insurance money could be selfish
   a. Obstacle: insurance money
   b. Complication: Ruth has to persuade Mama to keep the insurance money for herself
7. Conflict: Mama objects to Beneatha's irreligious remarks
   a. Obstacle: faith in God
   b. Complication: Mama has to keep Beneatha's liberal opinions in line

Poverty, parental responsibility, disreputable friends, unemployment, dreams deferred, and changing moral standards — each of the family's conflicts are spelled out. The opening scene furnishes much of the information needed for actors, directors, and designers to begin to understand the characters, situation, background story, and environment for what follows. It also introduces the main conflict, which centers on Walter's scheme to buy a liquor store with the life insurance money. This scene is a model of straightforward realistic craftsmanship, and the treatment of its conflicts, coupled with their obstacles and complications will reward patient analysis.

Climaxes

A *climax* is a prominent peak of emotional intensity that produces a significant change in the characters. As a rule, the highest peak of emotional intensity in the play is considered the most important or *main climax*. It is surrounded on either side by connecting scenes containing *minor climaxes* and governs all the other climaxes in the play. The main climax can appear at an assortment of distances from the end of the play, but always somewhere near the end for obvious reasons. In *A Raisin in the Sun* the main climax appears in the final scene with Walter, Mr. Lindner, and the family. The rest of the play occupies two and a half pages of dialogue after that. In *Oedipus Rex* the main climax occurs near the end of episode 4, and the last two scenes are devoted to the catastrophe (scene of physical violence) and the resolution. *The Wild Duck* has its main climax very near the end of the play, just after Hedvig kills herself. In *American Buffalo*, the main climax occurs near the very end of the play, when Don realizes that Teach is a fraud and says to him, "You have lamed this up real good." Berniece sitting down to play the piano to exorcise Sutter's ghost is the main climax of *The Piano Lesson*. In these examples, and many others readers can point to, the main climaxes are the most dramatic and memorable moments in the play.

A single climax may work all right for scholars or for reading purposes, but for actors, directors, and designers the idea of one big, solitary climax in the manner of Freytag is much too emotionally static. In the theatre, it is better to consider that every play exhibits three major climaxes that mark the beginning, middle, and end of the action, plus various minor climaxes supporting them. This way of thinking emphasizes the forward movement of the action, which is a distinguishing feature of a good professional-level performance. In *Hamlet*, for example, the beginning, the first major climax, occurs when the Ghost reveals the circumstances of his murder to Hamlet. The middle, or second major climax, occurs at the mousetrap scene in the middle of the play. With its tense, complicated interplay among Hamlet and Claudius, the Players, and the members of the court, it is one of the most effective scenes in all of drama. The end of the play, or third major climax, occurs in (5,3), with Hamlet's death and the arrival of Fortinbras. *The School for Scandal* contains five acts, but it also has three major climaxes. The first major climax occurs in 1,1, when Lady Sneerwell sets her plan in motion to break up the attachment between Charles Surface and Maria. The second major climax is the famous "screen scene" in 5,2, which many consider a model of comedy writing. The third major climax occurs in the final scene of the play when Joseph Surface is exposed as a hypocrite. In *Three Sisters*, there are three major climaxes for each of the three sisters. Which sister is the leading character and hence the main carrier of the play's meaning?

In addition to its three major climaxes, a play also contains an assortment of *minor climaxes* that occur every time an appreciable change takes place in the course of events. Minor climaxes show characters making or avoiding hard decisions about vital things in their lives, though not such life-changing decisions as found at the major climaxes. Let's examine the following moment where a character changes in this manner. There are seven conflicts in the first scene of A Raisin in the Sun, as we said earlier, but just one is significant enough to be considered a minor climax. It occurs when Beneatha reminds Walter that the insurance money belongs to Mama and that nothing he can say or do will ever tempt her to invest it in such a dubious enterprise as a liquor store. At this sharp reminder, Walter storms out of the apartment. It is a minor climax because if Walter had stayed there, he would have been obliged to confront his mother about his plans for the life insurance money, and the remainder of the play would have been different, to say the least. As it is, Walter exits angrily, and the critical issue of what will happen to the life insurance money remains unresolved. This minor climax shows Walter failing to deal with a vital issue in his life: his misguided ambition. Notice, too, that this minor climax is marked by a decisive physical action (slamming the door) that accentuates its climactic nature.

148

Recognition, Reversal, and Catastrophe

Before we move on to the remaining elements of dramatic structure, it will be helpful to pause and examine certain characteristics of climaxes in a little more detail. The word climax is a composite term used to describe two distinct processes that occur at the same time in performance: recognition and reversal. *Recognition*, according to Aristotle, is a change from ignorance to knowledge on the part of a character. At the third major climax (main climax) of A Raisin in the Sun, for example, Walter Younger recognizes that he has earned his family's shame and contempt, instead of their respect as he had wished. He has failed as a husband, father, and human being. The most effective kind of recognition is accompanied by a *reversal*, or drastic change of fortune. In Walter Younger's case the reversal is from bad fortune (humiliation) to good (respect). After great inner turmoil, he achieves self-respect and the respect of his family by letting go of his misguided dream of instant financial success. In view of his new status in the family, the loss of the insurance money (main obstacle) is no longer an important issue for him or them.

In *Death of a Salesman*, the recognition that Willy Loman experiences is similar in spirit to that of Walter Younger, but his reversal of fortune is in the opposite direction. Willy discovers that he has been a failure as a father as well, but instead of coming to terms with this, as Walter does, he decides to sacrifice his life so that Biff can obtain the life insurance money. Willy's fortune changes from good (life) to bad (death), although he believes otherwise. In classical tragedies, changes from bad fortune to good are accompanied by a *catastrophe*, or event of physical violence. In fact, the catastrophe is perhaps the single most distinguishing feature of classical tragedy. Willy's suicide is a catastrophe in this formal sense, as are Oedipus' self-mutilation and Hamlet's death. And these three plays are also considered tragedies in the classical sense. Although Walter Younger undergoes a terrible humiliation and loses the insurance money, there is no formal catastrophe in *A Raisin in the Sun*. How might the ending of this play be changed for it to be considered a tragedy? Whatever the case may be, the intense emotions that distinguish the third major climax are the result of feelings generated by a combination of recognition and reversal, either with or without a catastrophe. Incidentally, in both modern plays treated above, we are again reminded of getting or losing money as a widespread factor in the given circumstances.

149

Simple and Complex Plots

Aristotle described plots with traditional climaxes (those containing recognitions and reversals) as *complex*. He believed that complex plots were innately dramatic and therefore the most effective plots in the theatre. He described plots without climaxes (those without recognitions and reversals) as *simple*. Note that the terms simple and complex have no connection here with the intricacy of a play's story, which is a different issue. Most plays include recognitions and reversals, and for this reason their plots are considered complex in the formal sense. Aristotle believed that simple plots were not very dramatic, nevertheless many playwrights, even classical Greek playwrights, have made effective use of them. The plots of *Mother Courage*, *Happy Days*, *Three Sisters*, and *Rosencrantz and Guildenstern are Dead*, for example, are formally simple because they do not contain recognitions or reversals in their leading characters, yet no one would accuse these plays of being undramatic. Brecht, Beckett, Chekhov, and Kushner chose to employ other theatrical values in their plays instead of making use of the emotional excitement that accompanies recognitions and reversals. Brecht employed narration, poetry, music, and sharp social commentary. Beckett used pantomime, detailed character drawing, unusual moods, and sharp intellectual content. Chekhov used detailed character description, lyrical moods, contradictory actions, and multiple points of dramatic focus. Kushner's plays are noted for their wit, inventiveness, fantasy, fusions of topicality and history, and sharp social commentary. Undoubtedly, plays with complex plots have no built-in advantage over those with simple plots. In the hands of a skilled playwright either type can be effective. The main difference lies in the presence or absence of recognition and reversal in the leading character.

Resolution

The *resolution* comprises all the events following the main climax. Sometimes this feature is variously referred to as the denouement, outcome, falling action, or unraveling. The resolution is characterized by a gradual quieting of the tension and the emergence of a new relationship between opposing forces. The resolution in *Oedipus Rex* begins after the Messenger recounts the double catastrophe of Jocasta's suicide and Oedipus' self-mutilation. It consists of Oedipus' public expression of guilt and his banishment by Creon. The resolution in *Hamlet* is marked by the arrival of Fortinbras and the ceremonial removal of Hamlet's body from the stage. The resolution in *Tartuffe* is very brief, consisting of Tartuffe's arrest and the restoration of Orgon's possessions. The resolution in *A Lie of the Mind* consists of the folding of the flag and a fleeting moment of affection between Baylor and Meg. The final scene in *Death of a Salesman*, called the "Requiem" in the play, is its resolution. It also acts as a kind of epilogue (formal concluding scene) to the play. The resolution in *American Buffalo* consists of Don reproaching Teach and apologizing to Bob. The resolution in *Angels in America* includes everything that happens after Prior receives the blessing of the Angel, leading to the epilogue at Bethesda Fountain in Central Park. Note that a resolution is only an apparent re-balancing of the conflicting forces in a play. It is a useful object lesson to speculate what will happen to the characters after their play is finished.

Progressions and Structure in Nonrealistic Plays

Progressions

Nonrealistic plays are exactly like their realistic or classic siblings in the need to advance the dramatic action from one point to the next. They employ acts, scenes, French Scenes, units, and beats in the same way and with the same purpose. The difference lies not in

150

understanding the need to make use of progressions, but in identifying them and their interrelations. *Rosencrantz and Guildenstern are
Dead* by Tom Stoppard is a useful case in point. It has been variously described as "Samuel Beckett on speed," "an intellectual ten-
nis game," "regret for our insignificance in the universal void," and
"bewildering." It is a play where "the heroes drift helplessly toward
their inevitable demise" and in which "any choice can seem meaningless and therefore not worth making." Nonetheless, as the Player
reminds Guildenstern in act 2, "There's a design at work in all art —
surely you know that? Events must play themselves out to an aesthetic, moral and logical conclusion." In other words, logic is at
work, and it is understandable, but readers must have faith that it is
there in the first place.

Beats

We will begin with the treatment of beats. As the play opens,
Rosencrantz and Guildenstern are in the middle of a game of coin
toss. The prolonged run of heads is theoretically possible but highly
improbable, of course, and although Guildenstern is aware of the
strangeness of it, Rosencrantz shows no special feeling of surprise.

```
Beat 1

    ROS. Heads
        (He picks it up and puts it in his
        bag. The process is repeated.)
        Heads.
        (Again.)
        Heads.
        (Again.)
        Heads.
        (Again.)
        Heads.
    GUIL. (flipping a coin). There is an art to
        the building up of suspense.
    ROS. Heads.
    GUIL. (flipping another). Though it can be
        done by luck alone.
    ROS. Heads.
    GUIL. If that's the word I'm after.
    ROS. (raises his head at GUIL). Seventy-six
        — love.
```

> (*GUIL gets up but has nowhere to go. He spins another coin over his shoulder without looking at it, his attention being directed at his environment or lack of it.*)
> Heads.

GUIL. A weaker man might be moved to re-examine his faith, if in nothing else at least in the law of probability. (*He slips a coin over his shoulder as he goes to look upstage.*)

ROS. Heads.

> (*GUIL, examining the confines of the stage, flips over two more coins as he does so, one by one of course. ROS announces each of them as "heads."*)

GUIL. (*musing*). The law of probability, it has been oddly asserted, is something to do with the proposition that six monkeys (*he has surprised himself*)... if six monkeys were...

ROS. Game?

GUIL. Were they?

ROS. Are you?

GUIL. (*understanding*). Game. (*Flips a coin.*) The law of averages, if I have got this right, means that if six monkeys were thrown up in the air for long enough they would land on their tails about as often as they would land on their —

ROS. Heads. (*He picks up the coin.*)

GUIL. Which even at first glance does not strike one as a particularly rewarding speculation, in either sense, even without the monkeys. I mean you wouldn't bet on it. I mean I wouldn't, but you would...(*As he flips a coin.*)

```
ROS. Heads. (He looks up at GUIL — embar-
     rassed laugh.) Getting a bit of a
     bore, isn't it?
GUIL. (coldly). A bore?
ROS. Well...
GUIL. What about the suspense?
ROS. (innocently). What suspense?
          (Small pause.)
```

Beat 3

```
GUIL. It must be the law of diminishing
      returns....I feel the spell about to
      be broken.
      (Energizing himself somewhat. He takes
      out a coin. He takes out a coin, spins
      it high, catches it, turns it over on
      to the back of his other hand, stud-
      ies the coin — and tosses it to ROS.
      His energy deflates and he sits.)
      Well it was an even chance...if my
      calculations are correct.
```

153

These three beats constitute the first unit of the play in the standard way. What is their content? Beat one establishes the prolonged
run of seventy-six heads. It starts with the first line, reaches a small
peak when Rosencrantz says, "Seventy-six — love" and concludes
when Guildenstern gets up and walks away out of frustration. Beat
two begins when Guildenstern seeks to explain the situation by
means of the "law of probability" applied to "six falling monkeys."
Except that any thought of probability collapses when the run of
heads continues as before. In the third beat Guildenstern reaches for
another explanation, the "law of diminishing returns," and readies
himself for a promising outcome. When the run continues unbroken, "[h]is energy deflates and he sits," consoling himself with the
belief that "it was an even chance … if my calculations are correct."
What is the logic of this arrangement? (1) Guildenstern hopes for an
end to the run of heads, (2) Guildenstern places his hope in the law
of probability, and (3) Guildenstern is upset when the run continues
uninterrupted. This example shows that Stoppard makes use of beats
in the standard manner.

Units

Now let's shift perspective to the treatment of units. Four units transpire before offstage music points to the arrival of the Tragedians. The content of the units can be described in this way:

Unit 1: Guildenstern worries about the impossible run of heads
Unit 2: Guildenstern reproaches Rosencrantz for being unconcerned
Unit 3: Guildenstern examines their situation logically
Unit 4: Guildenstern reviews how they were sent for in the first place

What is the content of these units and how are they interrelated? First, the run of heads is impossible, yet there it is. (After all, anything is possible in a play, above all a nonrealistic play, and of course the characters do not realize they are objects of Stoppard's imagination.) Guildenstern is worried about the theoretical implications of the run of heads, while Rosencrantz is undisturbed. Guildenstern becomes more frustrated and seeks various other explanations. In his determination to find a logical explanation for their illogical situation, Guildenstern returns to the law of probabilities. He hypothesizes that the run of heads is "a spectacular vindication of the principle that each individual coin spun alone is as likely to come down heads as tails and therefore should cause no surprise each individual time it does." But this elaborate and over-subtle reasoning of his leaves him even more worried and confused than before. He tries to recover his bearings by going back over what has happened to them up to this time, but this proves to be worthless as well:

> GUILDENSTERN. [...]An awakening, a man standing on his saddle to bang on the shutters, our names shouted in a certain dawn, a message, a summons...A new record for heads and tails. We have not been...picked out... simply to be abandoned...set loose to find our own way. *We are entitled to some direction....* I would have thought.

Notice how logically the playwright has laid out the basic conflict of the play in these four units. On one hand is the amusing improbability of the situation, to which Rosencrantz adapts himself in a friendly way, and on the other hand is Guildenstern's obsession with finding a logical explanation in spite of all evidence to the contrary.

154

Later in the act the Player and his Tragedians add another attitude toward the play's reality.

French Scenes

Since the action is continuous in each act and occurs in a single, although unlocalized, setting, this play contains no formal scenes. Exits and entrances divide the action into French Scenes, which form the next range of progressions to study. Close reading reveals that their content is as concrete and their interrelations are as logical as the beats and units they contain. Here is the sequence of French Scenes in act one. The spotlight is on Guildenstern throughout the play, which is why the descriptions are formulated through his character.

Act 1 French Scenes:

1. Guildenstern looks for meaningful directions (Rosencrantz, Guildenstern)
2. Guildenstern rejects the Player's frivolous outlook (Rosencrantz, Guildenstern, Tragedians)
3. Although they are meaningless to him, Guildenstern nevertheless accepts the King's directions (Rosencrantz, Guildenstern, Ophelia, Claudius, Gertrude, Polonius)
4. Guildenstern rehearses the meaningless directions (Rosencrantz, Guildenstern)
5. Guildenstern begins to carry out the meaningless directions (Rosencrantz, Guildenstern, Hamlet)

Describing the French Scenes in this concise way reveals the framework of the action. The central issue is shown to be the meaningless (to them) instructions given to Rosencrantz and Guildenstern, and their contrasting outlooks toward those instructions. Formulating short and snappy descriptions like this is extra important in nonrealistic plays. It helps to place all the apparent wanderings and digressions in proper perspective and directs attention to the essential content and logic of the action.

Acts

Acts are the next group of progressions to consider and in Stoppard's nonrealistic play they illustrate the same careful attention to logic as beats, units, and French Scenes.

Act 1: Guildenstern obtains meaningless directions.
Act 2: Guildenstern carries out the meaningless directions.
Act 3: Guildenstern refuses to admit the directions were meaningless.

In this manner it can be seen that although *Rosencrantz and Guildenstern are Dead* is without doubt a play about the idea of meaninglessness, its progressions are scrupulously logical and crowded with real meaning. Again, Stoppard makes use of progressions in a standard manner.

Digressions

Earlier we stated that digressions are deviations from the plot, and that they need to be smoothed out in performance to make them correspond with the main idea. For nonrealistic plays, this statement is both true and not true. It is true in the sense that digressions need to correspond with the main idea, but it is not true that they need to be smoothed out to avoid calling attention to themselves. For what may be seen in standard plays as an interruption of the narrative becomes in nonrealistic plays an integral part of nonrealistic style itself. And while digressions may appear to depart from the main idea, they actually reinforce the main idea through scrupulous fidelity to it. The rules of plausible human behavior are disregarded in favor of fidelity to the main idea and its many possible variations. Seen from this point of view, digressions in nonrealistic plays are open representations of theme as opposed to that of character or plot. The analytical task in nonrealistic plays is to understand the thematic issues that lie behind the digressions, and then to find out if the issues are treated with approval, detachment, irony, ridicule, or whatever point of view.

In a nonrealistic play such as *Machinal*, the task is fairly easy because the main idea of the play is not difficult to understand. It is in the title: machinal literally means action without thinking, and the dehumanizing impulse of modern urban life (or attempts to escape from it) lies behind everything in the play. When this impulse bursts into elaborate, nonrealistic life, we may feel that such moments are digressions from the story, but actually they are volcanic eruptions directly from the main idea (inner life) of the play, unchecked by any notions of realistic plausibility. Some examples of such thematic eruptions in *Machinal* include the Mother's fixation on emptying the garbage, and the voices of the Boy and Girl calling for each other outside the Young Woman's apartment (scene 2); the Nurse's speech to the Young Woman about the joys of motherhood, and the Young Woman's nightmare monologue following the birth of her child (scene 4); the unfeeling, mechanical love relations among the characters in the bar, and the contrasting sympathetic relationship of the Young Woman and First Man later in the same episode (scene 5); the tune *Cielito*

156

Lindo (Little Heaven) played by the organ grinder and its emotional influence on the Young Woman, also the choreographed nature of her dressing and undressing (scene 6); and the pieties of the Priest and the indifferent comments of the Reporters as the Young Woman goes to the death chamber (scene 9). These moments might be considered as digressions, or at least detours, in a realistic or classic play, but in *Machinal* they serve as open windows into its deep meaning.

In *Fefu and Her Friends* (Fefu is the pet name for Stephanie), the task of finding the main idea supporting the digressions is not as easy because the play's style is both subtler and more complicated. In this respect, *Fefu and Her Friends* is a model of sophisticated non-realistic playwriting in a contemporary mode. The basic story is simple: eight women meet to rehearse an education project. Essentially, it is a pre-Freudian consciousness-raising group of the kind popularized in the 1960s by radical feminists. The main idea of the play is found in one of Fefu's statements. The women have been talking about the relationship between the sexes, and Fefu expresses her unconventional thinking about it:

FEFU. (*She stands there and speaks* [to CHRISTINA and CINDY] *reflectively.*) I still like men better than women. — I envy them. I like being a man. Thinking like a man. Feeling like a man. — They are well together. Women are not. Look at them [referring to the men in the backyard]. They are checking the new grass mower.... Out in the fresh air and the sun, while we sit here in the dark.... Men have natural strength. Women have to find their strength, and when they do find it, it comes forth with bitterness and it's erratic.... Women are restless with each other. They are like live wires...either chattering to keep themselves from making contact, or else, if they don't chatter, they avert their eyes ... like Orpheus... as if a god once said "and if they shall recognize each other, the world will be blown apart." They are always eager for the men to arrive. When they do, they can put themselves at rest, tranquilized and

in a mild stupor. With the men they feel
safe. The danger is gone. That's the closest they can be to feeling wholesome. Men
are muscle that covers the raw nerve. They
are the insulators. The danger is gone, but
the price is the mind and the spirit....
High price. — I've never understood it.
Why? — What is feared? — Hmm. Well... — Do
you know? Perhaps the heavens would fall.

Fefu has clearly been struggling with this problem for a long time. Her words embody it in a nutshell: the women are inside sitting in the dark, while the men are outside working in the sunshine and fresh air. The women are unable to come to terms with a reality that is different from their idealistic hopes and dreams. The men are happy fixing broken things (changing their reality) to make them work or acquiring new things that work better. Among the women, Fefu alone is struggling to come to terms with the world as it really is.

What are some of the curiosities, the digressions from the rehearsal meeting that forms the basic plot?

- Fefu shoots at her husband using a shotgun loaded with blanks.
- Christina can't decide if she wants bourbon and soda or ice with a drop of bourbon.
- Fefu does not call a plumber, but fixes the broken toilet herself.
- Christina is a "scaredy cat," who overreacts at every little hint of trouble.
- Julia used to hunt, but doesn't do so anymore ever since a hunter shot and killed a deer near her. She loves animals so much that even though the hunter's bullet never touched her, nevertheless she suffered a sympathetic spinal injury and has never recovered. Now she believes that men are persecuting her, but that she cannot talk about it or else they will torture her. She is confined to a wheelchair.
- Paula says to Fefu, "I liked your talk at Flossie Crit." Flossie Crit is college slang for feminist criticism. Fefu says half-jokingly that the subject of her lecture was "aviation," but Paula reminds them that the subject actually was the historical female anarchist Voltairine de Cleyre.
- Emma recites Shakespeare's complete sonnet 14, "Not from the stars do I my judgment pluck."

- In the four scenes comprising part two, the women participate in oddly one-sided conversations about their inability to
  come to terms with their broken dreams.
- Julia's hallucination in the bedroom in which she is tormented for disrespecting men.
- Emma's speech from Emma Sheridan Frye's book, *The Science
  of Educational Dramatics*. Its subject is the influence of environment on children's education.
- The childish water fight among educated, adult women.
- At the end of the play, Fefu shoots and kills a rabbit on the
  lawn outside, an action that seems to kill Julia inside the
  house at the same time.

These are digressions because they deviate from the narrative line of
the rehearsal meeting, which was the original purpose for the women
coming together. How do the digressions reinforce the main idea
of the play? In one way or another, they all represent the characters'
inability to deal with practical reality (whether from unwillingness,
ignorance, indifference, or outright fear), or else they represent Fefu's
restless attempts to come to terms with reality as it is, not as she would
like it to be. It is also important to notice that some digressions treat
the main idea approvingly, some ironically, some humorously, etc.

In nonrealistic plays such as this excellent example, the digressions are intended as entertaining distortions of various thematic
issues; not as realistic episodes in themselves, but as deliberate exag-
gerations, nightmares, daydreams, and comic or sentimental parodies of the main idea. Sometimes digressions are motivated by the
characters in a plausible manner. More often they are motivated by
theme, in which case the inner life of the play can take on a curious life of its own. In any case, digressions in nonrealistic plays are
intended to call attention to themselves frankly as digressions —
pauses for reflection about the main idea — and not "smoothed
out" for the sake of realistic plausibility. As a final point, notice that
Happy Days is a play with scarcely any conventional plot at all, but
consists almost totally of digressions.

Structure

Realism is the dramatic form most commonly associated with the
modern era. But as actors, directors, and designers, we should understand that realism is not a passive form of writing. It actively shapes the
kind of play that it "encloses." Consider all the dialogue and stage time
required to establish the time and place, move groups of characters on

159

and off the stage, disclose background story, set up and close down scenes, create "fully-developed" characters. A number of playwrights have questioned the need for these presumed requirements. And when they have done so, their plays have acquired new forms even as they explored new territory. It is possible to become mesmerized by this "new territory," however, and lose sight of the fact that, regardless of their potential for elusiveness, nonrealistic plays are still intended for performance before an audience — they are meant to be understood.

Literary scholars are inclined to treat nonrealistic plays mainly as intellectual exercises. They try to reach for meaning directly (intellectually) and in this way they attempt to escape the concrete world of the stage with its necessity for living human form. But actors, directors, and designers by definition have to remain grounded in the concrete world of the stage. We have to find meaning by working patiently and specifically with the materials of the plays in performance, with all their untidy and elusive originality. There is also the risk of giving too much attention to the exceptional features of nonrealism and not enough to the structure that supports them. In this case as well, it is possible to overlook what is most important. All these issues make dramatic structure in nonrealistic plays tricky to deal with, and they also illustrate why nonrealistic structure needs to be studied very closely. To avoid misreading and humdrum performance, it is more important than ever to look at nonrealistic plays bit by bit as well as in one piece, which means searching for the basic features of dramatic structure, clarifying them, and understanding how they all relate to each other. But how do the basic features of dramatic structure work in plays that seem to deal with dramatic structure in so many unusual ways?

Point of Attack

The point of attack is the moment when the play begins in relation to the timeline of the background story. And since nonrealistic plays tend to have less background story than realistic plays (see Chapter 3), they also tend to have an early point of attack. This is another way of saying that nonrealistic plays emphasize onstage events in preference to previous events. To understand how this difference works out in practice, it is necessary to consider the sort of influence that the background story exerts on the present action. Does its disclosure propel the stage action forward the way it does in realistic plays, or does it reinforce the totality of the surrounding conditions (thematic environment)?

In *Happy Days* Winnie and Willie have no past or future in the accepted sense. They live in an eternal present, unaffected by clock or calendar time. Background story is minimal, involving sentimental feelings and trivial events. The point of attack is early. Emphasis is on the present action and how Winnie and Willie are adjusting to their present reality. *The Birthday Party* is no different in this respect: minimal background story reinforces the milieu, and emphasis is on present action. From the background story we learn that Stanley has been in hiding since his piano concert was canceled, and that Goldberg and McCann have been searching for him. In the present action they find him, torment him, and take him away. The present action illustrating Stanley's tormented world takes place onstage before us. *Angels in America* also has an early point of attack. It seems to have a large amount of background story, and it does. With two exceptions, however, the background story does not exert significant influence on present action as such, but reinforces the totality of the play's environment. The two exceptions are Roy Cohn's embezzlement of a client's funds and Prior Walter's diagnosis with terminal AIDS, both of which do influence the stage action in significant ways. However, the remainder of the background story reinforces the play's thematic milieu more than it propels the present action. Past events such as Sarah Ironson's emigration to America; Prior Walter's ancestry; Ronald Reagan's presidency; Joe and Harper Pitt's religion, troubled childhoods, unstable marriage, and conflicted personalities; the disappearance of Prior Walter's cat; Roy Cohn's role in the trial and execution of the Rosenbergs; Joe Pitt's employment as a law clerk, and Louis Ironson's employment as a word processor; Prior Walter and Belize's former relationship — all these background story events work to reinforce the play's environment, its intellectual center, more than they drive the onstage action. In this case the thematic environment consists of the collapse of old ideals. Like other nonrealistic plays, the point of attack is early in the timeline of the background story.

Apparently, an early point of attack has become a defining feature of nonrealistic plays in general. Background story is used to establish the thematic environment, to establish a particular milieu. Nonrealistic plays show characters coming to terms with what is happening in this environment at this moment, onstage, before our eyes. It is what they are doing in the present that matters.

Primary Event

In nonrealistic plays it is not hard to discover the primary event (the most important incident in the background story) because there is so little background story to sort through. In *Fefu and Her Friends* the primary event is the mysterious injury Julia suffered from a shooting accident. (The women's get-together is also an attempt to assist in her rehabilitation.) Each character responds in a different way to Julia's accident: curiosity, indifference, flippant, apprehensive, and more. The primary event in *Top Girls* is Marlene's executive promotion. The summons from Claudius forms the primary event in *Rosencrantz and Guildenstern are Dead*. In *Mother Courage* it is the Chief's command that the Sergeant must assemble a squadron of new recruits because the war is killing too many soldiers. Jake's abuse of his wife, Beth, is the primary event in *A Lie of the Mind*. (Or could it be the death of Jake's father?) It is important to notice the prominence of these events in each play's background story. Such prominence is not always so apparent in the lengthy and complex background stories found in realistic plays. What is the primary event in *Happy Days*?

Inciting Action

It is not hard to see that Joe Pitt's visit to Roy Cohn's office in 1,2 is the inciting action, the event that sets the main action of *Angels in America* in motion. Cohn offers Pitt an influential position with the Justice Department in Washington, although in actual fact Cohn wants someone to represent his interests in the approaching disbarment proceedings. This particular inciting action is a classic illustration: its web of tensions extends throughout the entire play and it provides many opportunities for vivid dramatization. Moreover, the inciting action is plain to recognize here because it occurs in one of the play's realistic episodes. In *Mother Courage* it happens in the first scene, when Anna Fierling meets up with the Recruiting Sergeant who seeks to enlist her son. In *Machinal*, it is in episode one, when Mr. Jones proposes marriage to the Young Woman. Willie's emergence from his "hole" is the inciting action in *Happy Days*, and in *A Lie of the Mind* it is Jake's phone call to Frankie to come and get him out of trouble. Less easy to recognize, perhaps, is the inciting action of *The Birthday Party*. It occurs when Meg informs Stanley that "two gentlemen" have asked to come and stay for the night. Superficially, this moment is less dramatic than the actual arrival of Goldberg and McCann later on, but it is this event that puts Stanley on notice his life is in danger, initiating a major change in his temperament even before the new guests arrive. The inciting action in *Rosencrantz and Guildenstern are Dead* is sometimes seen as Claudius' command that Rosencrantz and Guildenstern must look into Hamlet's frame of mind. More accurately, it is the arrival of the Tragedians, in which the Player presents Guildenstern with an alternative way of dealing

162

with the uncertainty of their improbable situation. In short, nonrealistic plays make use of the inciting action just as realistic plays do and they present the same analytical challenges.

Conflicts

Screen-writing expert Robert McKee said it well: "Nothing moves forward in a story except through conflict" (McKee, 210). The problem of identifying conflicts in nonrealistic drama arises when faith is lacking in the absolute necessity of conflict, or when the idea of conflict is understood too narrowly. A representative example is 3,1 in *Angels in America*, which is the episode where two historical Prior Walters (thirteenth-century Prior Walter 1 and seventeenth-century Prior Walter 2) appear before the present-day Prior Walter as though in a terrifying vision. The word nightmare in the stage directions should be a clue that conflict is present, and studying the episode confirms it. Earlier in the chapter we said that conflicts arise from obstacles resulting in complications. The conflict in this episode is Prior Walter's objection to the frightening presence of Prior Walters 1 and 2. The obstacle is the task the visitors have been sent by Providence to carry out. And the complication is Prior 1 and 2's urgent need to persuade Prior Walter of its vital importance. Notice that to reveal the conflict all the basic elements must be performed actively, and not reactively. In other words, to illustrate the conflict here the phantoms must do more than just "deliver a message," and Prior Walter must do more than just "unwillingly receive a message." The first step in finding conflict is to have faith in its absolute necessity everywhere and at all times.

163

Climaxes

Some critics say that nonrealistic plays are deficient in climaxes, but close reading indicates otherwise. It is just that the climaxes tend to be more understated and ambiguous than they are in standard plays. Both plots in *Angels in America* (Joe and Harper Pitt, Louis Ironson and Prior Walter) contain three major climaxes that form the beginning, middle, and end of their storylines in a standard manner. The first major climax is always the inciting action. For the main plot with Joe Pitt and Roy Cohn, as we said earlier, this would be 1,2, when Cohn offers Pitt a position in Washington; and for the subplot with Louis Ironson and Prior Walter it would be 1,4, when Ironson learns about Prior's terminal illness. The second major climax for both plots occurs in 2,9, which the playwright tellingly labels a "split scene": Joe Pitt deserts his wife, Harper, and Louis Ironson deserts his partner, Prior Walter. This episode is the "tipping point" of the play, the event when the drive toward the remainder of the play becomes unavoidable. The two plots come together again at the third major climax (main climax), when Louis Ironson meets up with Joe Pitt in the park in 3,7 and they decide to live together. Minor climaxes are found in each of the remaining twenty-one scenes, a circumstance that is indicated by the way the play is subdivided into formal scenes. Each scene contains a minor climax. It is no accident that major and minor climaxes operate the same way in *Angels in America* as they would in realistic and classic plays. The content here is original, but the form makes use of climaxes in a standard manner.

Endings

Recognition, reversal, catastrophe, resolution, and simple or complex plotting mutually form a play's ending. It is the ending that shows how the characters come to terms with the world of the play and where the most characteristic expressions of nonrealism are found.

The climax of *Machinal* occurs in the courtroom scene when the Young Woman admits that she killed her husband. The recognition occurs after that, when "the enormity of her isolation comes upon her." Her imprisonment is the reversal of fortune, and the execution itself, which occurs after the curtain, is obviously the catastrophe. The resolution consists of the final episode, in which the indifference of the Matron, Jailer, Barber, Priest, and in particular the Reporters is exposed. The plot is technically complex because the Young Woman both recognizes the reality of her situation and suffers death as a result of it. Surprisingly, despite the assertive nonrealism of *Machinal*, the ending contains all the features of a classical tragedy.

At the climax of *The Birthday Party*, Goldberg and McCann torture Stanley with trite phrases from the lexicon of advertising, and then he collapses. Even though he has undergone a reversal of fortune (he is captured by Goldberg and McCann) and is experiencing a catastrophe (they torture him), Stanley's words are unintelligible and he is unable to reveal how he may have come to terms with his world. The resolution consists of Petey's hopeless protest when Goldberg and McCann take Stanley away. Left unanswered are the reasons for Goldberg and McCann's mistreatment of Stanley and the source of the dangerous power they exert over everyone in the play.

It appears that the climax of *Fefu and Her Friends* occurs when Fefu shoots and kills a rabbit in the backyard, concurrently killing Julia inside the house. It is a dramatic event certainly, but the prior conversation between Fefu and Julia is a more accurate choice for the climax. In this brief exchange, Fefu seeks a solution to her unhappiness from Julia, and Julia sympathizes but fears that her advice could be harmful to Fefu. After all, Julia has been permanently damaged by her own contact with reality. Julia blesses Fefu, after which Fefu asks for and receives her forgiveness and then goes into the backyard to shoot the rabbit. Fefu and Julia understand each other even though the exact subject of their conversation is not made clear in the dialogue. What is clear is that during this event the rules of the game have changed from realism to nonrealism without warning, and it will be necessary to step back from the particulars for a moment to recognize what is happening in more general terms. Taking place before us is a purification ritual whose purpose is to remove any traces of uncleanness prior to undertaking a special task. (See myth and ritual in the Introduction.) The "uncleanness" consists of the second-hand ideas that cloud the characters' thinking and make them unhappy despite their privileged circumstances and elite educations. The playwright has chosen to express the climax in nonrealistic ritual form to emphasize that the ultimate goal of consciousness raising is personal experience, not group meetings; action, not talk. Fefu recognizes this, takes action to reverse her unhappy fortune by shooting the "rabbit," and experiences a catastrophe displaced through Julia's death. The resolution consists of Julia's final line: "I killed it ... I just shot it ... and killed it.... Julia ..." and a poetic tableau of Fefu holding a dead rabbit with the women surrounding Julia's body. Recognition, reversal catastrophe, resolution, and a technically complex plot occur in mythic form beneath the seeable reality. The ending of A Lie of the Mind is structured as a symbolic ritual as well. It is the confession of a "sin" (Jake's violent behavior) accompanied by a "penance" (he relinquishes his wife, Beth, to his kindhearted brother, Frankie).

165

What is the practical outcome of all these formal patterns, this structural elusiveness and ambiguity? It is just this. The originality of nonrealistic plays derives precisely from their formal patterns, outward elusiveness, and ambiguity, and from their candid refusal to employ realistic specificity. Although nonrealistic plays treat most structural features in a standard manner, they have a propensity for handling endings in unusual ways to emphasize this formality, originality, and ambiguity. Characters may come to recognize the unusual nature of their worlds or they may not, and their ability or inability to do so is deliberately formal, novel, and ambiguous. Whatever novelty and ambiguity may be incorporated into the structure of these plays, however, it is not the result of lack of clarity in the writing. On the contrary, nonrealistic writing is strictly purposeful and rigorously, uncompromisingly thematic. Thus, even though nonrealistic plays may appear to be formal, elusive, and ambiguous, nevertheless they need to be carefully analyzed in the planning stages and vividly illustrated in production to give special emphasis to these features. Contradictions need to be analyzed and theatricalized, not "smoothed out" as in realistic or classic plays, and contrasts with realistic expectations in particular need to be highlighted.

Summary

In the study of plot, readers are inclined to devote most of their attention to understanding the basic external and internal actions, but as we have shown, this is not all that goes into crafting an effective plot. Besides identifying these features, readers will also need to explore the progress, disruptions, and arrangement of the story's progressions. At first, it may be tricky to catch the flow of dramatic progressions and develop a sense of how they relate to each other and to the whole play. The temptation is to read plays merely as sequential arrangements of scenes without much regard for their internal connections and patterns. But analyzing the progressions, digressions, and structure is essential for professional-level work and therefore should not be undervalued. Regardless of the kind of play or what it means, dramatic interest depends not only on the story itself but also on how it is told from moment to moment.

166

Questions

1. *Progressions.* Take time to subdivide the action of the play (or scene) into units (or beats if necessary) and ask, what is the basic story and how does each beat and unit contribute to its progress and development. How is the action divided into scenes (informal, formal, French Scenes) and acts? Describe how each of these larger progressions contributes to the logical advancement and development of the story. What do the progressions suggest about the mise-en-scene? How could the mise-en-scene contribute to the effectiveness of the progressions?

2. *Structure.* What is the motivating force that sparks the story (inciting action or first major climax)? What are the most important conflicts (the main obstacles and their associated complications)? What are the three highest points of emotional intensity

in the play (three major climaxes)? What are the less important points of emotional intensity (minor climaxes)? Does the leading character undergo a psychological recognition (complex plot)? If so, describe it. If not, why not (simple plot)? Is there an important change of fortune (reversal) for the leading character? If so, what is it? Does the reversal lead to better or worse fate for the leading character? What important actions, if any, occur following the highest peak of emotional intensity (resolution)? How can the change in tensions be described at this point in the play? What is the overall pattern ("cardiogram") formed by the inciting action, major and minor climaxes, and resolution? What does the structure suggest about the mise-en-scene? How could the mise-en-scene contribute to the effectiveness of the structure?

3. *After Action Analysis.* Search for the play's seed/theme at work in the progressions and structure. How does the seed/theme influence each beat, unit, scene, and act? How does the seed/theme influence the inciting action, major and minor climaxes, and resolution?

CHAPTER 6

Character

The term *character* has taken on assorted meanings over time. It developed from a Middle English root associated with something fixed and permanent, like an identifying mark or a sign on a building. During Shakespeare's time character was still considered a permanent feature. It was said to result from bodily fluids called *humours* that were once thought to control the tendencies of one's spirit (more about this below). In the nineteenth century character continued to mean a fixed state of development, though with added implications as in, "She has character." This meaning was associated with moral strength, self-discipline, and, most important to the Victorians, respectability. The modern meaning of character is more wide-ranging. Today we consider character the pattern of action that identifies a person, what Aristotle called *habitual action* (action acquired by habit or use). This is the understanding we will examine here. In drama, character is not a static object fixed forever in time, but rather a consistent pattern of actions associated with a particular figure in a play. Some writers think this suggests that characters actually change their individuality during a play, while others claim they only reveal traits hidden until that time. It is an interesting puzzle, but it need not detain us here. To recognize that character is composed of a habitual pattern of action identifying a figure in a play is satisfactory for practical purposes.

Although characters are sometimes studied as if they were real people, they are actually androids whose programming depends first upon the playwright and then upon the actor. That is why it is risky to depend too much on psychoanalytical methods, for example, to understand them. Psychoanalysis is a way of examining mental disorders in humans, and its main purpose is treatment of those disorders. Sometimes its methods can be useful in artistic circumstances, but character analysis is an artistic (artificial) enterprise, not a medical one. Dramatic characters may be embodied by real people, perform actions similar to those of real people, and have emotional lives similar to those of real people, but the resemblance stops there. Compared to real people, stage characters are exceedingly predictable. In life, few people are as absorbed with a single overpowering goal as the characters are in plays. The compact expressiveness of drama requires reduction to essentials. And to portray character, the whole array of ordinary human behavior is condensed into a few selected, pre-programmed features.

This chapter will study character under nine headings: (1) objectives equip the characters with goals; (2) actions are what they actually do to pursue those goals; (3) adaptations are behavior attributes applied to actions; (4) conflict describes the tensions between characters; (5) will power is the force characters use to pursue their goals; (6) values are the intangible things that characters consider good and bad; and (7) personality traits are those strokes of individuality that show how characters look, feel, and think. The topic of (8) complexity explains the degree of self-awareness in a character, and under (9) relationships are the primary and secondary associations among characters. These topics provide the general lines of inquiry that can be used to understand dramatic character. Some think of these topics as individual "layers" that stack up to form a functional character. Analyzing layer by layer is a useful way to come to terms with a character without having to deal with everything at once.

169

Objectives

In the last chapter, we studied the external features of progressions — how they tell the story of the play and how the playwright arranges them to make the story dramatic. Progressions have internal features too, called *objectives*. Like progressions, objectives are indispensable features of a play, and as a result can be identified in the text. Put another way, different readers analyzing the same play should arrive at the same, or at least comparable, character objectives. Objectives are also like progressions in that they are divided into larger and smaller degrees that correspond to beats, units, scenes, and acts. Indeed, progressions and objectives are complimentary and incapable of being separated.

Stanislavsky explained how to understand objectives properly. To greet someone with a nod, for example, would be an *ordinary objective*, he said. Not much psychology there because it is for the most part a mechanical process. A nod with the intention of expressing an emotion, let's say affection or dislike, is also of the ordinary variety, although it does contain a small amount of psychology. In contrast, a nod with the intention of apologizing for something you did wrong and asking for forgiveness would be a *psychological objective*. The most effective objectives are deeply and strongly psychological like this. They require careful thinking to devise and carry out. Stanislavsky understood that it can be difficult to work out objectives, which is one reason why he and Nemirovich developed the process of table work, patient analysis prior to rehearsal to find the right objectives and get comfortable with them.

We use the term objectives in this book because it was the term chosen by the original translator of Stanislavsky's works and is the term with which English-speaking actors, directors, and designers are most familiar. In the new translations of Stanislavsky, Jean Benedetti uses the word *task*. Problem is another alternative. Harold Clurman with the members of the Group Theatre and their students and followers use the words spine or intention. The differences can be puzzling and need not constrain us here. The words may vary, but they mean the same thing: what a character's efforts or actions are intended to attain or accomplish, that is, what a character wants, whether for a scene or for an entire play.

Objectives are best understood in relation to a specific play, and so we will study *Three Sisters* by Anton Chekhov. We will consider Irina the principal figure among the sisters. To learn her superobjective for the play, first find out what she says that she wants to do with her life. The play begins with her name day. (In Russia a person's birthday is celebrated on the day honoring the saint the person is named after.) It has also been one year since their father died, marking the end of the traditional Russian period of mourning. An end to black clothing and reverently restrained behavior. Today Irina, who is the youngest sibling, feels a new sense of freedom and hope. In the opening scene, she says to the others excitedly, "If only we could go back to Moscow! Sell the house, finish with our life here, and go back to Moscow." When their elderly friend, Dr. Chebutykin, encourages her youthful high spirits, she briskly responds, "When I woke up this morning [...] I suddenly felt as if everything in the world had become clear to me, and I knew the way I ought to live. [...] Man must work by the seat of his brow whatever his class, and that should make up the whole meaning and purpose of his life and happiness and contentment." From these lines and other evidence in the play we might agree that Irina's main goal, her *super-objective*, as Stanislavsky would say, is "to find happiness," perhaps through a fulfilling vocation. This would be essentially correct, but most readers would also agree that it leaves out a large part of Irina's character, her yearning for love. A stronger and more precise super-objective for her would be "to win the love of the man she was meant for." Several other alternatives are possible as well, but this is an accurate choice because it conditions everything Irina does in the play.

The family lives in a provincial town at some distance from Moscow. And in the narrow environment of provincial life, Irina's super-objective is one that requires patience, courage, and hopefulness. To accomplish it, she must break it up into more manageable pieces, the *minor objectives* that are tied to the individual progressions of her role in the play. For example, in the opening unit of the play, she disapproves of Olga's talk about their father's funeral. Her objective for this unit is "to remind Olga that their mourning period has ended." In the next unit, Irina's objective is "to encourage Olga's wish to return to Moscow (where they used to live). As soon as Irina remembers that their sister, Masha, would not be able to join them in Moscow because she is married to the local schoolmaster, her objective changes, "to play down Masha's unhappiness." In the event with Chebutykin that follows, Irina reveals how impatient she is to achieve her super-objective. She says to him, "I long for work. And if I don't get up early from now on and really work, you can refuse to be friends with me." Her objective here is "to encourage his kindly acceptance of her feelings." Each of Irina's minor objectives defines its own unique progression while also adhering to Stanislavsky's basic guidelines for objectives: the minor objectives follow from her super-objective, they are directed at specific characters and not at the environment in general, and they relate directly to her inner life.

It makes sense that a successful super-objective should logically relate to the main idea of the play, and Chapter 7 will explain the concept of the main idea in depth. For this chapter a convenient example will serve. Let's agree for now that the main idea of *Three Sisters* is *yearning for a dream*. (This was the main idea for Nemirovich-Danchenko's famous 1940 revival of the play. He was careful to note that yearning for a dream is different from aspiring for a dream or working for a dream.) It is easy to see how Irina's minor objectives relate to Nemirovich's description of the main idea. For this description to be persuasive for the entire play, however, the super-objectives of all the other characters must relate to it as well. And they do relate to it because every character in the play is yearning for a dream in their own way. Although each of their super-objectives contains its own separate feelings and thoughts as well as minor objectives, each one also relates to the main idea of the play: yearning for a dream.

Director Harold Clurman cautioned against the mistake of always looking for the minor personality traits in a character. Influenced by Stanislavsky, Clurman taught that the actor's most important analytical task should be to find the character's super-objective (the spine, in his terminology), the basic drive that determines the character's behavior in the entire play and throughout the acts, scenes, units, and beats of which the play is composed. Even though many of the characters will experience similar feelings of anger, joy, or sadness, it is their super-objectives that explain these changing feelings and thoughts by showing how they are all related to a single permanent goal.

Actions

For some readers objectives and actions are separate features; for others they are more or less the same thing. Since one of the purposes of this book is to encourage consistency of theatre vocabulary, this section will try to address the question. The concept of *action*, or dramatic action, comes from Aristotle, but it was Stanislavsky (by way of Nemirovich and the Russian Formalist critics) who applied it systematically to performance and production. To be precise, objectives are what a character wants, and actions are what the character does to get it. Furthermore, since action is a process of forcing, it is always directed toward another character. As Francis Hodge explains it, Character A forces Character B; B receives the forcing and adjusts to it; and then B forces A; A receives the forcing and adjusts to it; and then A forces B, etc., until the event is interrupted, delayed, or resolved either by A or B getting the better of the other or else by a deadlock. Each and every progression in a play is purposed to force someone to do something to someone else, and this forcing process is called action.

To express action, active (transitive) verbs are used because they convey aggressive forcing rather than passive (intransitive) receiving. For example, A encourages B, not B is encouraged by A. Certain verbs may feel like they ought to be active, but in reality they cannot be truthfully acted. Consider them *false active verbs*, or *false actions*. Some verbs that represent this group simply describe the form of communication going on in the dialogue (question, explain, announce, etc.). Others merely describe a physical activity (laugh, jump, run, etc.). Sometimes false active verbs can be useful as actions, but genuine active verbs always have the advantage because they are aimed at another character and have a sturdy, psychological foundation.

Although action is built into every moment of a play, we will limit the example here to a brief scene. We are further helped in this by Hodge's teaching and by a process called "actioning" developed by director Max Stafford-Clark, both of whom draw their thinking from Stanislavsky. In the example below, the action is underlined and placed in brackets after each character's name. The example is taken from the opening scene of the second act of *Three Sisters*. It dramatizes how the love between Andrey and Natasha has deteriorated in the two years they have been married. Natasha has grown petty and selfish, while Andrey has become withdrawn and unresponsive. She pampers their infant child, Bobik, and behaves arrogantly toward Andrey's sisters and the servents. The time is evening, and Natasha is prowling the house, looking for any candles that might be left burning. Andrey is hiding away, reading in his study. Objectives should be defined beforehand so that actions are purpose-driven instead of being arbitrary "choices." For this scene, Natasha's objective is "to keep close watch over the household," and Andrey's is "to relieve his boredom."

(It is eight o'clock in the evening. The
faint sound of an accordion is heard coming
from the street. The stage is unlit. Enter
NATASHA in a dressing-gown, carrying a candle. She crosses the stage and stops by the
door leading to ANDREY'S room.)

NATASHA [Distract]. What are you doing, Andrey?
Reading? It's all right, I only wanted to
know... (Goes to another door, opens it, looks
inside and shuts it again.) Must make sure
no one's left a candle burning anywhere...

ANDREY [Ignore]. (comes in with a book in his
hand) What is it, Natasha?

NATASHA [Criticize]. I was just going around
to see if anyone had left a light burning.
It's Shrovetide — carnival week, and the
servants are so excited about it...anything
might happen! You've got to watch them.
Last night about twelve o'clock I happened
to go into the dining-room, and — would

you believe it? — there was a candle alight on the table. I've not found out who lit it. (*Puts the candle down.*) What time is it?

ANDREY [<u>Neutralize</u>]. (*glances at the clock*) Quarter past eight.

NATASHA [<u>Warn</u>]. And Olga and Irina still out. They aren't back from work yet, poor things! Olga's still at some teachers' conference, and Irina's at the post office. (*Sighs.*) This morning I said to Irina: "Do take care of yourself, my dear." But she won't listen. Did you say it was a quarter past eight? I'm afraid Bobik is not at all well. Why does he get so cold? Yesterday he had a temperature, but today he feels quite cold when you touch him...I'm so afraid!

ANDREY [<u>Avert</u>]. It's all right, Natasha. The boy's well enough.

NATASHA [<u>Needle</u>]. Still, I think he ought to have a special diet. I'm so anxious about him. By the way, they tell me that some carnival party's supposed to be coming here soon after nine. I'd rather they didn't come, Andrey.

ANDREY [<u>Discourage</u>]. Well, I really don't know what I can do. They've been asked to come.

NATASHA [<u>Outwit</u>]. This morning the dear little fellow woke up and looked at me, and then suddenly he smiled. He recognized me, you see. "Good morning, Bobik," I said, "good morning, darling precious!" And then he laughed. Babies understand everything, you know, they understand us perfectly well. Anyway, Andrey, I'll tell the servants not to let that carnival party in.

ANDREY. [<u>Stifle</u>]. (*hesitatingly*) Well...it's really for my sisters to decide, isn't it? It's their house, after all.

NATASHA [<u>Sabotage</u>]. Yes, it's their house as well. I'll tell them, too... They're so

174

kind... (*Going.*) I've ordered buttermilk for supper. The doctor says you ought to eat nothing but buttermilk, or you'll never get any thinner. (*Stops.*) [Manipulates] Bobik feels so cold. I'm afraid his room is too cold for him. He ought to move into a warmer room, at least until the warm weather comes. Irina's room, for instance — that's just a perfect room for a baby: it's dry, and it gets the sun all day long. We must tell her: perhaps she'd share Olga's room for a bit...In any case, she's never at home during the day, she only sleeps there...(*Pause.*) [Appease] Darling, why don't you say anything?

ANDREY [Elude]. I was just day-dreaming... There's nothing to say, anyway...

NATASHA. [Pester]. Well... What was it I was going to tell you? Oh, yes! Ferapont from the Council Office wants to see you about something.

ANDREY [Tolerate]. (*yawns*) Tell him to come up.
(NATASHA *goes out.* ANDREY, *bending over the candle which she has left behind, continues to read his book.*)

Using the objectives defined prior to this passage, many if not most of these actions are evident in the lines themselves. However, depending on the objectives that were spelled out and the interpretive shrewdness of the performer, actions can sometimes be different from what is believed to be evident in the dialogue. What actions would Natasha make use of, for instance, if her objective was "to recover her husband's love?" What actions would Andrey make use of if his objective was "to relieve his emotional pain?" The differences are subtle, but imaginatively stimulating.

Verb choice is important in determining actions, but the analytical process is really one of perception, not vocabulary. Effective action is made up of basic human behavior that anyone should be able to understand. The question to ask is: what is happening outside and inside the line? Sometimes the answer can be hard to pin down, but then again the process of finding the actions will always be a challenge, like the process of script analysis itself.

Adaptations — An Aside

Actions in themselves cannot express all the emotional nuances involved in accomplishing an objective. Nonverbal performance attributes — facial expressions, gestures, body language, tones of voice — are also important to give special shading to dramatic actions. Stanislavsky calls these attributes *adaptations*, and devotes an entire chapter to the subject in *An Actor's Work*. Adaptations are useful, he writes, when a character spends a long time with a single objective, in which case it would be easy to become monotonous. Using different kinds of adaptations helps to avoid this performance problem. Some examples of mental states, moods, and emotions that could stimulate fresh adaptations include: anxious, bitter, dreary, gracious, impudent, lazy, playful, rough, soothing, stupid, warm, wistful, etc. Any of these adjectives and more could be used as the basis for fresh and unexpected adaptations. On the other hand, there is also a risk of enacting adaptations for their own sake. For example, instead of "I want to perform my action in a worried manner," an actor could unthinkingly slip into "I want to be worried," or worse, "I want to look like I am worried." In theatre parlance this would be called *indicating* (playing an emotion), a serious performance error that leads to generalized acting and clichés. To avoid such indicating, Stanislavsky and his followers recommend that adaptations should be perceived by instinct rather than pre-planned, or else used only in rehearsal or class exercises to expand an actor's personal range of emotional attributes.

Michael Chekhov and his followers agree with Stanislavsky about the need for nonverbal emotional attributes and that indicating is not good acting. However, they would avoid the risks involved with pre-planned adaptations by performing actions under the influence of specific *qualities*. Some would call this feature adverbs or tactics. Chekhov explained his approach by saying that actions are "what" the characters do and qualities are "how" they do them, whether anxiously, bitterly, drearily, graciously, etc. It is a subtle but important question, and readers wishing to understand it better should consult the works of Stanislavsky and Michael Chekhov, as well as instructive writings by their followers. In any case, it is important to know that adaptations and qualities are not inbuilt but added to actions by the actors, which makes them issues for classroom, rehearsal, and performance more than for script analysis as such. For that reason, adaptations are an aside to script analysis. We study the issue here to make the distinction clear and add to the effort of standardizing theatre vocabulary.

Conflict

The subject of *conflict* comes up so often in discussions about plays, it is important to examine it closely. In the last chapter talked about conflict in connection with the structure of a play. Here we address the subject of conflict in connection with character. The word conflict stems from a Latin root meaning to strike together, from which comes its current meaning of a battle, quarrel, or struggle for supremacy between opposing forces. Does conflict appear everywhere in every single play? If conflict is defined as big, open arguments between characters, the answer is no. There are few big arguments, for example, in *The Wild Duck, Happy Days,* or *Mother Courage.* Moreover, in some plays the characters do not seem to struggle very much to come to terms with their world in any way. Looking for traditional big arguments in situations like these is unrewarding.

Instead of being a single narrow concept, conflict actually appears in several different forms. There may be conflict between one character and another, between character and environment, between character and destiny or the forces of nature, between character and ideas, or even among the feelings within a single character. All these are legitimate types of conflicts, but not all of them produce the same kinds of tensions. Conflicts from intellectual abstractions such as environment, society, or destiny, for example, produce intellectual tensions. These conflicts are exploited in nonrealistic plays, where they are well theatricalized. They are useful primarily for directors and designers in their creative work, as will be seen in the next chapter.

177

To achieve the kind of vividness necessary for acting, however, conflict must be more than intellectual. It must be tangible and possess a human face. In other words, it must involve the behavior and emotions of the characters. This kind of conflict stems from specific conditions in the given circumstances and is grounded concretely in the world of the play. This is the most productive kind of conflict in the rehearsal hall because it provides the inner tensions that stir a performer's creative imagination. Conflicts in this concrete sense may be divided into two classes: (1) role conflicts stemming from characters' opposing views of each other and (2) conflicts of objectives stemming from their opposing goals. Role conflicts and conflicts of objectives are also part of the characters' outer selves, shaping the way characters relate to each other externally. That is why the subject of conflict occurs both in this and the preceding chapters.

Conflicts of Objectives

The concept of *conflicts of objectives* comes from the ideas of the nineteenth-century French writer and critic Ferdinand Brunetière (1849–1906). His so-called law of conflict states that drama is defined by the conflicts encountered as characters attempt to fulfill their desires. Desires considered as objectives, of course, occupy a central place in Stanislavsky's system, in which characters by definition have their own objectives, direct everything toward fulfilling those objectives, and try to bring everything in their lives into harmony with them. Accordingly, conflicts of objectives are the opposing objectives of other characters that stand in the way of this process. Major and minor climaxes occur at those points where the objectives of one character collide with those of another. These collisions in turn produce the events that make plays meaningful and entertaining.

To demonstrate this we will examine *A Raisin in the Sun* once more. Walter wants to use his father's life insurance money "to become a big success," and the question is whether he will succeed. He is prevented from fulfilling this super-objective by Mama's super-objective, which is to use the money "to help her family escape from poverty." This is their conflict of objectives. Walter eventually overcomes his mother's opposition, but he is defeated by his friend Willy, whose super-objective is "to get hold of the insurance money secretly for his own selfish purposes." This is their conflict of objectives. It is not hard to find conflicts of objectives; the real difficulty is in perceiving and expressing the force of their in-built opposition.

Role Conflicts

A *role conflict*, or self-image conflict, is a second type of character conflict. We all play many roles in life (parent, teacher, son or daughter, employee, etc.), and it is not difficult to see how this sense of the word role is related to the meaning here. Role conflicts arise from characters' opposing images of themselves and each other. They come from conditions in the given circumstances that cause one character's self-image to come into open disagreement with another's self-image. Just as with conflicts of objectives, there may be a number of different role conflicts among the characters throughout the play, each one defined by its own conditions in the given circumstances.

For an explanation of how role conflicts arise, return to the same scene between Walter and Ruth in *A Raisin in the Sun*. Walter's self-image is that of a good husband and father, and he considers Ruth to be an unsympathetic wife. In contrast, Ruth's self-image is that of a neglected wife, and she considers Walter to be an irresponsible husband and father. Their images of themselves and each other are in complete disagreement, yet their self-images govern how they interact with each other. Walter believes he is a responsible husband, yet Ruth treats him as an irresponsible husband. Ruth believes she is a neglected wife, yet Walter treats her as an unsympathetic wife. This identifies their role conflict. Their interactions are bound to clash because they are based on conflicting images of themselves and each other.

Of the two types of conflicts just studied, conflicts of objectives are used more often because they are easier to grasp and explain. Role conflicts impose a more severe analytical test, but the outcome is a larger assortment of performance options. Searching for either type of conflict will supply many useful alternatives. After the conflicts have been identified in the script, the final choice depends, of course, on the creative imagination of the artistic team and on what they decide to emphasize in production.

Will Power

The term *will* is defined as a strong wish, a firm intention, a power of choosing, a determination to do, and an inner force used to undertake conscious, purposeful action. The key words here are power, firmness, determination, and force. In script analysis, will is associated with strength, determination, and power because it takes characters with strong wills to create conflicts, to make things happen. Sometimes they are called *driving characters* because they control the action of the play so strongly. The leading characters in *Tartuffe* (Tartuffe and Orgon's wife, Elmire), *Top Girls* (Marlene), and *American Buffalo* (Teach), for example, are models of such strong-willed characters. They are identified by their determination to impose their wills on everyone, despite the outcome. They drive the action forward and force things to happen. Some characters may not have strong wills, but if the leading character is also devoid of a strong will, the results may be unsatisfactory unless other compensations are provided. Because conflict always requires resistance, characters without strong wills are unable to create traditional conflicts because they are incapable of resisting in the accepted sense. They may participate in conflicts, but they seldom seem to instigate or influence them. They do not seem to struggle against their situations, and they are often the victims of the more willful characters who control them.

Present-day sensibilities tend to sympathize with victims more than heroes, but it is not always easy to come to terms with passive,

179

victimized characters. Before sympathizing with them, it is necessary to try to understand the reasons for their apparent inactivity. Instructive examples of such characters appear in *Mother Courage* and *Hamlet*. In *Mother Courage* there is Anna Fierling, the canteen woman who earns a living by following armies on the march and selling necessities to them at inflated prices. The strength of her will shows up in the first scene of the play when she loses her son Eilif to the Recruiting Officer. She has been distracted by the chance to make a quick profit selling a belt buckle. We know that Fierling is a shrewd and single-minded businesswoman, yet she does nothing when her son is taken from her, a fact that Brecht emphasizes in stage directions that state, "she stands motionless."

Fierling is unable to prevent her second son, Swiss Cheese, from being sacrificed to the war either. She compromises with the same Recruiting Officer by permitting Swiss Cheese to enlist as a paymaster. She claims that at least he won't have to fight, but she knows he is simple-minded and will get himself into trouble because he can't count. She is troubled by these concerns, but she justifies her decision on the grounds that the war has been good for business. Soon she finds that Swiss Cheese has panicked during an enemy offensive and unthinkingly fled with the cash box. When he is arrested, Anna haggles over the bribe needed to save his life. Meanwhile Swiss Cheese is taken before a firing squad and shot. She observes, "Maybe I bargained too long," and the stage directions indicate once again that she "remains seated." Later, Fierling refuses to acknowledge the body of her son rather than risk arrest herself. She does attempt to file an official complaint about it, but after thinking it over, she changes her mind.

In another scene, Fierling's son, Eilif, arrives to say good-bye before being taken away to be executed for a petty crime. Just then the cease-fire is cut short by the renewed outbreak of war. Anna is so excited by the chance to make money again that she misses the chance to save Eilif's life. Further on in the play, Fierling finds herself in town on business when her remaining child, the mute Kattrin, is shot sounding an alarm to warn the town of an enemy attack. "Maybe it wouldn't have happened if you hadn't gone to town to swindle people," a peasant says to her. "I've got to get back in business," she replies. Then she hails a passing regiment and shouts "Hey, take me with you!" and the play ends.

Someone in Anna's predicament would normally invoke our sympathy, but Brecht attempts to dispel this expected tendency. He shows Anna Fierling as a character who lacks a mother's most basic power to protect her children. This would be a formula for certain failure in the theatre, but there are deliberate compensations that stimulate interest and sympathy. Brecht tries to show that Fierling's helplessness is not her fault. The play argues that her power for good has been exhausted by the brutal economics of war. Compelled to choose between peaceful poverty and wartime affluence, she chooses the latter. She believes that she can keep her family together despite the war by exploiting her business instincts. We are meant to feel that this choice hurts her even though she doesn't know why. Anna Fierling never learns that she is mistaken. For many readers, Anna's story is a vivid illustration of social and economic injustice.

Besides these thematic considerations, Fierling's apparent inactivity is further offset by other features in the play. The back-and-forth changes in the course of the war, for example, unsettle everyone. Also Anna's daughter, Kattrin, and the prostitute, Yvette, show remarkable strength of will and even heroism. Other offsetting features are the earthy humor and homespun intelligence of the characters, and the play's unusual production style, which employs signs, banners, musical interludes, poetry, and direct address to the audience. All these features give the play compelling social relevance, variety of feeling, and a special kind of excitement that compensate for the absence of traditional will power in the leading character.

Another seemingly weak character who is attractive to modern audiences is Hamlet. A sensitive person, he is burdened with the responsibility of revenging his warrior-father's murder. Hamlet had already neglected one of his royal responsibilities by standing aside while his uncle took the throne away from him. Nor did he do anything to put a stop to his mother's marriage to his uncle. By these examples of inaction, Hamlet seems to show weakness and even cowardice. At his first appearance in the play, Hamlet refuses to take part in the coronation ceremonies for the new king. His display of temperament is interpreted by the court as spitefulness stemming from immaturity and emotional instability. His strong conscience soon regains control over his grief, and he scolds himself for his inertia. He gets a chance to make up for his inaction when the Ghost appears and challenges him to take revenge, but here too Hamlet seems to miss one chance after another to carry out his duty. Instead of concentrating on revenge, he insists on assessing the moral implications of the events in which he is participating. It is Claudius who provides the force behind the play's conflict when he becomes worried about Hamlet's moodiness, interpreting it as suspicion of his own guilt.

Hamlet is sensitive, introspective, and outwardly inactive, at least compared to Claudius, Laertes, and Fortinbras. Despite appearances, however, his will is not weak, nor is he a coward. On the inside, where it counts, he's the strongest character in the play. It is his over-scrupulous conscience that drives him always to assess things and to undertake seemingly foolish schemes to test his assessments. This unusual characteristic is what makes him so attractive to us. We sympathize with his puzzlement about the world and feel that potentially he has the strength of will to do something extraordinary.

Hamlet has enjoyed success on the modern stage in spite of, or perhaps because of, its seemingly weak-willed leading character. It is the compensating features in the play, which provide the attractions. For one thing, Hamlet is likable. He loves his mother and honors his father. He has a sense of humor. He is a gentleman, a poet, a scholar, and a well-trained swordsman and soldier. He is not cowardly inside but morally brave, and of course he is always driven to assess the meaning of things. Many of the other characters in the play are also interesting in themselves. There are the strong-willed characters of Claudius, Laertes, and Fortinbras, whose crusades for power offset Hamlet's philosophical tendencies. It is the combination of all these features plus the comic interludes and the language that make the play dramatic.

As a final point, a distinction needs to be made between the concept of a character's will in the written script and that of *stakes* in an actor's performance. "Raising the stakes" means an actor should raise the emotional level of concern, want the objective more, and increase the energy level to make an event more compelling. Whether a character's will is strong or weak does not necessarily determine the level of emotional concern with which an actor should carry out that character's objectives. Characters such as Ophelia in *Hamlet*, Don in *American Buffalo*, or Prior Walter in *Angels in America* may not have strong wills according to the sense taught here. However, the level of emotional concern — the level of the stakes — with which actors perform these characters is an interpretive issue for actors and directors to sort out in practice.

Values

Values are the ideals the characters stand for or against in the world of the play, intangibles that form their ideas about good and bad, right and wrong. To achieve their objectives, characters embrace values that gratify them and they reject, or at least struggle against, those that do not do so. Values guide characters on the path where they wish to go. They affect their personal, family, and social lives, their work, and their leisure. They define their reasons for choosing to be who they are. Values arise from personal beliefs about such things as conscience, public- and family-mindedness, ambition, success, and pleasure. In some characters, the values may form a pattern of virtues, in others they may be vices, and in still others a mixture of virtues and vices. The deciding factor is whether the values are real, honest convictions or short-term tactics adopted for short-term ends.

Madame Pernelle, Orgon's mother in *Tartuffe*, is an example of a character whose values are more for social utility than they are for genuine virtue. On the surface her values seem to be honorable. She advocates good behavior, religious observance, modesty, and respect for authority. She reveals these values in the opening scene when she reproaches the family for what she believes to be their neglectful behavior. This is another way of saying that she disagrees with their values. She criticizes Elmire's clothes, which she believes are too showy for her position in society. Madame Pernelle criticizes Cleante, Elmire's brother, whose religious liberalism offends her. In spite of her protests, however, the most important value for Madame Pernelle is not virtue as such but the appearance of virtue, otherwise known as respectability. Her values are a form of behavior she has adopted to enable her to appear virtuous to other people, a fact she is probably not even aware of.

183

Values also play an important role in *Death of a Salesman*. As a salesman, Willy believes in the values held by many Americans, particularly during the period following World War II. He believes in the right of material prosperity, that America is essentially a just country, and that good friends and hard work will lead to success and happiness. In act 1, Willy tells Linda that he expects to find the same values in his son, Biff. He wants Biff to accomplish something in the all-American world of business. Although Biff has been on his own for ten years, Willy worries that he "has yet to take thirty-five dollars a week!" Willy believes that in "the greatest country in the world," someone with Biff's "personal attractiveness" and who is such a "hard worker" should be successful. Driven by his absolute faith in the importance of success in business, Willy is determined to help Biff get a job selling. In the first flashback scene, where Biff and Happy are young boys, Willy reminds them of the values he believes to be important in life: "The man who makes an appearance in the business world, the man who creates personal interest, is the man who gets ahead. Be liked and you will never want."

But if money and friends were all that Willy valued, he would not be a very sympathetic character. He values other things, too. First, he loves nature. Besides his garden, one of the things he enjoys most is the lovely New England scenery he can enjoy on his frequent sales trips. Respecting people as individuals is also important to him, though he senses that this value is declining in America and being displaced by competition and self-interest. He complains that selling is not as attractive as it once was for someone like him: "The competition is maddening!" Willy also values loyalty, hard work, and friendship, but perhaps most important of all, he values his family. He tells Linda that his deepest worry is not being able to support them as a father should do.

Willy's sensitivity, kindness, sense of duty, and love for his family coexist with his misplaced material values. That he does not value material success in itself but rather what he believes it can do for his family is clear. But his single-minded faith in the religion of business is at odds with his humane family values. In the end, his values are discredited. Willy dies for his son Biff, yet Biff is contemptuous of his father. It is the neglected (and self-centered) son, Happy, who dedicates himself to perpetuating his father's values. The central issue in *Death of a Salesman* is in large measure a conflict of values between a father and son.

Characters declare their sense of right and wrong all though *The Piano Lesson*, another play about clashing values. Doaker Charles, a retired railroad cook, expresses his values by using a railroad image.

> DOAKER. If everybody stay in one place I believe this would be a better world. Now what I done learned after twenty-seven years of railroading is this...if the train stays on the track...it's going to get where it's going. It might not be where you're going. If it ain't, then all you got to do is sit and wait cause the train's coming back to get you. The train don't never stop. It'll come back every time.

Which is to say, stick to what you know how to do, mind your own business, and go along with the way things are. Doaker's values are contested by his nephew, Boy Willie, who is from a younger generation and sees things differently.

> BOY WILLIE. See now...I'll tell you something about me. I done strung along and strung along. Going this way and that. Whatever

```
way would lead me to a moment of peace.
That's all I want. To be easy with every-
thing. But I wasn't born to that. I was
born to a time of fire.

      The world ain't wanted no part of me.
I could see that since I was about seven.
The world say it's better off without me.
See, Berniece accept that. She trying to
come up where she can prove something to
the world. Hell, the world a better place
cause of me. I don't see it like Berniece.
I got a heart that beats here and it beats
just as loud as the next fellow's. Don't
care if he black or white. Sometimes it
beats louder. When it beats louder, then
everybody can hear it. Some people get
scared of that. Like Berniece. Some peo-
ple get scared to hear a nigger's heart
beating. They think you ought to lay low
with that heart. Make it beat quiet and go
along with everything the way it is. But
my mama ain't birthed me for nothing. So
what I got to do? I got to mark my pass-
ing on the road. Just like you write on a
tree, "Boy Willie was here."
```

Boy Willie is a free spirit. In his speech, he also characterizes his sister's values. Berniece expresses these values when Avery asks her earlier in the play, "Who you got to love you, Berniece?"

```
BERNIECE. You trying to tell me a woman can't
      be nothing without a man. But you alright,
      huh? You can just walk out of here with-
      out me — without a woman — and still be
      a man. That's alright. Ain't nobody going
      to ask you, "Avery, who you got to love
      you?" That's alright for you. But every-
      body gonna be worried about Berniece. "How
      Berniece gonna take care of herself? How
      she gonna raise that child without a man?
      Wonder what she do with herself. How she
      gonna live like that?" Everybody got all
      kinds of questions for Berniece. Everybody
```

> telling me I can't be a woman unless I got
> a man. Well, tell me, Avery — you know —
> how much woman am I?

Berniece is bitterly down-to-earth; no dreams for her anymore. Avery understands that her values are more apparent than real, an expression of her inner pain. He is speaking about love, not bitterness, he says.

> AVERY. How long you gonna carry [your deceased
> husband] Crawley with you, Berniece? It's
> been over for three years. At some point
> you got to let go and go on. Life's got
> all kinds of twists and turns. That don't
> mean you got to stop living. That don't
> mean you cut yourself off from life.
> You can't go on through life carrying
> Crawley's ghost with you....
>   What is you [waiting] for, Berniece?
> You just gonna drift along from day to day.
> Life is more than making it from one day
> to another. You gonna look up one day and
> it's all gonna be past you. Life's gonna
> be gone out of your hands — there won't
> be enough to make nothing with. I'm stand-
> ing here now, Berniece — but I don't know
> how much longer I'm gonna be standing here
> waiting on you.

Berniece has cut herself off from the past and all the pain it represents to her. She is someone, perhaps like Willy Loman or the Prozorov siblings, who does not really know what she values. It takes someone who loves her, an Avery or a Boy Willie, to break through her self-imposed mask and encourage her authentic self to emerge. August Wilson's conception of authentic black values are the "lesson" of *The Piano Lesson*, and the many lines devoted to disclosing the characters' values are the evidence.

Personality Traits

The word personality comes from the Latin word *persona*, meaning mask or appearance, and so the meaning of personality as the manner in which a character is perceived by others, the way he relates to others. Personality has certain definable features called *personality traits* that identify outward appearance and behaviors. Personality traits may change in a character depending on the situation, but there is nevertheless a pattern that shows up under a variety of circumstances. This pattern allows for the collection of a personality profile. For some actors, personality traits are the issues that control how the character looks, sits, stands, walks, gestures, speaks, and behaves with other characters.

Personality traits can classify characters into one or more categories, or types. One of the earliest known personality authorities was Hippocrates (460 BC–370 BC), the Greek physician responsible for promoting ethical behavior in medicine through the Hippocratic oath. He proposed that the highest amount among four bodily fluids, or humours, determined one's personality type: blood (cheerful, active), phlegm (apathetic, sluggish), black bile (sad, brooding), and yellow bile (irritable, excitable). His theory was accepted in the West as late as the eighteenth century. Although Hippocrates' theory is obsolete, of course, speculation about personality remains fashionable because personality traits are simple to understand and talk about in daily life as well as in dramatic literature.

Personality traits, like other outcomes of play analysis, should be described as simply and clearly as possible. Although the list is perhaps endless, the process of determining them is not that difficult. First, list all the traits that the character shows in the play. Here it helps to think broadly better than narrowly. Next, reduce the list to manageable proportions by combining related traits and identifying those of central importance. The result will be a concise profile of personality traits. The most challenging part of the task is learning how to recognize personality traits from what characters actually say and do. Because personality is something all of us gossip about every day, close observation of human nature is required to distinguish clichés from genuine human behavior.

Willy Loman is a model character with which to explain this process. He reveals several of his most important personality traits in the opening scene. There Willy is impatient, indecisive, impulsive, and hurtful; "I said nothing happened. Didn't you hear me?" When he explains why he returned home unexpectedly, he is exhausted: "I'm tired to death … I couldn't make it. I just couldn't make it." His explanation is also absent-minded, "I suddenly couldn't drive anymore…. Suddenly I realize I'm goin' sixty miles an hour and I don't remember the last five minutes. I'm — I can't seem to — keep my mind to it." The confusion that underscores his line, "I have such thoughts, I have such strange thoughts," shows emotional anxiety. His rejection of Linda's appeal to him to ask for a desk job reveals inflated self-confidence; "They don't need me in New York. I'm the New England man. I'm vital in New England." Another important trait is cynicism, which appears when Linda reminds him that Biff and Happy have not been home for some time, "Figure it out. Work a lifetime to pay off a house. You finally own it, and there's nobody to live in it." There is also evidence of loyalty and faithfulness, traits reflected in his public values. More traits appear as the action unfolds, but these traits provide the raw material for Willy's personality profile.

What are the personality traits that distinguish the four Prozorov siblings in *Three Sisters*? Olga is generous, gracious, considerate, and intelligent. As the oldest sibling, she has assumed parental responsibility for keeping up everyone's collective spirits. This has come at the expense of her personal happiness, as expressed by her frequent migraines. Irina is the youngest of the four, excitable, sentimental, intelligent, spoiled and self-centered, and anxious about her future. The disintegration of her sentimental view of love forms the main action of the play. Masha is thoughtful and intelligent, bitter about her marriage, and desperate for companionship and affection. Their brother Andrey is cultured, scholarly, kind, introverted, poetical, naive, and insecure. Note their common personality traits of intelligence and good breeding, which is puzzling since they cannot even understand themselves or stand up for their own interests.

Complexity

Characters are appealing to us in proportion to how much they know about themselves. Their self-awareness or lack of it is what connects them with the play and determines their importance in the overall scheme of things. This capacity for self-knowledge indicates their *complexity*. Complexity is governed by what the characters respond to in their world, and more important, how they respond, whether ignorant, apathetic, and compliant or perceptive, intense, self-conscious, etc. The most complex character, the most "three-dimensional," the one with the most capacity to know him/herself, is considered the main character. The others are arranged around this character in different levels of complexity depending on their capacity for self-knowledge. This arrangement is not a defect in the writing but rather a technical principle resulting from the built-in economy of dramatic composition.

The least complex characters are regarded as *types*. They are often called "one-dimensional" because they display a single mental state, feeling, or action, throughout the play. One-dimensional characters are immediately recognized as belonging to certain well-known categories of people found in everyday life. In this group are domineering spouses, slow-witted or quick-witted servants, absent-minded professors, evil stepmothers, and so forth. A few examples in the study plays are Bob, the naïve wannabe crook in *American Buffalo;* Howard Wagner, the unfeeling businessman in *Death of a Salesman;* and Osric, the foppish dandy in *Hamlet.* One-dimensional characters show a minimum capacity for self-awareness and reveal very little about themselves apart from the narrow limitations of their type, that is, their single mental state, feeling, or action. They may be interesting and entertaining in themselves, but their real importance comes from their involvement with more complex characters, and their effectiveness in performance depends on the nature of this involvement.

The intermediate level of complexity (should we call it two-dimensional?) includes characters who are more self-aware than character types yet not as entirely aware of themselves or their world as they might be. Intermediate characters such as Linda and Happy Loman in *Death of a Salesman,* Mama and Ruth Younger in *A Raisin in the Sun,* Gertrude and Ophelia in *Hamlet,* Natasha Ivanovna in *Three Sisters,* and Doaker Charles in *The Piano Lesson* are some of the most engaging roles in dramatic literature. They are intermediate in terms of their complexity, but talented actors often create the impression that these characters are more complex than they actually are in the script itself. Sometimes the added complexity comes from playable potentials in the given circumstances, and other times it comes from the persona, or apparent personality, of the actors themselves. In any case, these actors are admiringly called "character actors" precisely because of their ability to add complexity to intermediate characters.

The most complex, fully developed, "three-dimensional" characters are those capable of completely understanding what is happening to them and allowing us to share in their knowledge. As a rule, the main character alone possesses this level of complexity. Plays are organized around them and most of the action is devoted to them. There are exceptions to this unitary principle, but not as many as some may think. Walter Younger is the single main character in *A Raisin in the Sun* as are Anna Fierling in *Mother Courage,* the Young Woman in *Machinal,* Joe Pitt in *Angels in America,* and Berniece in *The Piano Lesson.* Their capacity for self-awareness may or may not be actualized in the play itself, but self-awareness is one of the chief features that draws attention to them and identifies them at once as main characters.

Most plays may be considered biographies of one individual, but sometimes a play might contain more than one complex, fully-developed character, that is, more than one character capable of self-awareness. Identifying the main character in such plays can be problematical. Is *Death of a Salesman* about Willy or Biff? Is *The Wild Duck* about Gregers or Hjalmar? Is *Tartuffe* about Tartuffe or Orgon? Who is the main character in *Three Sisters*, or indeed is there one in the accepted sense? Some of the issues involved in identifying the main character are discussed below. At any rate, even if there is but one main character, there may be more than one character capable of self-awareness. We will learn more about this issue next.

Relationships

The focal point of dramatic interest in a play is the conflict between the main character and his/her chief opponent. Citing the Greek term used by Aristotle, writers call these characters the protagonist (*for* the argument) and the antagonist (*against* the argument). The relationship formed by these two characters is the *main relationship* in the play. Oedipus and Teiresias form the main relationship in *Oedipus Rex*, Hamlet and Claudius in *Hamlet*, Walter and Mama in *A Raisin in the Sun*, Willy and Biff in *Death of a Salesman*, Berniece and Boy Willie in *The Piano Lesson*, and Joe Pitt and Roy Cohn in *Angels in America*. The relationship between the protagonist and antagonist is purposely written to be the center of dramatic attention. Incidentally, the fact that some plays contain only one character does not do away with the concept of a main relationship. In such cases, the antagonist may be offstage (the wife in Anton Chekhov's monodrama *On the Harmfulness of Tobacco*, for example) or may be a different aspect of the same character (young Krapp in Samuel Beckett's play *Krapp's Last Tape*).

The protagonist and antagonist's contacts with other characters can be considered *secondary relationships*. Although these pairings sometimes can be as interesting and entertaining as the main relationship, they are nonetheless secondary to it for reasons of thematic focus. Secondary relationships exist primarily to add force and clarity to the main relationship, and only enough of the secondary relationship is furnished to fulfill this function. For example, Oedipus has secondary relationships with Creon and Jocasta; these relationships, however, are a direct outcome of his main relationship with Teiresias.

Walter Younger and his mother have secondary relationships with Ruth, Beneatha, and Bobo. Walter and Mama are not always on stage together, but their main relationship is developed by implication through these secondary relationships. In *American Buffalo*, Don has a special relationship with Bob, but the main relationship, the one that governs the meaning of the play, is that of Don and Teach.

Of course, there are differences of opinion about main relationships. Artistic sensibility presumes that no single understanding of a play is fixed forever. Specific productions need to be single-minded, of course, but apart from that, interpretations can be diverse. It is true that some alternative main relationship choices are little more than entertaining or thought-provoking departures from the original. But theatre is not science. There is no law against a fresh understanding of the main relationship, as long as it is based on a conscientious appraisal of the play and consistent with the sense of the production as a whole. A fair understanding of *Hamlet*, for example, might suggest other options for the main relationship — Hamlet and his deceased father, Hamlet and Horatio, Hamlet and Laertes, Hamlet and Fortinbras, or (according to playwright Tom Stoppard) not Hamlet and anyone else, but Rosencrantz and Guildenstern. What about the relationship between Walter and his deceased father in *A Raisin in the Sun*? Or between Jake and his deceased father, or Jake and his brother Frankie, or Jake and his mother Lorraine in *A Lie of the Mind*? All of these are options and yet all are based on a fair assessment of the information in the plays themselves. The key to identifying the main relationship is a conscientious analysis of the script.

Character in Nonrealistic Plays

At the beginning of the chapter we said that character is a distinctive pattern of actions, or what Aristotle called habitual action. But action cannot exist in a vacuum; to be dramatized action must be performed by characters. Thus stage characters are essentially "action-figures," that is, artificial objects designed to carry out certain actions, not real human beings. In realistic and classic plays characters perform actions based on plausible human behavior, but in nonrealistic plays they perform actions based primarily on an idea, the main idea. Plausible human behavior is not neglected or ignored, of course; otherwise the play would be arbitrary and incomprehensible. Even extreme examples of nonrealism, such as *Machinal* and *Happy Days* among the study plays, depend on characters performing plausible human actions to be understandable. The point is that characters in nonrealistic plays are less dependent on the realistic plausibility of their behavior than on the harmony of their behavior with the main idea. It is this emphasis on idea rather than realistic behavior that gives nonrealistic characters the freedom to behave in the unexpected ways they do. To some extent, of course, everything in a play is influenced by its main idea. What we are talking about here is a matter of degree. Characters in standard plays *tend* to be influenced more by plausible human behavior than by idea, whereas those in nonrealistic plays *tend* to be influenced more by an idea than by plausible human behavior.

Tendencies aside, sometimes it can seem as though nonrealistic characters are entirely abstract, with little concrete connection to normal human behavior. This viewpoint may be all right for novels, where a reader's imagination can transform abstractions into realizable images; or for movies and television, where technology can do the much the same thing. Theatre is very different. Its special purpose, its special appeal, necessitates the presence of live actors, and actors have to perform specific actions. Otherwise they will be reduced to indicating, performing generalized emotional states without authentic feeling and artistic truth. Theatre also calls for scenery, costumes, and lighting to add clarity and force to these actions. Otherwise designers would be reduced to the role of mere decorators, illustrators of pretty conceptual motifs with little connection to the main idea of the play. For even though the intuitive responses of actors, directors, and designers may be accurate and exciting in themselves, nevertheless they still need to be worked out in the concrete world of the play itself. The answer to this seeming paradox is professional analysis and explicit attention to fundamentals in performance and production. This book is about those fundamentals.

Since nonrealistic characters are conditioned by the main idea, it follows that their objectives, actions, conflicts, will, values, complexity, and relationships should come from the main idea as well. Undoubtedly, there are as many ways of doing this as there are nonrealistic plays, but by careful analysis it should be possible to understand how it is done in specific plays.

If the main idea in *Rosencrantz and Guildenstern are Dead* is "the impossibility of certainty," it is dramatized through a farcical treatment in which Guildenstern is obsessed with certainty, Rosencrantz is submissive to uncertainty, the Tragedians make a living from uncertainty, and Hamlet is able to transform uncertainty into tragedy.

The main idea is "abuse of power" in *The Birthday Party* and it is dramatized through a mysterious treatment in which Goldberg and McCann possess a secret power, which Stanley fails to escape from, Petey meekly protests against, and Meg blithely ignores. *Angels in America* is about "the disintegration of outdated social, political, and religious ideals" and all its characters are governed by this main idea. It is dramatized through a fantastic treatment in which Joe Pitt and Louis Ironson struggle with deeply held personal ideals, Harper Pitt falls to the wayside as a helpless victim of her ideals, Roy Cohn defends his cynical ideals and dies in the process, Rabbi Chemelwitz is pragmatic about his religious ideals, while Belize is without the narrow-minded idealism of the other characters and is therefore able to adjust to the world as it is becoming. In *Top Girls*, the characters are dramatized variants of "materialistic ambition" — for, against, or trapped within this main idea.

Characters in nonrealistic plays are each unique in the way they embody the main idea. They may explain themselves or not, and even if they attempt to do so the conclusion may be elusive and ambiguous. Moreover, characters are not "fully developed" as in realistic and classic plays. Character and idea are a single entity, a mutual embodiment of the play's special world.

193

The Score of a Role

The *score of a role* is one of the most important contributions of Stanislavsky's system. He defined it as "the small and large tasks, pieces, scenes and acts [...] created from the physical and elementary psychological tasks which firmly set the emotional experiences." In other words, the score of a role is an *organized arrangement* of all the playable information that can be found about a character in a play. Just as action analysis applied to an entire play is equivalent to what Stanislavsky called the score of a production, so also action analysis applied to a single character is equivalent to the score of a role. Actors and costume designers will find working on the score one of the most useful ways to see a character whole. A score is not a substitute for all the details and layers that can be discovered through formalist analysis, but it can provide sufficient information with which to begin creative rehearsals or design work.

To give a demonstration of the score of a role, we will analyze the character of Ophelia from *Hamlet*. Setting down the score in the form of an outline reinforces the logic of the seed, which is its controlling feature. Chapter 1 provided definitions for all the parts of action analysis and the procedures for determining them. The practical value of the score of a role should become self-evident from the following account.

Sequence of External Events

The score of a role is only concerned with those events in which the selected character appears on stage, whether speaking or silent. Ophelia is not in every scene of *Hamlet*; few characters are always onstage in a play. She takes part in six external events:

1,2: Claudius takes over the throne
1,3: Laertes departs for France
2,1: Polonius gives instructions to Reynaldo
3,1: Claudius eavesdrops on Hamlet and Ophelia
3,2: The "mousetrap scene"
4,5: Laertes returns to Elsinore

The above list shows how we defined the external events in Chapter 1, when dealing with action analysis for the entire play. To establish the score for Ophelia, we need to revise the descriptions and concentrate on her. The following descriptions do so while using the same kind of brevity and simplicity promoted earlier.

1,2: Ophelia attends the accession of Claudius
1,3: Ophelia says good-bye to Laertes
2,1: Ophelia seeks help from Polonius
3,1: Ophelia returns Hamlet's gifts
3,2: Ophelia meets Hamlet in public
4,5: Ophelia presents flowers to Claudius and Gertrude

Reviewing the Facts

The broad outlines of Ophelia's role are already emerging: her father stops loving her, her brother abandons her, her lover rejects her, her father forces her to give up the person she loves, her lover torments her, and she escapes into the past where she used to be happy.

Seed and Theme

Previously, we determined that the seed of *Hamlet* is idealism. Because the seed by definition influences all the characters, it follows that idealism also influences Ophelia. In her own way she is an idealist as well. But while the theme of the play is impossible idealism, that formulation applies to Hamlet more than it does to Ophelia. Her idealism is not of the impossible variety. She only asks that Hamlet, Laertes, and Polonius love and understand her as they used to do. Moreover, she does not attempt to impose her idealism on others, as Hamlet does. It is the others who assault her with their distorted brands of idealism and cynicism. In this respect, her fate may be compared to that of unfortunate Hedvig in *The Wild Duck*. Thus, Ophelia's personal variant of the theme (her personal response to the seed) might be described as "betrayed idealism."

Sequence of Internal Events

One by one, Ophelia's ideals are betrayed. The internal events below describe this process.

1,2: External: Ophelia attends the accession of Claudius
Internal: Ophelia sees that Polonius supports Claudius and that Hamlet is distressed. Two of her ideals have suddenly become distorted.

1,3: External: Laertes says good-bye to Ophelia
Internal: Laertes, another of her ideals, deserts her

2,1: External: Ophelia seeks help from Polonius **195**
Internal: She vainly seeks her Father's help when Hamlet, her most sacred ideal, rejects her

3,1: External: Ophelia returns Hamlet's gifts
Internal: Her father forces her to lie to Hamlet and Hamlet warns her against the world

3,2: External: Ophelia meets Hamlet in public
Internal: Hamlet, once her ideal gentleman-courtier-lover, publicly torments her

4,5: External: Ophelia presents flowers to Claudius and Gertrude
Internal: Ophelia bids farewell and returns to the ideal world in the past, where she remembers being happy

Three Major Climaxes

A role has a beginning, middle, and end just as a play does. Having only six events to deal with, these climaxes are not difficult to recognize here. The first major climax occurs when Ophelia's world — composed of her father, her brother, and Hamlet — changes with the accession of Claudius to the throne. The second major climax — the middle or tipping point of her development — occurs in 3,1, where she is forced to act in opposition to everything she holds good and true by lying to Hamlet about her love for him. The third major climax — the end for her — is in 4,5, where she says her farewell to this world of innocent ideals betrayed.

Super-Objective

To discover Ophelia's super-objective, it is necessary to ask what she wants from life. Let's make several tries at it. She wants Hamlet to love her, she wants to obey her father, she wants to please her brother, she wants things the way they were before Claudius took over, and she wants to be happy once again. What unites these alternatives is Ophelia's belief that something has gone terribly wrong and that, despite her best efforts, she cannot discover what it is. Maybe she has done something wrong herself, something to make everyone hate and abuse her? Therefore, her super-objective could be "to find out what she has done wrong." Being so innocent and idealistic, it is logical for her to feel that she is the one who has done something wrong instead of the others. The goal "to find out" is consistent with her innocent idealism. Ophelia is not in a position to influence the actions of others. There may be further choices for Ophelia's super-objective, but this description is supported by a great deal of evidence in the play and offers a strong, unifying line of development for her character.

Through-action

Ophelia's through-action is her story in the play, her main conflict stated in a single concise sentence. Who is Ophelia? The innocent daughter of a government official. What is she doing? Trying to come to grips with her strange, new world. Where is she doing it? In the corrupt court of Denmark. Hence, her through-action: the innocent daughter of a crooked official comes to grips with the corrupt environment she is forced live in. Ophelia is the daughter of a criminal and she is forced to choose whether she wants to live in her father's corrupt world. She chooses not to do so.

Counter Through-action

Hamlet's chief opponent in the play is Claudius, the ultimate source of corruption in the court. His relationship with Claudius forms the main relationship of the play. But Claudius does not directly influence Ophelia's behavior. Her actions are influenced more by Polonius, Laertes, and, above all, Hamlet — each of whom betrays her idealism in one way or another. Most readers would agree that Hamlet is the character who influences her most and the person who betrays her innocence most hurtfully. He occupies the other position in Ophelia's main relationship. Accordingly, the counter through-action may be described like this: an angry young prince ruthlessly abandons the innocent woman who loves him. Ophelia sees Hamlet through her own innocently idealistic eyes, not through his impossibly idealistic eyes.

Summary

Objectives are the specific goals that characters strive to achieve. They help make sense of a character's different feelings and thoughts by relating them to a select controlling desire. Actions are the behaviors that characters employ to achieve their objectives. Role conflicts consist of the tensions that arise from characters' opposing images of each other. Conflicts of objectives result from their opposing goals. The force with which characters pursue their goals is their will power. Although classic drama depends on strong-willed characters to make things happen, modern plays often include characters with weak or vacillating wills. When the leading character is weak-willed, there are compensating factors to sustain the play's interest. The characters' choices of the good and bad things in life define their values. A character's situation in relation to other characters and his or her response to the world of the play is determined by his/her values. Personality traits are a character's physical and vocal identification marks together with the impulses and inhibitions that reveal his/her individuality and how he/she relates to others. To focus attention, playwrights compose their list of characters in progressive levels of complexity. Ordinarily, the more self-aware a character is, the more important that character is in the play. The main character is most capable of self-awareness, or at least potentially so, although there are exceptions. Playwrights also arrange character relationships to further concentrate dramatic attention. The conflict between the main character and his/her strongest opponent is the main relationship. Other relationships are considered secondary but contribute to the main relationship by comparison and contrast.

All these features are crafted by the playwright and form the collective pattern (habitual action) that we refer to as character. Strictly speaking, playwrights create the written form of the characters, and actors create the physicalized form, called characterization, based on the written form.

197

Questions

1. *Objectives*. What is each character's super-objective? What are the minor objectives for each scene, unit, and beat? What does

the main character's super-objective suggest about the mise-en-scene? How could the mise-en-scene contribute to the effectiveness of the main character's super-objective?

2. *Conflicts.* What are the characters' images of themselves and each other (role conflicts)? Do the characters' super-objectives and minor objectives clash with those of other characters (conflicts of objectives)? Where specifically do those conflicts occur? What complications arise from these conflicts? What does the main conflict suggest about the mise-en-scene? How could the mise-en-scene contribute to the effectiveness of the main conflict?

3. *Will Power.* How strongly does each character work to carry out his/her objectives? Is the character's will steady, does it vacillate or gain or lose strength in certain circumstances? If so, where in the play does it do so? What do the characters' wills suggest about the mise-en-scene? How could the mise-en-scene contribute to the effectiveness of their wills?

4. *Values.* What does each character stand for and against? What does each character consider to be right and wrong? Good and bad? How do each character's values relate to those of the other characters? To the world of the play? What do the values of the characters suggest about the mise-en-scene? How could the mise-en-scene contribute to the effectiveness of these values?

5. *Personality Traits.* What is each character's energy level? Is it consistent or does it vary from one scene to another? How old is each character? What occupation? How does each character look? How does each character move? How does each character sound? What is each character's mental and emotional outlook? What are each character's internal impulses and inhibitions? What do the personality traits of the characters suggest about the mise-en-scene? How could the mise-en-scene contribute to the effectiveness of their personality traits?

6. *Complexity.* How self-aware is each character? Is the character a type, intermediate, or complex figure? Who is the most complex (main) character? Why? Who are the minor characters? Why? What does the complexity of each character suggest about the mise-en-scene? How could the mise-en-scene contribute to the effectiveness of this complexity?

7. *Relationships.* What is the main character relationship? Why? Could any other relationship be interpreted as the main relationship? Why? What are the secondary character relationships? Why? How do they contribute to the main relationship? What do the character relationships suggest about the mise-en-scene?

How could the mise-en-scene contribute to the effectiveness of their relationships?

8. *After Action Analysis.* Search for the play's seed/theme in each character. How does the seed/theme influence the character? In what way does associating the seed/theme with each character help the entire play to develop?

199

CHAPTER 7

Idea

The word *idea* comes from a Greek source, meaning the inner form of a thing as opposed to its physical reality. From this root comes the current meaning of a thought or a mental image. Idea is also related to the word ideal, meaning a model or an original pattern. To some extent, idea has been discussed already in connection with given circumstances, background story, plot, and character. Earlier chapters treated the contribution that each of these features made to idea, however, not the element itself. This chapter will concentrate on idea as one of the basic elements of drama.

Many people think of idea in drama in connection with idea plays, sometimes called problem plays, thesis plays, propaganda plays, or social dramas. Idea plays first appeared in France during the early nineteenth century with the works of Alexander Dumas the younger (1824–1895), Henri Becque (1837–1899), and Eugene Brieux (1838–1932). The tradition was expanded by Henrik Ibsen, George Bernard Shaw, and later dramatists. Idea plays are a part of today's theatre tradition. They are identified by the way they treat topical questions from a didactic, or instructional, point of view and offer, or at least suggest, a solution. Sometimes idea plays call attention to shortcomings in society; at other times, their intention is more radical. Shaw originated the discussion play, a kind of idea play in which current social, political, or economic issues are debated as part of the play's action.

Although idea and discussion plays aim at social reform, the concept of idea under consideration here is broader than that. Here idea means the thought pattern expressed by the whole play. Some would refer to this as the theme, super-objective, spine, meaning, outlook, or world view of the play. Idea is present in all plays in one form or another, but we should stress that not all ideas in plays are as meaningful as those found in *Oedipus Rex*, *Hamlet*, *The Wild Duck*, or *American*

Buffalo, for instance. Idea is most important in serious plays and satires. Idea appears in comedies, too, but in these plays character and plot are more important. Idea is least important in farce and old-fashioned melodrama. However, the playwrights associated with Theatre of the Absurd even managed to invest farce with intellectual significance.

According to critic Francis Fergusson, idea in action "points to the object which the dramatist is trying to show us, and we must in some sense grasp that if we are to understand his complex art" (*The Idea of a Theatre*, 230). In other words, idea controls the path analysis and subsequent artistic work should take. Learning to deal with idea is also a useful mental exercise because it tests the quality of the reader's thinking about a play. Idea lays the foundation for intelligent discussions about a play, which is indispensable for effective communication among the members of the creative team.

Differences of opinion about the concept of idea illuminate one of the major differences between studying plays for performance as opposed to intellectual study alone. For despite the centrality of idea in script analysis, it is seldom everything in a production. Theatre is above all an emotional experience, and the intellectual issues expressed in most plays seldom provide sufficient entertainment value in themselves. Idea illuminates character and plot, however, which in turn provide the entertainment value. Accordingly, actors, directors, and designers should guard against the belief that playwrights — at any rate, realistic and classic playwrights — think that plays are meant to demonstrate intellectual issues. Idea is rarely imposed on a play by the author but rather formed from within it. Nonrealistic plays have a somewhat different perspective on this question, which will be discussed later in the chapter.

Plays express idea both directly and indirectly. The idea in *Death of a Salesman* is expressed directly because it is stated openly in the words of the characters. The same may be said of *Tartuffe*, *The Piano Lesson*, *Angels in America*, and *Hamlet*. On the other hand, idea in *American Buffalo* is expressed indirectly through the plot and characters. The same is true for *A Lie of the Mind* and *Three Sisters*. Intellectual issues as such are not apparent in these plays. Nevertheless, the use of direct or indirect presentation does not exclude the use of its flipside at the same time or in the same play.

Idea in the Words

The customary verbal devices for conveying idea include titles, discussions, aphorisms, allusions, set speeches, imagery, and symbolism.

In some standard plays the need to talk about idea is so strong that the plot seems just a pretext for a discussion of intellectual issues — for example, in the plays of George Bernard Shaw or Tom Stoppard. Characters talk about ideas in such a way that their words can almost be removed intact from the dialogue and used for a composition on the intellectual issues in the play. But most playwrights avoid this approach. Instead, they integrate discussions or comments about idea within the dialogue so that a feeling of plausible realistic speech is maintained. Playwrights may turn their attention to intellectual issues, but they seldom overlook the principal need for dialogue to advance the plot and reveal character.

Titles

Very often playwrights embed idea in play *titles*. The title of *A Raisin in the Sun* is from a poem by Langston Hughes about frustrated dreams. The titles of *The Wild Duck, Happy Days, A Lie of the Mind, The Piano Lesson,* and *Mother Courage* indicate dramatic idea by implication. The important task with implications, of course, is interpreting them within the proper context. Is the title meant to be taken at face value, metaphorically, ironically? Often the title points to the main character of the play as in *Oedipus Rex* and *Hamlet.* A title that refers to both the main character and the idea is *Death of a Salesman.* Willy Loman, the salesman, is the main character of the play, but the title also points by implication to idea. We would expect a formal phrase like "The Death of…" to refer to an important person such as a member of royalty or a famous artist. However, a salesman is an ordinary person, an illustration of the so-called common man. Thus Miller's decision to emphasize the word salesman (ordinary businessman) instead of someone customarily more important is a clue to the idea of the play. The titles of *Machinal, The School for Scandal,* and *Angels in America* were probably chosen as much for their curiosity value as their ability to connect with the dramatic idea.

Discussions

Characters sometimes step back from the plot and engage in open *discussions*, or earnest conversations, about ideas. When this happens, the principle of artistic unity ensures that the discussion topics will relate in some important way to the main idea of the play. As mentioned earlier, such discussions are a characteristic of discussion plays, but briefer examples may occur in any sort of play. In *Oedipus Rex*, Sophocles included discussions about the capriciousness of the gods, the nature of political power, the role of chance in human affairs, and the credibility of oracles. Shakespeare is not considered an intellectual dramatist as such, but he included discussions about a wide assortment of ideas in *Hamlet*. Some of them deal with the nature of grief, love, duty, afterlife, revenge, Providence, indecision, ennui, ambition, suicide, acting, public office, forgiveness, honor, and guilt. The working-class characters in *Mother Courage* discuss war, economics, means and ends, military strategy, religion, and politics. *The Piano Lesson* contains discussions about moral issues in the form of homespun anecdotes.

Discussions exist in comedies as well as in serious plays. Discussions about religious principles and tolerance in *Tartuffe* have already been pointed out. In *The School for Scandal*, there are discussions about reputation, literary fashion, and class relations. *Three Sisters* contains discussions about how best to conduct one's life, which may or may not be reflected in the actions of the characters. Discussions may not always point straight to the main idea, but they can lead the way to it through careful consideration of their content and the given circumstances in which they occur.

203

Aphorisms

The word *aphorism* comes from a Greek source meaning the short statement of a principle, truth, or sentiment. We use this word to refer collectively to axioms, maxims, adages, saying, mottoes, sententious statements — all the brief, quotable statements that compress human experience into a concise verbal generality. For example, architect Miës van der Rohe's observation, "God is in the details," is an aphorism, as is Thoreau's, "It is never too late to give up your prejudices." Unlike the issue of discussions explained earlier, aphorisms are not mini-debates or reports of specific matters. They are concise remarks about general principles.

Sophocles used a number of aphorisms in *Oedipus Rex*. Some of notable ones are:

— There is no fairer duty than that of helping others in distress.
— No man can judge the rough unknown or trust in second sight, for wisdom changes hands among the wise.
— Time, and time alone, will show the just man, though scoundrels are discovered in a day.

Hamlet's enjoyment of aphorisms is one of his personality traits:

— Frailty, thy name is woman.
— Foul deeds will rise, though all the earth o'erwhelm them, to men's eyes.
— That one can smile and smile and be a villain.
— To be or not to be, that is the question.

He takes so much pleasure in aphorisms that he writes them down in his table book (a personal accessory Elizabethan gentlemen kept handy for this purpose): "My tables — meet it is I set it down/ That one may smile, and smile, and be a villain."

The value of aphorisms in illuminating the main idea depends on the context as well as acuteness and credibility of the character that is speaking. When an unscrupulous character pronounces an aphorism, it can express an opposite meaning from what was intended by the speaker. For instance in *Hamlet* Polonius is also fond of aphorisms. His famous farewell advice to Laertes is often cited out of context as a set of model aphorisms for sound moral behavior. Knowing what a hypocrite Polonius is, however, it is hard to take him seriously when he says things like "To thine own self be true, and it must follow, as the night the day, thou, canst not then be false to any man."

In modern plays, aphorisms are often distinguished by irony, conveying a meaning opposite of their literal meaning. In *Mother Courage*, Brecht uses aphorisms ironically in the form of humorous folk sayings:

— If you want the war to work for you, you've got to give the war its due.
— On the whole, you can say that victory amid defeat cost us plain people plenty.
— The best thing for us is when politics gets bogged down.

A humorous and ironic aphorism appears in *Angels in America* when Rabbi Isador Chemelwitz declines to hear Louis Ironson give vent to his feelings of guilt from abandoning his ailing partner, Prior Walter. The aphorism is underlined.

> RABBI ISADOR CHEMELWITZ. You want to confess, better you should find a priest.
> LOUIS. But I'm not a Catholic, I'm a Jew.
> RABBI ISADOR CHEMELWITZ. Worse luck for you bubbalah. <u>Catholics believe in forgiveness; Jews believe in guilt.</u>

204

Astute readers will find in this aphorism a clue about the different world views expressed in part 1 and part 2 of this remarkable play. Dramatists employ aphorisms in this way to highlight specific ideas that form a pattern of meaning in the play.

Allusions

An *allusion* is a reference to another work of literature or to a person or an event outside the play. It is a way of sending an idea-signal not only to listening characters, but also to the more knowledgeable members of the audience. Not everyone in the audience may recognize these allusions. On the other hand, those who do recognize them are rewarded with the pleasure of additional insights. Historically, the most common allusions came from religion, classical literature, history, and mythology. Today there may be a variety of such references in a play, including many that refer to current affairs and popular culture.

A playwright who is widely known for his distinctive use of allusions is Samuel Beckett. His play *Happy Days* contains many examples. Sometimes they are openly set off from the dialogue as allusions and other times they are integrated into the dialogue and require very close reading to recognize. Over two dozen sources have been discovered for the allusions in *Happy Days*, ranging from the works of classical Greek playwright Menander to songs by Viennese composer Franz Lehar. Even the physical action of the play is an allusion to Dante's *Inferno*, where characters in one level of hell lie half-buried in the earth as punishment for their sins. All the allusions relate in some way to the nearness of death and the transitory nature of life, issues that are connected approvingly or ironically to the main idea of the play.

In *Angels in America*, Tony Kushner was fond of using allusions from all kinds of highbrow and lowbrow sources, including politics, religion, camp homosexual culture, and popular culture, to cite some of the obvious examples:

Annie Hall	*Clinique*
Bayeux tapestry	*Come Back, Little Sheba*
Belle Reeve	Conran's
Berlin Wall	D Train
Big Mac	*Democracy in America*

CBS Mike Wallace	Ed Koch
Cecil B. DeMille	Ed Meese
Central Park	Ethel Rosenberg
Chernobyl	George Schultz
Christian martyr	Grace Jones
Henry Kissinger	Morticia Addams
in vitro	Newt Gingrich
J. Edgar Hoover	Ollie North
Jacob and the Angel	Pepto Bismol
Jesse Helms	Perestroika
Jessie Jackson	Prodigal son
Joe McCarthy	*Profiles in Courage*
Kaddish	*Rosemary's Baby*
King Lear	the Rosenberg case
Land of the free, home of the brave	Roy Cohn
Lazarus	San Francisco
Legionnaire's disease	Stephen Spielberg
Louis Farrakhan	Tab
Macy's	The Ramble
Mikhail Gorbachev	*The Twilight Zone*

Individually, these allusions help to establish the play's time period, but together they expand the thematic environment of the play — the collapse of old political, social, and religious ideals.

Sometimes allusions may be a challenge to identify, but they are meant to be more than mind games. In the hands of a skilled playwright, allusions enlarge the scope of plays. The Yellow Dog talked about so much in *The Piano Lesson* is a piece of Southern folklore that refers to an ill-tempered dog, one that turns on its owner. This has a bearing on our understanding of the play, in particular our understanding of Berniece, who appears to be rejecting her heritage. A subtle allusion is found in David Mamet's play *American Buffalo*, when Teach sings a tune to himself from *H.M.S. Pinafore*. The fact that this tune is from a comic opera by Gilbert and Sullivan is a clue to the meaning of the play and to Mamet's droll sense of humor in general. Comparable to other accepted conventions discussed in this chapter, allusions such as these can unite to form a coherent pattern of meaning that points to the main idea, if not directly illuminating it. Moreover, allusions are a practical test of artistic awareness because understanding them depends on our cultural literacy, the knowledge of our common cultural heritage.

Set Speeches

Set speeches are formal or methodical speeches that emphasize specific intellectual issues in the play. They stand out from the surrounding dialogue because they are extended and composed like operatic arias, court pleadings, or arguments at a formal debate. There may be one or several set speeches (or none) in a play, touching on a variety of subjects and viewpoints. In all cases, however, they embody at that moment the thematic essence of the scene or play, accenting the general meaning in addition to the particular moment.

Because of their formal workmanship, set speeches appear more often in classic plays, where formal language is the norm. Laertes' admonition to Ophelia in 1,3 of *Hamlet*, in which he warns her against expecting too much from Hamlet's affections, is partly a set speech. In the context of saying good-bye to his sister, he explains the weighty responsibilities of kingship in general. Laertes' speech changes the episode from that of particular characters to the general political environment of the play. There are three conspicuous set speeches in *Tartuffe*. The first two appear together in act 1, when Cleante describes the ideal traits of a religious person, and the third takes place at the end of the play when the Officer pays tribute to the wisdom and generosity of the King.

207

Set speeches are less common in realistic plays because their obvious formality can interfere with the need to sustain realistic plausibility. Unless they are analyzed carefully, they can appear mawkish, over-sentimental, or affected. Modern playwrights tend to introduce compensating features to overcome this possibility. Arthur Miller managed to include one each by Linda ("attention must be paid...") and Charley ("No one dast blame this man...") in *Death of a Salesman*. The first occurs when Linda is justifiably upset about Biff and Happy abandoning their father in a restaurant so they could be with their girl friends. The second occurs in the epilogue, where the characters are gathered to say some final words at Willy Loman's gravesite. In the context of *American Buffalo's* clipped dialogue, a rather long line by Teach near the end of the play could be considered a set speech. It is formally written and openly expresses the idea of the play, but it is darkly ironic because the speaker is a prime example of what he is railing against. Notice the use of capital letters, too, which underlines this sense. Here Teach is upset when he learns that Bob has actually been lying about the whole setup.

```
TEACH. [...] The Whole Entire World
        (TEACH picks up the dead-pig-sticker and
        starts trashing the junk shop)
        There Is No Law.
        There Is No Right And Wrong.
        The World Is Lies.
        Every Fucking Thing.
        (Pause.)
        Every God-forsaken Thing.
DON. Calm down, Walt.
TEACH. We all live like cavemen.
```

Because set speeches call attention to the intellectual issues in a play, they can be reliable sources of information about the main idea if they are treated attentively. Moreover, as openings into the heart of the play, they also provide excellent acting opportunities. Set speeches are longer than adjacent speeches, are formally written to achieve specific emotional effects, and emphasize crucial issues in the play.

Imagery

Imagery is the use of sensory language to represent objects, actions, or ideas. "The air smells sweet." "He could still see her in his imagination." By expressing issues in sensory form like this, imagery increases our resources for understanding plays. Imagery can be expressed in several ways. A *simile* is a figure of speech in which two unlike things are explicitly compared: "She is like a rose." A *metaphor* is a figure of speech in which a word or phrase that ordinarily designates one thing is used to designate another: "A mighty fortress is our God."*Personification* represents a person as an inanimate object, creature, or abstraction: "Art is a jealous mistress." And *assonance* is a resemblance of sound in words or syllables: "June moon."

G. Wilson Knight (*The Wheel of Fire*) and Caroline Spurgeon (*Shakespeare's Imagery and What It Tells Us*) have found that imagery plays a powerful role in Shakespeare's plays. *Hamlet,* for example, contains many images of decay. Note Marcellus's line (1,4,90): "Something is rotten in the state of Denmark." (A fish rots from the head down, and the leadership of Denmark is corrupt.) Various post-apocalyptic images are found in *Happy Days*, and imagery about basic physical activities is apparent in *Mother Courage*. Images of frontier America can be found throughout *A Lie of the Mind*.

Apart from intellectual knowledge, imagery, like music, appeals directly to the imagination. As such it plays a crucial role for designers in their development of the mise-en-scene. Incorporating a play's imagery through the mise-en-scene has the potential to illuminate a large range of feelings and ideas from the play in fresh ways, evoking a feeling of the whole.

Symbolism

A *symbol* is something that is both itself and something more — a thought-sign. The word itself comes from a Greek verb meaning "to throw together," and its noun form means a mark or a sign. Unlike a metaphor, which compares two different things, a symbol automatically associates something with itself. Symbols vary in complexity and purpose, of course, but we only need to consider two kinds for script analysis. *Intentional symbols* are those in which there is a direct equation (scales = justice, owl = wisdom), either because of an accepted meaning or because they are designated as a symbol in the play. *Incidental symbols*, by contrast, originate from readers and are subject to change according to their sensibilities.

Normally, an author who uses intentional symbols slips them in cunningly. If they stand out too much their handling will feel like a sermon or book report instead of a play. But in the hands of a skilled playwright, intentional symbols can enrich by fresh associations, working like allusions or imagery, except more noticeable and therefore more potent. By evoking abstract ideas and feelings in concrete form, intentional symbols function as connections between the play and the outside world. Many times they can expose an idea, and reveal it more quickly and emphatically, than other elements.

The wild duck in the play of the same name is an example of an intentional symbol. We learn from the play that when a Scandinavian wild duck is wounded, it does not try to escape but dives into the water and clings to the weeds on the bottom. We also learn that a wild duck is tamed without difficulty and thrives in captivity despite its name. Notice that Gregers Werle, the radical idealist, is the one who designates the wild duck as a symbol of Hjalmar Ekdal when he says to him in act 2, "I almost think you have something of the wild duck in you." Idealists, Ibsen seems to be saying, like to find symbols of their ideals in the world around them. The symbol of the wild duck reinforces behavior patterns that Gregers thinks he sees in Hjalmar. According to Gregers, the wild duck represents Hjalmar's inability to cope with the misfortunes in his life. He also believes that Hjalmar has forsaken his youthful ideals for a comfortable existence. The meaning of the wild duck is clear because the playwright has described it as such in the story.

Other intentional symbols in the study plays are the office machines in *Machinal*, Mama's potted plant in *A Raisin in the Sun*, the pregnant ant in *Happy Days*, Anna Fierling's canteen wagon in *Mother Courage*, the spinning top that Fedotik gives to Irina in *Three Sisters*, the piano in *The Piano Lesson*, Bethesda Fountain in *Angels in America*, and the name Oedipus (wounded foot) in *Oedipus Rex*.

What was stated above about the relation of imagery to mise-en-scene also holds true for symbols. Intentional symbols by definition go straight to the imagination, often calling to mind specific elements of the mise-en-scene. Apart from being practical, accurate, and attractive, production values that take advantage of this fact are *artistically functional* as well. That is, mise-en-scene invested with symbols (and imagery) from the play evokes intangible, experiences, further inducing a feeling of the whole."

210

Prologue and Epilogue

The prologue and epilogue are additional literary devices used for presenting an idea directly. The *prologue* (literally, the speech before) is a small scene, formally separate from the play, in which the main idea is subtly introduced. The *epilogue* (the speech after) summarizes the main idea by restating it at the end of the play within a wider context. In a classical Greek tragedy such as *Oedipus Rex*, the prologue and epilogue frame the action according to what was then accepted dramatic form. They highlight the main idea by their characteristics as formal openings and closings and through the words of the Chorus. The Requiem at the end of *Death of a Salesman* is a formal epilogue with a similar function. The nature of the funeral scene leads us to expect a summing up, which we find in the words of Linda, Biff, Happy, and Charley.

Idea in the Characters

Idea may also be expressed through certain kinds of conventional characters. Expressing idea in this way involves definite technical restrictions, however, because characters cannot speak about the play's meaning too much without straining plausibility. Such characters may say only what is permitted within the limits of their own identities and while addressing other characters. With these limits in mind, over time certain conventional characters have developed that may embody idea without straining logic or entertainment value. These conventional characters do not appear all the time or in every play. Moreover, when they do appear there is no rule against a single character fulfilling several playwriting functions at one time. In other words, sometimes they act simply as clear-cut dramatic characters, and are not always as thematically functional.

All the same, readers should not depend too much even on these conventional characters to learn about idea, for that practice comes close to the intentional fallacy discussed in the Introduction. Interest in the ideas that characters express and the technical functions some characters carry out should not lead to misunderstanding the characters as characters. Some characters may give emphasis to idea, but in the best plays, they are seldom merely mouthpieces for the meaning. Characters behave as characters because they are governed first by artistic considerations and only later by technical requirements.

Narrator and Chorus

A *narrator* is a character that adds spoken commentary to a play, and a *chorus* is a group of characters that serve as participants, commentators, or supplements to the main action. Because a narrator and chorus by definition always know more about the story than the other characters, they can be studied for information about idea. In *Mother Courage*, Anna Fierling, Eilif, Yvette, and the Chaplain step out of the action several times and speak or sing to the audience as narrators. They communicate ideas from the play through songs, such as "The Song of the Old Wife and the Soldier," "The Song of Fraternization," and "The Song of the Great Capitulation." These songs are about ideas central to the play — over-romantic heroism, associating with the enemy, admission of defeat, and more. The chorus in Greek tragedies also plays dual roles of narrator during the choral odes and citizens of the polis during the episodes. When narrators or choruses interrupt the action, they are likely to explain something important about idea.

Raisonneur

Another conventional character that knows more than the other characters is the *raisonneur*, a type of narrator, but one who always remains within the action. Although participating in the action, the raisonneur has little direct effect on it, thus furnishing this character with objectivity and credibility. The raisonneur is often a doubter, wishing to offer sound advice or to convince through reasoning. The character of Cleante in *Tartuffe* is a classic example of a raisonneur. As Orgon's brother-in-law, he remains plausibly within the action, but his liberal viewpoint permits him to speechify while continuing to maintain his place in the story. He has no major influence on the plot, but he does defend his opinions about the main intellectual issues in the play. Another example of a raisonneur is Dr. Relling in *The Wild Duck*. After his introduction during the lunch scene in act 3, he appears four more times in the play. He objects to Mrs. Sorby's marriage plans (they used to be lovers), admonishes Gregers' misguided idealism, tracks down the missing Hjalmar, and provides medical help for Hedvig. Dr. Relling says that he is "cultivating the life illusion" in others, that is, helping them to be able to live with themselves. Despite an inclination to moralize, raisonneurs like Relling are most valuable when they are understood as part of the world of the play and not just as sermonizers. For example, as a character Cleante expresses indignation when Orgon treats his religious skepticism as the ranting of an atheist. Dr. Relling expresses similar feelings of indignation when Gregers Werle accuses him of being indifferent to the welfare of their mutual friend, Hjalmar. The words of raisonneurs should be understood as expressions of their character, not merely stuck on to explain the meaning of the play.

Confidant

A *confidant* (fem., *confidante*) is a close friend or associate with whom the main character shares secrets or discusses personal problems. Resembling a raisonneur, a confidant has little direct influence on the action even though always remaining within it. Because others open their hearts to this character, the confidant is more often a trusted friend than a skeptical observer like the raisonneur. Confidants tend to be well-adjusted characters without serious personal conflicts in respect to the world of the play. In this capacity, confidants want to help the main character adjust to that world. They provide an opportunity for main characters to seek sympathetic help for their problems.

Charley, Willy Loman's next-door neighbor in *Death of a Salesman*, is a typical confidant. In act 1, Charley listens sympathetically and helps Willy to take his mind off his problems. He genuinely feels sorry for Willy. In act 2, he gives Willy practical help with offers of money and a job. Other examples of confidants are Horatio in Hamlet and Belize in *Angels in America*. By definition, confidants function outside the main action most of the time. This apparent passiveness is offset by their strong desire to help other characters. By offering others a chance to talk in safety about vital ideas, confidants provide support and encouragement unobtainable from anyone else.

Norm Character

The term *norm* or *normative character* is borrowed from the social sciences. It describes someone who is prudently adjusted to the world of the play. The norm character is another example of a character that knows more about the situation than the other characters, but in this case greater awareness results more from intuitive understanding than from direct knowledge. Norm characters do not appear in every play. They appear most often in comedies, where their common sense serves as a reference point against which to compare the eccentric behavior of other characters. Playwrights know that eccentricity is illumined best if it is displayed against a background of cheerful common sense.

In *Tartuffe*, the norm character is Orgon's wife, Elmire. Despite Madame Pernelle's unsympathetic opinion of her, Elmire is sensibly adjusted to the capricious standards of her society. She is independent-minded, tolerant, and shrewd in the ways of the world, and, above all, good-natured. For Elmire religion (the main obstacle in the play) is a private matter, not a commodity for public discussion or a hoax to defraud people of their money. Although Elmire strongly disapproves of Tartuffe, she does not overreact by publicly condemning him. Tartuffe is a shrewd character, after all, and trying to expose him directly could backfire (and does backfire when Damis tries to unmask him). Instead, she attempts to set Orgon free from his obsessive hero-worship by leading Tartuffe to expose his own hypocrisy. This is one part of her super-objective, which might be "to get the family's life back to normal, the way it used to be before Orgon became obsessed with Tartuffe." Notice the importance of normalcy in the super-objective of this norm character.

In *The School for Scandal*, Rowley performs the dual functions of norm character and confidant, as does Charley in *Death of a Salesman*. Mrs. Sorby is the norm character in *The Wild Duck*, as is Joseph Asagai in *A Raisin in the Sun*. For sound dramatic reasons, norm characters are of central importance in their plays. A crucial point is that they are too intelligent to be pressured by social

213

conventions. And since they do not take themselves too seriously either, they often display a well-developed sense of humor. They are interesting, attractive characters in themselves, not colorless or insipid, or else the meaning of the play is liable to be weakly played up.

Having reviewed the ways playwrights present idea through the characters, we still should be careful about assuming that any characters point inevitably to the main idea. This does not mean that characters never say anything trustworthy. It is only that they have their own objectives, and what they say is shaped by those objectives from moment to moment. Their words may be appropriate in one set of circumstances, yet they may not explain the entire play all the time.

Idea in the Plot

Although dramatists may sometimes present the idea in the words of the characters, successful plays work primarily through action, not verbal statements. Plays are not literary or philosophical essays, and there is seldom much obvious talk in them about ideas. Playwright Thornton Wilder said that playwriting springs from an instinctive linkage between idea and action. To this extent, no matter how intellectual a play may seem on the surface, the main idea is presented most persuasively through the plot, the pattern of actions. Plot is part of the expressive system of drama. Just as conventions in the dialogue and characters can express idea, so also can certain conventions in the plot. This section will study these plot conventions in an effort to understand how dramatists may express idea through them.

Parallelism

Playwrights who feel the need to express a series of equivalent or similar ideas sometimes use a plot device called *parallelism*. When characters or events in a play have matching counterparts in other characters or events in the same play, the issues connecting them may be reinforced by means of parallelism, that is, through repetition or contrast or both. Parallelism calls attention to idea.

Shakespeare often used parallelism to point up idea in his plays. An analysis of *Hamlet*, for example, reveals a number of parallelisms linking the characters of Hamlet, Laertes, and Fortinbras. The fathers of Hamlet and Fortinbras are both deceased warrior-kings, while their sons are both princes and rightful heirs to the throne, yet neither holds the throne in his own country because their uncles have taken them over underhandedly. Polonius, by contrast, is a pale reflection of these two fathers. There are, or were, close relationships between all these fathers and sons: between Hamlet and King Hamlet, and Fortinbras and King Fortinbras, Laertes and Polonius. Hamlet has embarked on a course of revenge for his father's murder. For equivalent reasons, Fortinbras threatens to retake lands his father lost to Denmark and Poland, and Laertes threatens to revenge the murder of Polonius. Characters involved in parallelisms are considered *foils* for one another, meaning they point out some features of each other. From these and other connections, it seems clear that Laertes, Fortinbras, and Hamlet could be considered mutual foils. Although the three parallel foils in *Hamlet* aim to revenge the deaths of their fathers, Fortinbras and Laertes are unshakable in their tasks. The absence of a similar commitment in Hamlet points up the fact that he is more poet or philosopher than a soldier. The parallelisms also highlight the complex personality traits Hamlet displays compared to those few simple traits displayed by Fortinbras and Laertes.

Parallelism appears in modern plays too. In *The Wild Duck*, the activities of the Werle and Ekdal families constitute parallelisms. The main idea expresses itself through the contrasting ideals of Gregers and Hjalmar and through their relationships with their parents, above all with their fathers. Notice the feminine influence in their family backgrounds as well. Three parallelisms in *Death of a Salesman* also reinforce the relations between fathers and sons: Willy and Biff, Charley and Bernard, and the founder of the Wagner Company and his son Howard. The sub-plots indicate that father–son relations reinforce issues associated with the main idea. The two families in *A Lie of the Mind* form obvious parallelisms and their connections are brought to our attention by the alternating construction of the plot. The question is, what should be compared or contrasted about the two families and how does it help us to understand the play? The same question arises with *Angels in America* in the parallelism between Harper and Joe Pitt on one hand and Prior Walter and Louis Ironson on the other. Of course readers should not look for parallelisms all the time or in every play, but whenever parallelisms can be accurately identified, readers would be justified in studying them for clues about idea.

Conflict

Chapter 6 treated conflicts that motivate the characters — role conflicts and conflicts of objectives. Here we are talking about *intellectual conflicts*, conflicts that generate ideas, producing intellectual tensions that are especially valuable for directors and designers. Intellectual conflicts stem from opposition between societal systems or between characters and the world of the play.

Consider the ideas that can be drawn from the intellectual conflict in *American Buffalo*. At first reading, petty criminal behavior appears to be the sole interest in the play, but after closer analysis this behavior begins to illuminate a significant societal issue, an intellectual conflict: devotion to an ideal that clashes with reality. Don is devoted to the thinking and methods of a professional crime as distinguished from amateur crime. In some ways he is devoted more to the concept of professionalism than he is to the actual criminal act of stealing. He esteems Teach because he believes him to be professionally skilled at what he does, at stealing. But Teach only talks about professionalism. At heart he is a violent and selfish petty crook who cloaks the stupidity of his behavior in the disguise of craftsmanship, professionalism. Don learns this lesson when Teach makes a mess of their scheme to steal the rare coins, trashes Don's shop, and critically injures Bob. Don's idealism clouded his thinking and blinded him to the reality of Teach's behavior. Don has fallen in love with an idea and therefore allowed his life and Bob's to be thrown away; it is an intellectual conflict that goes to the heart of the play. And in the form of ignorant idealism, it is found in public life all around us as well, unfortunately. Combined with the supporting tensions of crime and violence, *American Buffalo* offers a rich supply of intellectual tensions. By setting the play in an intellectual context larger than itself, such conflicts can contribute to the kind of directing and design that helps to theatricalize the play in its imaginative entirety.

216

Main Climax

Director Elia Kazan said that the *main climax* of a play is the most concrete illustration of its main idea. All the parts of the play converge at this point, and everything appears in its most vivid theatrical form. The quality of a play's main climax is judged by how well it fulfills these functions. All the essential forces of the play should be found at work there.

This point may be explained by studying a typical example in detail. In *The Wild Duck*, the main climax occurs almost at the end of the play when Hedvig shoots herself. She has killed herself, but it is the various responses to her death that actually form the main climax. Old Ekdal attributes her death to forest demons. He flees into the garret to console himself with liquor. Reverend Molvik is always drunk anyway. He mumbles a few prayers over Hedvig's body, but this gesture is embarrassing rather than consoling. Hedvig's father, Hjalmar Ekdal, reacts in his usual way by thinking of himself first. When Dr. Relling tries to console Hjalmar by assuring him that Hedvig's death was painless, Hjalmar says melodramatically, "And I! I hunted her from me like an animal.... She crept terrified into the garret and died for love of me!" Super-idealist Gregers Werle interprets Hedvig's death as the symbolic validation of his mission in life. "Hedvig has not died in vain," he says to Dr. Relling, "Didn't you see how sorrow set free what is noble in him [Hjalmar]?" Relling, for his part, scoffs at this. He warns Gregers that even Hedvig's suicide will not change Hjalmar's juvenile selfishness, but Gregers refuses to believe it. "If you are right and I am wrong," he says, "then life is not worth living." But Relling sees things more skeptically. He recognizes that Hedvig's death has become little more than an opportunity for extravagant self-pity in Hjalmar. In addition, he knows that Hedvig would not have died if Gregers had not misled Hjalmar with his foolish notions of "the claim of the ideal."

The death of an innocent child is always a heartbreaking event. It should draw out feelings of unaffected sorrow and remorse in the characters and the audience. The family picture Ibsen provides at the climax of *The Wild Duck*, however, is one of drunkenness, petty vanity, and thoughtless insensitivity. Gregers had hoped to inspire Hjalmar with renewed idealism; instead, he has had the opposite effect. This climax shows through concrete human behavior that Gregers is a dangerous type of radical idealist. Although Relling provides a few significant remarks about the situation, Ibsen has chosen to express the main idea of the play theatrically, that is, through the actions and attitudes of the characters. Notice as well that Dr. Relling can only talk about the others' indifference to suffering; long ago he lost the ability to feel anything himself. He can only stand by and watch. Ibsen shows that behind every authoritative assertion of ideals, including Relling's, stands an insecure psyche.

The climax of *A Lie of the Mind* is another useful example. Three moments at or near the end of the play offer possibilities for the main climax: the moment when Lorraine learns from her daughter, Sally, that her son Jake murdered his father; the moment when Baylor kisses Meg, thereby reversing their uncaring relationship; and the moment when Jake relinquishes his wife, Beth, to the care of his brother Frankie. Sam Shepard described this play as "a love ballad...a little legend about love." Which moment best expresses that statement most strongly in terms of human behavior? Studying the main climax can help to give an understanding about how idea itself works in the theatre. It shows how to understand that idea in drama is not an abstract literary concept but rather the philosophy of the play expressed in terms of human action.

The Main Idea

Some think it is necessary to see a play in concrete physical terms, and then somehow rise above it into an abstract world of meaning. On the contrary, dramatic ideas are too complicated to be expressed by abstract thinking alone. Rather by using selection and compression, playwrights transform ideas into concrete human experience. They do this by putting the characters through a controlled series of events intended to illustrate a specific view of the world. When theatricalized well, this can also induce audiences to feel as the characters do in the given circumstances. Every word in the play exists for this reason, and every detail and incident has been prepared with this end in view. The result is that even though the dramatist is not there in person, the *main idea* is understood by the actors, director, designers, and audience as an obvious conclusion. Thus, the main idea is the outcome of the entire presented experience of the play, both performance and mise-en-scene. And since plays are biographies of the main character, it is he/she that by default forms the principal focus of this experience. Incidentally, the main idea should not be confused with the production concept, which is an original idea, design, or plan for performing a play and governing its mise-en-scene. The main idea is an intellectual matter present in the script itself. Ideally, a production concept should be based on a sound understanding of a play's main idea, but this does not always happen in practice.

To be studied for itself the main idea must be changed from its concrete human expression in the play into some type of verbal understanding. This is done by applying a process of radical reduction to the entire play so as to disclose its underlying form. An automobile, for example, stripped to its bare frame is still recognized functionally as an automobile. Though most of the details have been removed, it still retains its underlying form. Its other parts are extensions and elaborations of this basic framework. Similarly, the main idea represents the essence of the underlying framework that unites all the parts of the play. This process of extreme reduction is more than academic, it is artistically essential. By stating the idea in a simple, condensed way it remains as close as possible to its original unified expression in the play. As soon as minor qualifications (more

218

words) are added, information enters that may obscure the main idea's basic clarity. Moreover, whenever the formulation of the main idea is too drawn out or contains too many conditions, there is a strong chance that some misunderstanding exists about the play at the basic level.

Radical reduction comes after the fact, when the playwright's work is already finished. There are wide differences in the mentalities of working playwrights. For some, writing is an intellectual experience, planned and worked out through careful logic. For others, writing is a intuitive experience. And many gradations in between. Whatever the case, most playwrights do not create their works backward; that is, they do not begin with an intellectual conception of the play's meaning then work backward to the finished play. In the initial stages of work, playwrights generally have only an incomplete awareness of what they have written, at least in intellectual terms. Nonetheless, this does not mean their finished plays lack coherent main ideas. Nor does it lessen the importance of the main idea for the creative needs of actors, directors, and designers, who, after all, are the fortunate recipients of the playwright's finished work.

Although there are no fixed rules governing how to state the main idea in reduced form, in formalist analysis it is usually expressed as a super-objective, action summary, thesis sentence, or theme. (See Chapter 1 for the super-objective and through-action, too.) No single method has any particular advantage over any other, and any or all of them may be used for just about any play.

The *super-objective* (some say spine or super-task) is Stanislavsky's way of describing a play's main idea. It is used even by those who are not knowingly influenced by Stanislavsky, and therefore we will begin with it. Since we already know about character objectives, the principle of the super-objective is not that difficult to understand. According to Stanislavsky, all the individual minor objectives in a play should come together under the command of a single, controlling objective called the super-objective of the play. We might think of the relation between the super-objective and all the minor objectives as the popular Russian nesting dolls (matryoshka dolls), graduated in size, each fitting inside the next larger doll. Note again that the super-objective of the play is actually that of the main character, whose biography forms the play.

Like other objectives, the super-objective is seldom frankly observable in the dialogue but must be deduced from the action. It is the reader's responsibility to search for the logic that frames all the objectives and relates them to the super-objective. Any objective, no matter how small, that does not relate to the super-objective is considered inaccurate or at least lacking in coherence. To repeat a discussion from an earlier chapter, it is important to choose for objectives the infinitive form of an active verb to energize the action in the right direction (always toward another character). The same principle applies in the formulation of a super-objective.

How does this process work? One reasonable super-objective for *Hamlet* might be "to search for a father's murderer" or "to revenge a king's death." It is possible to imagine how all the objectives could relate to these options because a great deal of information in the play supports them. Strictly speaking, however, they are incomplete as super-objectives. The problem is that by treating the play essentially as a murder mystery or a revenge play, the other issues in it will have only accidental importance. The play's social, political, moral, and spiritual consequences will be afterthoughts. If the super-objective is "to rescue Denmark from wickedness," the super-objective would be more complete. Hamlet's love for his country would receive stronger emphasis. The social ideas would also grow in importance, giving the whole play larger social and political significance. The play can be enriched still further if the super-objective is "to reawaken everyone's conscience." This is a paraphrase of the formulation Edward Gordon Craig defined for his famous Moscow Art Theatre production in 1924. It proved to be effective for him because it unified all the objectives under an appropriate commanding idea without omitting anything he believed to be significant in the play. Hamlet's goals become broader, and the whole play becomes more voluminous and less personal than it is if the leading character is preoccupied with his father or his country alone. The implications behind Craig's super-objective are no longer merely social or political but moral in scope. Moreover, the poetic dimensions of the play take on special significance, an important issue for Craig because of his affection for highly conceptual mise-en-scene.

We can see that these super-objectives were described in three ways: personal (to search for a father's murderer); social and political (to save a country from wickedness); and universal (to reawaken the sense of morality). Each option had a great deal in the play to support it, but each was also progressively broader in scope and expressed more of the play's meaning. In the classroom, the exact wording of the super-objective is up to the individual reader. For production, however, everyone on the creative team should be able to work with the same super-objective and contribute to its unified expression in the play, although the director is usually responsible for defining its final form. The scope of the super-objective can be within any range of meaning — personal, social, political, moral — but to be effective in production it should be based on information from the play itself and not unthinkingly laid on.

For some plays, readers may choose to state the main idea as an *action summary*, without bothering about Stanislavsky's requirements for a super-objective. An action summary is just what it says: a brief summary of the play's main action as it is understood for a specific production. Actor Laurence Olivier used an action summary for his film version of *Hamlet* as "the story of a man who could not make up his mind." Olivier's main idea obviously highlights the psychological dimensions of the play. Readers who are more socially or politically inclined may choose to express the main idea as a *thesis statement*, a single declarative sentence that asserts a lesson about the subject of the play forcefully. For example, Ibsen may have written *The Wild Duck* to demonstrate that "impractical idealists always go wrong," or Brecht may have written *Mother Courage* to show that "capitalism destroys human feeling." *Three Sisters* may be a demonstration that "love always gives back much less than we expect," and *Angels in America* is evidence that "freedom that fails to grow will not last." All four examples show that a thesis statement is often useful for highlighting social or political issues. In contrast to a thesis sentence, a *theme* is not an arguable message but rather an expression of the main idea in abstract universal terms. For example, the theme of *Machinal* might be "a struggle for freedom" or that of *Oedipus Rex*, "a quest for truth." Themes seem to work best when they are expressing the broad philosophical and poetic aspects of a play. (Chapter 1 presents somewhat different but related explanations of super-objective, through-action, and theme.)

All these formulations are reasonable definitions of the main idea for their respective plays. The logic behind them should be obvious: it is an effort to describe in condensed form the basic conflict at the heart of the play, the conflict that revolves around the main character. Regardless of the verbal form, it is crucial to state the main idea as a single declarative statement. The main idea will be free from cloudiness if its formulation boldly asserts or denies something about the meaning of the play. And if it is concisely expressed.

Developing a statement of the main idea tests artistic awareness because it forces the creative team to determine what it is they want to express with their work. It stimulates ideas about acting, directing, and design, but it takes considerable practice to acquire the skill needed to define it accurately and concisely. This skill can be

221

nurtured by making it a habit to identify the main idea for whatever plays (including films, TV shows, and novels) are read or seen. As said earlier in this chapter, occasionally the playwright states the main idea somewhere in the dialogue. The task is to find that statement among all the many words in the play. In most cases, however, the main idea is not openly stated and so must be extracted from the action by means of implication. The ability to draw out implications (patterns of meaning) in this way is one of the most challenging skills in script analysis. If actors, directors, and designers can learn to extract the main idea in an accurate and convincing way, it is likely that they will be more consistently successful in their creative work.

Idea in Nonrealistic Plays

Playwright Thornton Wilder said that realism is the theatre of the Unique Occasion. In standard plays the events happen to one set of persons, at one moment in time, and in one place. By contrast, nonrealistic plays attempt to show how each human being is both an individual and the representative of a group, an archetype (see Introduction). Nonrealistic plays have developed from the premise that today we sense intuitively how each of us is part of a larger human experience in the world. Knowingly or unknowingly, in daily life we take into account the past, present, and future of the entire world.

To dramatize this collective frame of mind, nonrealistic playwrights seek to place their works within a larger field of reference made up of myths and archetypes, history, dreams, symbols, art, music, literature, popular culture, current events, and all sorts of other sources. On one level, these references draw from the shared meanings essential for cooperation within nations and cultures, from what we call general knowledge or cultural literacy. On another level, they draw from what is known in psychology as the collective unconscious (impressions in the unconscious that are always present in everyone everywhere). In nonrealistic plays, this collective viewpoint is intentional.

As stated earlier, James Joyce's major novels, *Ulysses* and *Finnegan's Wake*, are considered primary examples of this principle. Samuel Becket was a colleague and admirer of Joyce, and his plays *Waiting for Godot, Happy Days, Endgame*, and *Krapp's Last Tape* are considered the purest form of modern nonrealistic playwriting. How is the collective viewpoint achieved in his plays? Realistic and classic plays illustrate their vision, their main idea, through the plot and character, but

222

in Beckett's plays, the features of plot and character are negligible. As a nonrealistic writer, Beckett was not interested in conventional plots, that is, in anecdotes about entertaining incidents. Nor was he interested in individual personalities, that is, in characters as such. He was interested in the great myths and archetypes, in histories, great literature, dreams, and symbols, but — and this is vital — presented in sharp, contemporary form. Accordingly, while plot and character may be slight in Beckett's plays, the intellectual patterns found in them are always of considerable importance.

In *Happy Days* Beckett evokes the collective impulse through the use of formal interlocking patterns just as Joyce did in his famous novels. Beckett lists no less than twenty-five of these patterns in his production notebook for the play:

1. Winnie's various voices
2. Her turns to Willie
3. Her self-reflections
4. Her glances toward Willie
5. Her turns to the shopping bag
6. Her emotional contractions
7. Her emotional expansions
8. Her moments of weakness
9. Her use of the term "happy day"
10. Her searches for the right word
11. Her repetitions of "those" and "that"
12. Her literary references:
    a. *Hamlet*
    b. *Paradise Lost* (Milton)
    c. *Romeo and Juliet*
    d. *Cymbeline*
    e. "Ode on a Distant Prospect of Eton College" (Gray)
    f. *Life of Johnson* (Boswell)
    g. *The Rubaiyat of Omar Khayyám*
    h. *Paracelsus, III* (Browning)
    i. "Ode to a Nightingale" (Keats)
    j. *Twelfth Night*
    k. "Go! Forget Me" (Wolfe)
    l. "At the Hawk's Well" (Yeats)
    m. "To the Virgins, to Make Much of Time" (Herrick)
13. Her references to songs
14. Her references to time
15. Her repetitions of the words "old style"

16. Her pauses
17. Her repetitions of the word "strange"
18. Her repetitions of the word "reason"
19. Her repetitions of the word "wonderful"
20. Her repetitions of the word "understandable"
21. Her repetitions of the word "mercies"
22. Her repetitions of the word "no"
23. Her smiles
24. The bell
25. Her tidying

We have taken the space to print the complete list because these formal patterns are what give *Happy Days* its wider significance — and its nonrealistic genius. Like Joyce, Beckett creates his patterns from the mise-en-scene (scenery, costumes, properties, and physical activities) and from literary sources (word repetitions, myths and archetypes, and literature itself). The patterns create intellectual motifs of space, time, habit, memory, inactivity, and change, which examine the play's main idea of "absurd dreams" from different perspectives — approving, sympathetic, ironic, parodic, ridiculous, tragic, farcical, sentimental, etc. It is important to recognize that the play's response to its theme is deliberately ambiguous, not as explicit as it would be in a standard play. In music, theme and variations is a form of composition where an initial theme is stated and each section thereafter is a modification of that theme. Nonrealistic plays, of which *Happy Days* is a prime example, are composed along the same lines. In *Happy Days* the theme of absurd dreams is stated at the outset through the dialogue, mise-en-scene and acting, and thereafter it forms the background for variations of itself through the numerous motifs listed above.

Happy Days is an excellent example of nonrealism to study because it consists almost entirely of variations on a theme. The majority of nonrealistic plays, on the other hand, tend to combine theme and variations with at least the minimal features of a standard plot. *Fefu and Her Friends* combines both forms in almost equal measure. *Top Girls* begins with a theme-and-variations scene (a contemporary dinner party with historical and imaginary characters), followed by a comparatively standard plot. *Machinal*, *Mother Courage*, *The Birthday Party*, *Angels in America*, and *A Lie of the Mind* are essentially standard plots broken up by episodes of theme and variations. Consequently, while plot and character may be slight in nonrealistic plays, the intellectual patterns found in them are crucial to their meaning. More than a manipulative experience intended to confuse, nonrealistic plays are composed of premeditated thematic variations, fully and clearly expressed, intended to place the plays within specific visions of the world. In practical terms, nonrealistic plays are theatricalized ideas in which the meaning is physicalized, externalized, and objectified. And in doing so, a constant alternation is established between everyday reality and large collective generalizations, like keeping two balls in the air at the same time.

It is also worth keeping in mind that nonrealistic plays are generally engaged in satiric social criticism of one kind or another. Today more than ever ours is a culture of ideas. Public discourse is filled with theories and explanations about everything, and we are brought up to know them all. Or more accurately, to half-know them, a situation that itself has become the source of much satire in nonrealistic plays.

Sophie Treadwell was a sharp social critic when she pointed a satirical finger at Mr. Jones, whose money-oriented way of life created a society of androids. In *Machinal* the entire era of fanatical commercialism is represented, with its impressive efficiency and single-minded concentration on profit-making at the expense of human relations. Brecht did more with this theme than Treadwell did, since the commercialization of politics was a natural subject for his assaults on unprincipled capitalism. And when Tony Kushner portrays representatives of liberalism and conservatism in *Angels in America*, he is not so much inventing his own drama of ideas as making fun of *their* drama of ideas, which is an act his characters put on before the world.

225

The category of unthinking half-idealists is even larger than that dramatized by Brecht, Treadwell, and Kushner. At first sight, nonrealistic playwrights seem to share the same opinions as some of the characters who stand apart in their plays. But by putting these characters at the heart of the action they turn out to be counterfeits themselves. Marlene in *Top Girls* is an example. At first she appears to be the model contemporary feminist who has achieved material success in a capitalist patriarchal society that oppresses women. But she is shown to be just as much of an amoral cynic and fraud as the economic power system over which she has prevailed. So also, the characters in *A Lie of the Mind* are shown to be foolish in the matter of their misguided or sentimental ideals about life and love. Their long-established values are exposed as hopelessly wrong-headed. The values they conform to, and expect others to live by, are not the way people live and think today, if in fact people ever did so. Thus, while standard plays tend to sympathize with their people and their ideas, nonrealism shows how these people and their ideas have lost their original meanings. They have now become opportunities for parody and satire. Not comical in the usual sense, but darkly comical, where events usually treated seriously are treated in a strangely humorous manner. The value systems of these people and their ideas are even pointedly capitalized today to show that they are not used in their time-honored sense: The American Dream, Individualism, Modern Culture, Democracy, The Old West, Television, Liberalism, Conservatism, Faith; and even more significant, Family, Home, Children, and, of course, Love. When closely studied, many of the ideas that are thought to be the most venerated in nonrealistic plays are actually shown in a negative or at least a satiric light. As a consequence, when studying nonrealistic plays, readers should always look for the idea behind the ideas.

A final point worth noting is that in a practical sense all plays — realistic, nonrealistic, and any combination thereof — are examining life. Realism tends to examine life openly and frankly. On the other hand, nonrealism tends to examine life from the inside, grasping the concentrated essence of its meaning, and then from this essential interior creating a sharply mythic theatrical form. Nonrealistic authors reach for this concentrated essence in different ways. As pointed out earlier, James Joyce was inclusive, putting into his works as much of the history, literature, daily news, geography, biology, and popular culture that his extraordinary mind could grasp. Samuel Beckett was minimalist, reducing his works almost to the bare minimum needed for comprehension, but still wide-ranging by playwriting standards. Most other nonrealistic playwrights fall somewhere between these two poles — at times filling their works with complex patterns, concentrating on a certain range of associations, or reducing selected elements to their smallest possible state. Some describe this method as being inside-out, that is, theme rather than plot or character controls the dramatic form. Although the results can appear illogical and distorted, they are united by their close relationship to the play's concentrated essence, its mythic center, its main idea. The task is to discover and theatricalize the coherence that lies beneath the bewildering arrangement of contrasts and counterpoints.

Summary

This chapter concerned itself with some of the ways in which the main idea emerges in plays. It takes considerable experience to develop the ability to understand and describe a play's main idea with clarity and simplicity. Nevertheless it is a skill that needs to be acquired if we expect to communicate with others involved in the artistic process, not to mention with the audience as well. Sometimes the clearest understanding of the main idea may not occur until late in the process of analysis or even during rehearsals. Sometimes the main idea does not become clear until after the play has opened, and it can at last be comprehended whole as it was originally intended. Nevertheless, for professionals the search always continues. Most of the audience will never judge the play on the basis of its main idea but rather as drama and feeling. But one way or another, for reasons already explained, the main idea shows the path for actors, directors, and designers in their work. The main idea controls the play and gives each play its unique identity. It is the starting point and focusing device that propels the artistic team toward its final result. Regardless of whether a particular statement is definitive, the practice of determining the main idea is one of the major goals of play analysis.

Questions

1. *Words.* Does the title reflect the meaning? If so, does it do so directly, indirectly, poetically, ironically? Any discussions about ideas in the dialogue? If so, who is involved? What specific ideas are discussed? Are there any examples of aphorisms? If so, who speaks them? What ideas do they illustrate? Any literary, religious, or cultural allusions? If so, who speaks them? What are the sources? What ideas do they illustrate? Any speeches formally putting forward specific ideas (set speeches)? If so, who says them? What ideas do they illuminate? Are there any images or intentional symbols in the dialogue? If so, what are they? What ideas do they suggest? Is there a prologue or an epilogue? If so, how does it point up the main idea of the play?
2. *Characters.* Is there a narrator or chorus? If so, when and how do they express the main idea? Is there a skeptical character that offers advice or tries to reason with others (raisonneur)? If so, how does the character express the main idea? Is there someone in whom the leading character confides private feelings (confidant[e])? If so, how does that character relate to the main idea? In a comedy, is there a character that has adjusted to the behavior code of the world of the play (norm character)? If so, how does that character illustrate the main idea?
3. *Plot.* Are there any characters or situations that repeat or highlight others (parallelisms or foils)? If so, how do they relate to

the main idea? Are there any intellectual conflicts involving the social order, destiny, or the forces of nature? Can any intentional symbolism be found in the dialogue or action? If so, how does it relate to the main idea? How does the main climax embody the main idea?

4. *Statement of the Main Idea.* What is the main idea of the play? Frame the description in the form of an action summary, a super-objective, a thesis sentence, or a theme. Justify the response with detailed information from the play itself.

5. *Mise-en-Scene.* What does the main idea suggest about the mise-en-scene? How could the mise-en-scene contribute to its effectiveness?

6. *After Action Analysis.* As a test of artistic awareness, employ the seed to describe the main idea according to all the various ways explained in this chapter: super-objective, action summary, thesis statement, and theme.

Postscript on Action Analysis

This chapter on idea finishes study of the formalist origins of action analysis (Chapter 1), of which the theoretical underpinnings should by now be evident. The sequence of events and three major climaxes emerge from the external and internal action (Chapter 4) and progressions and structure (Chapter 5). Reviewing the facts stems from the given circumstances (Chapter 2) and background story (Chapter 3). Through-action and counter through-action are outcomes of the study of character (Chapter 6). And idea (Chapter 7) can be seen as a comprehensive treatment of the concepts of the seed, theme, super-objective, and through-action.

The following chapters continue to teach formalist analysis; however, they deal with subtler and more complex issues than action analysis can address. Because action analysis depends by definition on the study of action, by itself it can provide few practical insights into Dialogue (Chapter 8), Tempo, Rhythm, and Mood (Chapter 9), or Style (Chapter 10). Formalist analysis is equipped to sort out advanced subjects such as these. The going will be slower because it involves a microscopic look at numerous fine points in the play.

Dialogue

Dialogue is the conversation that takes place among the characters. It includes all the talk, monologues, soliloquies, narration, choral odes, songs, and anything else spoken by the characters. It does not include stage directions. Enough has already been said in earlier chapters to show how important it is to study the dialogue for information about given circumstances, background story, plot, character, and idea. Yet even when the dialogue is clear about all this, it still deserves to be studied for its own sake. In addition to being the play's primary means of communication, dialogue is also the playwright's sole means of expression. Dialogue can be merely workmanlike or it can display a high degree of virtuosity.

Although most readers do not pay much attention to the language as such in a play, it does exert a subtle influence. The language may evoke comments such as

- The dialogue is easy to understand.
- The words come from the characters naturally.
- The play uses lots of short sentences.
- I was so bored by the long and complicated sentences that I skipped whole passages.

Most of these opinions are too general to be useful. Script analysis needs to be more specific to offer anything that can be helpful in the rehearsal hall or design studio. When scholars use the term *diction*, they mean the technical and artistic qualities of language, and the selection and arrangement of words, phrases, sentences, lines, and speeches. This chapter treats dialogue as diction, starting with the basic technical building blocks and progressing to more creative qualities. Some features are relative and opinions about them vary,

229

but most dialogue can be studied in the same open-minded way already recommended in this book.

Often the analysis of dialogue uncovers a hidden task. To understand the language in a play, readers need to know basics of grammar, syntax, punctuation, sentences, paragraphs, and so forth. Therefore, before starting to work, it might be necessary to review these fundamentals. Although the rules of language usage can be subtle and complex, their subtlety and complexity appears in the way writers stretch the rules. Readers should know what the rules are, how they are being stretched, and why. Fortunately, the subject is not that difficult. Any serious student can cover the basics with a good manual. Highly recommended are: *The Elements of Style* by William Strunk, Jr. and E. B. White and its companion works, *The Elements of Grammar* by Margaret Shertzer.

Words

There may be many characters in a play, and they may speak in various ways, but in the best work each character preserves a certain manner of speech identified as that character's and no one else's. Since characters speak in their own voices, the words they use can tell a great deal about them. This distinctiveness is achieved in part by the choice of words, that is, characters can be understood to some extent by certain features of the words they speak.

Abstract and Concrete

One of the first features to search for in words is their quality of abstraction or concreteness. *Abstract words* describe things that cannot be perceived by the senses — ideas and feelings such as love, honor, experience, heritage, democracy, or materialism. Creon in *Oedipus Rex* and Cleante in *Tartuffe* use abstract words such as power, knowledge, justice, hypocrisy, and self-sacrifice. Characters that use such words have a tendency to be reserved, aloof, or affected. By contrast *concrete words* describe things that can be seen and touched, such as flowers, smiles, thumbtacks, and hammers. They are vivid and emphatic, and the characters that use them tend to display comparable traits. Oedipus and Orgon speak in concrete terms like this. They express their hasty judgments and rash decrees using strong, concrete language that differs from Creon and Cleante's cautious abstractions.

Formal and Informal

Another feature of conversational speech is the level of formality or informality in the words. *Formal words* make generous use of elevated language of the kind often found in books (satisfactory, illuminate, preserve, contribute) and literary language (however, nonetheless, consequently, moreover, inasmuch). Formal language aims at precision, but in doing so it deliberately restricts emotion. *Informal words* are simple everyday words, the kind we use at home (OK, lit up, jelly, give) and can be more emotionally direct.

Comparing the words of Joseph Surface with those of his brother Charles in *The School for Scandal*, we can see an illustration of these different word types. Joseph's frequent use of "indeed," "certainly," "however," and similarly formal words may tell us that he is class-conscious and pompous and that he values literary style over sincerity. By contrast, his brother Charles's use of words such as "bumper," "blockhead," "wench," and similar kinds of everyday words arise naturally from his egalitarian feelings. He does not worry about how he sounds to others. The down-to-earth characters in *A Lie of the Mind* and *American Buffalo* by and large use such informal words to express themselves as well.

Related to formal and informal language is the *syllabic composition* of words. Polysyllabic words are longer and often come from Latin, historically the language of scholars. Joseph Asagai is the Nigerian exchange student who is Beneatha Younger's boyfriend in *A Raisin in the Sun*. He enjoys displaying his new American education with polysyllabic words (mutilated, accommodate, assimilate). In *Angels in America*, Louis Ironson's affected speech-making (comparatively, inexorably, ontologically) contrasts with Roy Cohn's unaffected low-class language ("So, baby doll, what? *Cats?* Bleah."). The uneducated characters in Brecht's *Mother Courage* often speak in single-syllable words (in translation): "Halt, you scum!" "He's pulled a black cross. He's through." "You've left your hat." Formal, polysyllabic words tend to be associated with emotional restraint, while short, informal words carry a feeling of emotional freedom.

Jargon and Slang

Jargon (professional specialized language) and *slang* (nonstandard everyday words) have special appeal in dramatic dialogue because they sound unusual, vivid, and colorful. Our recognition of such language as dramatic is just as important as is the realism it lends to a play. *Mother Courage* and *American Buffalo* acquire some of their dramatic value from the use of professional jargon from military life and petty crime, and from everyday slang. They employ *good–bad speech*, meaning bad speech that is written to achieve good, expressive effects. The obscenities in *Angels in America* are shocking, of course, but they also keep the political ideas of the play operating on a basic human level. Characters in *Machinal* speak the jargon of the commercial world and the big city. African-American slang is found in *A Raisin in the Sun* ("bread" for money and "ofay" for white person, which the movie version disallowed), and *The Piano Lesson* ("country farm" for prison and "studying" for "concerned with"). In *The Birthday Party* the characters speak in a variety of British slang ("bloke" for man, "bird" for woman). Communication is enriched by jargon and slang from these social groups and from many more besides. On stage, jargon and slang entertain as much as they help to identify characters within a particular social context.

Connotation

Recall from the Introduction that "to connote" means to suggest or convey associations in addition to the explicit (denoted) dictionary meaning. *Connotative words*, therefore, are words that convey more than their dictionary meaning. For example, the words "gentleman" and "lady" mean more than the words "man" and "woman," "snake" means more than "serpent," and "gossip" means more than "talk." Extra meaning has been attached to these words from our collective personal experience. Dramatists like to use connotative words because they add vividness without necessarily adding more words.

Some words are almost solely connotative, with little or no dictionary meaning at all. Linguists describe them as *snarl and purr words*. They may look like normal words, but their literal meanings are of negligible importance. Words like "damn" or "ouch" or "wow" are little more than snarls that express pure feelings. Similarly, "wow" or "oooh" or "aaah" express little more than pleasure. Since emotion plays such a large part in dramatic dialogue, play readers should be alert for the connotative as well as the literal meanings of words.

In *Happy Days*, "Brownie" means more than "revolver" and "emmet" means more than "ant." The obscenities in *American Buffalo*, *A Lie of the Mind*, and *Angels in America* may offend some readers, but no one will deny that obscenities express thoughts and feelings impressively. They shock, but they connote strong feelings too.

Sentences

The next type of language device is that of the *sentence*, the primary verbal tool of a play. Studying the various features of a play's sentences can reveal dramatic potentials that are sometimes overlooked by nonprofessional readers.

Length

Sentence length can reveal information about character. This can be done by counting the number of words and sentences in a continuous section of the play and then dividing the number of words by the number of sentences. After estimating the average number of words for each sentence, more important considerations can be worked at, namely, the relation between sentence length, context, and character.

The potential value of sentence length for character analysis is shown in the episode between Polonius and Reynaldo (1,2) of *Hamlet*, in which Polonius instructs Reynaldo to keep an eye on Laertes while he is in France. In this brief exchange Polonius says seven times as many words as Reynaldo, his sentences are over four times longer, and he uses many abstract words. Of course, we would expect Polonius to say more in this scene because he is giving instructions, but even so, the numerical calculations tell us that Polonius talks too much in a misplaced attempt to sound important, or perhaps he believes that Reynaldo is not as clever as he is himself. Reynaldo speaks in short sentences; he is a simple and down-to-earth person who is trying to bring an end to Polonius's wearisome talk.

American Buffalo offers some playable dramatic values from sentence length as well. Don and Bob appear together in the first episode of act one. The average sentence length is nine words, and most sentences are even shorter. True, in modern plays, characters say what must be said using the fewest words possible. These sentences, however, are much shorter than we might expect even in a modern play and many of the lines are also fragments. This might show a lack of education or strong feelings. Together with the street jargon, abusive slang, and connotative words, the short length of the sentences in *American Buffalo* contributes to the charged emotional atmosphere that is so characteristic of plays by David Mamet.

Lengthier sentences may be governed by a halting, insecure feeling of anxiety or perhaps by unrestrained hysterics. They may also be governed by the complexity of the thinking or the richness of the images, as in the case of Shakespeare. Short sentences and sentence fragments can be tough and piercing, or suggest weariness or dullness. From the context of the situation, readers should be able to recognize both extremes and the variations in between.

233

Type

Sentences can be grammatically *simple, compound, complex,* or *compound-complex;* rhetorically *loose, periodic, balanced,* or *antithetical;* or functional *statements, questions, commands,* or *exclamations.* The various types of sentences used in a play and their relative proportion to each other can be the source of playable values. Dialogue in classic plays is formally composed, like music. Sentences show noticeable patterns, flow logically from one point to another, and are accentuated by prominent stops. Typically there is enough expressive matter in them to make up several sentences in a modern play. By contrast, nearly all the sentences in modern plays seem like ordinary speech and do not call attention to themselves as the carefully written dialogue they really are. Sentences tend to be short and stop when the basic sense is complete. Yet within these two broad limits, there can still be different types of sentences. This is not the place for a long discussion about the way language is constructed (grammar), its rules (syntax), and its effective use (rhetoric). The point is that sentence types can be studied, and this study can be dramatically productive, depending on the quality of the language in the play.

To illustrate this issue, we will study the sentences in a passage from one classic, one modern realistic, and one late-modern realistic play, evaluating the sentence types in each passage. The first passage is from *The School for Scandal.* Rowley is persuading Sir Peter Teazle that he is mistaken in his opinions of Charles and Joseph Surface.

> ROWLEY. You know, Sir Peter, I have always taken the liberty to differ with you on the subject of these two young gentlemen. I only wish you may not be deceived in your opinion of the elder. For Charles, my life on't! he will retrieve his errors yet. Their worthy father, once my honored master, was, at his years, nearly as wild a spark; yet when he died, he did not leave a more benevolent heart to lament his loss.

> SIR PETER. You are wrong, Master Rowley. On their father's death, you know, I acted as a kind of guardian to them both till their uncle Sir Oliver's liberality gave them an early independence. Of course no person could have more opportunity of judging their hearts, and I was never mistaken in my life. Joseph is indeed a model for the young men of the age. He is a man of

sentiment and acts up to the sentiments
he professes; but, for the other, take my
word for't, if he had any grain of virtue
by descent, he has dissipated it with the
rest of his inheritance. Ah! my old friend
Sir Oliver will be deeply mortified when
he finds how part of his bounty has been
misapplied.

The modern realistic example involves a similar situation in *The Wild Duck*. Dr. Relling is attempting to refute Gregers Werle's opinion of the integrity of Hjalmar Ekdal.

GREGERS. What is your explanation of the spiritual tumult that is now going on inside
Hjalmar Ekdal?

RELLING. A lot of spiritual tumult I've noticed
in him.

GREGERS. What! Not at such a crisis, when
his whole life has been placed on a new
foundation? How can you think that such an
individuality as Hjalmar's—

RELLING. Oh, individuality — him! If he ever
had any tendency to the abnormal developments you call individuality, I can assure
you it was rooted out of him while he was
still in his teens.

GREGERS. That would be strange indeed — considering the loving care with which he was
brought up.

RELLING. By those two high-flown, hysterical
maiden aunts, you mean?

GREGERS. Let me tell you that they were women
who never forgot the claim of the ideal —
but of course you will only jeer at me
again.

RELLING. No, I'm in no humor for that. I know
all about those ladies, for he has ladled
out no end of rhetoric on the subject of
his "two soul mothers." But I don't think
he has much to thank them for. Ekdal's misfortune is that in his own circle he has
always been looked upon as a shining light.

GREGERS. Not without reason, surely. Look at
the depth of his mind!
RELLING. I have never discovered it. That his
father believed in it I don't so much wonder; the old lieutenant has been an ass
all his days.

The passage from *The School for Scandal* features abstract words ("lib-
erty," "honored," "benevolent," "mortified," etc.) and various sentence types (simple, compound, complex, etc.). The sentences are
quite long and contain an assortment of twists and turns (dependent and independent clauses). The tempo of the dialogue is slow
and measured. In the passage from *The Wild Duck* there are fewer
sentence types and fewer twists and turns. The dialogue in the second passage also contains (in translation) a few broken sentences,
missing links, and nonstandard grammar. The characters speak rap-
idly, and the stresses are crowded together unevenly ("Oh, individuality — him!"). The sentence types in the first passage show Rowley
and Sir Peter disagreeing in a reasonable and polite manner. The
sentences in the second passage show Gregers and Dr. Relling disagreeing with more feeling. Also notice that in both passages the
important information generally comes at the end of a sentence. Of
course here we are comparing an English play with a Norwegian play
translated into English, but the practical consequences still apply.
Most plays in English-speaking countries are read and performed in
English.

The third passage is from *American Buffalo*. It is the episode where
Don teaches Bob a lesson about a character named Fletcher, whom
Don respects for his professionalism. Watch for the radical change in
sentence length, word choice, and sentence types in *American Buffalo*
compared to those same features in *The School for Scandal* and *The
Wild Duck*.

DON. Now lookit Fletcher.
BOB. Fletch?
DON. Now, Fletcher is a standup guy.
BOB. Yeah.
DON. You take him and put him down in some
strange town with just a nickel in his
pocket, and by nightfall he'll have that
town by the balls. This is not talk, Bob,
this is action.
(Pause.)

```
BOB.  He's a real good card player.
DON.  You're fucking A he is, Bob, and this
      is what I'm getting at. Skill. Skill and
      talent and the balls to arrive at your
      own conclusions. The fucker won a hundred
      bucks last night.
BOB.  Yeah?
DON.  Oh yeah.
BOB.  And who was playing?
DON.  Me...
```

Five simple sentences and six plain compound sentences (two independent clauses connected by the word "and"), broken sentences ("*Me...*"), sentence fragments ("Skill and talent and the balls to arrive at his own *conclusions.*"), and hardly any formal links between lines. Of course this is a short passage, but readers familiar with Mamet's plays will agree that it is generally representative of his dialogue. Upper-class aristocrats, middle-class business people, and lower-class hoodlums. It takes a little careful reading to see how sentence types are associated with character and situation.

Rhythm

Rhythm is a pattern of thought pulsations. Although there is no reliable method for objectively identifying the rhythm of prose, rhythm plays a large part in producing emotional effects. Howeover, scanning prose sentences for rhythm in the manner of poetry may not be a very valuable exercise if it is practiced for very long. The rhythm of prose sentences must be heard to be appreciated. It is no doubt better for play readers to get into the habit of reading aloud. Oral reading allows for hearing the difference between melodious and clashing rhythms, and between agreeable and awkward sound combinations.

But for learning purposes, try to scan the rhythm of the prose passages above. Now turn to this famous prose passage from *Hamlet*, which has been scanned informally here for rhythmical accents.

```
HAMLET.  Speak the speech, // I pray you, //
         as I pronounc'd it to you, // trippingly
         on the tongue; // but if you mouth it,
         // as many of our players do, // I had
         as lief the town crier spoke my lines. //
         Nor do not saw the air too much with your
         hand, // thus, // but use all gently; //
```

for in the very torrent, // tempest, // and, as I may say, whirlwind of your passion, // you must acquire and beget a temperance // that may give it smoothness. // O, it offends me to the soul to hear a robustious periwig-pated fellow tear a passion to tatters, // to very rags, // to split the ears of the groundlings, // who, // for the most part, // are capable of nothing // but inexplicable dumb shows and noise. // I would have such a fellow whipp'd for o'erdoing termagent; // it out-herods Herod. // Pray you avoid it. //

And for further comparison, here is a prose speech from *Death of a Salesman*:

BIFF. I am not a leader of men, Willy, // and neither are you. // You were never anything but a hard-working drummer // who landed to the ash can // like all the rest of them! // I'm one dollar an hour, Willy! // I tried seven states // and couldn't raise it. // A buck an hour. // Do you gather my meaning! // I'm not bringing home any prizes anymore, // and you're going to stop waiting for me to bring them home! //

And a speech from *A Lie of the Mind*.

JAKE. (Staring.) There's this thing // this thing in my head. // This thing that the next moment // the moment right after this one // will blow up. // Explode with a voice. // A scream from a voice I don't know. // Or a voice I knew once but now it's changed. // It doesn't know me either. // Now. // It used to but not now. // I've scared it into something else. // Another form. // A whole other person who doesn't see me anymore. //

There are other ways to scan these passages, but at least this shows how certain important thoughts are stressed and how they help to create rhythm. The language in *Hamlet* is formal and rhetorical like that in *The School for Scandal,* but its rhythm is more evident than its eighteenth-century counterpart. The rhythm of the passage from *Death of a Salesman* shows itself to be carefully planned as well and yet closely linked to grammatical rules. The convulsive rhythm of the prose passage from *A Lie of the Mind* is striking by comparison. Its rhythm is based not on grammar but on pulses of feeling. The sentences in all three passages require a feeling for spoken rhythm to express the musical potential from top to bottom.

Speeches

A *line* is a single continuous statement by a character. Normally a line consists of a few sentences or less. A line becomes a *speech* when it contains more than a few sentences, which is a sure sign that crucial issues are at stake. It makes sense that characters talk at greater length about crucial issues than they do about routine issues, and so speeches warrant extra attention in script analysis. Their punctuation, linking, internal organization, and relationship to neighboring dialogue can communicate in distinct ways. Despite appearances, speeches are not just lengthy expressions of emotion, but are carefully orchestrated to convey specific intellectual and emotional results.

239

Punctuation

Punctuation has unique features that require both understanding from readers and special intonations from actors for *accurate expression.* Periods, commas, exclamation points, question marks, ellipses, and single and double dashes all have distinctive meanings. The vocal drop that accompanies a period shows the end of a thought or feeling. The vocal rise of a question mark requires a reply. Commas and semicolons are warnings that call for pauses of certain lengths. A colon demands attention to what follows it. An exclamation point signals approval or disagreement. Dashes indicate an interrupted thought. Ellipses hint at something left unsaid. Director and Shakespeare scholar B. Iden Payne often reminded his students that punctuation in dramatic dialogue is not just grammatical, but "dramatical." By this he meant that playwrights employ punctuation not merely for reasons of good grammar but also to signal dramatic action. (Notice the difference, for example, between the punctuation in Shakespeare's original quartos, which were written for actors, and the later editions, which were "corrected" by literary scholars.) The expressive qualities of punctuation marks are meant to help actors feel the texture of the dialogue by adding extra expressiveness to the words.

We might study this passage from *A Raisin in the Sun* to show the expressive use of punctuation in a speech. Recall that Walter Younger is irate over his friend Willy's theft of the $10,000 in insurance money that he (Walter) was planning to use to buy a liquor store. To replace the money, Walter has agreed to accept a realtor's payoff to keep his family from moving into a white neighborhood. Obviously, this is humiliating for Walter and his family.

> WALTER. What's the matter with you all! I didn't make this world! It was given to me this way! Hell, yes, I want me some yachts someday! Yes, I want to hang some real pearls 'round my wife's neck. Ain't she supposed to wear pearls? Somebody tell me—, who decides which women is suppose to wear pearls in this world. I tell you I am a man — and I think my wife should wear pearls in this world!
>
> MAMA. Baby, how you going to feel on the inside?
>
> WALTER. Fine!... Going to feel fine ... a man...
>
> MAMA. You won't have nothing left then, Walter Lee.
>
> WALTER. I'm going to feel fine, Mama. I'm going to look that son-of-a-bitch in the eyes and say — and say, "All right, Mr. Lindner — that's your neighborhood out there. You got the right to keep it like you want. You got the right to have it like you want. Just write the check and — the house is yours." And, and I am going to say — And you — you people just put the money in my hand and you won't have to live next to this bunch of stinking niggers!...Maybe — maybe I'll just get down on my black knees ... Captain, Mistuh, Bossman. A-hee-hee-hee! Yassssuh! Great White Father, just gi' ussen de money, fo' God's sake, and we's ain't gwine come out deh and dirty up yo' white folks neighborhood...

240

To point up the emotion and meaning in this passage, Lorraine Hansberry has used exclamation points, commas, ellipses, and

---

dashes in dramatical fashion. As Walter exposes his deepest feelings, each punctuation mark becomes more meaningful. The exclamation marks in the first line show his anger. At the word "man," significantly, he begins to hesitate, and his speech becomes halting and troubled. He falters several times during the last sentences as the depth of his humiliation settles into his consciousness. His voice breaks, he stumbles, falls to his knees, and breaks down. The ellipsis shows that the speech ends with an embarrassing silence. Hansberry has provided dramatical punctuation to underscore the different phases of Walter's thoughts and feelings. The punctuation is dramatical as much as grammatical, and more than a sign of slang and nonstandard speech. Compare it with August Wilson's dialogue in *The Piano Lesson*, for example, which also contains slang and nonstandard speech, but has very few dashes or ellipses even though it contains many more long speeches.

Linking

The idea of *linking* comes logically after sentences and punctuation. We know from composition classes that linking in prose is performed by antecedents and tenses, phrases and clauses, and other forms of backward and forward reference to knit sentences together. Linking is a basic principle of writing in general. When there is no linking, or when it is weakly done, meaning stumbles. Linking is also an important feature of dramatic writing because it helps to maintain the feeling of forward motion necessary for good dramatic structure. Moreover, dialogue linking also encourages line-to-line communication among characters, called give-and-take, reciprocation, or communion.

Dramatic dialogue uses thoughts or words to link lines together. Ordinarily, the method is one complete idea to one line of dialogue, with the last thought of one line suggesting the first thought of the next. This is not a rigid rule, but whenever something breaks the connection, it will most likely have a purpose of its own. The following passage shows dialogue linking at work in *The School for Scandal*. Here Snake has just reported to Lady Sneerwell that he managed to place scandalous reports about Charles Surface in the newspapers. Lady Sneerwell and Charles were once lovers. She wants to win Charles back from his current lover by damaging his reputation. Charles' brother, Joseph Surface, joins the scene. Careful reading will show how the final thoughts in each line suggest the initial thoughts in the succeeding line.

JOSEPH SURFACE. My dear Lady Sneerwell, how do you do today? Mr. Snake, your most obedient.

LADY SNEERWELL. Snake has just been teasing me on our mutual attachment; but I have informed him of our real views. You know how useful he has been to us; and believe me, the confidence is not ill placed.

JOSEPH SURFACE. Madam, it is impossible for me to suspect a man of Mr. Snake's sensibility and discernment.

LADY SNEERWELL. Well, well, no compliments now; but tell me when you saw your mistress, Maria — or, what is more material to me, your brother.

JOSEPH SURFACE. I have not seen either since I left you; but I can inform you that they never meet. Some of your stories have taken good effect on Maria.

LADY SNEERWELL. Ah, my dear Snake! The merit of this belongs to you. But do your brother's distresses increase?

JOSEPH SURFACE. Every hour. I am told he has had another summons from the court yesterday. In short, his dissipation and extravagance exceed anything I have ever heard of.

LADY SNEERWELL. Poor Charles!

JOSEPH SURFACE. True, madam; notwithstanding his vices one can't help feeling for him. Poor Charles! I'm sure I wish it were in my power to be of any essential service to him; for the man who does not share in the distresses of a brother, even though merited by his own misconduct, serves —

LADY SNEERWELL. O Lud! You are going to be moral and forget that you are among friends.

JOSEPH SURFACE. Egad, that's true! I'll keep that sentiment till I see Sir Peter. However, it is certainly a charity to rescue Maria from such a libertine, who, if he is to be reclaimed, can be so only by a

242

> person of your ladyship's superior accom-
> plishments and understanding.
> SNAKE. I believe, Lady Sneerwell, here's com-
> pany coming. I'll go and copy the letter
> I mentioned to you. Mr. Surface, your most
> obedient.
> JOSEPH SURFACE. Sir, your very devoted.

It will be worthwhile to study this passage closely. Sheridan's dialogue is a model of straightforward dialogue linking. Each line connects with the line before and the line after, and the conversation moves from one topic to the next without any breaks in logic or feeling. The two lines without verbal links are linked nonverbally. Lady Sneerwell's expression ("Poor Charles!") seems to end her line before furnishing a link with Joseph Surface's next line. Actually, the two lines are linked by the unspoken thought of Lady Sneerwell's secret love for Charles. The dramatist expects the actors to provide a facial expression, gesture, or stage business to fill the pause. At first glance, Snake's line announcing the arrival of visitors also seems unlinked; however, the offstage sounds of the approaching guests provide the link here.

We have seen that linking is not always openly expressed in the dialogue. This is especially true in modern plays, where psycho-physical expression is often more important than verbal expression — subtext is as much or more important than text. Much of the dialogue in *A Lie of the Mind, Angels in America, American Buffalo,* and *The Birthday Party,* for example, seems to skip from one line to another in unlinked fashion, almost telegraphic in its brevity. In performance, where the subtext becomes energized, the effect is less formal and more lifelike, as well as more emotionally provocative.

Internal Arrangement

Just as dramatists arrange conflicts leading to a climax, they also arrange the internal dynamics of speeches to achieve the strongest effects. Most speeches build toward a single climax; however, they may do so in different ways. The beginning may be bold, as in the previous example from *A Raisin in the Sun,* or it may be a low-conflict point of departure. A resting point usually occurs somewhere in the middle of a long speech, followed by the final progression to the climax at the end. (This is another example of the eternal principle of beginning, middle, and end.) Sometimes the climax may be followed by a simple, quiet close. Of course, the actor's interpretation can never be overlooked, but in any event, the internal arrangement of a speech is governed by writing considerations like these.

At the close of *Death of a Salesman*, Arthur Miller arranged Linda's final speech beside Willy's gravesite in a skillful climactic fashion. The speech intensifies as it builds toward the end.

> LINDA. Forgive me, dear, I can't cry. I don't
> know what it is, but I can't cry. I don't
> understand it. Why did you ever do that?
> Help me, Willy, I can't cry. It seems to
> me that you're just on another trip. I keep
> expecting you. Willy, dear, I can't cry.
> Why did you do it? I search and search and
> I search, and I can't understand it, Willy.
> I made the last payment on the house today.
> Today, dear. And there'll be nobody home.
> (A sob rises in her throat.) We're free and
> clear. (sobbing more fully, released) We're
> free. (Biff comes slowly toward her.) We're
> free…We're free…

244

Linda's speech begins quietly, then builds to a small crest ("Willy, dear, I can't cry"). After a brief emotional rest, the intensity builds to a final peak of emotion ("We're free and clear"), then it ends with a simple, quiet close ("We're free…"). Carefully arranged speeches also distinguish the dialogue in *The Piano Lesson*, *A Lie of the Mind*, and many other plays by writers with a musical ear.

External Arrangement

Chapter 5 mentioned that scenes are arranged like miniature plays. Now let's analyze a scene to learn how the *external arrangement* of the dialogue supports this process. The climax of *Death of a Salesman* is the quarrel between Willy and Biff near the end of the play. In this scene, Biff summons the courage to challenge his father's mistaken ambitions for him. This is the confrontation between Willy and Biff that the entire play has prepared us to expect. Prior to this moment, the dramatist stockpiled (loaded) a large inventory of dramatic tensions in the earlier scenes. He created the necessary suspense for this scene by revealing information about Willy and Biff's relationship in small increments and by inserting complementary scenes with the other characters.

The scene begins when Biff comes into the backyard, where Willy is working in the garden, and tells him that he is leaving home for good. Biff is trying to appear calm, withholding his real feelings because he does not want to provoke another argument with his father. Willy is preoccupied at this point and does not understand what Biff is saying anyway. In the next unit, the tension accumulates. They go into the house together, and Biff describes his plans to his mother in the same restrained way. Then Biff extends his hand to Willy to say good-bye, and the first emotional eruption occurs as Willy refuses Biff's gesture. When Linda intervenes, Willy curses Biff and refuses to accept any responsibility for Biff's failures. At this point, Biff cannot restrain his feelings any longer, and he challenges Willy openly: "All right, phony! Then let's lay it on the line." Then Biff brings out the rubber hose that Willy planned to use to commit suicide (by connecting it to the gas line from the water heater in the basement). This is the second emotional flare-up in the scene. When Happy tries to stop him, Biff turns on his brother, ridiculing his fake dream of becoming a successful businessman. Now Willy grows even more distressed, and Happy and Linda begin to panic. Biff turns on Willy and condemns him: "I never got anywhere because you blew me so full of hot air I could never stand taking orders from anybody!" While Willy still does not understand what is happening, Biff explodes into self-reproach. It seems that Biff is going to strike Willy: "Pop, I'm nothing! I'm nothing, Pop!" but then he breaks down and collapses in his father's arms instead. This is the major climax of the play. At last Willy begins to understand: "What're you doing? Why is he crying?" Biff struggles to contain himself, pulls away, and moves to the stairs, "I'll go in the morning," he says to Linda, "Put him — put him to bed," and he goes to his room. After a long pause, Willy says quietly, "Isn't that — isn't that remarkable? Biff likes me!"

This is only one example of how a very good playwright arranges the emotional peaks and valleys in one brief, if significant, scene. Other writers arrange their plays in different ways to correspond with their own characters and situations. Moreover, readers should never overlook the crucial interpretive contributions to a scene that the actors, director, and designers provide.

Special Qualities

From the preceding discussions it should be clear that theatrical dialogue involves scrupulous attention to words, sentences, and speeches, as well as their internal and external arrangement. Our awareness increases if we can also recognize when dialogue has literary attractions of its own. Dialogue that merely asserts the facts of

245

plot, character, and idea may be no more than workmanlike and satisfying. Yet many dramatists love language very much as language, and for this reason they are artists in words as well as in action and character.

To understand how dialogue can be innately pleasing, consider the following questions. Does the dialogue merely reveal the basic facts in a practical way, or does it also display a pleasing style of its own? Does it contain colorful speech? Is it poetic? Not every analysis needs to deal with these topics extensively, but most plays require at least some understanding of the potential appeal of the dialogue as dialogue.

Poetry

Anyone who is serious about the theatre cannot help being interested in the dramatic potentials of *poetry*. Since most of us are not used to reading poetic dialogue, however, many of its dramatic potentials tend to be overlooked. Prose dialogue, for all its possible complexity, generally runs straight ahead. Poetry, on the other hand, is always calling up associations from within itself, a practice that enriches its patterns of sound and meaning. Moreover, prose dialogue reveals plot, character, and idea, while poetic dialogue adds extra pleasure as literature. There is no need to spend time here discussing the catalogue of literary features that can be found in poetry. (See *Break, Blow, Burn* by Camille Paglia.) But play readers should at least be aware that poetic dialogue has more expressive potentials at its command than does unadorned prose.

Poetic plays by definition ought to be more exciting than are their prose counterparts. Their emotional peaks and valleys are more vivid, and they contain more obvious rhythmic pulses. Short selections from two plays will help to illustrate this. One play is formally poetic, the other written in poetic prose. The first passage is from 4,7 of *Hamlet*. Claudius and Laertes have been plotting to murder Hamlet when suddenly Queen Gertrude enters with news of Ophelia's death. We will explain in a moment why the plot lines are underlined.

> QUEEN. One woe doth tread upon another's heel.
>   So fast they follow.
>   *Your sister's drown'd, Laertes.*
> LAERTES. Drown'd?
>   O, *where?*
> QUEEN. *There is a willow grows ascant the brook*

That shows his hoar leaves in the glassy
stream;
<u>There</u> with fantastic garlands did she make
Of cornflowers, nettles, daisies, and long
purples
That liberal shepherds give a grosser name,
But our cold maids do dead men's fingers
call them.
There, <u>*on the pendant boughs*</u> her cornet
weeds
Clamb'ring to hang, <u>an</u> envious <u>*sliver broke;*</u>
<u>When down</u> her weedy trophies and <u>herself</u>
<u>Fell in the</u> weeping <u>brook</u>.
<u>Her clothes</u> spread wide,
And, mermaid-like, <u>awhile they bore her up;</u>
<u>Which time she chanted snatches of old
lauds,</u>
As one incapable of her own distress,
Or like a creature native and imbued
Unto that element;
<u>but long it could not be</u>
<u>Till that her garments</u>, heavy with their
drink,
<u>Pull'd the poor wretch</u> from her melodious
lay
<u>To muddy death.</u>
LAERTES. Alas, then <u>she is drown'd!</u>
QUEEN. Drown'd, drown'd.

247

The passage develops in seven stages: (1) the Queen's emotional
distress, (2) the news of Ophelia's death, (3) where it happened
and what Ophelia was doing there, (4) her collapse into the water,
(5) how she sang as her clothes held her afloat, (6) how she sank
beneath the water and drowned, and (7) Laertes' grief. As the underlining shows, the bare plot information could have been conveyed
with less than fifty words, yet Shakespeare has provided over one
hundred additional words to convey the feelings and thoughts that
Ophelia's suicide calls up in the characters. We could further analyze the literary features of this passage, but no written description
could do justice to its poetic beauty. For full expression, it must
be performed by an actress who can express its music as well as its
drama. Incidentally, although this passage contains excellent poetry,

the same principles apply to poetry that is poor by design. Doggerel or negligent grammar or syntax can be as effective in poetry as is the good–bad prose speech discussed earlier.

The tradition of poetry has not disappeared from the modern theatre. In the last hundred years, various playwrights have made attempts to achieve in the theatre the expressive feelings of which poetry is capable. Some authors, like William Butler Yeats, T.S. Eliot, and Maxwell Anderson, returned to writing openly poetic dialogue. Others, like August Strindberg, Eugene O'Neill, Tennessee Williams, Samuel Beckett, August Wilson, David Mamet, Harold Pinter, August Wilson, and Sam Shepard have written prose that can often be as expressive as poetry. In some of the best plays the dividing line between prose and poetry is not easy to draw. Modern poetic dialogue does not conform to rules; its poetic flavor is all its own. But it is poetic in the sense of how it is used in the play and from the context, not just from content or form.

A few lines from *Happy Days* will illustrate this idea. Winnie passes the entire time with trivial activities in the absurd belief that her life is happy. Among the objects in her handbag is a revolver. This is how the passage is printed in the script:

> WINNIE. But something tells me, do not overdo
> the bag, Winnie, make use of it of course,
> let it help you … along when stuck, by all
> means, but cast your mind forward, some-
> thing tells me, cast your mind forward,
> Winnie, to the time when words must fail —
> (Pause. She turns to look at the bag.)—
> and do not overdo the bag.

Winnie is speaking of suicide, of course. In view of this, her everyday words, her pantomime, even her imperfect grammar and syntax, suggest important meanings in this passage. In fact, it would be instructive to recast the passage as a free verse poem about the futility of happiness.

> But something tells me,
> Do not overdo the bag, Winnie,
> Make use of it, of course,
> Let it help you … along,
> When stuck,
> By all means,
> But cast your mind forward,

```
Something tells me,
Cast your mind forward, Winnie,
To the time when words must fail —
And do not overdo the bag.
```

One of the distinctive rhythmical features of this passage is Beckett's way of repeating simple phrases, bouncing them in the air like a ball: "do not overdo the bag," "something tells me," "cast your mind forward." Once again this points up the difficulty of dealing with poetic speech in the theatre. We know that dialogue should not be considered exclusively as literature, yet in many cases it is written as much for evocative sound as it is for explicit sense.

Charm

Another feature of dialogue is its power to please through wit, irony, gracefulness, or surprise. For lack of a better term, we will call these collected qualities *charm*. The prose dialogue of many dramatists appeals to the imagination, the appreciation of beauty, and the sense of humor in this way. Some of the most attractive qualities of *The School for Scandal* and *Angels in America,* for example, are the clever remarks and graceful turns of phrase spoken by the characters. The large measure of ironic humor in *The Wild Duck* and *Three Sisters* is one reason these early realistic plays sustain their appeal for contemporary audiences. Brecht may be a social dramatist, but the surprising literary inversions ("How can you have morality without a war?") and musical interludes found in *Mother Courage* are important parts of its verbal appeal.

249

The poetic quality of Sam Shepard's prose has been well-documented. Here is a passage from *A Lie of the Mind* in which Sally interrupts her brother Jake, who is secretly preparing to run away to find Beth. Jake is shaving in front of a mirror.

```
JAKE. (Whispers.) Don't think about her feet
      or her calves or her knees or her thighs
      or her waist or her hips or her ribs or
      her tits or her armpits or her shoulders
      or her neck or her face or her eyes or her
      hair or her lips. Especially not her lips.
      Don't think about any of these things.
      You'll be much better off.
      (He turns upstage just as SALLY enters
      through the up left door, wearing a jacket,
      jeans, and western boots and carrying
```

> a suitcase. Pause. SALLY *closes the door,*
> *then turns back to JAKE. She keeps hold of*
> *the suitcase.)*

SALLY. How're you feelin', Jake?

JAKE. Me?

> *(Pause. He moves fast to the bed, pulls*
> *the flag off his neck as he crosses, kneels*
> *down beside the bed, stuffs the flag under*
> *the bed, pulls out a small black toilet*
> *case, unzips it, puts the shaver inside,*
> *zips it back up, and shoves it back under*
> *the bed. He rises to his feet, then sits*
> *on the edge of the bed, facing SALLY, and*
> *rubs his knee as he stares at her. Pause.)*

SALLY. *(Sets her suitcase on floor.)* Where's
Mom?

JAKE. *(Rapid speech.)* I don't worry anymore
about where anybody is. I don't think
about that. Anybody can move wherever
they want. I just try to keep track of my
own movements these days. That's enough.
Have you ever tried that? To follow yourself around? Like a spy? You can wind up
anywhere. It's amazing. Like, just now I
caught myself shaving. I was right over
there. Shaving my face. I didn't know I
was doing that until just now. It's kinda
scary, ya know.

SALLY. Scary?

JAKE. Yeah. I mean there's a possibility that
you could do something that you didn't
even know about. You could be somewhere
that you couldn't even remember being. Has
that ever happened to you?

SALLY. No. No, it's the opposite with me.
Everything just keeps repeating itself.

JAKE. Oh. Well, then you don't know what I'm
talkin' about.

A poetic mood is established with Jake's opening remarks. Sally's abrupt questions interrupt the mood. Jake follows with curt rapid speech in which he makes up a lame excuse for shaving. Jake is suspicious of Sally, whom he believes will prevent him from leaving. The plot is not complicated here, but the mood created by the dialogue lends the moment a disturbing quality. The special charm of Shepard's dialogue is part of what elevates his plays to the level of modern parables.

Dialects and Accents

A *dialect* is a verbal departure from standard language. Dialects are characteristic of a particular group of speakers and have their own charm as well. "Y'all" in the South, "Yah" in Minnesota, "Eh?" in Canada. The regional dialects of Brooklyn, the rural South, New England, and Appalachia, not to mention the greater contributions of Canada and Britain, and those of various ethnic cultures, have certainly enriched the English language. An *accent* is a particular way of pronouncing standard language. "Warsh" for wash in Cajun Louisiana, "Noo Yawk" for New York among native new Yorkers, "aboot" for about in Canada. The appeal of dialects and accents comes from our appreciation of their musical intonations, imaginative word choices, and emotive speech rhythms. Playwrights have shown great skill in using these charming features of language. Dialects and accents enhance plausibility, aid in rapid recognition of given circumstances, and provide additional opportunities for emotional expression.

251

Theatricality

Besides its literary features, good stage dialogue also possesses *theatricality*. This does not mean sensational, melodramatic, or artificial, but effects achieved through the actors and production values. Any lay reader can find literary meanings on a printed page, but it takes professional skill to perceive the budding dramatic and physical action, emotion, and subtext present in dramatic dialogue. This kind of perception requires theatrical imagination as well as literary acuteness.

External Action

As explained in Chapter 4, an intrinsic quality of stage dialogue is its ability to convey external action. Lorraine Hansberry has provided a great deal of such external action in the dialogue of *A Raisin in the Sun*. Mama's first appearance in act 1 offers a good illustration. It is morning and everyone is getting ready for the day's activities.

MAMA. Who that 'round here slamming doors at this hour.

RUTH. That was Walter Lee. He and Bennie was at it again.

MAMA. My children and they tempers. Lord, if this little old plant don't get some more sun than it's been getting it ain't never going to see spring again. What's the matter with you this morning, Ruth? You looks right peaked. You aiming to iron all them things? Leave some for me. I'll get to 'em this afternoon. Bennie, honey, it's too drafty for you to be sitting around half dressed. Where's your robe?

BENEATHA. In the cleaners.

MAMA. Well, go and get mine and put it on.

BENEATHA. I'm not cold, Mama, honest.

MAMA. I know — but you so thin ...

BENEATHA. Mama, I'm not cold.

MAMA. (*Seeing the make-down sofa-bed as young Travis has left it.*) Lord have mercy, look at that poor bed. Bless his heart — he tries, don't he.

RUTH. No — he don't half try at all 'cause he knows you going to come along behind him and fix everything.

The author has provided a busy round of physical actions (blocking and use of properties) for Mama in this short selection of dialogue. During these ten lines, Mama enters the room to begin her chores, waters the plant in the kitchen, moves to help Ruth with her ironing, and crosses to Bennie at the table and fusses over her clothing. Then she closes the window, moves to the sofa bed, and begins straightening the covers. These external activities characterize Mama as an energetic, hard-working caregiver who thinks of others first. Some of the activities are openly stated, others implied.

Much of Winnie's role in *Happy Days* consists of external actions (use of properties) that Beckett arranged with considerable attention to detail. Since Winnie scarcely moves in the entire play, her external actions and use of properties are a necessary expressive accompaniment to her dialogue. Think as well of all the properties (external actions) associated with the act of dining in *The Wild Duck, Three*

Sisters, Mother Courage, Death of a Salesman, A Raisin in the Sun, Top Girls, A Lie of the Mind, and *The Piano Lesson.* External actions like these and more have become increasingly important in modern drama. Some professional actors, directors, and designers possess amazing ability to devise expressive external action to accompany the dialogue. Readers as well should be alert for opportunities to reinforce the dialogue by addition of external action.

Internal Action

Dialogue is also a form of *internal action.* It is used by characters to shape attitudes and provoke actions in other characters. Recall that this principle was introduced in Chapter 4 (assertions, plans, commands) and again in Chapter 6 (actioning). The principle of dialogue as internal action is important enough for more attention. We will go over it again here, but this time with a classic play. In the following passage from *Tartuffe* there is little obvious external action, but the moment is comical performance because of its conflicting internal actions. Keep in mind that defining objectives is necessary before starting this type of work.

Ever since the arrival of Tartuffe in the house, Dorine has been trying to persuade Cleante that Orgon has taken leave of his senses. When Orgon returns from a short visit to the country, Dorine uses the opportunity to prove the truth of her assertion to Cleante. Her objective here is "to incite Orgon to reveal his obsession with Tartuffe." Orgon has been away from home and is worried about how Tartuffe has been treated in the interim. His objective is "to look after the welfare of Tartuffe," and of course he interprets every incident as an offense to Tartuffe. Broadly speaking, Orgon is giving commands and Dorine is responding with assertions, but actioning discloses further shading for each line. The internal action is in brackets after the characters' names.

> ORGON. [Test] Has everything gone well the few
> days I've been away? What have you been
> doing? How is everyone?
> DORINE. [Provoke] The day before yesterday the
> mistress was feverish all day. She had a
> dreadful headache.
> ORGON. [Prod] And Tartuffe?
> DORINE. [Shock] Tartuffe? He's very well: hale
> and hearty; in the pink.
> ORGON. [Amaze] Poor fellow!

DORINE. [Alarm] In the evening she felt faint
and couldn't touch anything, her headache
was so bad.
ORGON. [Pump] And Tartuffe?
DORINE. [Incite] He supped with her. She ate
nothing but he very devoutly devoured a
couple of partridges and half a hashed leg
of mutton.
ORGON. [Horrify] Poor fellow!
DORINE. [Torment] She never closed her eyes
all through the night. She was too fever-
ish to sleep and we had to sit up with her
until morning.
ORGON. [Search] And Tartuffe?
DORINE. [Startle] Feeling pleasantly drowsy,
he went straight to his room, jumped into
a nice warm bed, and slept like a top
until morning.
ORGON. [Astonish] Poor fellow!
DORINE. [Incite] Eventually she yielded to our
persuasions, allowed herself to be bled,
and soon felt much relieved.
ORGON. [Test] And Tartuffe?
DORINE. [Overwhelm] He dutifully kept up his
spirits, and took three or four good swigs
of wine at breakfast to fortify himself
against the worst that might happen and
to make up for the blood the mistress had
lost.
ORGON. [Outrage] Poor fellow!

254

This episode entails some external action as Orgon arrives, takes
off his coat, sets down his traveling bag, etc. He might also pursue
Dorine around the room with his questions. Nonetheless, this external action would not generate much interest in itself without the
internal action of Dorine poking fun of Orgon at his own expense.
The humor arises from the internal action, which is based on the
specific given circumstances. In a recent production at the Moscow
Art Theatre, external action was introduced to reinforce the internal
action of this episode: Orgon clasped in his arms a small bust of
Tartuffe (external action) to express his obsessive fondness for him
(internal action).

Emotion

An important function of dialogue — some would say its most important function — is the expression of *emotion*. Characters do not just state facts; they also express their feelings about the conditions of those facts. The most intense emotional dialogue is often a free release of feelings stemming from an open clash of conflicting wills. Moliere has provided a tense emotional clash like this between Orgon and his son Damis in *Tartuffe*. Damis has discovered Tartuffe attempting to seduce his stepmother, Elmire. He hopes that his father will condemn Tartuffe when he finds out, but Tartuffe outwits him. By openly admitting the accusation, Tartuffe seems to humbly take the blame for Damis' false accusation. This causes Orgon to interpret Damis's accusation as slander, and he turns his anger on Damis instead.

> ORGON. (*to Damis*) Doesn't your heart relent, you dog!
>
> DAMIS. What! Can what he says so far prevail with you that...
>
> ORGON. Silence, you scoundrel! (*raising up Tartuffe*)
>
> Rise, brother — I beg you. (*to his son*) You scoundrel!
>
> DAMIS. He may—
>
> ORGON. Silence!
>
> DAMIS. This is beyond bearing! What! I'm to...
>
> ORGON. Say another word and I'll break every bone in your body!
>
> TARTUFFE. In God's name, brother, calm yourself. I would rather suffer any punishment than he should receive the slightest scratch on my account.
>
> ORGON. (*to his son*) Ungrateful wretch!
>
> TARTUFFE. Leave him in peace! If need be, I'll ask your pardon for him on my knees ...
>
> ORGON. (*to Tartuffe*) Alas! What are you thinking of?
>
> (*to his son*) See how good he is to you, you dog!
>
> DAMIS. Then I...
>
> ORGON. Enough!
>
> DAMIS. What! Can't I ...
>
> ORGON. Enough, I say!

Orgon and Damis come into open conflict at this moment. They almost get into a brawl, yet their apparent loss of self-control is carefully orchestrated for them in the dialogue. Moliere has provided accusations and counter-accusations, epithets, connotative words, and broken sentences to guide and reinforce their strong feelings.

We explained before as well how dialogue can narrate and explain ideas. Characters under stress, however, seldom stop to describe and analyze their thoughts. Dialogue is rarely a cool intellectual debate. Instead it reveals strong emotions the characters feel about the practical outcome of their ideas. In *The Wild Duck* when Dr. Relling scoffs at Gregers Werle's idealistic image of Hjalmar Ekdal, he does so with strong feeling. He believes that Gregers is ruining people's lives with his meddlesome brand of idealism. Relling is not just debating abstract ideas here; he's talking about the welfare of his friends.

> GREGERS. (*indignantly*) Is it Hjalmar Ekdal you
> are talking about in this strain?
> RELLING. Yes, with your permission; I am sim-
> ply giving you an inside view of the idol
> you are groveling before.

256

> GREGERS. I should hardly have thought I was
> quite stone-blind.
> RELLING. Yes, you are — or not far from it.
> You are a sick man, too, you see.
> GREGERS. You are right there.
> RELLING. Yes. Yours is a complicated case.
> First of all, there is that plague of
> integrity fever, and then — what's worse —
> you are always in a delirium of hero wor-
> ship; you must always have something to
> adore, outside yourself.
> GREGERS. Yes, I must certainly seek it outside
> myself.
> RELLING. But you make such a shocking mistake
> about every new phoenix you think you have
> discovered.
> GREGERS. If you don't think better than that
> of Hjalmar Ekdal, what pleasure can you
> find in being everlastingly with him?
> RELLING. Well, you see, I'm supposed to be a
> sort of a doctor — God help me! I have to
> give a hand to the poor sick people who
> live under the same roof with me.

Relling may be intelligent, but he is not the coldhearted cynic Gregers thinks he is. He chose to be a doctor because he wanted to help people. Unfortunately, he started drinking and then lost his fiancée (Mrs. Sorby) as well his medical practice. Now his lingering sympathy for the suffering of others shows through in the strong emotion of this passage. For Dr. Relling, as for other characters who speak about their most cherished beliefs, ideas have practical consequences.

Another example of a deluded idealist like Gregers Werle is found in *Angels in America*, where Louis Ironson rarely misses an opportunity to speak out about his political ideals. Act 2,2 starts with Louis provoking Belize, "Why has democracy succeeded in America?" Belize sees that Louis' political speechmaking is a pretense to cover his guilt from abandoning his partner, Prior Walter, who is seriously ill. Belize brings their one-sided conversation to a close with his account of a cheap romance novel that declares, "...real love isn't ever ambivalent." The politics in this dialogue disguises the latent emotion, which is what makes the scene effective on a theatrical level. Without the underlying emotion, however, the dialogue here would simply be political talk and not very entertaining.

Subtext

Some plays reveal plot, character, and idea directly through the text itself. The acting, directing, and design are straightforward illustrations of the text, and the basis of the play's dramatic interest is controlled by it. Many of these are excellent plays, yet in the theatre the spoken word is not always as valuable in itself. Sometimes it is the unspoken *subtext* that is, or should be, the most important source of dramatic interest.

Stanislavsky explained subtext as the internally-felt life a character, which continuously flows beneath the words of the text, all the time justifying and animating them. It is what forces the characters to speak the words of their role. Subtext is one of Stanislavsky's most widely honored contributions to the understanding of plays. It stems from two basic premises. First, that characters speak only a small part of what they are thinking. Second, that a point-to-point association exists between what the characters are saying and what they are thinking. Subtext is much more than "reading between the lines;" it is a concrete feature of the dialogue. In many plays, studying the dialogue alone is not enough; knowledge of the subtext is essential to energize the dialogue and make it theatrical. Success depends on the vocal intonations, facial expressions, gestures, and other illustrative measures that can be provided only by expressing the subtext right along with the text. One of the professional reader's most serious tasks is to understand the subtext so that it may take explicit form in performance.

Subtext plays an important role in *The Wild Duck*. Not much of an external nature happens in the play. There are none of the big scenes we normally associate with the stage. The major confrontations between Gregers and his father, Hjalmar and Gina, and Gregers and Relling are brief and subdued, not climactic in the usual sense. Even Hedvig's death occurs off stage; we only see its aftereffects in the characters. The real drama is expressed in the subtext. Uncovering the subtext means close reading for all evidence of conflicts, whether direct, implied, or inferred. In this play it is chiefly the conflicts involving Gregers and his father, whom he believes was responsible for his mother's death. A large part of Gregers' so-called mission in life is to punish his father for this perceived misdeed. In fact, Gregers sees his father's malicious handiwork everywhere he turns. Most of the information necessary to identify this issue comes from the background story, which is among the most intricate in all of Ibsen's plays. *The Wild Duck* becomes dramatic only when its subtext is first understood and then expressed through performance and mise-en-scene.

A contemporary playwright whose plays often languish from the absence of subtext in performance is Sam Shepard. The subtext of *A Lie of the Mind*, for example, is frequently under-expressed in production, leaving audiences and actors in a muddle. A clear and steady look at what happens in the play can solve such problems. *A Lie of the Mind* is about an abusive husband who finds out what love means only after he almost kills his wife. The subtext throughout the play is plugged into the transforming power of love. Without this subtext — without the undercurrent of love lost, distorted, diverted, and misguided — the play's dramatic potential becomes dissipated and falls off to little more than a perplexing narrative.

Subtext is not restricted to modern plays. An instructive example is provided by Stanislavsky from his production of *Tartuffe*, which is well described in Vasily Toporkov's book, *Stanislavsky in Rehearsal*. The passage happens to be the one between Orgon and Dorine studied above in the discussion of internal action. In the context of a rehearsal, Stanislavsky furnishes fresh and imaginative subtext for each line to help the actors find and express the latent dramatic value. His comments about the subtext are worth close attention.

Dialogue in Nonrealistic Plays

The varied types of writing that Vladimir Nabokov identified in James Joyce's nonrealistic novels can be extended by inference to nonrealistic plays as well.

Leisureliness

Passages of straightforward realistic writing in the nonrealistic study plays are both obvious and numerous, but what is distinctive at this point is their quality of *leisureliness*. Unhurriedness, a retarded tempo, is the general picture presented in *Happy Days*, *Rosencrantz and Guildenstern are Dead*, *The Birthday Party*, and *Fefu and Her Friends*, though similar examples occur in the other nonrealistic study plays as well. Consider also the opening scene of *Top Girls*, where a collection of real and imaginary historical women at a dinner party share their life histories. Often nonrealism feels undramatic and lacking in power because the characters seem to talk just to kill time, talk for the sake of talking, as Eric Bentley said about mistaken readings of Beckett's plays. Conflict apparently evaporates, and nothing important seems to be going on — except expression of the given circumstances of the play's special world.

259

But this seemingness and this exception are important. They produce one of the chief characteristics of nonrealistic dialogue: *thematic resonance*. It makes no difference that the plot recedes into the background and there is minimal progress in the storyline. Internal action is vividly present — not in the customary sense, but in a sufficient amount to allow us to perceive the big picture. In spite of opinions to the contrary, nonrealistic playwrights have not run out of things to say, and so fill up the time with aimless conversation. Their plays are packed with meaning, like other good plays are (see Chapter 5). To paraphrase Bentley again, they are writing about characters that find it difficult to fill *their* time with meaning. The passages where characters seem to ramble or run out of important things to talk about should be seen as disruptions of *their* continuity, not that of the author. Playwrights work long and hard to draw special attention to these moments. As stated in the previous chapter, such moments set up an alternating motion between the seeable reality of the play and its internal reality, between what is being said and done and the underlying meaning. This so-called leisurely quality has a fascination and dramatic potential of its own, which means that the points of thematic resonance need to be analyzed accurately at the table and illustrated attentively in performance.

Incomplete, Rapid, Broken, Stream-of-Consciousness

Examples of this type of writing are found throughout nonrealistic plays, although they are most often associated with the main characters. The longer speeches of the Young Woman in *Machinal* and Julia in *Fefu and Her Friends* are prominent examples. It is important to recognize that stream-of-consciousness soliloquies (Nabokov would say "stepping stones" of consciousness) such as these emphasize the verbal aspects of thinking; however we do not always think in words but also in images. Thus, stream-of-consciousness takes for granted that such a torrent of words, words, words is plausible even though it is not realistic to suppose that characters would or could talk in this way. In other words, incomplete, rapid, broken and stream-of-consciousness passages are not realistic events. They are plausible only in that they reinforce the main idea of the play. By definition, characters in all plays, including nonrealistic plays, think and speak by using words and sentences. But in nonrealistic plays their mental and verbal processes are governed principally by the thematic needs of the play.

Mistakes, Ambiguities, and Stoppages

To Nabokov's categories we append one more. Nonrealistic plays seem to present worlds in which the characters scarcely communicate with each other. The mechanical statements of the supporting characters in *Machinal*, the flighty digressions of Winnie in *Happy Days*, the talk at cross purposes in *The Birthday Party*, the inarticulate eloquence of the characters in *American Buffalo* and *A Lie of the Mind* — these examples give tangible form to the idea that the characters have lost touch with their authentic selves, with their humanity, and therefore with each other as well. Nonrealistic dialogue is only a thin covering. Its accepted meanings have dried up or become buried beneath a lifetime of false impressions about self-identity and reality. Characters often speak in trite, stereotyped expressions that have lost their originality and impact, either from careless overuse or from fear of interfering with their frightening private worlds. Again, the object here is not just "inability to communicate," but what sort of world causes miscommunication to occur in the first place.

Summary

Dramatic dialogue is a very strict form of writing. Normally, it is denied any expressiveness that is not exclusively devoted to the practical workings of the play. Even when dialogue employs special literary qualities of its own, they cannot be artificially applied or else the play may lose its dramatic momentum. From beginning to end, good dialogue is crafted so that each line advances the action, adding to the harmony and strength of the whole. Readers can be successful at analysis of dialogue because there is usually enough time to do so at the table prior to production. Studying the literary features of dramatic dialogue at the table, however, should not be cause to overlook its dramatic function in performance. Drama is in danger when too much theoretical interest is taken in language or when language becomes the continuous subject of study. If theatre is really to happen, language must be an integral part of it, not independent from it. It is important to understand the dialogue, but it is also necessary to guard against thinking too much about it. Dramatists are generally more concerned with what they have to say than with the way they say it.

Questions

1. *Words.* Does the dialogue use a noticeable amount of abstract words? Concrete words? Formal words? Informal words? Do any of the characters especially do so? Are there any examples of professional jargon or slang? Are there many words that convey more than their dictionary meanings (connotations)? If so, who speaks them? What associations do the words suggest?

2. *Sentences.* How long is the average sentence in the play? Does anyone speak sentences that are longer or shorter than the average? What types of sentences are generally represented? Are the sentence types generally similar, or is there a variety of sentence types? Do any characters speak in distinctive sentence types? What do the sentences in the play sound like? Is their rhythm special or memorable in any way?

3. *Speeches.* Is punctuation strictly grammatical, or is it also used for dramatic purposes? Can examples of dramatic punctuation be cited? How are the speeches linked to each other? By words? By thoughts? Are there any examples of dialogue linking by means of action instead of words or thoughts? How are the sentences emotionally arranged within the longer speeches? How are the lines emotionally arranged within units and scenes?

4. *Special Qualities.* Is the dialogue written in verse? If so, what types of verse are represented? Is the dialogue written in carefully composed prose? If so, what makes it special or memorable? Is the

dialogue appealing in any other way? If so, how? Are there any examples of dialects or accents? If so, what kinds?

5. *Theatricality*. How does the dialogue express external and internal action? Is the dialogue highly emotional? If so, how is emotion expressed? Does the dialogue contain a great deal of unspoken inner tension (subtext)? If so, how is it expressed?

6. *Mise-en-Scene*. What does the dialogue suggest about the mise-en-scene? How could the mise-en-scene contribute to the effectiveness of the dialogue?

262

CHAPTER 9

Tempo, Rhythm, and Mood

The words *tempo, rhythm,* and *mood* are used here to describe the feature Aristotle called music or song. Greek tragedies were written in verse that was sung with music, and scholars believe that Aristotle's term referred to this music as well as the rhythms of the verse itself. He observed that music and rhythm were capable of directly inciting emotions and he concluded that these emotions enhanced the dramatic impression of plays. From this idea he deduced that "the music of the language" is one of the six basic elements of drama.

Although not many plays are written in verse today, plays continue to employ tempos, rhythms, and moods to express feelings just as verse and music do. The rhythmical cadences of speech can stimulate overt emotional responses such as laughter, tears, and applause. Think of some of the great modern orators, such as John F. Kennedy, Martin Luther King, Jr., and Winston Churchill, among others. Tempo, rhythm, and mood can also stimulate subtle physical changes in breathing, heartbeat, blood pressure, and muscular tension, all of which we associate with emotion. Whether they acquire their powers from poetry, music, or biology, the features of tempo, rhythm, and mood can and do convey authentic feelings.

Some might argue that these features cannot really be observed in a script. They would say that tempo, rhythm, and mood are metaphysical issues and do not represent material reality. Others disagree. Psychologist William James maintained that there is no reason to call emotional sensations unreal just because they may be for the most part unseen. If something produces real effects — and most people would agree that emotions are real enough — then it must be a form of reality itself. Stanislavsky was aware of James's ideas and seems to have agreed with him, if only unknowingly. In the second part of *An Actor's Work*, Stanislavsky devoted several chapters to tempo, rhythm, and mood, and their role in production. His principle of tempo-rhythm stems from the tension between external and internal tempos, rhythms, and moods in a character. Michael Chekhov's practical understanding of tempo, rhythm, and mood is important too. In his book *To the Actor*, he draws a distinction between the *individual feelings* of a character and *atmosphere* stemming from tempos, rhythms, and moods in the script itself. And so it appears that there are some knowable issues involved. They may be subtle and complex, but they need to be studied because they help to shape the emotional experience of a play.

Tempo

First some definitions and distinctions. Timing, speed, pace, tempo, and rhythm are separate but related concepts. They have no precise definitions in the theatre, but the definitions presented here could be considered representative. *Timing* is the temporal relationship between one spoken word and another, between a spoken word and a physical action, or between two physical actions. *Speed* is the measurable rate of movement or speech in real time. And *pace* means the observer's subjective perception of speed. These three terms deal with features of time in a live performance. This chapter deals with tempo, rhythm, and mood in the play itself. These issues are all interconnected, of course, and are separated here only for teaching purposes.

As discussed in earlier chapters, every moment in a play is aimed at expressing plot, character, and the main idea. How these features emerge from within the script has also been examined. *Tempo* at this point refers to how much and how often this type of information occurs in the play, that is, the amount and frequency of such information. In this special context, tempo is not related to the usual meanings of velocity or measurable speed but is closer to the concept of density, the quantity of information in a passage. When dialogue is crowded with information about plot, character, or idea, the tempo is slow (very dense) because there is a large amount of such information to deal with. When such information is limited, the content is thinner (less dense), and the tempo is quicker because there is less new information to sort out. The questions to ask are where and when does the play present important dramatic information, what kind of information is it, and how much of it is there. The answers to these questions, according to the sense intended here, describe tempo in the script.

In the Plot

Chapter 3 explained that background story is the secret part of the plot. In Chapter 4 we learned that plot in the dialogue consists of entrances and exits, blocking, use of properties, special physical activities, and in particular assertions, plans, and commands. Chapter 5 said further that plot develops in progressions arranged in an escalating pattern of major and minor climaxes. These are also issues to deal with when determining *tempo in the plot*. The following examples are drawn from *The Wild Duck* and *Oedipus Rex*, which are prototypes for modern and classic plays.

Ibsen was an excellent craftsman when it came to conveying plot information through dialogue and arranging it in clear, logical progressions. In the scene between Gregers and his father near the end of the first act of *The Wild Duck*, the chief dramatic interest is plot. Although some character information is revealed, very few lines express information about character as such. One line in the scene relates to the main idea of the play, none contain any special literary qualities (in the English translation at least), and there is little obvious external action. The scene occurs on stage while a dinner party takes place in the adjoining room. The assertions, plans, and commands in the dialogue advance the plot in four steps: (1) Gregers blames his father for the collapse of the Ekdal family, (2) Gregers threatens to disclose his father's relationship with their former housemaid, who is now Hjalmar Ekdal's wife, (3) Werle informs Gregers of his engagement to Mrs. Sorby, and (4) Gregers condemns his father and announces his intention to leave home and embark on his life's mission. The analysis below is slow and detailed because the information is densely packed.

The first beat sets up Gregers' urgent wish to speak privately with his father.

> GREGERS. Father, won't you stay a moment?
> WERLE. (*stops*) What is it?
> GREGERS. I must have a word with you.
> WERLE. Can't it wait until we are alone?
> GREGERS. No, it can't, for perhaps we shall never be alone together.
> WERLE. (*drawing nearer*) What do you mean by that?

265

Notice the suspenseful link to the next beat in the last line: "What do you mean by that?"

Next follows a beat of twelve lines composed of six rhetorical questions by Gregers (assertions about the background story) and six angry replies by Mr. Werle (counter-assertions about the same events). The main topic here is the illegal timber harvesting incident, but seven related topics are also introduced and expressed in two or three lines. Each small topic forms its own sub-beat, so to speak, because each adds its own fragment of new information to advance the plot: (1) the decline in the fortunes of the Ekdals, (2) the former friendship between Lieutenant Ekdal and Mr. Werle, (3) their mutual involvement in the timber incident, (4) Ekdal's responsibility in drawing up the fraudulent boundary map, (5) Ekdal's illegal cutting of the timber, (6) Werle's alleged ignorance of Ekdal's actions, and (7) the guilty verdict handed down against Ekdal and the acquittal of Mr. Werle for lack of evidence. Sub-beats are indicated by a double bar // for clarity.

GREGERS. How has that family been allowed to go so miserably to the wall?

WERLE. You mean the Ekdals, I suppose?

GREGERS. Yes, I mean the Ekdals. // Lieutenant Ekdal was once so closely associated with you.

WERLE. Much too closely; I have felt that to my cost for many years. It is thanks to him that I — yes I — have had a kind of slur cast upon my reputation. //

GREGERS. (softly) Are you sure that he alone was to blame?

WERLE. Who else do you suppose?

GREGERS. You and he acted together in that affair of the forests — //

WERLE. But was it not Ekdal that drew the map of the tracts we had bought — that fraudulent map! // It was he who felled all the timber illegally on government property. In fact the whole management was in his hands. // I was quite in the dark as to what Lieutenant Ekdal was doing.

GREGERS. Lieutenant Ekdal himself seems to have been very much in the dark as to what he was doing.

WERLE. That may be. // But the fact remains
that he was found guilty and I was
acquitted.

GREGERS. Yes, I know that nothing was proved
against you.

WERLE. Acquittal is acquittal.

The topic of the next beat is Mr. Werle's counter-offensive. It consists
of four new sub-beats expressed in two or three lines each and totaling nine lines: (1) Werle's wish to put the timber affair behind him
for good, (2) Ekdal's emotional collapse after being released from
prison, (3) Werle's attempt to assist Ekdal with money and a job,
and (4) Werle's decision not to record this generosity in the financial
accounts of his business.

WERLE. Why do you rake up these old miseries
that turned my hair gray before its time?
Is that the sort of thing you have been
brooding over up there all these years? I
can assure you, Gregers, here in the town
the whole story has been forgotten long
ago — as far as I am concerned. //

GREGERS. But that unhappy Ekdal family—

WERLE. What would you have me do for those
people? When Ekdal came out of prison he
was a broken man, past all help. There are
people in the world who dive to the bottom
the moment they get a couple of slugs in
their body and never come to the surface
again. // You may take my word for it,
Gregers, I have done all I could without
positively laying myself open to all sorts
of suspicion and gossip.

GREGERS. Suspicion? Oh, I see.

WERLE. I have given Ekdal copying work to do
for the office, and I pay him far, far more
than his work is worth.

GREGERS. (without looking at him) H'm; that I
don't doubt.

WERLE. You laugh? Do you think I'm not telling
you the truth? // Well, I certainly can't

> refer you to my books, for I never enter
> payments of that sort.
> GREGERS. (smiles coldly) No, there are certain
> payments it is best to keep no account of.

The first unit ends here and contains two beats. The remainder of the scene contains seven more units: Gregers presses Werle to admit he paid for Hjalmar Ekdal's photography lessons and helped to set him up in business; Gregers accuses Werle of having an affair with their former housemaid and then arranging her marriage to Hjalmar Ekdal; Werle accuses Gregers and his deceased mother of conspiring against him; Werle informs Gregers of his illness and his forthcoming marriage to Mrs. Sorby; Werle offers Gregers a partnership in his firm (a payoff?); Gregers criticizes his father's immoral behavior; Gregers announces he has found his mission in life and departs. Because Ibsen's dialogue in this scene is jam-packed with detailed plot information, the tempo of the plot is slow. It unfolds gradually, fact by fact, in very small increments, and each fact adds a little more information to the plot. Without a doubt, this scene reveals a very high level of realistic playwriting craftsmanship.

Naturally, the tempo of the plot influences the speed with which a scene is performed. Accordingly, this scene would probably be performed at a snail's pace, with the actors painstakingly accenting everything they talk about. It is also quite possible that the plot may not need as much emphasis in a modern performance as this early realistic play seems to indicate. After many years of experience with realism, audiences have been conditioned to deal with the complicated background story that is the hallmark of realistic playwriting. This being the case, in the contemporary theatre this scene might be performed faster than it was done in the past. Perhaps there would be more emphasis on the zigzags of the emotional relationship between Gregers and Werle, building to a climax at the end of the act. Of course, this is a matter of interpretation. Nonetheless, beats that are too long can oversell a topic and weaken the tension. They may have to be performed quickly to sustain the appropriate level of tension. Beats that are too short may need to be expanded in performance with illustrative external action. In either case, the slow tempo of the plot in the script itself would remain unchanged.

Compare this scene with the similar father–son confrontation from *Death of a Salesman* that was studied in Chapter 8. In that scene, except for Biff's announcement to leave home, neither Biff nor Willy supply any new information to advance the plot. Essentially, they go over in more forceful terms important facts spoken under different circumstances earlier in the play. The inner tempo of the plot is swift there because most of the facts are already known. Once again, however, the speed of the actual performance will depend on the interpretive considerations of those involved.

In the Characters

As seen in Chapter 6, many scenes contain information introduced to express character. When examining character in terms of tempo, it is again necessary to study what sort of character information is introduced and how much. Look for information about objectives, qualities, conflicts, values, personality traits, and relationships. For obvious reasons, the largest amount of character information tends to occur near the beginning of the play or when important characters appear for the first time.

The dialogue in Sophocles' *Oedipus Rex* is an instructive example of character tempo in a classic play. Creon's first appearance is in episode 2, where Oedipus demands to know if Teiresias accused him of murdering King Laius many years ago. This information consists of background story and assertions. Most of the scene, however, is devoted to illustrating the characters of Creon and Oedipus — their behavior qualities, conflicts, values, personality traits, and relationship. In the first beat, Creon reacts to Oedipus' accusations of treason. Creon asserts that he values citizenship, honor, and loyalty above everything else. Character information is underlined.

```
CREON. Men of Thebes:
  I am told that heavy accusations
  Have been brought against me by King Oedipus.
  I am not the kind of man to bear this tamely.
  If in these present difficulties
  He holds me accountable for any harm to him
  Through anything I have said or done — why,
      then,
  I do not value life in this dishonor.
  It is not as though this rumor touched upon
  Some  private  indiscretion.  The  matter  is
      grave.
  The fact is that I am being called disloyal
  To the State, to my fellow citizens, to my
      friends.
```

In the next beat the Choragos (leader of the Chorus) tries to persuade Creon that Oedipus did not really mean what he said. He is implying that Oedipus is impulsive and hot-tempered. He is reluctant to say this openly, however, and Creon becomes impatient. The excuses that the Choragos offers to explain Oedipus' behavior reveal as much about him (the Choragus) as they do about Oedipus.

> CHORAGOS. He may have spoken in anger, not
>   from his mind.
> CREON. But did you not hear him say that I was
>   the one
> Who seduced the old prophet into lying?
> CHORAGOS. The thing was said; I do not know
>   how seriously.
> CREON. But you were watching him! Were his
>   eyes steady?
> Did he look like a man in his right mind?
> CHORAGOS. I do not know.
> I cannot judge the behavior of great men.

270

Oedipus enters in the next unit, whose first beat contains eight balanced lines of dialogue. Oedipus' first five lines recap what is already known about the plot. The remainder of the beat is devoted to the expression of character. We see Oedipus' stubborn pride contrasted with Creon's stubborn reasonableness. In the final four lines of dialogue, Oedipus ridicules Creon's educated style of speech.

> OEDIPUS. So you dared come back.
>   Why? How brazen of you to come to my house,
>   You murderer!
>   Do you think I do not know
>   That you plotted to kill me, plotted to steal
>   my throne?
>   Tell me, in God's name, am I a coward, a
>   fool,
>   That you should dream you could accomplish
>   this?
>   A fool who could not see your slippery game?
>   A coward, not to fight back when I saw it?
>   You are the fool, Creon, are you not? Hoping
>   Without support or friends to get a throne?
>   Thrones may be won or bought: you could do
>   neither.

CREON. Now listen to me. You have talked; let me talk, too. You cannot judge unless you know the facts.

OEDIPUS. You speak well: there is one fact; but I find it hard To learn from the deadliest enemy I have.

CREON. That above all I must dispute with you.

OEDIPUS. That above all I will not hear you deny.

CREON. If you think there is anything good in being stubborn Against all reason, then I say you are wrong.

OEDIPUS. If you think a man can sin against his own kind And not be punished for it, I say you are mad.

CREON. I agree.

The next beat reinforces plot information from the previous scene with Teiresias, but the beat after that returns to expression of character. It contains a lengthy speech in which Creon stands up for himself by defending his values. Note how he uses formal speech and supports his arguments with aphorisms. The final beat is devoted to an exchange of short lines that emphasize the character differences between Oedipus and Creon.

CREON. But now it is my turn to question you.

OEDIPUS. Put your questions. I am no murderer.

CREON. First, then: you married my sister?

OEDIPUS. I married your sister.

CREON. And you rule the kingdom equally with her?

OEDIPUS. Everything that she wants she has from me.

CREON. And am I the third, equal to both of you?

OEDIPUS. That is why I call you a bad friend.

CREON. No. Reason it out, as I have done. Think of this first: Would any sane man prefer Power, with all a king's anxieties, To that same power and the grace of sleep? Certainly not I. I have never longed for the king's power — only his rights.

Would any wise man differ from me in this?
As matters stand, I have my way in everything
With your consent, and no responsibilities.
If I were king, I should be a slave to
    policy.
How could I desire a scepter more
Than what is now mine — untroubled influence?
No, I have not gone mad; I need no honors,
Except those with the perquisites I have now.
I am welcome everywhere; every man salutes me.
And those who want your favor seek my ear,
Since I know how to manage what they ask.
Should I exchange this ease for that anxiety?
Besides, no sober mind is treasonable.
I hate anarchy
And never would deal with any man who likes
    it.
Test what I have said. Go to the priestess
At Delphi, ask if I quoted her correctly.
And as for this other thing: if I am found
Guilty of treason with Teiresias,
Then sentence me to death! You have my word
It is a sentence I should cast my vote for—
But not without evidence!
You do wrong
When you take good men for bad, bad men for
    good.
A true friend thrown aside — why, life itself
Is not more precious!
In time, you will know this well:
For time, and time alone, will show the just
    man,
Though scoundrels are discovered in a day.
CHORAGOS. This is well said, and a prudent man
    would ponder it.
OEDIPUS. But is he not quick in his duplicity?
And shall I not be quick to parry him?
Would you have me stand still, hold my peace,
    and let
This man win everything, through my inaction?
CREON. And you want — what is it, then? To
    banish me?

272

```
OEDIPUS. No, not exile. It is your death I want.
   So that all the world may see what treason
      means.
CREON. You will persist, then? You will not
      believe me?
OEDIPUS. How can I believe you?
CREON. Then you are a fool.
OEDIPUS. To save myself?
CREON. In justice, think of me.
OEDIPUS. You are evil incarnate.
CREON. But suppose that you are wrong?
OEDIPUS. Still I must rule.
CREON. But not if you rule badly.
OEDIPUS. O city, city!
CREON. It is my city, too!
```

The plot tempo in this unit is swift because little is revealed about
the plot that is not already known. The tempo of character disclosure
is very slow, however, because so much of the dialogue is devoted to
expressing character as such. The stately character tempo and reliance
on words instead of external actions are common practice in classic
plays. When speaking in public or in a court of law, classical conventions often required speakers to establish their credibility by stating their family heritage and personal values. If these beats revealing
character seem too long for modern tastes, they might be sped up in
performance and supplemented with illustrative character business.

273

When modern dramatists write dialogue devoted to character,
they generally do so in shorter passages. They are also inclined to
supplement the dialogue with opportunities for external action.
A useful example of this is found in *American Buffalo*. Here is the opening unit again (remember it from Chapter 5), where Don and Bob
are sitting at last night's poker table in Don's Resale Shop. They are
talking about a blunder Bob made in their planning for the burglary.

```
DON. So?
   (Pause.)
   So what, Bob?
BOB. I'm sorry, Donny.
   (Pause.)
DON. All right.
BOB. I'm sorry, Donny.
   (Pause.)
```

DON. Yeah.

BOB. Maybe he's still in there.

DON. If you think that, Bob, how come you're in here?

BOB. I came in.

(*Pause.*)

DON. You don't come in, Bob. You don't come in until you do a thing.

BOB. He didn't come out.

DON. What do I care, Bob, if he came out or not? You're s'posed to watch the guy, you watch him. Am I wrong?

BOB. I just went to the back.

DON. Why?

(*Pause.*)

Why did you do that?

BOB. 'Cause he wasn't coming out the front.

DON. Well. Bob, I'm sorry, but this isn't good enough. If you want to do business...if we got a business deal, it isn't good enough. I want you to remember this.

BOB. I do.

DON. Yes, *now*...but later, what?

(*Pause.*)

Just one thing, Bob. Action counts.

(*Pause.*)

Action counts and bullshit walks.

BOB. I only went around to *see* he's coming out the back.

DON. No, don't go fuck yourself around with these excuses.

(*Pause.*)

BOB. I'm sorry.

DON. Don't tell me you're sorry. I'm not mad at you.

BOB. You're not?

DON. (*Pause.*) Let's clean up here.

(BOB *starts to clean up the debris around the poker table.*)

An entire chapter could be devoted to the craftsmanship of this little episode. But for the time being, notice the concise way in which the dialogue illustrates character. Don is an idealist who wants everything to work just right, and Bob is a blunderer. Each line (in fact the entire play) dramatizes this role conflict and its corresponding conflict of objectives. More character information can be seen in Bob's naiveté, which we later find out is the result of drug addiction and mental incapacity, and in Don's misplaced compassion. The short and snappy dialogue is dense with character information and the character tempo is slow.

In the Idea

When ideas are expressed openly in the dialogue, the tempo slows to conform to the type and amount of intellectual information presented. The slowest tempos arising from idea are found in classic plays, where the practice was to present ideas in speeches composed according to formal principles. Cleante's initial scene with Orgon in the first act of *Tartuffe*, for example, includes two very long idea speeches (set speeches). Together they total twenty-five sentences averaging over twenty-five words each. Close reading shows them to be expressions of the chief ideas at stake in the play. Whatever tempos may be found elsewhere in the play, the idea tempo is slow and deliberate in these speeches.

275

Modern dramatists are inclined to incorporate talk about ideas less formally, more plausibly, within the character and situation. In *Death of a Salesman*, Arthur Miller demonstrates considerable skill at expressing intellectual issues in the dialogue without obviously appearing to do so. His characters convey ideas in the form of aphorisms that sound like expressions of simple personal values. Willy offers this advice to his sons: "The man who makes an appearance in the business world, the man who creates personal interest, is the man who gets ahead. Be liked and you will never want." "Start big and you'll end big." Ben advises young Biff: "Never fight fair with a stranger ... You'll never get out of the jungle that way." Linda admonishes Biff: "A small man can be just as exhausted as a great man." Charley warns Willy: "When a deposit bottle is broken, you don't get your nickel back." These simple sayings are not meant to slow down the plot as Cleante's formal speeches do. Instead they delay things only for a moment, like a brief retard in music, while they harmonize or counterpoint the main idea of the play.

Chapter 7 explained that epilogues provide opportunities for the characters to speak about the important ideas in the play. In the epilogue for *Death of a Salesman*, Biff says about his father, "He had all the wrong dreams. All, all, wrong." Then Charley admonishes him for failing to understand Willy.

> CHARLEY. Nobody dast blame this man. You don't understand. Willy was a salesman. And for a salesman, there is no rock bottom to life. He don't put a bolt to a nut, he don't tell you the law or give you medicine. He's a man way out there in the blue, riding on a smile and a shoeshine. And when they start not smiling back — that's an earth-quake. And then you get yourself a couple of spots on your hat, and you're finished. Nobody dast blame this man. A salesman got to dream, boy. It comes with the territory.

The way in which idea is expressed in this passage is characteristic of realistic playwriting in general. Charley's line is a statement about the main idea ("A salesman got to dream..."), but it sounds like an emotional outburst. The idea tempo is slow because his speech is lengthy and filled with intellectual content, like Cleante's above. Charley's speech, however, is realistically plausible because Miller has placed it in a solemn situation and divided it into eleven short sentences averaging only nine words each. The mood of the situation plus the halting progress of the words mask the intellectual content of the speech and help it sound like an expression of character and feeling.

Rhythm

Rhythm is a pattern of recurring stresses, and dramatic rhythm is a pattern of tensions in the beats, units, scenes, and acts — a pulsing sensation that occurs when the dramatic intensity rises and falls in each progression. Rhythm is capable of directly inciting feelings, and because it is based in natural human instincts, it induces these feelings effortlessly. Most of us are inclined to accept rhythm's emotional effects without even thinking about them. Rhythm operates the same way in drama as it does in poetry and music. It uses recurring stresses and variations in the placement of accents to stimulate feelings and associations that reinforce the meaning. Rhythm assists progressions in building interest, maintaining suspense, developing idea, and concluding interest in the work. But dramatic rhythm does not depend on regular metrical pulses like those found in poetry or music. As already seen, there is a large variety in the way that tensions are built up and released in progressions.

In the Plot

To some extent, *plot rhythm* was treated at the same time we were considering Freytag's principles of dramatic structure. Recall in Chapter 5 his point that a plot is not a flat, featureless arrangement of events. On the contrary, it consists of various obstacles and complications arranged to convey specific dramatic effects. Freytag's pyramid was an attempt to visualize an idealized arrangement of these features. But in doing so, he also gave a picture of plot rhythm. By visualizing as he did the maximum and minimum tensions, it is possible to obtain a tangible picture of the rhythm of the plot. Of course this is not the only way to study rhythm. Readers could also scan the emotional pulses in a series of events, something like scanning verse. (Director Louis Jouvet classified such pulses as emotionally "masculine," "neutral," or "feminine.") Collecting the pulses into coherent groups can furnish a narrative description of the rhythm. In any case, what we are attempting to discover here is how the pulses of tension collect and develop to understand plot rhythm.

Director Tyrone Guthrie believed that anyone who wishes to know a play well ought to be able to observe the rhythm of a play as a graph similar to a patient's hospital chart or a company's sales statistics. In other words, the reader should see the emotional peaks and valleys and picture the shape of the scene in a graphic form that helps to make the plot rhythm clear. The vertical axis would show emotional tensions, and the horizontal axis would show acts and scenes. Graphing like this can also help to show the relationships among adjoining scenes. Ideally, each scene would have its own small graph and in the end a graph of each act would emerge. In this way it is possible to grasp the rhythmic peaks and valleys of the play visually.

To understand plot rhythm in a narrative way, we will study the opening scene from *The Wild Duck*. It takes place in Werle's study, where the servants are putting things in order (1st rhythmic pulse) and a dinner party is under way in the adjoining room (ongoing rhythmic counter-pulse). Petersen lights a lamp and says resentfully, "Listen to them, Jensen!" Then he starts a whispered conversation about Mr. Werle and his son, Gregers (2nd). During the conversation, other hired waiters can be seen at work through the doorway upstage center, with chatter and laughter coming from the room. As the two servants on stage are speaking, the side door opens and Old Ekdal bursts in, drunk. Petersen says, "Good Lord! — what do you want here?" and Ekdal asks to be allowed into the office to pick up his salary (3rd). After Ekdal goes into the office, Jensen asks skeptically, "Is he one of the office people?" Next is a restrained conversation about Old Ekdal (4th). Soon Petersen hears the dinner party breaking up and warns Jensen, "Sh! They're leaving the table" (5th). The double doors are thrown wide open, and Mrs. Sorby enters (6th). The two servants stop their conversation and hurry on to perform their duties. The rhythm in this scene is controlled by the tension of the first whispered conversation about Werle and Gregers, the increase in suspense accompanying Ekdal's surprise appearance, the tension of the second whispered conversation about Ekdal, and the interruption of the conversation when Mrs. Sorby appears with guests. All the time accompanied by a rhythmic counter-pulse from the adjoining room.

Plot rhythm arises from the structure of the play itself, but it takes performance and mise-en-scene to actualize this rhythm in production. Therefore, although awareness of plot rhythm begins with knowing what is going on in the script, it also requires awareness of the contributions to be made by all the creative elements involved with the performance.

In the Characters

Character rhythm is the pattern formed by the psychological changes in a character. How much change occurs in a character from beginning to end? How much from one entrance to the next? In his valuable handbook, *Acting: The First Six Lessons*, Richard Boleslavskygave this explanation of character rhythm. He and his student took a nonstop elevator ride to the top floor of New York's Empire State Building. When they emerged from the elevator on the 102nd floor, they were exhilarated by the view. Boleslavsky explained that the reason they were exhilarated was because the sensation was so different from that at street level. He said that if they had ascended one floor at a time instead of nonstop, they would still know where they were and how high. They would continue to see the change, but there would be none of the earlier feeling of exhilaration because the view from one floor to the next does not change very much. The final view would be the same, but the gradual, step-by-step manner of getting there would make it different, less exhilarating.

The thrill Boleslavsky and his student experienced after taking the elevator to the top floor came from several sources: (1) the sudden shutting-out of the complex sights and sounds at street level when they stepped into the quiet elevator; (2) the silent, accelerated ascent through space; and (3) the infinite expanse of open space that greeted them when they emerged onto the top-floor viewing deck. They were transported from a noisy world of chaotic impressions, placed in an isolation chamber, and then thrust into a new world of openness, freedom, and silence.

Boleslavsky's lesson illustrates how rhythm operates in the expression of character. Hamlet is a different character at the end of the play, for example, than he is at the beginning. We will not argue whether he has actually changed or only revealed traits that were hidden at the outset. The point is that however they may occur, the changes in Hamlet's character have occurred in small increments, one scene at a time. The rhythm of Hamlet's character development is slow and steady, and the final effect is cumulative rather than surprising. Character rhythm is also like this in *Death of a Salesman*, *American Buffalo*, and *The Piano Lesson*. On the other hand, Oedipus changes from an arrogant dictator to a blinded outcast in five enormous leaps. His character is markedly different in each episode, and the emotional impact of his final appearance is that much greater because of the rhythmic leaps. Orgon has a similar character rhythm in *Tartuffe*, as does Walter in *A Raisin in the Sun*, and Jake in *A Lie of the Mind*.

Character rhythm in *Three Sisters* changes in similar leaps. There are three plots, three love triangles, in the play: Masha Kulygin–Vershinin, Andrey–Natasha–Protopopov, and Irina–Tuzenbach–Solyony. At most, each relationship has only one or two scenes in each of the four acts, each separated by a year or more. Our composite picture of these relationships is based on a total of four or five brief encounters. The separate love affairs are woven together in such a seamless fashion that we scarcely realize how little we know of them or how far each relationship has progressed since its previous episode. Each one progresses over great leaps of time, from which we see a few carefully selected events. Chekhov leads us to fill in the gaps for ourselves. Again, character rhythm only starts with the script, and must be physicalized in performance through acting and mise-en-scene.

Mood and Atmosphere

First, let's try to standardize some definitions. *Mood* here refers to the particular feeling of a character, and *atmosphere* refers to the general feeling of a scene or an entire play. Some moods and atmospheres are suggested by the play script itself, and some are suggested by the performance and mise-en-scene. Script, performance, and mise-en-scene come together in production, of course, but the subject treated here is mood and atmosphere in the closed system of the script itself — the starting point for physicalizing these features in performance and mise en scene. The principle sources of atmosphere are given circumstances, plot, and idea. The principal source of mood is the characters.

In the Given Circumstances

The main purpose of the *given circumstances* is to set up the conditions in which the play takes place. As a side-effect, however, the given circumstances form the world of the play, which strongly suggests the general atmosphere. Seventeenth-century, war-torn Europe creates an atmosphere of vigilance and danger in *Mother Courage*. The seasons (fall and winter) and the locales (an empty highway, a half-demolished church, an army camp, etc.) suggest atmospheres for individual scenes. *American Buffalo's* untidy collection of useless items in Don's Resale Shop creates an atmosphere of shoddiness and failure. In *The Wild Duck*, the luxurious atmosphere in the dining room — a dinner party, bustling servants, chatter and laughter, sparkling candles, piano music, expensive furnishings, and party decorations — counterpoints the tense atmosphere of the action in the study. Compare this to the atmosphere created by the given circumstances in the rest of the play, which takes place in Hjalmar Ekdal's flat. Instead of wealth and family conflict, there is an atmosphere of poverty and family harmony.

Chekhov is often considered a playwright of atmospheres. In *The Joy of Rehearsal*, Russian director Anatoly Efros explained his understanding of this feature for each act of *Three Sisters*. Notice that the mood/atmospheres are not laid on by Efros, but generated from the given circumstances, specifically the time of day.

The first act of **Three Sisters** takes place in the morning. The second in the evening. The third at night. And the fourth again in the morning.
Morning: hopes, sunshine, Sunday breakfast, name days. But in the morning there is also melancholy. Because of yesterday's unfortunate events, yesterday's suffering.
Evening: company, the table full of food, chit-chat, disputes, quarrels, cheerfulness, and nervous uneasiness.

Night: sleep, nightmares, hysterics, overwrought impressions. Morning again: departures, hangovers, denouement. The pallor of the faces and ennui in the postures. The need for work. And again hope.

Readers can almost certainly come up with many more examples to show how the given circumstances can suggest atmosphere.

In the Plot

The emotional dynamics of the plot supply some of the most noticeable examples of atmosphere. Murder mysteries and thrillers are good examples of this principle at work. The atmospheres created by the tensions, suspense, and surprises in whodunits and horror stories are a major part of their popularity and appeal. Though character is the dominant element in *Hamlet*, the broad scope of its plot has an influence on the general atmosphere as well. It contains scenes of mystery, intrigue, lyricism, humor, horror, pomp and circumstance, irony, and conspiracy and concludes with savage killings and a military funeral procession. *Machinal* and *Angels in America* are other examples of voluminous plot dynamics influencing atmosphere. Some playwrights take the opposite approach. The comparatively inactive plots of *Happy Days* and *American Buffalo* are the keys to their characteristic atmospheres. In these plays and many others, the tensions released and withheld in the plot itself contribute to the suggestion of atmosphere.

In the Characters

Characters evoke moods through their motives, actions, and desires. Moliere's characters are excellent examples. Think of Tartuffe's audacious and clever hypocrisy, Dorine's merry rebelliousness, Mariane's romantic affection, and Orgon's impulsive temperament. *A Raisin in the Sun* also displays a wide range of character moods: Mama's moral strength, Walter's longing, Ruth's forbearance, Asagai's optimism, and Beneatha's exuberance. The leading characters in *Mother Courage* and *Death of a Salesman* are also memorable for their particular moods.

Some characters are so compelling that their individual moods influence the general atmosphere of the entire play. Oedipus and Hamlet, for example, strongly influence the atmosphere of their individual plays. In like manner, Jake's quirky moods influence the atmosphere of *A Lie of the Mind*, and the boisterous and disorderly mood of Boy Willie influences the atmosphere of *The Piano Lesson*. The individual moods of Goldberg and McCann evoke atmosphere of mystery and danger in *The Birthday Party*. The moods of Winnie in *Happy Days* and the Young Woman in *Machinal* each influence the atmosphere of their respective plays.

In the Idea

Idea can suggest strong atmospheric values, depending on what is going on in the mind of the observer and in the world outside the play. Spirited feelings arise when ideas in the play make direct contact with real-world ideas about politics, economics, science, religion, and art. The ideas in *Mother Courage* were so provocative that its initial productions in this country angered audiences in the politically conservative 1950s. When *Death of a Salesman* was produced in 1949, it was not unusual for men in the audience to weep openly. Its ideas were sharp and moving in the post-World War II economic boom. The anti-capitalist implications of *Death of a Salesman* were also a subject of spirited debate in the press. Tony Kushner's 1992 play *Angels in America* is another instance of idea creating strong atmospheric values. Today the play is understood as a compassionate plea for understanding. In 1992, however, the gay liberation movement was still in its formative stages and its ideology provoked serious and widespread public opposition. Moreover, the presidency of Ronald Reagan (1981–1989) and Margaret Thatcher's election as Prime Minister (1979–1990) seemed to herald a new atmosphere of ultra-conservatism in the West. The motifs of homosexuality and political conservatism in the play incited audiences emotionally and at the same time made them think. As discussed in Chapter 7, dramatists employ ideas in the belief that they will not just interest audiences intellectually, but will mainly evoke atmospheric values.

Tempo, Rhythm, and Mood in Nonrealistic Plays

The unusual tempos, rhythms, and moods in nonrealistic plays are a result of intentional *displacements*. By displacement we mean something surprising, either because it is side by side with something it is not usually coupled with or because it is seemingly illogical. Ordinary things take on unusual qualities when they are displaced in a different context. A friend from work seen at a dinner party or a movie star seen mowing the lawn are within the range of ordinary experience, but in the world of nonrealistic plays unusual feelings can be stirred up through such displacements. Consider the displacements in Edward Hopper's paintings. They may look like ordinary life because they show ordinary people in ordinary locales, but they stir up unusual feelings of loneliness, isolation, and pain because their inhabitants are emotionally displaced from the ordinary life otherwise present in the paintings. It feels like something disturbing has just happened or is about to happen.

A birthday party normally evokes feelings of happiness, but in Pinter's play the presence of Goldberg and McCann — displaced as they are from their usual environment — stir up feelings of fear, mystery, and danger. The ordinary married couple in *Happy Days* is displaced in an expanse of scorched earth. In *Top Girls* the historical and mythological figures are displaced in a restaurant at a dinner party with Marlene. Associations between a line of dialogue and its accompanying action can be a source of displacement. "Haven't you got anything better to do than to monkey around with weapons and [American] flags?" Baylor says to his son, Mike, in *A Lie of the Mind*. Locales are another potential source. Sometimes nonrealistic plays provide information about a specific or general locale, yet since little reference is usually made to the outside world, the overall impression feels displaced. The "Sweden, Poland, Germany" of *Mother Courage and Her Children*; the generic locales in *Machinal*, *Angels in America*, and *Fefu and Her Friends*"; and the "place without any visible character" in *Rosencrantz and Guildenstern are Dead* — these locales could be somewhere, nowhere, everywhere, or all places simultaneously. The absence of a tangible connection to the outside world displaces the action and creates unusual feelings of separation, farness, mystery, and sometimes danger.

283

It can be a challenge to recognize and then physicalize the tempos, rhythms, and moods in nonrealistic plays. However, accurate understanding and insightful mise-en-scene are essential for accurate theatricalization of these features. The so-called ambiguity of the tempos, rhythms, and moods in these plays is specifically what gives them their special fascination.

Closing Notes on Nonrealistic Plays

This chapter concludes the separate treatment of nonrealistic plays. The next chapter studies the question of style, which is an issue applicable to every play equally and without exception. Below is a summary of the issues to consider when analyzing nonrealistic plays for production.

Audiences might be able to feel the ambiguity in nonrealistic plays, but actors, directors, and designers must be able to understand and illustrate it.

Nonrealism requires super-specificity in analysis, acting, directing, and design.

Actors, directors, and designers need to do more than brainstorm about thematic issues, they need to theatricalize them.

Montage is the technique of combining in single composition elements from various sources to give the impression that the elements belonged together originally, or to allow each element to retain its separate identity as a means of adding interest or meaning to the work.

Actors, directors, and designers must clearly illustrate the dots for the spectators to be able to connect them.

Nonrealistic plays need to be theatricalized, not explained in program notes, lobby displays, talk-backs, or post-play discussions.

Theme and variations is a form of composition where an initial theme is stated and each section thereafter is a modification of that theme.

It is a paradox: while performing it is important for actors to be able to step outside their characters and at the same time to identify with them (Bertolt Brecht, Michael Chekhov).

Nonrealism depends on formal patterns.

Nonrealistic plays deliberately establish a distance between the audience and the work. By maintaining an obvious artificial quality instead of trying to illustrate realistic plausibility, nonrealistic playwrights make sure that audiences will retain an objective point of view. In this sense, nonrealistic plays are intended to be analytical and question the world rather than try to explain it.

The structures of nonrealism are the structures of the mind itself, consciousness. To accomplish this, nonrealism often reaches for established forms in other arts and the sciences, including literary criticism (notably structuralism), music, the novel, jazz, theme and variations, monologues, descriptions, expositions, lists, digressions, biology, astronomy, physics, etc. Nonrealism is not an imitation of seeable life but an imitation of consciousness.

It is up to the audience to decide for themselves whether the stage experience is helpful or unhelpful in their future actions. But the options should be theatricalized for the audience to perceive.

Samuel Beckett's plays are excellent examples of nonrealism to study because for the most part they are based on theme and variations. The majority of nonrealistic plays, however, tend to combine theme and variations with at least the minimal features of a standard plot.

Nonrealism requires real-time dual awareness of the inside and the outside of the play.

Entertainment value lies in the ironic contrast between surface and depth. The surface appears insignificant only if the observer lacks insight into the depth. Both levels are equally "real."

Nonrealism is a game, with the audience playing along too.

Samuel Beckett: "Find a form to accommodate the mess."

Social setting is minimal, but awareness of the social setting in production is maximal — without self-awareness in the characters, however.

Reality is not a romantic quest anymore, since it is already only a heritage. Nonrealism shows how this heritage still conditions our lives, although in ignored, forgotten, mutated, or distorted forms.

Summary

Plays employ tempo, rhythm, and mood to express feelings just as poetry and music do. While this chapter dealt with tempo, rhythm, and mood in the play itself, all the same tempo, rhythm, and mood have important outcomes in performance and mise-en-scene. Indeed, for many designers tempo, rhythm, and mood are often the most important links between the text and their creative work. Tempo is the amount of information presented in a selected passage and is recognizable in the given circumstances, the characters, and the ideas — the density of presented information. Rhythm is the pattern of tensions illustrated in the plot and characters. Mood and atmosphere are suggested through the given circumstances, plot, characters, and idea. Displacement of customary tempos, rhythms, and moods is one of the most distinctive traits of nonrealism. Tempo, rhythm, and mood may be hard to pin down ahead of time, but it is important make an effort to do so to define performance goals and maximize the expressiveness of the mise-en-scene.

285

Questions

1. *Tempo.* Studying the beats and units closely, how often is information presented about plot? About character? About idea? Is the given passage crowded with such information and what kind appears most often? Or is there comparatively little of this information? Where in the play is most of this information presented? Which characters or scenes express this information most? What does the density of plot, character, or idea information

suggest about the mise-en-scene? How could the mise-en-scene contribute to the effectiveness of this issue?

2. *Rhythm.* How do the emotional tensions collect and develop in each scene? Each act? The entire play? Can the rhythmical pattern of tensions be described? Graphically represented? How much, if at all, do the leading characters change or develop from one scene to the next? From the beginning of the play to the end? What do the patterns of emotional tension suggest about the mise-en-scene? How could the mise-en-scene contribute to the effectiveness of these rhythmic patterns?

3. *Mood.* Are there any atmospheric feelings associated with the given circumstances? Any strong moods associated with specific characters? Any atmospheric feelings associated with the major or minor ideas? What is the controlling atmosphere of the world of the play? Is the controlling atmosphere associated with the moods of a particular character? With a particular set of given circumstances? What do the character moods and general atmosphere suggest about the mise-en-scene? How could the mise-en-scene contribute to the effectiveness of the character moods and general atmosphere?

CHAPTER 10

The Style of
the Play

The preceding chapters studied the issue of form, that is, the separate parts of a play and how they work. This chapter studies the issue of style. In production, style is the personality of the actors, directors, or designers imprinted on their work. Also related to production is historical style, which is based on the period in which a play originated and aims to recreate an illusion of historical authenticity. In the play script itself, on the other hand, style is a special way of expressing plot, character, idea, dialogue, and tempo–rhythm–mood that is characteristic of a particular play, playwright, or group of playwrights. It is what makes plays, playwrights, and groups of playwrights different from each other. This is what is meant here by the term style, and to understand it this chapter will return to the basic parts of a play to reconsider them. Except this time we will study how they are shaped and how they relate to each other and to the entire play, instead of what they are and how they work singly. Separating script analysis into form and style phases involves some repetition, but we hope to show that it has its benefits.

Given Circumstances

Time

Any feature that differs from standard expectations has the potential of becoming a point of style. In *Death of a Salesman*, for example, *time* is a point of style. Besides the standard forward progress of time, there are also flashbacks (scenes from the past inserted into the flow of the present) and reveries (dreamy meditations) that take place outside of clock or calendar time. There are also no realistic transition scenes to clarify the changes between present, past, and non-time. The changes occur almost unnoticeably, creating the impression of a continuity among past, present, and future. Time is treated with similar freedom in *Angels in America*. The dramatic time covered by this play is about six months between 1986 and 1987. Within these limits, time generally moves forward chronologically, but there are also split scenes that take place in two places at the same time, flashbacks, and hallucinatory scenes that occur in imaginary time. Since little information about time as such is provided in the dialogue, time appears to jump irregularly from scene to scene. Readers and audiences are expected to fill in the gaps. Nonstandard treatment of time is also a stylistic feature of *A Lie of the Mind* and *Rosencrantz and Guildenstern are Dead*.

Dramatists who write in this manner do not pay much attention to scenic linkage and other features that make things appear to happen in a standard way. Instead they go straight to the central events, scene by scene, without delay. They emphasize the essential issues and restrict themselves to those alone, without the need to deal with the writing requirements of standard realism. Shepard and Kushner take this issue even further than Miller did by eliminating almost any references to time of day in their plays. Taken away are most of the usual entrances and exits, the lighting or dimming of lamps, the putting on or taking off of coats and hats, the "Good mornings" and "Good nights," and all the other details needed to indicate time realistically. As a result, we are dropped into the stream of the action in the manner of the movies. This is a departure from the standard treatment of time found in *The Wild Duck* and *The Piano Lesson*, but it is not new. It is a return to the emancipated way that Shakespeare handled time in his plays. What is stylistically different is the application of Shakespeare's free treatment of time to modern plays.

Dramatic time in Beckett's *Happy Days* stands still throughout the entire play. The harsh white light never changes, and there is no actual passage of time. A loud bell is the signal for Winnie and Willie to wake and sleep. Winnie often speaks about time, but when she does, it only emphasizes the fact that time in the conventional sense no longer exists for them.

In these several plays, the treatment of time departs from standard (realistic) expectations and by this means becomes a point of style.

Place

To answer the question "Is *place* stylistically important in the play?" it is necessary to learn if one of the chief interests in the play is its general or specific locale. The attic in *The Wild Duck* is a useful example. Ibsen describes it in detail. The room contains "odd nooks and corners, stovepipes running through it from the rooms below and a skylight through which clear moonbeams shine in." Inside are doves flying about, hens cackling, rabbits and other small animals, assorted small trees, and the wild duck. Access is through a sliding door in the back wall of the studio through a special see-through curtain — "the lower part consisting of a piece of old sailcloth, the upper part of a stretched fishing net." All through the play, the dialogue, action, visual interest, and sound effects are associated with this specific locale. Old Ekdal treats the attic as if it were a place of pilgrimage, Hjalmar uses it as a hideaway, and Hedvig shoots herself there. In *The Wild Duck*, the attic has symbolic importance and its understanding, design, and use should be stylistic points in production.

Beyond special locales, style can also be found in the use of multiple locales or complex changes of locale. The Loman house in *Death of a Salesman* needs to suggest a realistic sense of place, but it should also provide enough scenic flexibility to permit the fluid expression of time in the play. This calls for a unique scenic design that has become one of the hallmarks of this play in production. How, for example, do the characters manage to change their costumes when they appear in adjacent scenes but in different time frames? How are the lighting changes handled? These will be important stylistic features in any new production design.

Machinal contains multiple locales: an office, a kitchen, a hotel bedroom, a room in a hospital, a bar, a "dark room," a sitting room, a courtroom, and a prison cell. The succession of locales, generically urban in nature, contributes to the feeling of busy, noisy activity in the play, which reinforces the Young Woman's dilemma. The multiple locales in *Mother Courage* also contribute to the style of that play. The action travels all over central Europe, yet the constant presence of the canteen wagon adds a note of timelessness to the various locales. Multiple locales are also characteristic of *Hamlet* and *Angels in America*. *Hamlet* occurs in and around the castle of Elsinore, while *Angels in America* occurs in and around New York City. What is the emotional difference between Shakespeare's historical castle and Kushner's modern metropolis? The effect of multiple locales — individually, sequentially, and collectively — adds stylistic uniqueness to a play.

Society

Interesting observations about a play's style and a playwright's thinking can be uncovered by studying the *society* portrayed in the given circumstances. In his book *Mimesis*, Erich Auerbach discusses the special role of society in Shakespeare's plays, notably the aristocratic classes of society. Auerbach explained that when members of the middle or lower classes appear in Shakespeare's plays, they almost always speak and behave in comic, or at least unserious, ways. Shakespeare's aristocratic characters may fall into unserious ways of expression or behavior, but the reverse seldom happens. Auerbach asserts this is evidence of the dominant ruling-class social values implicit in Shakespeare's plays. The plays of Sophocles and Moliere show similar stylistic tendencies. On the other hand, the plays of Sheridan, Miller, Brecht, Hansberry, Wilson, Shepard, Fornes, Pinter, and Kushner suggest a deep-seated mistrust of ruling-class culture. In plays by these writers, the sympathetic ("positive") characters are mainly from middle- and lower-class social groups, and they speak and behave in serious, meaningful ways. The unsympathetic ("negative") characters are from wealthy, upper-class, or bourgeois social groups and talk and act in comic, satiric, or unserious ways. This stylistic feature can be read as an implied critique of wealthy, or at least of conformist bourgeois, culture.

290

The choice of fashionable social groups or fashionable values may lead to other stylistic insights. *The School for Scandal* is a satire about a small circle of characters that entertain themselves by passing judgment on the reputations of others. A leading member of this circle is Joseph Surface, whom Sheridan has singled out for special disapproval. Joseph admits to being a "sentimentalist." The sentimentalists were a fashionable group current in eighteenth-century London. They were distinguished by their aristocratic class-consciousness, their flamboyant moral self-righteousness, and their habit of sprinkling conversations with clever aphorisms drawn from popular sentimentalist literature. Joseph displays all these traits. In contrast to Joseph and his sentimentalists, Sheridan places his brother, Charles Surface, with his classless circle of friends. They disdain social distinctions and sentimentalist vocabulary, and champion democratic ideals. Sheridan's style in this play is marked by the contrast between these two social groups and their conflicting values.

Three Sisters deals with Russian educated society, the so-called intelligentsia. *A Lie of the Mind* deals with proletarian society, one of whom (Frankie) is first-generation college-educated. He is disdained by the all the others except his brother, Jake, and Jake's wife, Beth. While the leading characters in *Angels in America* are of course gay, the social groups include lawyers, doctors, religious figures (including angels), their families and associates — members of America's so-called ruling classes. The women in *Fefu and Her Friends* are well-to-do and college-educated. *American Buffalo* deals with the culture of petty criminals. *The Piano Lesson* and *A Raisin in the Sun* concentrate on African Americans relegated to the lower economic and educational ranks of society — the disenfranchised classes. How and why do these plays focus on these specific social groups? The answer is an important feature of their individual styles.

More Style Possibilities

A close study of other given circumstances can uncover more features that contribute to style, depending on the play. Under the category of learning and the arts (subdivision: science and technology), for example, there are details about late nineteenth-century photography described in *The Wild Duck*. Hjalmar's studio contains "photographic instruments and apparatus of different kinds, boxes and bottles of chemicals, instruments, tools, photographs and small articles, such as camel's-hair pencils, paper, and so forth." Act 3 opens with Hjalmar colorizing and retouching photographs. At the beginning of act 4 Gina has just finished a photographic session. She is shown "with a little box and a wet glass plate in her hand," and later she "slips the plate into the box and puts it into the covered camera." Hjalmar's photography business is a motif of external action that runs throughout the play.

291

A little supplementary study reveals that Ibsen has described the practice of wet-plate photography used during the period. Historians say that photography was initially considered a shortcut for artists to avoid learning basic drawing and painting. With a little imagination, readers should be able to recognize the stylistic possibility of these details. Photography was still novel in 1884, and Hjalmar's studio may have been one of the first in his city (financed by Mr. Werle, of course). The fact that photography was considered a shortcut to art calls to mind Hjalmar's desire to be treated as an artist without having to do the hard work of actually making art. He maintained this "life illusion" about himself by leaving to Gina the messy work of taking pictures and developing them while reserving for himself the "artistic" work of touching up and adding color to the results. The scientific dimension of photography also provided him with public proof of his desire to be thought of as an inventor, another life illusion of his. The fact that in this play about sexual infidelity Hjalmar specializes in wedding pictures is an example of Ibsen's wry sense of humor. This is how the given circumstances connected with photography can reveal some interesting features about Hjalmar's personality — and about the level of detail present in Ibsen's plays and a point of his style.

Special treatment given to select given circumstances can be a sign of style in other plays as well. Further examples from the study plays include small-time commerce in *Mother Courage*; back-room politics in *Angels in America*; go-getting free enterprise in *Death of a Salesman*, *Top Girls*, and *Machinal*; genteel culture in *Three Sisters* and *Fefu and Her Friends*; petty thievery in *American Buffalo*; and ethnic traditions in *The Piano Lesson*. Each of these given circumstances is treated with the kind of care that warrants special stylistic attention in analysis and production.

Background Story

In realistic and classic plays, *background story* provides at least as much dramatic potential as the onstage action. Alternatively, background story in nonrealistic plays is nearly absent. In either case, because background story in some form is always essential to onstage action, the way it is handled is an important feature of a play's style.

Content

What is the *content* of the background story? Generally it is composed of events, but it is also true that events as such can play a minor role in the background story, even in a realistic play such as *American Buffalo*. Feelings, character descriptions, and sensory responses are the more important features of the background story here. The only important previous events are the coin collector's purchase of the buffalo-head nickel from Don, and the setting up of the burglary by Don and Bob. The other events disclosed in the background story — last night's card game, the dispute between Fletch and Ruthie about the stolen pig iron, the cheap diner run by Ruthie and Gracie, the fact that Teach pawned his watch — have no major bearing on the plot. The background story in this play mainly shows the environment the characters inhabit (which is always on the edge of falling apart), the characters' circle of friends, the volatile emotional relationships among the characters, the bad weather, the omnipresent threat of the police, and the characters' feelings about the instability of life in general. The relative insignificance of most of the background story, and yet the significance the characters attribute to it, is an important part of the play's meaning and unusual comic style.

292

Technique

The *technique* used to disclose the background story is another likely style feature. As we have seen, in classic plays the practice was to reveal the background story in long speeches near the beginning of the play, and this method continues to be used to the present day. *Death of a Salesman* is admired for its realism, but Arthur Miller relies on the classic technique of early long speeches to disclose the background story. True, sometimes the background story is presented onstage in flashbacks, but by and large the background story is disclosed in the classic manner. The content is mainly events: Willy's mental lapses, the transformation of the old neighborhood, Biff's empty life, Happy's selfish careerism, and Willie's secret suicide plans. The majority of the background story is revealed in quite a few long speeches in the early episodes. August Wilson and Sam Shepard also use long speeches to disclose background story. In *The Piano Lesson*, the characters of Doaker, Boy Willie, and Wining Boy disclose the background story in long speeches written almost as sermons or arias. And in two scenes with long speeches in *A Lie of the Mind*, Jake informs his brother, Frankie, about the abuse of his (Jake's) wife, and Sally informs her mother, Lorraine, about Jake's murder of their father. In neither play are these speeches disguised as anything other than frank disclosures of background story.

Modern realism tends to disguise the background story by disclosing it in a fragmented manner, which does not noticeably interrupt the advance of the action. Chapter 3 discussed the ways in which Ibsen placed special emphasis on background story and altered the way it is handled. Also discussed in that chapter was the minimalist practice of withholding, concealing, or ignoring background story. Samuel Beckett minimized background story so well that it became one of the leading features of his style. The background story in *Happy Days*, for instance, is either hidden behind elliptical suggestions and accidental remarks or else it has been purged altogether. This technique places the play in an unlocalized world, which nonetheless has a special style value of its own. It is interesting to note that even though background story plays a big role in *Angels in America*, it does not involve the type of striking events found in other modern plays. There are few big events, for example, with which to create opportunities for onstage action. What rationale lies behind this style decision?

Reasons for Disclosure

One complexity involved with realistic playwriting is the time and effort needed to establish ordinary plausibility. In addition to considerations of the mise-en-scene, characters must be occupied with ordinary tasks and speak in ordinary ways. They must observe all the details of ordinary life to make what is going on realistically plausible. This is above all true for background story. It takes a great deal of stage time and amazing writing skill to fit in all the technical devices, flourishes, formulas, and conventions — which any type of playwriting is full of — and shape them into a plausible picture of reality. This means that, besides the content and type of background story, there is also the possibility of style in the reasons used for disclosing it. P.F.D. Tennant explained how Ibsen used confidants, the meetings of old friends, inquiring strangers, raisonneurs, and written correspondence (letters, notes, messages) as reasons for talking about the background story while maintaining realistic plausibility.

Ibsen's methods worked so well that they have become models for dramatists ever since. In *Death of a Salesman*, Arthur Miller uses arrivals and confidants as reasons to disclose the past. Willy's surprise return from a sales trip in the opening scene gives a plausible reason for him to explain why he came back home. In the same scene Willy talks about Biff's return home after a long absence. In the next scene, Biff's return furnishes a plausible reason for him to talk with his brother, Happy, about their childhood and about what has happened to them in the intervening years. Later in the act a confidant appears in the form of Charley, the Lomans' next door neighbor. Charley's arrival is a plausible reason for Willy to unburden himself about Biff and related worries. The flashback arrival of Willy's deceased brother Ben supplies the reason for him and Willy to discuss their childhood. The use of returning characters and confidants to give plausible reasons for disclosing the background story is a feature of this play's style.

In *Three Sisters* the arrival of Colonel Vershinin provides an opportunity to talk about his earlier life in Moscow, which arouses nostalgic feelings in the sisters as well. The initial arrivals of Lorraine, Frankie, and Baylor provide plausible reasons for talking about Jake and Beth's rocky marriage in *A Lie of the Mind*. Later in the play, Sally acts as a confidante when she reveals to Lorraine the circumstances surrounding the death of her father, that is to say, Lorraine's husband. In *The Piano Lesson* August Wilson uses the visits of Boy Willie and Wining Boy as reasons to talk about events in the South that occurred before everyone moved up to Pittsburgh.

Style can sometimes appear in the absence of such plausible reasons, or more accurately, in the expansion of our understanding of what constitutes a plausible reason. In *American Buffalo, The*

Birthday Party, Fefu and Her Friends, and *Rosencrantz and Guildenstern are Dead,* the past is often disclosed seemingly without plausible reasons. Characters talk about the past any time they wish, often at outwardly illogical moments in the play. And since we seldom bother about plausible reasons to talk about the past in everyday life, this writing practice (style) seems to give plays an extra dose of "reality." The style point here is that many playwrights do not bother much about surface realism. They dole out background story whenever and wherever it is necessary and use whatever method suits the needs of the moment. This does not mean that background story is handled clumsily, but simply that it is handled pragmatically to devote more attention to emergent plot, character, and idea.

Plot

Type of Actions

In practical terms, *genre* is the collective emotional spirit of a play, and it is obvious that there is a need for understanding it. However, this book is not concerned with the theoretical definitions of tragedy, comedy, melodrama, and farce. The purpose behind studying genre here is not to comply with theoretical categories, but to understand the emotional spirit of a play as the groundwork for acting, directing, and design. For the time being, it is enough to recognize that in comedies unhappy situations are prevented from becoming so unhappy that they undermine the comic mood, and in tragedies serious situations develop to the fullest possible extent to reinforce the tragic mood. The differences among genres are more of degree than they are of kind. In the practical treatment of plot, character, idea, dialogue, and other features, dramatic genres are essentially alike. And it is always at the climaxes where the emotional spirit of a play continues to be expressed most vividly.

295

Having said that, the *type of actions* depicted in a play can contribute to an understanding of its genre, which most would agree is a major part of any play's style. In the past, plays depicted actions that were consistent with classical principles. Comedies, such as *The School for Scandal,* depicted unserious incidents and concluded with unserious (happy) endings. Tragedies, such as *Oedipus Rex,* contained serious incidents and concluded with serious (unhappy) endings. But enforced uniformity never has been a good thing in art, and even in classic plays, unserious actions are found in the most serious of plays and vice versa. In fact, one of the chief characteristics of Shakespeare's style, and his stylistic point of departure from other writers of his time, was his mixture of unserious and serious actions within a single play. For example, although most of the incidents in *Hamlet* are serious, nevertheless unserious or ironic moments continually intrude. This is true at the level of individual speeches, characters, scenes, or indeed the entire play. Moliere's writing shows a similar stylistic tendency. *Tartuffe* is unserious in spirit even though some scenes contain serious actions. Certainly, to maintain dramatic coherence most plays sustain a single overall type of action, even if they contain contrasting actions as well. *Death of a Salesman, Three Sisters,* and *A Lie of the Mind,* for instance, contain unserious and ironic moments, but their controlling actions are for the most part serious.

Many modern plays combine serious and unserious actions more noticeably. In the final scene of *The Wild Duck,* Hedvig's suicide shares the stage with the drunkenness of Old Ekdal and Molvik, the sarcasm of Doctor Relling, and the sentimental self-pity of her father, Hjalmar. In the final scene of *Machinal* the somber tone of the final moments before the Young Woman's execution is combined with the mournful tone of an African American spiritual, the strident sound of an airplane flying overhead, the absurd moralizing of the Priest, the empty-headed indifference of the Guards, and the bloodthirsty curiosity of the Reporters. *Angels in America* contains many serious events, but on the whole its actions are unserious, or at any rate life affirming, and not tragically serious. Mixing actions that are usually not mixed can be disorienting, but it makes an important style statement. Few plays today maintain the consistency of action types once found in classic plays. Instead, like *Machinal* and *Angels in America,* they employ unexpected combinations of actions, and the disorienting feelings that arise from them are part of their style.

Organization

For most plays, cause-and-effect is the means of *organization.* They lead through a series of successive, apparently inevitable events without anything missing or out of place, from an initial situation to its logical conclusion. This chain of events and consequences is the essence of causally organized dramas such as *Tartuffe, The School for Scandal, The Wild Duck, Death of a Salesman, A Raisin in the Sun, The Piano Lesson,* and *Three Sisters.* Starting with the opening lines, questions, forebodings, and possibilities are raised that carry interest from scene to scene and act to act on the way to a logical conclusion.

Cause-and-effect is among the most common organizing principles, but to be effective this principle needs to be seen at work in performance as well as at the table. Think of *The School for Scandal*. Plot summaries tend to rate the influence of Lady Sneerwell too low in the play, but her wish to undermine the love between Charles Surface and Maria is the logical source of the entire tangled story. Unless Lady Sneerwell's motive has a logical reason behind it, however, she is not a credible character, and the play becomes little more than a collection of nonsense. Several motives could account for her behavior: love, hate, envy, revenge, or even boredom. The task is to determine which specific reason logically motivates her throughout the entire play, and then to illustrate it through vivid illustration of her super-objective.

The clue is in the opening scene. At one time Lady Sneerwell was herself the victim of a scandal stemming from a love affair with none other than Charles Surface. What reinforced the scandal was the class distinction between her and Charles and rumors of an illegitimate child. To recover from her misfortune and social disgrace and win Charles back, or at least settle the score with him, she says she would "sacrifice everything." This crucial information is disclosed in a brief, almost casual conversation with Mr. Snake, and yet it is the source of her super-objective. It is a logical motive and it is strong enough to explain the dramatic nature of its consequences. But for cause-and-effect to work in practice, Lady Sneerwell needs to disclose her motive and portray it in such a way that her character is seen to govern the outcome of the play (even if behind the scenes). She is the source of the logic that drives the chain of events and consequences that leads to the play's comic conclusion.

Actors, directors, and designers need to be aware of the principles of cause-and-effect and should be able to recognize how they are intended to work in a play. As the example from *The School for Scandal* shows, special care needs to be taken when dealing with cause-and-effect in plays with complicated plots. However, not all plays maintain the logic of cause-and-effect so strictly. Sometimes events intrude to break up the persistent forward motion of the plot. *Oedipus Rex* is interrupted by choral interludes that retard the flow of action to comment on its wider implications. The forward motion of the story in *Hamlet* often comes to a stop while the leading character speculates about the philosophical meaning of his actions. Signs, songs, and journalistic and cabaret devices interrupt the forward progress of *Mother Courage*. The logic of such interruptions is not necessarily found in their relationship to the plot, but in their relationship to the main idea.

Certain plays depict causally related events only partially or even not at all. Instead they move ahead by varieties of set speeches and conventional scenes governed largely by the main idea. This is especially true of nonrealistic plays. The hallucination episodes in *Angels in America* seem to defy ordinary cause-and-effect, as do many of Jake's actions in *A Lie of the Mind*, Goldberg and McCann's actions in *The Birthday Party*, and more. In other words, some plays work by a form of abstract logic, not realistic cause-and-effect. Take *Fefu and Her Friends*. The play is presented in three parts. In part 1 the characters meet and greet each other in a typical genre scene (scene from everyday life). Part 2 contains three simultaneous genre scenes (on the lawn, in the study, and in the kitchen) in which set speeches comprise most of the dialogue. Part 3 is a genre scene governed largely by realistic cause-and-effect, but it is interrupted by several set speeches that seem to defy the logic of its identity as a genre scene. This is because Fornes' play is not organized by realistic cause-and-effect. Like most nonrealistic plays, it is the demonstration of an idea in dramatic terms. And this idea is demonstrated by means of associations created between itself on one hand, and the plot and characters on the other. Everything exists for the sake of the main idea, which in turn needs to be reasoned out from the situations and relationships demonstrated. Some readers find this kind of organization disorienting. Nevertheless, the number of examples has been increasing for years, and so it would be worthwhile for actors, directors, and designers to understand how such theatricalized demonstrations work to achieve their effects.

Simple and Complex Plots

Chapter 4 explained that a technically *complex plot* contains a reversal in the leading character's fortunes and a change in that character's state of self-awareness. Think of *Tartuffe* and note that the plot is technically complex in this way. At the moment when Orgon understands how foolish his devotion to Tartuffe has been, he concurrently suffers the loss of his personal fortune and reputation, not to mention the respect of his family. The plot of *Death of a Salesman* presents some interesting considerations in this respect. The playwright has stated that he believes Willy Loman comes to a profound understanding of himself. This would mean the plot is technically complex and Willy is elevated to the stature of a tragic hero (classical tragedy employs a complex plot). According to critic Francis Fergusson, however, it is not clear that Willy achieves this sort of self-awareness. The answer to this question lies in the scenes where

Willy is planting in his garden. Does he attach any special significance to his actions in these scenes? Does he associate the garden symbolically with his role as a father? Is the garden representative of the future (his son, Biff) to him? If the answer to these questions is yes, the play could be considered a tragedy in the classical sense. If the answer is no, then it is not tragic in the classical sense, but nonetheless still serious in its emotional spirit. Since the type of action sets the emotional tone for the performance, the issue of complex or simple plots is more than theoretical. It has a practical influence on the actions in a play and the ways in which actors, directors, and designers interpret and illustrate them.

In a *simple plot*, there is no significant reversal either in the nature of the situation or in the self-awareness of the leading character. *The Wild Duck* is an example of a play with a technically simple plot. Hedvig's death appears to be a major change of fortune for Hjalmar Ekdal and Gregers Werle. Ibsen points out the error of this assumption, however. When Gregers insists that Hedvig's suicide has changed Hjalmar's character, Dr. Relling corrects his sentimental viewpoint, "Before a year is over, little Hedvig will be nothing to him but a pretty theme for declamation." Nor does Gregers give any indication that Hedvig's death has had any serious effect on himself either. Censured by Relling for interfering in other people's lives, Gregers replies: "I am glad that my destiny is what it is...to be thirteenth at table." The style issue behind the use of a simple plot here is Ibsen's skepticism and his avoidance of traditional climactic endings. By declining to provide a conventional resolution, the action of the play underscores his belief that people do not change, unfortunately, no matter how much others may wish them to do so.

Bertolt Brecht was aware of the same question at stake in *Mother Courage*. He observed at its premiere that audiences tended to sympathize with Anna Fierling, viewing her as a type of heroine, which is not the meaning of his play. Brecht wanted to show that Fierling does not prevail over her environment and that she continues to surrender to the situation just as she has done throughout the play. She has unthinkingly "internalized" the dehumanizing standards of her world. She even has a song in the play titled "The Song of the Great Capitulation." In other words, since the leading character does not change (does not become self-aware), the plot is technically simple. Brecht adjusted the ending to ensure that audiences would recognize her as the unfeeling businesswoman that she really is.

Chekhov employed simple plots too. Despite the obvious intelligence and culture of the Prozorov siblings in *Three Sisters*, for example, at the end they understand no more about themselves than before. In the last words of the play, Olga states their problem: "If only we knew, if only we knew…!"

Plays with simple plots show a situation growing from bad to worse, but unfortunately no one becomes any the wiser for it. That is the point they are trying to make and what is so compelling about them. For those readers who expect characters to come to terms with their world, it can be frustrating to see that they do not do so in plays with simple plots. To express the meaning of such plays, it is necessary to express the technically simple nature of the plot as plainly as possible. It could be a style mistake to interpret simple plots as complex or vice versa.

Scene Linking

Chapter 8 treated *linking* as one of the basic features of dialogue. As parts of a whole, scenic actions are also linked by the repetition of selected features from one scene to the next throughout the play. These connections prepare for the logical arrangement of events and help to form a coherent world within the play. The ways in which plot, character, dialogue, and idea promote scene linking determine the style feature to be emphasized. In classic plays, direct statements placed at the ends and beginnings of scenes link them together. The last topic in one scene forms the first topic in the next.

Scene linking operates this way in *Oedipus Rex*, where important facts like the murder of Laius, Oedipus' past, and the prophecies of the oracles are also repeated inside scenes as further linking devices. The same method is employed in realistic plays. Close reading of *The Wild Duck* reveals frequent accenting of select plot incidents — Hjalmar's youth, Ekdal and Werle's pasts, Gina's past, Hjalmar's marriage, Hedvig's birthday, Werle and Hedvig's weak eyesight, the wild duck, and the fatal pistol. The links converge in the final misfortune of Hedvig's suicide. Ibsen's style of scene linking uses allusions, direct and indirect statements, and chance remarks. In nonrealistic plays, the scene linking is more subtle because it stems from the main idea and not necessarily the speech or behavior of the characters. Scene linking may not be as apparent in these plays as it is in their more standard counterparts.

Scene linking in plays is more than literary foreshadowing to arrange things so that later events are prepared for audiences beforehand. By intentional repetition, scene linking reinforces the main idea and ensures logical coherence in the play.

300

Scene Openings and Closings

In classic plays, a scene was identified by the introduction and development of a single complete topic. A new scene opened either with the entrance of a new character or with the reappearance of an earlier character with new information. It closed after the new information was introduced, developed, and concluded. A quick review of *Hamlet, Tartuffe,* or *The School for Scandal* will show this pattern. The scene openings and closings are influenced entirely by plot considerations like this, but they are plausible in performance because other features distract from whatever "realistic" questionability they might have. Similarly utilitarian openings and closings are used in modern plays. The scene openings and closings in *A Lie of the Mind, Angels in America,* and *Rosencrantz and Guildenstern are Dead* are controlled entirely by the mechanics of the plot. Yet because of the advance connection with the main idea and the emotional continuity of the performance, any realistic questionability dissolves in the flow of the story. The same holds true for the openings and closings in almost every drama on television and in films. Actors, directors, and designers can learn useful lessons from observing the ways in which scene openings and closings are handled in these other dramatic forms.

The appearance of the modern realistic style of playwriting altered this practice somewhat. In modern realism, characters are often introduced not only to present new information but also to interrupt conversations before they are developed. This practice creates suspense by delaying the full disclosure of important information until later in the play. It can be seen at work in *American Buffalo*, where the story of the planned burglary emerges in bits and pieces because it is always being interrupted by characters entering and exiting. The full story does not come out until the end of act one. In *Death of a Salesman*, the action is interrupted by the flashbacks and the appearances of Uncle Ben. The flashbacks in turn are interrupted by a return to the main action. In this way, the reason why Biff did not graduate from high school is not disclosed until late in act 2, just before the final build toward the main climax. Scene opening and closings in *The Piano Lesson, Three Sisters,* and *A Raisin in the Sun* work in a similar manner. Characters do not turn up or depart on demand as they do in classic plays. The realistic style of frequent interruptions calls for the utmost tension and suspense in the scene openings and closings. Whodunits and thrillers depend for their success on this style of scene openings and closings.

Character

Objectives

Style is often the result of what the characters want and the forces that oppose those wants. In other words, the nature of the *objectives*. Oedipus strives for knowledge in opposition to the will of the gods. Although he loses on the physical level, he nonetheless achieves tragic stature by a heroic exertion of his will. By contrast, both Willy Loman and Walter Younger strive for material objectives in a world controlled by material values. Willy becomes a victim (perhaps) of his materialistic goals, but Walter overcomes his materialistic objectives and leads his family to a new beginning. Jake wakes up to the distorted American myths that govern his violent tendencies in *A Lie of the Mind*, and then he rejects them. Berniece in *The Piano Lesson* strives to separate herself from her own culture, but finally learns a lesson about her rightful place in that culture. The Young Woman in *Machinal* strives to find herself in a hostile materialistic world, but she is only a pawn in a larger social struggle beyond her understanding or control. Style in these plays results from the nature of the characters' objectives, from what opposes them (self-governing truth, materialistic ideals, phony myths, socioeconomic forces), and from their final victory or defeat.

Values

Values (standards of right and wrong) were apparently more widely accepted in the past, or at least tolerated, than they seem to be today. There was little obvious effort on the part of dramatists to challenge the dominant values of their times in their plays. On the contrary, dramatists tended to endorse established conventions of good and bad. Moreover, they were expected to do so or else risk losing their aristocratic support, or worse. The characters of Hamlet and Orgon exist within societies where established standards of good and bad were generally acknowledged as true. Their personal challenges consisted of striving to understand and conform to these normative values.

Modern dramatists, on the other hand, tend to challenge accepted ideas of right and wrong. This is not the place to consider the historical circumstances that led to such a shift in the general view of the world. Whatever the reasons, the results are there for everyone to see. The aim of many modern dramatists is to replace, or at least reconsider, old values in light of new values based on the conditions of life here and now. Plays such as *The Wild Duck, Death of a Salesman, Mother Courage, American Buffalo, A Lie of the Mind,* and *Angels in America* attempt to reveal the secreted impulses behind accepted standards of good and bad. In doing so, accepted values are turned upside down. What was considered good becomes bad, and what was bad becomes good. The clash of old versus new values forms a major part of the style appeal of these plays.

Depiction

Characters are revealed through narration and action, and the relative balance between the two methods is part of a play's style. That two of the major requirements of playwriting are time and proportion has already been shown. Since most plays are written to conform to a two-and-a-half-hour time limit, attention must be focused on the most important features of the characters. Moreover, a play must be devoted mainly to showing the actions of a single character. Supporting characters need to be presented as economically as possible, which often means through narration. This fact is apparent every time the secondary characters in a play are studied.

When narration furnishes the majority of the information about major characters, however, the reasons may be other than practical. George Pierce Baker pointed out that the essential distinction between character depiction in drama and fiction is the difference between narration and action. A corollary to this is that narrated characters are by definition more literary (static) than they are dramatic (dynamic). Certain major characters in *Mother Courage, A Raisin in the Sun, American Buffalo,* and *The Piano Lesson* fall into this category. Whether this is from dramatic necessity or slips in technique are a matter for the reader to determine after studying other features in the plays.

A typical example of a character that is almost entirely narrated for sound dramatic reasons is Haakon Werle, Gregers' father and the alleged father of Hedvig in *The Wild Duck.* The paradoxes of his personality are disclosed through the judgments of Gregers, Hjalmar, Gina, and Mrs. Sorby, all of whom have conflicting opinions of him. The only concrete actions he performs in the play are the announcement to Gregers of his engagement to Mrs. Sorby in act 1 and his visit to the Ekdals' flat to offer Gregers a job in the firm in act 3. Everything else known about him comes through the words of others. Of course, Ibsen's use of narration in this case should not be attributed to faulty or excessively literary writing. He avoided

303

showing too much of Werle's real character deliberately to suggest an ambiguous impression of him. Werle's character is a diversionary tactic, and what he did in the past matters little to the outcome of the play. The key issue is what others think of him, in particular what Gregers and Hjalmar think of him. Ibsen's choice of a narrative style for depicting Werle is in harmony with the main idea of the play. Other examples of calculatingly narrated characters include the fathers in *Oedipus Rex*, *Death of a Salesman*, *A Lie of the Mind*, *Machinal*, *A Raisin in the Sun*, *Top Girls*, and *Three Sisters*. Is there also a style point in the fact that all these purposely ambiguous characters are fathers?

In classic plays, it was often the practice to depict certain characters through a formally balanced combination of narration and action. Notable among them is *Tartuffe*. The title character forms the chief topic of conversation in acts 1 and 2 of Moliere's play. By the time of his first appearance in act 3, a very considerable amount is known through other people's statements about him. Unlike Haakon Werle, however, Tartuffe's personality is explicitly revealed in his own words and actions in the remainder of the play. The audience has ample opportunity to test the impressions of the other characters by witnessing Tartuffe play at piety, seduce Elmire, and swindle Orgon. The point of style here is that the play is about everyone's response to Tartuffe, and not about the character of Tartuffe himself.

304

Narration defines Mr. Werle and a balance of narration and action defines Tartuffe, but action is the chief method of depicting most major characters in plays. It is by their actions that it is possible to understand major characters such as Oedipus, Hamlet, Orgon in *Tartuffe*, Gregers Werle and Hjalmar Ekdal in *The Wild Duck*, Willy Loman in *Death of a Salesman*, Winnie in *Happy Days*, Walter in *A Raisin in the Sun*, the Prozorov siblings in *Three Sisters*, Prior in *Angels in America*, and Jake in *A Lie of the Mind*. Nevertheless, the manner in which narration or action is used to depict these characters is an important feature of a play's style.

Idea

The dramatist selects and arranges everything in the play to express *idea* with maximum force and clarity. It follows that the ideas playwrights choose to deal with are important features of a play's style. The principles of logic help to understand idea, but plays are emotional experiences and the value of emotional truth is always more important than logical truth. This is because the word "truth" has a broader meaning in art than it does in philosophy or science. Truth means not merely that the play is logically accurate but mainly that we agree with it or that the feelings it evokes can lead to better self-understanding.

Persuasiveness

The *persuasiveness* of the playwright's ideas stems from the suitability of the ideas to the actions and characters and from how the ideas stand up to close study. But psychological consistency is not the sole reason ideas can be persuasive. Sometimes ideas may be compelling for conventional reasons. The exaggerated ideas in broad comedies, for instance, are enjoyable even though they will seldom stand up to close study. Comic ideas have fleeting appeal merely as entertaining premises for plot, though they must be at least consistent.

The religious hypocrisy in *Tartuffe* is more than momentarily enjoyable, it is also psychologically consistent, as is the economic pragmatism in *Death of a Salesman*. These ideas are persuasive because they arise plausibly from their dramatic contexts. For similar reasons, the racial discrimination that forms a large part of the worlds of *A Raisin in the Sun* and *The Piano Lesson* is plausible. On the other hand, certain readers may be doubtful about the economic determinism depicted in *Mother Courage*, the apparent scientific materialism in *Happy Days*, or the all-inclusive tolerance advocated in *Angels in America*. They may feel that the actions and characters have not justified these ideas satisfactorily. The ideas in some plays strain credibility despite the best efforts of dramatists. In any case, the persuasiveness of a play's ideas is potentially a style point to consider.

305

Scope

The *scope* of the idea's practical relevance is another part of its style. Many dramas attempt to deal with universal truths. These are feelings or understandings that are valuable to society under all circumstances. Solving sharp political, social, or moral questions is not part of their style. Although social and political ideas are present in *Oedipus Rex*, Sophocles does not depict his characters on this basis exclusively. Most readers would also agree that even though Shakespeare deals with ideas about society and politics in *Hamlet*, his play is more concerned with the characters trying to solve their own problems than with solving them himself. Some critics have attempted to label Anton Chekhov as a social dramatist, but most readers would see beyond this viewpoint. These dramatists observe, select, and combine ideas for the sake of art, and their styles are based on the assumption that theatre is an artistic experience. Interpreting their plays otherwise is a risky exercise, although there are many exceptions.

Socially responsive playwrights question whether universal ideas stand the test of time. The world has changed, they rightly argue. The stylistic theory of "art for art's sake" may be a noble ideal, but it leaves much to be desired in the contemporary world. Consequently, these writers believe they should make a stand in their plays on the vital social and political questions of the day. Dramatists from Ibsen to Kushner have come out on one side or another of important moral and political issues. The ideas in *The Wild Duck*, *Mother Courage*, *Machinal*, *The Piano Lesson*, and *Angels in America*, for example, attempt to contribute toward the creation of a new and more humane social order. The style of these ideas suggests dislike for, or at least dissatisfaction with, outmoded values that are perceived as detrimental to society. Consequently, the ideas are sharply decisive in these plays, and audiences look forward to being challenged by such works.

But there are questions with this stylistic approach as well. George Bernard Shaw was one of the most articulate representatives among the socially responsible playwrights. Yet even Shaw expressed concern about the authority of a playwright to pronounce judgment on social or political issues, his own work notwithstanding. He pointed out that dramatists tend to lead literary lives. They dwell for the most part in the world of the imagination (like Hamlet?) instead of the world of politics, business, law, and statecraft. Shaw argued that although such authors may seek to raise social or political issues in their plays, some of them remain surprisingly unaware of real life as it is lived by ordinary people. Many modern playwrights present moral and political ideas with high degrees of conviction, imagination, sympathy, and a sharp sense of observation, but the key issue for readers here is more than one of technical skill. It is necessary to assess whether authors have the wisdom to make the ideas in their plays practical as well as desirable.

Dialogue

Since *dialogue* is the most conspicuous part of the script, it certainly is an important component of a play's style. Its features can appeal to audiences as strongly as does any other element in the play. Apart from its literary aspects, however, dialogue also functions as the container for plot, character, and idea. These theatrical functions may be less obvious to an untrained observer, but they are no less important in determining style.

Literary Features

Literary features in the dialogue include all of those traits studied in Chapter 8, including verse forms, rhetorical or telegraphic or emotional speech, imagery and symbolism, songs, jokes, colorful and unusual words, idiomatic phrases, dialects, and anything that calls attention to the dialogue as dialogue. There are many plays that employ such features. *Oedipus Rex, Hamlet,* and *Tartuffe* contain numerous different verse forms as well as rhetorical speech, aphorisms, and historical charm. These literary features show that, even though the chief elements in these plays are character and idea, dialogue still contributes significantly to the overall style.

The expectation of everyday talk in modern plays may lead some readers to find slight literary merit in realistic speech. A number of modern realistic dramatists, however, also use literary features in their dialogue, though less obviously than their nonrealistic counterparts. Arthur Miller's dialogue in *Death of a Salesman,* as mentioned earlier, contains pronounced rhythms, colorful words and phrases, and emotional speeches that contribute to its style. Dialogue is one of the main stylistic attractions of Brecht's plays, although with Brecht the language has a more unexpected result because of its contrast with the homespun nature of the characters. Treadwell's use of tempos and rhythms is not as important as is character revelation and idea in *Machinal,* yet the telegraphic nature of the dialogue appeals to the ear as well. Intelligence and wit are very much part of the appeal of the dialogue in *Angels in America.* Poetic language plays a large role in the success of *The Piano Lesson* and *A Lie of the Mind.* David Mamet's dialogue is noteworthy for its wit and terseness. Both classic and modern playwrights have used a rich variety of literary devices to focus attention on the stylistics of their language.

Text and Subtext

The question of speech rhythm brings up another element of style found in dialogue. One of the chief differences between classic and modern dialogue is compression. Modern plays tend to use language economically. They dispense with formal modes of expression and cut out everything that is not essential. This radical reduction of the number of words in modern plays has had important stylistic outcomes. It has caused a corresponding enlargement of unspoken inner tensions. Stanislavsky identified these inner tensions as *subtext*, the unspoken words beneath the text.

An important question for Stanislavsky was how to determine the relative balance between spoken dialogue on one hand and unspoken subtext on the other (external vs. internal life). Literary dialogue places more emphasis on spoken words, less on unspoken subtext. By contrast, economical modern dialogue capitalizes on subtext to express character, feelings, and ideas. Thus, some realistic dialogue may sound conversational, but in reality it may be far different from relaxed, everyday speech. Forceful subtext revealed through vocal rhythms and word choices energizes the dialogue and makes it dramatic in a modern way. In the plays of Beckett, Shepard, and Pinter, for instance, characters say what they mean using the fewest possible words, yet they seem to understand subtle hints and veiled allusions at first hearing. When this occurs in a play, it has a style function and is a sure sign that subtext is a prominent element of the play's style.

308 Atmosphere

The previous chapter explained *atmosphere* as the dominant emotional spirit of a scene or an entire play. Atmosphere is a special combination of tempos, rhythms, and moods working in harmony to create an all-inclusive emotional impression. Atmosphere becomes an important stylistic factor when it is sustained and potent enough to be memorable in itself. (Once more, we are talking here about features in the play itself, not necessarily in performance or mise-en-scene, although obviously they are closely related.)

Atmosphere in realistic and classic plays is usually associated with the leading character. His/her emotional life spreads all through the play, which in turn comes to be identified with his/her personality. The atmosphere of *Hamlet* could be described as sharp, nervous, and excitable, stemming from those same feelings that identify Hamlet. The atmosphere of *Death of a Salesman* is suggested by Willy Loman's desperation, and that of *The Piano Lesson* by Boy Willie's exuberance. The same situation obtains in *Three Sisters*, where the moods of anguish and longing in the siblings influence the atmosphere of the entire play. In these plays the controlling atmosphere comes from the tempos, rhythms, and moods expressed through the actions of the leading characters.

As we might expect, the situation is somewhat different in non-realistic plays. Since they are controlled by the main idea instead of plot or character, it follows that the controlling atmosphere would come from the same source. In fact, one of the distinguishing features of nonrealistic plays is the way in which the main idea controls the characters, and not the other way around. When this happens, ordinary events employ tempos, rhythms, and moods in ways that create extraordinary atmospheres. Consider the atmosphere of sinister menace in *The Birthday Party*, which has no reckonable basis in the ordinary events taking place on stage, but comes from the mysterious power everyone seems to acknowledge in Goldberg and McCann. A strange, severe emptiness identifies the atmosphere of *Happy Days* — strange because it is controlled by the main idea and not by Winnie and Willie's behavior. The atmosphere of *Fefu and Her Friends* is that of captivity and loneliness, which forms an intentional counterpoint to the "tasteful mixture of styles" in the living room of a New England country house. Critics call such atmospheres "absurd" because they do not seem to arise from the characters or events in the plays themselves, but from something "outside." Actually, it is just the opposite. The unusual atmospheres come from deep inside the plays, from the main ideas that govern them, and which they are written and dramatized to illustrate.

Summary

Playwrights are self-conscious artists. They know what they want to do and have the skills to achieve their goals using the most effective means possible. They shape plot, character, idea, and dialogue as well as tempo, rhythm, and mood to focus attention on the important features in their plays. In many plays, the dominant style element might be character, with supporting interest in idea, plot, or dialogue. In others, style could be dependent on idea, with characters, dialogue, and plot in supporting positions. In still other plays, the plot itself might be the major point of style, and "What's going to happen next?" becomes more important than who the characters are, what they are saying, or even what it all means. In a few plays, the primary style feature has so much appeal that the subordinate elements may have almost no intrinsic interest at all. Whodunits and thrillers, for instance, or musicals.

Plays make their style statements apparent in various ways. The length and number of scenes devoted to a particular element, the

qualities of thoroughness and detail, and the spirit of the main idea —
all these issues contribute to style focus. Studying the artistic reasons
behind these decisions may seem abstract and theoretical compared
to the crisp kind of analysis presented in the earlier chapters, but
nonetheless it is necessary for the discovery of still more playable
dramatic values.

Questions

1. *Given Circumstances.* How is time handled? Is it continuous or
   interrupted? Does it flow chronologically from beginning to
   end, or is there another pattern? How is continuity of time maintained? Is there anything special about the general locale? The
   specific locale? How many locales are presented? How is continuity of place maintained? What social groups are presented?
   What is the point of view of the play toward each social group?
   Are any unusual or outsider groups presented? Anything special
   about the economic circumstances? Political and legal circumstances? Educational and artistic circumstances? Spiritual circumstances? Any special scientific or technological details in the
   plot? Any unusual social or professional customs?
2. *Background Story.* Does the background story consist of events?
   Character descriptions? Feelings? Sensory impressions? Character
   descriptions? Is the background story disclosed in long passages?
   Short passages? Retrospectively? Fragmented? Is it openly stated, or
   is it disclosed through hints and allusions? What situations in the
   play are used to justify disclosure of the past? Who discloses most
   of the background story?
3. *Plot.* What types of actions are depicted? Are the actions serious?
   Comic? Ironic? Why? Are conflicting types of actions presented
   simultaneously? How is the introductory portion of the play
   managed? How is the main conflict introduced at the beginning
   of the play? What is the play's point of view toward its subject?
   Serious? Comic? Ironic? Critical? Parodic? How is the play's point
   of view introduced? Are the incidents arranged by cause-and-
   effect? Chronologically? In progressively more intensive scenes?
   From familiar to unfamiliar? How is the conclusion managed?
   Restatement? Amplification? Emotional rallying call? Positive or
   negative? Does the plot contain a reversal of fortune for the leading character? Does the leading character come to a new understanding of him/herself? How are the scenes linked? How are the

scene openings and closings treated? Is the story completed in each scene? Interrupted? How are the act endings handled?

4. *Character.* Do the characters want power? Knowledge? Love? Wealth? Fame? Personal fulfillment? What do the characters consider good and bad in the world of the play? How completely are the characters depicted in the script? Are the characters revealed through action? Narration? Both?

5. *Idea.* What ideas are dealt with in the play? How are they related to one another? Is the main idea persuasive? How credible is the playwright's authority to speak out on the idea? Is the main idea artistic? Practical? Idealistic? Moralistic?

6. *Dialogue.* Does the dialogue have literary merit in itself? If so, what are its main literary features? Is the dialogue conversational? If so, what are its main conversational features? How important is the text compared to the subtext? What is their relative balance in the play?

7. *Atmosphere.* Is a single predominant emotional tone sustained throughout the play script? If so, what is it? Are the atmospheres mixed or contrasting? If so, in what ways? What features in the play script create the controlling atmosphere? Any sequences of unusual, interesting, or effective atmospheres? If so, what are they and how do they come about? Any contrasting atmospheres within the same or adjacent scenes? Are the atmospheres independent of one another? Is the source of the atmosphere found in the plot? Character? Idea?

8. *Style Statement.* What is the single most important element in the play script? Plot? Character? Idea? Dialogue? Atmosphere? Why? What are the secondary elements? Why? Describe the overall style of the play script in a concise, one-sentence *style statement,* comprising the main character, main relationship, main conflict, and atmosphere. What does the overall style of the play script suggest about the mise-en-scene? How could the mise-en-scene contribute to the effectiveness of the play's intrinsic style?

A Final Word

This is the end of a long, close look at the wide-ranging subject of script analysis. Yet one of the difficulties with analytical principles when they are defined and explained in a textbook is that they can remain inactive on the printed page. Or worse, the intellectual frame of mind required for analytical study interposes itself between the actors, director, and designers on one hand and the human behavior and mise-en-scene that are the lifeblood of drama in performance on the other. When this happens readers will remain just as mystified about how plays work as they may have been before they read the book, despite the best efforts of author and teachers. One remedy is to consider that the principles might work better as questions that encourage a search for answers. The questions at the end of each chapter are a guide to what should be included in script analysis. They are meant to encourage as much familiarity as possible with all the dramatic potentials of a play and all the possible relationships among them. The questions also encourage study of the facts behind the automatic assumptions any reader faces in an encounter with a play. Questions also reinforce the practice of systematic study, which after all will ordinarily be conducted without the benefit of an expert guide.

Even though not all of the topics will be helpful all the time, readers should determine for themselves which ones are more valuable and which ones less so for each play. This means completely answering all the questions, or at least striving to do so. It means thinking out the subtle implications of what the characters say and do, the world they inhabit, and what the play means. By the same token, script analysis should never be allowed to become fussy or overwrought. The ultimate goal is to stir up the imagination and provide suggestions for acting, directing, and design. As much as possible, this goal should be kept foremost in mind, and other considerations should be kept in the background.

I hope to have shown that there is a wonderful artistic self-sufficiency to a play latent with meaning. Economy, control of shape and details, the search for a structure with independent beauty — all are worked into excellence by the playwright. It is not always clear what is meant by form in a play. It has something to do with a beginning, middle, and end; with harmony and sharp thematics;

with the relationship of different features to the events of the plot; and with the properties of theatre itself. Formalist analysis heightens awareness of these features. It invites us to admire the undividable coexistence of form and content. As professionals, we should be capable of developing a sense of form as an integral part of the total experience of play production, the summation of what is meant by the art of theatre.

Appendix

Further Questions for Script Analysis

Throughout this book a play has been treated as an independent object with its own self-contained context. A good play becomes even better, however, when its external associations as well as its internal features are understood. After studying the life of the author, his or her other works, and the author's world, a play becomes more fascinating, the characters grow, the plot thickens, and the whole work becomes more voluminous. It becomes part of something on a scale greater than itself. In other words, while formalist analysis and action analysis can reveal the internal qualities of a play, outside information is always necessary for a completely professional understanding.

Topics to guide the initial steps of this process are provided below, at least insofar as I have been able to comprehend them. Some of the more radical critical approaches are omitted because they are notoriously hard to pin down. In any case, my own prejudices as a director and critic should be clear from this book. Consequently, readers should be sure to consult other books for more authoritative information about the individual approaches discussed here. Wilfred Guerin's comprehensive survey, *A Handbook of Critical Approaches to Literature*, is a good place to start.

A word of advice should be added before finishing this preamble. Theories of criticism, the biography of the author, the historical and social context, the history of the play and its productions, variations of the text, and so on — evidence that goes beyond the play — obliquely suggest ideas *about a play*. Actors, directors, and designers should always consider such information secondary and confirm results by studying directly what is *in the play*. External information should be tested against internal information to be used productively in the rehearsal hall and design studio.

Biography and History

A play is certain to be more meaningful when its historical environment and the biography of its author are understood. How are the playwright's life and times reflected in the play? Consider personal, social, political, economic, religious, and artistic circumstances of the author and the period when the play was written. Do the biography of the dramatist and the historical context in which the play was written suggest anything about the mise-en-scene? How could the mise-en-scene contribute to the effectiveness of this biographical and historical context? Note that point-to-point correlations between the author's life and his/her works seldom exist, at least not as often as it might seem. Authors are too skillful and subtle to employ such simplistic methods. The search for biographical influences will be more rewarding if this tip is kept in mind.

Text

Try to establish an authoritative text of the play. Are there any other editions or translations? If so, compare and contrast the differences, including spelling, punctuation, capitalization, and italicization as well as any more substantial variations which might appear in the dialogue, characters, scenic arrangements, and endings. Study the commentary of editors and translators for additional insights.

Philosophy and Morality

Some writers believe that the final purpose of literature, including dramatic literature, is to teach morality and inquire into philosophical issues. How does the play relate to the philosophical and moral ideas of its era? Of the present era? Of a particular school or circle? Of the author? What philosophical and moral issues does the play seem to promote or criticize? Do the philosophical and moral issues in the play suggest the mise-en-scene? How could the mise-en-scene contribute to the effectiveness of these issues?

Psychology

The psychoanalytic theories of Sigmund Freud and his followers emphasize the unconscious aspects of the mind, the sexual motives of behavior (libido), and the involuntary repression of unwelcome memories. Additionally, mental processes may be assigned to three different regions, called the id (the source of dangerous aggressions and desires), the ego (the conscious controlling agent of the id), and the superego (conscience and pride). Other features include the reality principle, the pleasure principle, the morality principle, and the Oedipus complex, to name only the most well known. What insights can be gained from applying Freud's theories to the characters in the play? Do any psychoanalytic associations suggest the mise-en-scene? Could the mise-en-scene contribute to the effectiveness of these associations in production?

Myth and Archetype

As stated in the Introduction, myths are stories of allegedly historical events. They bond social groups together through common activities and beliefs and are found everywhere in society. Certain mysterious elements related to myths can arouse universal reactions. Furthermore, some myths summon common meanings or responses or serve similar functions throughout many different societies. These common images or themes are called archetypes, or universal symbols.

Does the play promise to become a classic? Does it express the kind of reality that generates a universal response? Is the play based on a well-known myth? What archetypal patterns does the play highlight that could summon a deep emotional response? What symbolic expressions of hope, fear, morality, and desire are expressed in the play? Does the play correlate with any prehistorical spiritual forces or rituals? What is the myth, the abstract core of action, that gives the play its form or meaning? Does myth and archetype in the play suggest the mise-en-scene? How could the mise-en-scene contribute to the effectiveness of myth and archetype in production?

Feminism

Did a man or a woman write the play? What male–female issues may have conditioned the play? What are the concealed male–female power imbalances, patriarchal premises, gender prejudices, and other signs of misogyny in the play? How are they reflected, endorsed, or questioned by the play? Are the women in the play constrained in their environment? Are the women in the play exploited in ways related to their economic circumstances? Do the women in the play experience any additional oppression as members of a minority group? Do the feminist issues suggest anything about the mise-en-scene? How could the mise-en-scene contribute to the effectiveness of these issues?

Structuralism and Post-structuralism

What deep structures, or systems of relationships, are found in the play? What words or physical items in the play gain special meaning from these relationships? Can the play be equated with language forms, architecture, landscaping, kinship, marriage customs, fashion, restaurant menus, timetables, calendars, street maps, furniture, popular culture, politics, or any other well-known social or cultural phenomenon? If so, what additional meanings are obtained? On the other hand, what internal contradictions or self-contradictions may be found in the play? Is there any kind of concealed power in the author that may unintentionally undermine the immediate meaning of the play? Do the structural issues suggest anything about the mise-en-scene? How could the mise-en-scene contribute to the effectiveness of these issues?

Marxism

Locate the play within the context of larger social, political, economic, and historical forces. Does the play reflect, endorse, or question any of these enormous forces operating in opposition to each other? In particular, can any negative social effects of the capitalist system be found in the play? How does the play (or the characters in the play) come to terms with issues of class, race, sex, oppression, and liberation? Does the play provide a workable solution to well-known socioeconomic problems? Do the Marxist issues suggest anything about the mise-en-scene? How could the mise-en-scene contribute to the effectiveness of these issues?

Communication and Rhetoric

Consider the possible interactions between the play, the author, and the audience. How does the process of communication in the play operate among these three groups? What does the play communicate to the audience and how does it do so? What can the play reveal about the author? Whom is the playwright addressing with the play? How is the audience expected to respond? Is there a distinction between the beliefs of the author and those expressed by the characters in the play? Do the communication and rhetoric issues suggest anything about the mise-en-scene? How could the mise-en-scene contribute to the effectiveness of these issues?

Bibliography

Appia, Adolphe. *Adolphe Appia: Essays, Scenarios, and Designs.* Tr. Walther R. Volbach. Ed. Richard C. Beacham. Ann Arbor, MI: UMI Research Press, c1989.

———. *Music and the Art of the Theatre.* Tr. Robert W. Corrigan and Mary Douglas Dirks. Intr. Lee Simonson. Ed. Barnard Hewitt. Coral Gables, FL: University of Miami Press, c1962.

Aristotle. *Poetics.* Tr. S. H. Butcher. Ed. Francis Fergusson. New York: Hill & Wang, 1961.

Aronson, Arnold. *Looking into the Abyss: Essays on Scenography.* Ann Arbor: University of Michigan Press, 2005.

Ball, David. *Backwards and Forwards: A Technical Manual for Reading Plays.* Carbondale, IL: Southern Illinois University Press, 1983.

Ball, William. *A Sense of Direction.* Hollywood: Drama Publishers, 1984.

Barry, Jackson G. *Dramatic Structure: The Shaping of Experience.* Berkeley: University of California Press, 1970.

Barthes, Roland. *S/Z: An Essay.* New York: Hill & Wang, 1991.

Bentley, Eric. *The Life of the Drama.* New York: Atheneum Press, 1964.

———. *The Playwright as Thinker.* New York: Harcourt, Brace & World, 1967.

Boal, Augusto. *Theatre of the Oppressed.* New York: Theatre Communications Group, 1985.

Bogart, Anne and Tina Landau. *The Viewpoints Book: A Practical Guide to Viewpoints and Composition.* New York: Theatre Communications Group, 2005.

Boleslavsky, Richard. *Acting: The First Six Lessons.* New York: Theatre Arts Books, 1977 (1933).

Brook, Peter. *The Empty Space.* New York: Touchstone, c1968.

Brooks, Cleanth and Robert B. Heilman. *Understanding Drama.* New York: Henry Holt and Company, 1948.

Cahoone, Lawrence, Ed. *From Modernism to Postmodernism: An Anthology.* Malden, MA: Blackwell Publishers, 1996.

Caldarone, Marina and Maggie Lloyd-Williams. *Actions: The Actors' Thesaurus.* Hollywood: Drama Publishers, 2004.

Carnicke, Sharon M. *Stanislavsky in Focus*. London: Routledge, 1998.

Carra, Lawrence. *Controls in Play Directing*. New York: Vantage Press, 1985.

Chekhov, Michael. *On the Technique of Acting*. New York: Harper Collins, 1991.

———. *To the Director and the Playwright*. New York: Harper & Row, 1963.

Clay, James H. and Daniel Krempel. *The Theatrical Image*. New York: McGraw-Hill, 1967.

Clurman, Harold. *On Directing*. New York: Macmillan, 1974.

Craig, Edward Gordon. *On the Art of the Theatre*. New York: Theatre Arts Books, c1911.

Driver, Tom F. "Beckett by the Madeleine." *Columbia University Forum* IV.3 (Summer 1961): 21–25.

———. *Romantic Quest and Modern Query: A History of the Modern Theatre*. New York: Delacorte Press, 1970.

Durham, Weldon. "Functional Analysis [for Designers]." *Fine Arts.Michigan Technological University.Debra Bruch*. <http://www.fa.mtu.edu/~dlbruch/scriptanalysis/funct.html>, Accessed 14 August 2008.

Eagelton, Terry. *After Theory*. New York: Basic Books, 2003.

———. *Literary Theory: An Introduction*. Minneapolis: University of Minnesota Press, 1996.

Efros, Anatoly. *The Joy of Rehearsal*. Tr. James Thomas. New York: Peter Lang Publishers, 2005.

Eisenstein, Sergei. *Film Form: Essays in Film Theory*. New York: Harvest Books, c1949.

———. *The Film Sense*. New York: Harcourt/Harvest, c1942–1975.

Eliot, T.S. "The Function of Criticism," *Selected Essays: 1917–1932*. New York: Harcourt, Brace and Company, 1932.

Falls, Gregory A. "Intellect and the Theatre." *Educational Theatre Journal* 18.1 (March 1966): 1–6.

Fergusson, Francis. *The Idea of a Theatre*. Garden City, NY: Doubleday Anchor Books, 1949.

Fornes, Maria Irene. "Interview." *Performing Arts Journal* 2.3 (Winter 1978): 106–111.

Freytag, Gustav. *Technique of the Drama: An Exposition of Dramatic Composition and Art*. Tr. Elias J. MacEwan. Chicago: Scott Foresman, 1900.

Frye, Northrop. *Anatomy of Criticism*. Princeton, NJ: Princeton University Press, 1957.

Gardner, John. *The Art of Fiction*. New York: Alfred A. Knopf, 1984.

Gass, William H. *Fiction and the Figures of Life*. New York: Alfred A. Knopf, 1970.

Gassner, John. *Directions in Modern Theatre and Drama: An Expanded Edition of Form and Idea in Modern Theatre*. New York: Holt, Rinehart and Winston, 1965.

Ginkas, Kama. *Provoking Theatre*. Tr. John Freedman. Hanover, NH: Smith and Kraus, 2003.

Gorelik, Mordecai. *New Theatres for Old*. New York: Samuel French, c1940.

Greenberg, Clement. "Modernist Painting," *Clement Greenberg: The Collected Essays and Criticism*. Ed. John O'Brian. Chicago: University of Chicago Press, (v. 4) 1995.

Guerin, Wilfred L., et al. *A Handbook of Critical Approaches to Literature*. Oxford: Oxford University Press, 2005.

Haring-Smith, Tori. "Dramaturging Non-Realism." *Theatre Topics* 13.1 (March 2003): 45–54.

Herrington, John. "Directing with the Viewpoints." *Theatre Topics* 10.2 (September 2000): 155–168.

Hirsch, E.D., Joseph F. Kett and James Trefil. *The New Dictionary of Cultural Literacy: What Every American Needs to Know*. New York: Houghton Mifflin, 2002.

Hodge, Francis. *Play Directing: Analysis, Communication, and Style*. Englewood Cliffs, NJ: Prentice-Hall, 2004.

Hornby, Richard. *Script into Performance: A Structuralist View of Play Production*. Austin: University of Texas Press, 1977.

Howard, Pamela. *What is Scenography?* London: Routledge, 2002.

Ingham, Rosemary. *From Page to Stage: How Theatre Designers Make Connections between Scripts and Images*. Portsmouth, NH: Heinemann, 1998.

Innes, Christopher. *Avant Garde Theatre: 1892–1992*. London: Routledge, 1993.

Jonas, Susan S., Geoffrey S. Proehl and Michael Lupo. *Dramaturgy in America: A Sourcebook*. Boston: Wadsworth, 1996.

Jones, Robert Edmond. *The Dramatic Imagination*. New York: Theatre Arts Books, c1941.

Joyce, James. *Ulysses*. New York: Vintage Books, 1990 (1922).

Kernan, Alvin. *The Death of Literature*. New Haven: Yale University Press, 1990.

Knebel, Maria. *O tom, chto mne kazhetsia osobenno vazhnym*. [What is Especially Important to Me]. Moskva: Isskustvo, 1971.

Knight, George Wilson. *The Wheel of Fire*. London: Oxford University Press, 1930.

Kozintsev, Grigori. *Shakespeare: Time and Conscience*. Tr. Joyce Vining. London: Dennis Dobson, 1966.

Larson, Orville K. *Scene Design for Stage and Screen: Readings on the Aesthetics and Methodology of Scene Design*. Westport, CT: Greenwood Press, 1976.

Leach, Robert. *Stanislavsky and Meyerhold*. New York: Peter Lang Publishers, 2003.

Lemon, Lee T. and Marion J. Reis, Ed. and Tr. *Russian Formalist Criticism: Four Essays*. Lincoln: University of Nebraska Press, 1965.

Liberman Susan. "A Roof without a House: Assessing Current Graduate Design Training." *Theatre Crafts* (March 1985): 26–56.

Lipovetsky, Gilles. *The Empire of Fashion: Dressing Modern Democracy*. Princeton: Princeton University Press, c1994.

Lotman, Yuri. *Semiotics of Cinema*. Tr. Mark E. Suino. Ann Arbor: Michigan Slavic Contributions, 1976.

Mamet, David. *3 Uses of the Knife: On the Nature and Purpose of Drama*. New York: Columbia University Press, 1998.

Marowitz, Charles. *Recycling Shakespeare*. New York: Applause Books, 1991.

McKee, Robert. *Story: Substance, Structures, Style, and the Principles of Screenwriting*. New York: HarperCollins, 1996.

McMullan, Frank. *The Directorial Image*. Hamden, CT: Shoestring Press, 1962.

Merlin, Bella. *Beyond Stanislavsky*. London: Nick Hern Books, 2001.

Nabokov, Vladimir. *Lectures on Literature*. Ed. Fredson Bowers. New York: Harcourt Brace, 1980.

Parks, Suzan-Lori. "Elements of Style." *The America Play and Other Works*. New York: Theatre Communications Group, 1995, 6–18.

Payne, Darwin Reid. *Scenographic Imagination*. Carbondale, IL: Southern Illinois University Press, 1993.

Ransom, John Crowe. *The New Criticism*. Norfolk, CT: New Directions, 1941.

Reid, Francis. *Lighting the Stage: A Lighting Designer's Experiences*. London: Focal Press, 1995.

Rosen, Carl. "Silent Tongues: An Interview." *Sam Shepard: A Poetic Rodeo*. London: Palgrave Macmillan, 2004.

Rush, David. *A Student Guide to Play Analysis*. Carbondale, IL: Southern Illinois University Press, 2005.

Sharp, William L. *Language in Drama: Meanings for the Director and the Actor*. Scranton, PA: Chandler Publishing Co., 1970.

Shukman, Ann. *Literature and Semiotics: A Study of the Writings of Yuri M. Lotman*. Amsterdam: North-Holland Publishing, 1977.

Simonson, Lee. *The Stage is Set*. New York: Theatre Arts Books, c1963.

Smiley, Sam. *Playwriting: The Structure of Action*. Englewood Cliffs, NJ: Prentice-Hall, Inc., 1971.

Sontag, Susan. "Against Interpretation" and "On Style." *A Susan Sontag Reader*. New York: Farrar-Straus-Giroux, 1963.

———. "Artaud: An Essay." *Antonin Artaud: Selected Writings*. Ed. Susan Sontag. Berkeley: University of California Press, 1976, xvii–xlii.

Spurgeon, Caroline. *Shakespeare's Imagery and What It Tells Us*. Cambridge: Cambridge University Press, 1935.

Stanislavski, Konstantin. *An Actor's Work* (aka An Actor Prepares and Building a Character). Tr. Jean Benedetti. London: Routledge, 2008.

———. *Creating a Role*. Tr. Elizabeth Reynolds Hapgood. New York: Theatre Arts Books, 1961.

———. *Stanislavsky Directs*. Ed. Nikolai Gorchakov. Tr. Miriam Goldina. New York: Minerva Press, 1954.

———. *Stanislavsky in Rehearsal*. Ed. Vasily Osipovich Toporkov. Tr. Christine Edwards. New York: Theatre Arts Books, 1979.

Sutherland, Donald. "Gertrude Stein and the Twentieth Century." *A Primer for the Gradual Understanding of Gertrude Stein*. Ed. Robert Bartlett Haas. Los Angeles: Black Sparrow Press, 1971.

Tarkovsky, Andrey. *Sculpting in Time: Reflections on the Cinema*. Tr. Kitty Hunter Blair. London: Faber and Faber, 1986.

Tennant, P.F.D. *Ibsen's Dramatic Technique*. New York: Humanities Press, 1965.

Thomas, James. "Its Hour Has Arrived: Rosalia Tolskaya and the 'Theatre of Players' Method." *Contemporary Theatre Review* 18.2 (May 2008): 236–249.

Thompson, Ewa M. *Russian Formalism and Anglo-American New Criticism*. The Hague: Mouton, 1971.

Tovstonogov, Georgi. *The Profession of the Stage Director*. Tr. Bryan Bean. Moscow: Progress Publishers, 1972.

Whitmore, John. *Directing Postmodern Theatre*. Ann Arbor: University of Michigan Press, 1994.

Whyman, Rose. *The Stanislavsky System of Acting: Legacy and Influence in Modern Performance*. Cambridge: Cambridge University Press, 2008.

Wilder, Thornton. "Joyce and the Modern Novel." *American Characteristics and Other Essays*. Ed. Donald Gallup. New York: Harper & Row.

Wiles, Timothy J. *The Theatre Event: Modern Theories of Performance*. Chicago: University of Chicago Press, 1980.

Wimsatt, William K. *The Verbal Icon*. Lexington: University of Kentucky Press, 1954.

Wimsatt, William K. and Cleanth Brooks. *Literary Criticism: A Short History*. New York: Alfred A. Knopf, 1965.

Wolfe, Tom. "Stalking the Billion-Footed Beast." *The Best American Essays: 1990*. Eds. Justin Kaplan and Robert Atwan. New York: Ticknor & Fields, 1990.

Young Thomas Daniel, Ed. *The New Criticism and After*. Charlottesville: University Press of Virginia, 1976.

Index

327

329

330

334

335

336

337

339

Rosencrantz and Guildenstern are Dead
(Stoppard) (*Continued*)
timelessness, 63
units, 154–155
unlocalized place, 63
Russian Formalist critics, 133, 172

S

Satires, 201
Scene linking, 300
Scenes
below-stairs scene, 75
formal, 136
French, 94, 136–139, 155
mise-en-scene, see Mise-en-scene
openings and closings, 301
The School for Scandal (Sheridan)
assertions, 103–104
background story technique, 74
character descriptions, 79
climaxes, 147
dialogue charm, 249
digressions, 140
discussions, 202
economics, 56–57
formal scenes, 136
formal words, 231
inciting action, 144
linking, 241–243
normative character, 213
occupation, 52
plot organization, 296–297
point of attack, 143
scene openings and closings, 301
sentence rhythm, 239
sentence types, 234–236
social rank, 53
society as style, 290
specific locale, 48–49
style and actions, 295
titles, 202
use of properties, 99
The Science of Educational Dynamics
(Frye), 159
Scope, idea and style, 305–306
Score of the role, 193–197
Screenwriting, conflicts, 163
Scribe, Eugene, 74–75
Secondary relationships, 190–191
Second major climax, 19, 32–33, 147,
163, 195
Second plan, 102

Seed
in action analysis, 7–12
author's plan, 8
definition, 7
Hamlet, 11, 13–14
moral commandment, 9–10
nonrealistic plays, 28–29
score of the role, 194–195
Stanislavsky/Nemirovich-Danchenko
concept, 7–8
and theme, 20–21
Self-contained plays, 136
Self-pity, 217, 296
Semicolon, 239
Sentences
definition, 232
length, 233
rhythm, 237–239
types, 233–237
Sentimentality
feelings, 79, 161
idea plays, 224–225
parodies, 159
personality traits, 188
self-pity, 296
set speeches, 207
simple plot, 299
society, 290
Serious plays, 201, 203
Set speeches
idea plays, 207–208
idea in words, 201–202, 275
organization, 298
Shakespeare, William
acts concept, 138
entrances and exits, 95
external events, 6
idea scope and style, 305
imagery, 208–209
moral commandment, 10
parallelism, 214–215
place as style, 289
punctuation, 239
society as style, 290
style and actions, 295–296
theme, 21
Shakespeare Our Contemporary
(Kott), 21
Shakespeare's Imagery and What It Tells
Us (Spurgeon), 208–209
Shaw, George Bernard, 76, 200, 202, 306
Shepard, Sam, 217, 248–251, 288, 290

341

342

343

344

345